The Human Context

RUDOLF H. MOOS
Stanford University Medical Center
and Veterans Administration Hospital
Palo Alto, California

THE HUMAN CONTEXT
ENVIRONMENTAL DETERMINANTS
OF BEHAVIOR

IN COLLABORATION WITH EVELYN BROMET,
ROBERT BROWNSTEIN, JAMES KULIK, RICHARD PRICE,
PAUL SOMMERS, AND BERNICE VAN DORT.

A WILEY-INTERSCIENCE PUBLICATION

JOHN WILEY & SONS, New York ● London ● Sydney ● Toronto

Library of Congress Cataloging in Publication Data

Moos, Rudolf H   1934-
      The human context.

      "A Wiley-Interscience publication."
      Includes bibliographical references and index.
      1. Human ecology. I. Title. [DNLM: 1. Behavior.
2. Social environment. BF352 M825h]

HM206.M66   301.31   75-36905
ISBN 0-471-61504-8

Printed in the United States of America

10 9 8 7 6 5 4 3 2 1

To

ALBERT EINSTEIN

Humanitarian

Preface

This book reviews the major ways in which human environments have been treated. It summarizes and attempts to integrate existing knowledge about environmental impact on human behavior. Part One presents a historical and conceptual overview. Parts Two and Three, respectively, discuss the major ways in which physical and social environments have been characterized. Part Four integrates the material through a discussion of utopias and an attempt to draw practical conclusions useful to individuals in coping with their current environments. Issues relating to the development of optimum human environments and to the limits of man's ability to shape and transcend environments are examined.

The book presents a conceptualization in search of a theory. In my view, there is no adequate theory of how human environments and human beings interact and shape one another. Lacking a theory to guide my decisions about the organization and content of the chapters, I used my own sense of what was relevant. No doubt others would—and will—do it differently. The division between physical and social environments is arbitrary, since different environmental characteristics mutually influence each other. The distinction simply provides a convenient way to organize what have until recently been distinct substantive areas. In this connection, the chapter on behavior settings could just as easily be placed in Part Two as in Part Three, or in a separate section of its own. I believe that the major thrust and application of behavior setting theory relates to the organization of the social environment, and I have thus elected to place this chapter in Part Three.

I have taken other liberties. I have emphasized environmental impact when I know that people shape environments as much as environments shape people. My defense is that most of us cannot shape our environments as much as we would like. We must often deal with the environment as it is. However I redress the balance somewhat in Part Four, where I focus on human utopias and consider how individuals can cope with (and presumably change) environmental impact. Human utopias serve as models to guide our attempts to restructure our environment. Practical conclusions about environmental influence will also help us make necessary choices. It is my hope that this material can enhance each individual's control of his or her own environment.

Although I sketch the broad outlines of what I call "a social ecological approach," I do not mean to enhance the development of a new field of inquiry. I do not believe that either environmental psychology or ecological psychology stands as a separate field of inquiry. I do feel the need for a broad integrative approach, in which the individual is the basic unit of study. I believe that the study of the physical and social environment should be synthesized. I believe that individual adaptation, adjustment, and coping with the environment must be emphasized. I believe that more attention should be placed on the mechanisms by which the environment acts on man. I also believe that we need an approach that is applicable to current individual and societal problems and has an explicit value orientation in that it attempts to promote the quality of human life. These principles indicate the outline of a social ecological approach. My aim is to integrate this approach in ongoing substantive fields of inquiry rather than to set it apart.

From a more personal perspective, this book represents a developmental stage in my own endeavor to understand our environment. My initial concern was with the social climate, or what I call the "personality" of the environment. As I worked in this area it became increasingly clear that one could not fully understand the social climate of an environment without focusing on the types of people in that environment (the human aggregate) and on the organizational structure within which they functioned. But the types of available behavior settings are also important. Furthermore, the architectural environment may influence (and be influenced by) the social climate, the organizational structure, the behavior settings, and so on. I thus found it necessary to broaden my search for relevant dimensions of human environments. In this search I found myself wandering as Alice in Wonderland, fascinated by new areas I did not fully understand. I touch here on work relevant to such fields as history, geography, meteorology, human ecology, cultural ecology, anthropology, sociology, architecture, and urban planning. I hope I have kept the inevitable inaccuracies to a minimum.

Although this is a book about environments, it is a book for the individual. If you learn as much from reading this book as my colleagues and I learned from writing it, our endeavor will have been worthwhile.

I have dedicated this book to the memory of Albert Einstein, who gave my parents and me an affidavit that enabled us to come to the United States during the darkest days at the beginning of World War II. This kindness and concern provided me with the opportunity that eventually led to my academic career and to my writing of this book. I have always thought of Einstein more as a humanitarian than as a scientist. His dedication, his simplicity, his integrity, and his intellectual honesty have helped me chart a course for my life. I like to think that he would have been sympathetic to my efforts to understand the human environment.

RUDOLF H. MOOS

Palo Alto, California
July 1975

Acknowledgments

This work was supported in part by grant MH16026 from the National Institute of Mental Health, grant AA00498 from the National Institute on Alcohol Abuse and Alcoholism, and by Veterans Administration Research Project MRIS 5817-01. Some of my ideas were developed in discussions with Richard Price, who also read and cogently criticized the entire manuscript. Robert Luft contributed to the reorganization and rewriting of Chapter 4. I could not have written this book without my colleagues, Evelyn Bromet, Robert Brownstein, James Kulik, Richard Price, Paul Sommers, and Bernice Van Dort, who collaborated with me on various chapters. The relevant fields of inquiry are simply too broad for any one person to comprehend adequately.

Vivien Tsu competently and efficiently handled the majority of the proofreading, editing, indexing, and bibliographic details. Louise Doherty and Susanne Flynn typed the myriad drafts of each chapter faster than I could write and rewrite them. This facilitated the completion of this book much more than they realized.

Bernice tried to create a home environment in which I could be productive. Luckily, Karen and Kevin did not follow her advice to leave me alone. Luckily, neither did she. The delays and interruptions always facilitated my writing.

R. H. M.

Contents

PART ONE   *Historical and Conceptual Overview*   **1**

Chapter 1.   **Conceptualizations of Human Environments**   **3**

Chapter 2.   **Environment and Man: Perspectives from Geography**   **36**

PART TWO   *Physical Environments: Natural and Man–made*   **71**

Chapter 3.   **The Weather and Human Behavior**   **73**

Chapter 4.   **The Architectural Environment: Physical Space and Building Design**   **108**

Chapter 5.   **Population Density, Crowding, and the Use of Space**   **141**

Chapter 6.   **Noise and Air Pollution**   **175**

PART THREE   *Social Environments*   **211**

Chapter 7.   **Behavior Setting Theory and Research**   **213**

Chapter 8.   The Impact of Organizational Structure
              and Change   248

Chapter 9.   The Human Aggregate   284

Chapter 10.   Social Climate: The "Personality" of the
              Environment   320

              PART FOUR   *Toward an Optimum Human Milieu*   357

Chapter 11.   Utopian Environments   359

Chapter 12.   Coping with Environmental Impact   394

Index   433

The Human Context

PART ONE

Historical and Conceptual Overview

CHAPTER ONE

Conceptualizations of Human Environments

The Need for a Broad Perspective. The current upsurge of interest in the human environment is remarkable. More books treating man and his environment from a holistic and ecological point of view have appeared within the past few years than appeared during the prior three decades.[1] Within the broader society, this interest is largely due to technological advances whose "side effects" raise critical issues about the delicate ecological balance existing on "Spaceship Earth." Major human problems such as environmental deterioration, water and air pollution, increasing population and population density, and resource depletion have aroused grave concern.

New developments in the social and behavioral sciences reflect these concerns. Architects and city planners focus on the optimum construction and physical organization of urban centers and new towns. Human ecologists and geographers are concerned with the ways in which entire communities adapt and grow in their unique surroundings. Psychologists and sociologists attempt to design environments that will maximize effective functioning and personal competence. Psychiatrists and social workers, believing that disorders of human functioning are partially rooted in dysfunctional social systems, want to identify the ways in which social environments can facilitate the constructive handling of life crises.

An integrated perspective regarding the human environment is essential for the central task of the social, behavioral, and biological sciences. This task may be broadly conceived as furthering man's struggle to create an optimum human environment. The arrangement of environments is probably the most powerful technique we have for influencing behavior. From one point of view, every institution in our society sets up conditions that it hopes will maximize certain types of behavior and certain directions of personal growth. Families, hospitals, prisons, business organizations, secondary schools, universities, communes, groups, and, for that matter, entire societies are all engaged in arranging environmental conditions to maximize certain intended effects. There is, of course, serious disagreement about which effects should be maximized and which environmental conditions should maximize them.

What are the criteria by which an environment can be judged as favorable? Lewis Mumford viewed an ideal environment as "seeking continuity, variety, orderly and purposeful growth" as opposed to an environment that "magnifies authoritarian power and minimizes or destroys human initiative, self-direction and self-government."[2] Others have conceived of optimum environments as highly structured and controlling, since they must provide the organization necessary for a plentiful existence. There are no clearly defined criteria for an ideal environment that can meet everyone's requirements. But we are much more likely to achieve an optimum environment when critical decisions about constructing and changing the environment are in the hands of the people who live and function in it. These decisions are currently in our hands, and to make them wisely we urgently need more reliable information about human environments and their impacts on human beings.

What are the principal ways in which environments and their impacts have been conceptualized? In this chapter we discuss seven major trends that underlie the recent upsurge of interest in man's surroundings. We identify certain recurrent issues, with the goal of synthesizing different approaches to man-environment relations into a social ecological perspective.

The seven trends are as follows. First is a broad historical and geographic perspective that attempts to explain the rise and fall of entire civilizations. Our major example is Arnold Toynbee's notion that men need "stimulus and challenge" from the environment to develop advanced societies. The second trend is the development of ecology and the associated outgrowth of human ecology and cultural ecology. These developments are linked to conceptions of the environment as currently used in anthropology, sociology, and epidemiology. The issues raised here are discussed further in Chapters 2 (human ecology), 6 (pollution), and 9 (epidemiology).

The third trend, the notion that environmental factors influence health and disease, has an old tradition beginning with the ancient Greeks. It is relevant to material covered in Chapters 3, 8, and 10. The study of organizations, the fourth trend, emerged from the Industrial Revolution and the rise of the bureaucratic society. This trend, as historically represented by Karl Marx and Max Weber, is discussed in Chapter 8. The fifth trend is due mainly to experimental psychology and personality theory. Personality theorists and mental health practitioners have found that personality traits do not explain as much about individual behavior as these investigators had originally thought. This has led to important shifts in emphasis in these fields and to the development of community-oriented and environmental perspectives, as discussed in Chapters 9, 10, and 12.

The sixth trend stems from the architectural and building design profession. Architects conceive of buildings as actively shaping the behavior that occurs in them. Buildings and the spaces in them encourage some behaviors and inhibit others. In Chapters 4, 5, and 6, we consider how environmental psychology has arisen partly from this development and partly from the increased emphasis on environmental variables in personality theory and social psychology.

The seventh trend is represented by recent interest in conservation and the "quality of life." Conservation issues are not the primary focus of this book, but the quality of the environment, especially as it affects individual human beings, is of central concern. The issue arises, in particular, in Chapters 4, 5, 6, and 12. A review of all seven trends provides a broad introduction to the major ways in which human environments have been characterized.

A conceptually related but historically separate trend concerns the development of utopias and of utopian thought. Utopian thought, which is as old as recorded history, deals with the fundamental question of how to structure an optimum human environment. This issue is treated in Chapters 11 and 12.

The First Trend: The Rise of Advanced Civilizations. Man has lived on earth for at least 2 million years. But the earliest recorded civilizations date back only about 6000 years. What is it that has impelled—or allowed—man to develop higher civilizations? The British historian Arnold Toynbee asks this question in his monumental 12-volume *Study of History*. He tries race, then environment, as explanatory factors. On analysis he discards both factors in favor of a relational theory of man and milieu.

Toynbee identifies the major civilizations of which we have knowledge: the Egyptian and Minoan in Europe and the Near East, the Inca and

Mayan in the Americas, and so on. He finds that two civilizations were created by contributions from three different races, nine by contributions from two different races, and ten by the contributions of a single race. Both Caucasians and non-Caucasians have created the great civilizations of the past. On this evidence, Toynbee rejects the idea that the development of great human civilizations depends on a particular race.

Can the environment explain the genesis of advanced civilizations? Have the geographic and/or climatic conditions in which human societies have lived accounted for the emergence of great civilizations in some cases but not in others? Toynbee rejects the environment as the explanatory factor, since he finds that similar environments have not necessarily produced similar human cultures. For example, the vast grasslands of Europe and Asia have given rise to a nomadic society. However the prairies of North America, the pampas of Argentina, and the vast Australian grasslands have not. Some historians believe that the fertile riverbed of the Nile Valley was partly responsible for the rise of Egyptian civilization. Toynbee points out (but there is some debate about this) that a similar environment exists in the valleys of the Rio Grande and the Colorado River in the southwestern United States, yet great civilizations did not arise in these areas.

How can one say that the high plateau of the Andes Mountains is the cause of the Inca civilization when geographically similar highlands in East Africa show evidence of ancient man's presence but not of comparable civilization? Did the tropical rainfall and lush vegetation of northern Guatemala and southern Mexico (the Yucatan) stimulate the development of the Mayan civilization? If so, how can we explain why no comparable civilization developed in the basically similar environments of the Amazon and the Congo? And, finally, how can we say that the Russian civilization is a product of the Russian forests, rivers, and cold climate when no comparable civilization flourished in the basically similar Canadian environment.

These examples indicate that there is no simple correspondence between the characteristics of the physical or geographic environment and whether a great civilization developed in that environment. But what of the human or social environment, which basically consists of the other societies with which any given society has contact? Could it be that civilizations develop in similar geographic-social environments? For example, one might argue that Canada did not have the same human environment as Russia because Canada was not influenced by the early development of Christian civilization.

Certain that the inclusion of the human element is not enough to account for the development of civilizations, Toynbee concludes that virtually identical combinations of the human and the nonhuman environment may give rise to a civilization in one case but not in another. Civilizations have emerged in exceedingly diverse environments. The nonhuman environment can take many forms: the fertile river valley type (Egyptian and Sumeric), the plateau type (Inca and Aztec), the archipelago type (Minoan and Greek), the continental type (Chinese), or the jungle type (Mayan). The same diversity of conditions is found in the surrounding human environment. Thus "any kind of climate and topography is capable of serving as an environment for the genesis of a civilization if the necessary miracle is performed by some positive factor which still eludes our search."[3]

Toynbee suggests that the histories of individuals, of communities, and of entire civilizations fall into successive stages. In each stage some groups of people are confronted by a specific challenge that imposes an ordeal, and different individuals react to these common ordeals in different ways. The majority succumb. Some barely manage to survive. Some, however, discover a response to the challenge that not only allows them to cope with the ordeal of the moment but puts them in a favorable position for undergoing the next ordeal. Other people follow these leaders into the next stage of civilization. Toynbee proposes the basic idea of *challenge and response* as a mechanism stimulating the evolutionary process. The role of the "external factor" (i.e., the environment) is to supply the "inner creative factor" with challenging stimulus sufficient to evoke a creative response.

What challenges from the environment produced creative human civilizations? Toynbee speculates that the Egyptian civilization was a creative response to the challenge of increasing dessication or lack of water after the last Ice Age. Certain communities met this challenge by changing their habitat and their way of life. The grasslands overlooking the lower valley of the Nile turned into desert. Some heroic pioneers migrated to the jungle swamps of the valley bottom, became food-cultivators rather than food-gatherers, and built new civilizations. Thus lack of water represents a challenge from the physical environment that can cause people to adapt and to develop new ways of civilization.

What are some of the other challenges that may have stimulated the development of advanced civilizations? The Chinese civilization developed in a wilderness marked by marshes and floods and by a temperature that varied from extreme heat in summer to extreme cold in winter. The civilizations of the Mayas and the Incas, respectively, developed in response to the challenges of a tropical forest and of a bleak climate and barren soil on the plateau, as well as heat and desert on the coast. The Minoan civilization developed because of the challenge of the sea, and so on. Toynbee labels these characteristics of the geographic environment the challenges of "hard countries."

There is also the challenge of "new ground"—as, for example, when people migrate overseas to a new land. Great natural disasters such as earthquakes, volcanic eruptions, and floods, also present a challenge from the natural environment. Comparable challenges come from the human environment. There is the challenge of "blows," which includes war and politics; the challenge of slow, continuous "external pressure," usually from another civilization; and the challenge of "social penalizations" such as enforced migration, slavery, and racial or religious discrimination. These challenges often result in creative, adaptive responses by man.

Thus Toynbee sees nature (the environment) as presenting a challenge. Man can conquer nature for a time, as shown by the existence of many great civilizations. But nature often reasserts her supremacy. For example, there is dense jungle where the Mayan civilization once flourished. The desert can be conquered by man, as indicated by the achievements of the Syrian civilization. But the ruins of this civilization attest to the ultimate victory of the desert over man. In this view there is a continual contest between two opposing forces, man and nature. A stunning victory by man (i.e., the development of a great society) is often only a moment of fleeting glory.

The conditions offered to man by the environments that have been the birthplaces of civilizations have been unusually difficult, not unusually easy. There is some evidence that although unusually easy environments may contribute to a comfortable and happy life, they may at the same time engender laziness and weakness. In this view, man needs to be exposed to challenges from either the physical or the human environment. Toynbee concludes that "the greater the ease of the environment, the weaker the stimulus towards civilization which that environment administers to man."[4]

On the other hand, certain challenges from the environment may be too extreme. This is difficult to prove, since the mere fact that certain civilizations failed a particular challenge does not mean that that challenge will always be excessive. For example, man has only recently conquered the atom and developed air and space travel. But there is a law of diminishing returns. According to Toynbee, "there is a mean range of severity at which the stimulus of a challenge is at its highest . . . we shall call this degree of severity the optimum."[5] Furthermore, "there are challenges of a salutary severity that stimulate the human subject of the ordeal to a creative response; but there are also challenges of an overwhelming severity to which the human victim succumbs."[6]

Thus in Toynbee's view the environment presents a challenge to which man must respond. If the challenge is too weak (i.e., the environment is too easy) human potential will remain unfulfilled. If the challenge is excessive, human attempts to cope with it will result in failure and decline. When the challenge is optimal, human beings will be stimulated to new creative heights. The challenge of the environment is a necessary condition for man to grow and to develop higher civilizations. It is the stimulus of the battle that allows people to prove their potential.

The Second Trend: Evolution and Human Ecology.   Human ecology developed mainly out of Charles Darwin's evolutionary perspective. The two essential elements in Darwinian theory are variation in the reproduction and inheritance of living organisms and natural selection, or the survival of the fittest. One factor is internal, the other is external. The inner factor, variation, is thought of as positive and creative. It produces the variations that are needed for human progress. The external factor, natural selection, is conceptualized as negative and destructive. It eliminates the harmful, the less fit, the less useful variations, leaving the beneficial, the more fit, or the more useful variations to develop and multiply. Living organisms exist in the "web of life" in which they "struggle for existence" in relation to the environment. This process fits and adapts the individual to the particular character of its environment. Thus the environment has a limiting or constraining impact on the organism.

Darwin's ideas first inspired work on the classification of animals and plants. Different species of animals and varieties of plants had to be accurately identifiable before they could be effectively studied in relation to their environment. Three phases of scientific ecology developed —botanists studied plant ecology, zoologists studied animal ecology, and sociologists (in the main) studied human ecology. The German biologist Ernst Haeckel first used the term "ecology" in 1868 in relation to his study of plants. Plant ecology developed first because, as one pundit put it, plants were more stable than animals in relation to their environment and thus were more easily studied.

Ecology itself has been defined as the study of the relation of organisms or groups of organisms to their environment. As Hawley succinctly stated:

> . . . every organism, plant and animal—including man—is in constant process of adjustment to an environment external to itself. The life of an organism in other words is inescapably bound up with the conditions of the environment which comprise not only topography, climate, drainage, etc. but other organisms and their activities as well . . . all organisms are engaged

in activities which have as their logical conclusion adjustment to environment.[7]

Two other areas of interest also influenced the development of human ecology. The first emerged in Western Europe, particularly England and France, around the beginning of the nineteenth century. This area constituted social (epidemiological) studies concerned with the spatial distribution of various human characteristics, particularly illness and crime. For example, the prevalence of crime, suicide, and so on, varied considerably between cities and towns and among different sections of cities. Realization of this led to studies of the distribution of crime and mental illness discussed in Chapter 9 and, indirectly, to the development of the epidemiological frame of reference, to the development of demography, and to the collection of census data and census tract studies.

The other intellectual root of human ecology was in human or cultural geography. In the twentieth century geographers began to study the structure of cities. This work which was concerned with the geographical analysis of urban structure, was known as urban morphology or urban geography, and the investigators tried to answer the question of whether environmental factors, particularly geographical and cultural factors, favored certain physical sites and facilitated the growth of particular cities. Theodorson points out that geographic and sociological studies of human ecology developed in relative isolation from each other. However, they actually described cities and their growth in basically similar ways.[8]

The sociologists of the so-called Chicago school of the 1920s and 1930s coined the term "human ecology." Believing that competition was the basic process in human relationships, they applied the theoretical schemes of plant and animal ecology to the study of human communities. The competition largely involved a struggle for space, but survival of the group demands that competition be tempered and some degree of mutual cooperation be practiced. Thus people form interdependent or "symbiotic" relationships. Robert Park viewed human society as organized on two levels: the biotic (biological) and the cultural. The struggle for existence results in the organization of the biotic level of society and determines the spatial distribution of people. The cultural level of society, on the other hand, is based on communication and consensus among people. Park defined society as that area "within which biotic competition has declined and the struggle for existence has assumed higher and more sublimated forms."[9] The biotic level of human organization was initially thought to be the proper concern of human ecology. Cultural factors were not included in the first ecological investigations.

Some classical ecologists felt that economic factors were as important as a biological orientation and that cultural factors should be included in human ecology. This position gave rise to many ecological community studies—for example, the notion of the dominance of the central business district of a city, the idea of concentric circular zones of city growth, and the notion that cities could be divided into small units or "natural" areas, which were thought to be the "unplanned" result of natural growth processes. These ideas stimulated studies of the distribution of particular social variables in relation to the natural areas and concentric zones of the city. The best known studies related to the distribution of crime and mental illness, which varied from one city zone to another. The original idea was that something about the environment of particular city areas fostered mental illness and crime (see Chapter 9).

One of the many criticisms of classical human ecology that appeared was that many cities did not fit the general pattern of concentric circular urban growth. In a book entitled *Social Ecology*, Milla Alihan criticized the distinction between the biotic and cultural levels of human organization.[10] She also criticized the assumption that competition is the basic process in human relationships. Others stressed the importance of culture in all human relationships. Many conceived of man as a social animal with cultural factors surrounding and influencing all his activities. This made it impossible to isolate a subsocial or noncultural (i.e., biotic) level of behavior.

Some authors saw human ecology not as a branch of sociology but rather as a general perspective useful for the scientific study of social life. Human ecology is distinguished from plant and animal ecology specifically by the unique characteristics of man and the human community. Unlike plants and animals, human beings can construct their own environment. They are not necessarily attached to the immediate environment in which they are placed by nature. Men also have an elaborate technology and culture. They are regulated by conscious controls, by rules, norms, laws, and formal organizations. At the minimum, these factors introduce complications in the study of human ecology which are not present in the plant and animal worlds.

Thus human ecology was slowly reconceptualized as a social and cultural science. According to Hawley, the unique aspect of human ecology is the study of communal adaptation. Unable to adapt to their environment alone, human beings are highly dependent on their conspecifics. Adaptation to the conditions of the physical environment is facilitated by adaptation to (and cooperation with) other living beings. Human beings confront the environment as a "human aggregate" and make cooperative efforts at adaptation. It is this communal adaptation which is the distinctive subject matter of ecology. Human ecologists study aggregate populations of human beings rather than individuals. The distinctive hypothesis of human ecology is that the human community is an essential adaptive mechanism in man's relation to the environment.[11]

Theodorson[8] indicates that there are three major trends in human ecology. In one view, the main task of human ecology is the analysis of community structure, which is primarily conceived of in terms of the division of labor. Community structure, from the ecological point of view, is the study of the way in which a population organizes itself for survival in a particular ecological niche. This view of human ecology has a strong economic orientation.

A second trend is social area analysis, a technique that rests on the classification of the census tracts of a city according to certain variables (i.e., social rank, urbanization, and segregation). These variables are easily assessed by regularly collected census tract indices and are thought to measure crucial factors in the development of modern industrialized societies.

The third approach, that of the sociocultural or social ecologists, emphasizes culture as a primary explanatory concept. For example, Walter Firey maintains that space has symbolic value and takes on meaning for man through cultural definition. Cultural values always intervene between the physical environment and the human community. Firey finds that symbolic values are the only adequate explanation of what he calls "space fetishes" such as the Boston Common, free cemeteries, old churches, and old meeting houses, which are all maintained in the central business district of Boston despite their contribution to serious economic dysfunction.[12] From a purely economic perspective, large office buildings and apartment houses would be much more valuable.

Anthropologists, like their colleagues in geography and sociology, have also come to recognize the promise of employing ecologic factors in their studies. Since they view man as a culture-bearing animal, they are not content with explanations in which *Homo sapiens* is described as merely another species of biological organism. This view has implications for the possible autonomy of cultural dynamics on theories on man-environment relationships.

The "culture area" was one of the first concepts employed by American anthropologists to comprehend the linkage between man and nature. This notion simply attested to the presence of relatively homogeneous cultural groups in particular geographic regions. Otis Mason, applying the concept to North American Indians, observed that the distinct climatic zones corresponded to areas occupied by linguistic families, which in turn corresponded to generally similar cultures. He distinguished 12 regions, which he designated "ethnic environments."[13] The culture area perspective produced the insight that the environment somehow sets boundaries to cultural activity.

A major development in anthropology's approach to man-environment relationships occurred with the appearance of Julian Steward's concept of cultural ecology. Steward was dissatisfied with previous efforts at ecological analysis and with historical explanations of the development of human culture. The former, he felt, failed to comprehend the significance of culture as a nonorganic factor.

> Human beings do not react to the web of life solely through their genetically derived organic equipment. Culture, rather than genetic potential for adaptation, accommodation and survival, explains the nature of human societies. . . . In states, nations and empires the nature of the local group is determined by its larger institutions no less than by its local adaptations. Competition of one sort or another may be present but it is always culturally determined and as often as not cooperation, rather than competition, may be prescribed. If, therefore, the nature of human communities is the objective of analysis explanations will be found through use of cultural historical concepts and methods rather than biological concepts. . . .[14]

Steward studied primitive societies in an attempt to estimate the extent to which their environments required particular modes of behavior for adaptation and survival. One major development, then, in evolutionary thought as well as in human and cultural ecology, is the increased emphasis on the human environment (i.e., on social and cultural determinants of man's adaptation).

The Third Trend: Environmental Determinants of Health and Disease. The notion that the physical and social environment influence health and disease has a long and varied history. For example, in the Book of Proverbs one finds the following: "A merry heart doeth good like medicine; but a broken spirit dryeth the bone" (Chapter 17, verse 22) and "A sound heart is the life of the flesh but envy is the rottenness of the bones" (Chapter 14, verse 30). These and similar quotations indicate that the ancients believed that emotional factors played an important role in disease processes.[15] Presumably these emotions were aroused by the social context in which the individual lived.

Hippocrates believed that there was a direct causal connection between elements of the physical environment and health and disease in man. He thought that the changes of the seasons, the risings and settings of the stars, and the changing patterns of the wind and temperature, all had an important impact on health and disease.

Health problems have always been linked to the political, social, and economic conditions of different groups of people. The apparent influence of various occupations on health had been noted in Greek and Roman times. The notion that various diseases and plagues occur more frequently in densely settled cities, partly through the "corruption of the air" (climate) and through rapid population growth, was prevalent in the Middle Ages.[16] Interest in the relationship between environmental factors and health grew rapidly. Illness and death represented a significant economic problem and a loss of productive labor.

More specific studies, which began about 150 years ago, dealt with the physical geography and natural history of particular areas. Nutrition, housing, the customs of the people, and other variables were related to the occurrence of disease. For example, in 1828 Louis René Villerne produced evidence that mortality rates in France were closely linked to the living conditions of different social classes. There was also a clear relationship between conditions of poverty and disease. Income, nutrition, and housing conditions were shown to have an impact on growth and physique.

When the fields of public health and social medicine grew out of such notions, they were based on the idea that a society has an obligation to protect and enhance the health of its members. Also basic was the belief that social, economic, and other environmental conditions have an important impact on health and disease. As far back as 1847, Virchow concluded that social, economic, and political factors had as much to do with causing a typhus epidemic as did biological and physical factors. The final force that brought the field of public health into being was the realization "that the steps taken to promote health and to combat disease must be social as well as medical."[17] The notion was that public health would help care for society by alleviating environmental conditions that adversely affected health. For example, the spread of communicable diseases could be attributed to environmental factors such as nutrition, working and living conditions, education, and income, as well as specific infectious agents.

Some of the basic principles underlying these notions were formulated by Alfred Grotjahn, who suggested four ways in which social conditions and disease conditions might be linked. (1) Social conditions may create or favor a predisposition for a disease. (2) Social conditions themselves may cause disease directly. (3) Social conditions may transmit the causes of disease. (4) Social conditions may influence the course (and treatment) of a disease. Preventing diseases or influencing their course by public health measures requires attention to the social and economic environment.[18] Thus the notion that aspects of the physical and social environment may have an important impact on health is by no means new. Today the fields of epidemiology, public health, preventive medicine, social medicine, and medical sociology are concerned with these issues.

The field of psychosomatic medicine represents a separate but related development. The psychosomatic perspective classically asserts that the emotional experience of an individual can affect his bodily functions, his health status, and the onset, course, and treatment of his disease. This formulation is immediately connected to the individual's environment, since emotional experiences are aroused by the characteristics of the social environment in which one lives. Recent studies have shown that almost every physiological system in the body may be affected by psychological and environmental stimuli. To put it another way, our reactions to the situations we encounter every day affect our internal bodily processes in important ways. This is supported by the frequent clinical observation that diseases may get better or worse depending on the life situation of the patient.

A series of studies by Hinkle and Wolff aptly illustrate this logic. They studied illnesses in three groups of subjects over long time periods (e.g., 20 years). Some people exhibited much greater susceptibility to all forms of illness than did others. The illnesses often came in clusters, and the majority of illness clusters occurred when people perceived their life situations to be unsatisfying, threatening, and overdemanding. There were disturbed relations with family members, threats to security and status, and no satisfactory methods of adapting to these situations. A person's susceptibility to illness is influenced by his relation to the society in which he lives and to the people in it. Efforts to adapt to the social environment are involved in the majority of all illness situations. Thus there is good reason to believe that all disease processes "may be to some extent influenced by the host's adaptation to his social environment."[19]

Sargent has suggested that health is not a characteristic of man per se. Man and environment constitute a system.[20] Health is a process of man-environment interaction within a specific ecological context. In this view, health is defined in terms of the adaptive capacity of man in relation to environmental circumstances. When adaptation succeeds, man can be considered healthy. When adaptation fails, he is ill. Health is thus the "ability of the organism to function effectively within a given environment . . . since the environment keeps changing, good health is a process of continuous adaptation to the myriad of microbes, irritants, pressures and problems which daily challenge man."[21]

A related line of development concerns the impact of the physical and social environment on mental health and illness. Some reformers during the eighteenth century felt that inequalities of physical and mental abilities might be alleviated by exposure to an optimum environment (e.g., a temperate climate, a democratic government, a liberal education, adequate religious training). In a sense the concern of these social reformers was similar to the concerns of workers in the field of public health; that is, securing the "sanitation" of both the physical and social environment was thought to be helpful in preventing and alleviating mental illness.

This point of view was particularly well developed in the notion that the social environments of mental hospitals have an important impact on the patients who live within them. In 1806 the Quaker William Tuke established the York Retreat in England, emphasizing an atmosphere of kindness and consideration, meaningful employment of time, regular exercise, a family environment, and the treatment of patients as guests. This era of the recognition of the importance of "moral" or environmental treatment is well documented in America. Samuel Woodward, the first superintendent of the Worcester (Massachusetts) State Hospital, believed that insanity resulted from social and cultural factors. The hospital instituted "moral therapy," which consisted of individualized care that included occupational therapy along with physical exercise, religious services, amusements, and games. Moral treatment implied that the creation of a healthy psychological environment for the individual patient was itself curative. The assumption was that an appropriate social milieu could eliminate undesirable patient characteristics that had been acquired because of "improper living in an abnormal environment."[22] These theories have received renewed impetus by the recent development of the "therapeutic community," which is based on the belief that the social environment may affect the outcome of psychiatric treatment.

The Fourth Trend: The Rise of Modern Organizations. Modern governmental bureaucracies evolved out of the royal households of Western Europe.[23] The variety of retainers who accompanied the British and Prussian kings performed different administrative services for the royal families. For example, the king might appoint retainers to take charge of supplies, finances, clothing, horses, and weapons. The size and complexity of these tasks steadily increased because political bodies grew larger. These groups of officials gradually separated physically from the royal household and were paid money instead of in kind. Future grants of noble titles and fiefs were often given to retainers for their services.

In the sixteenth century European rulers began to employ university-trained jurists and humanists in administrative positions. These officials worked on a strictly contractual basis, subject to cancellation by either party. Temporary public service in exchange for future grants of nobility and fiefdoms were gradually replaced by life-long public employment, guaranteed by contract.

In Prussia and France a third trend contributed to the development of bureaucracies. Military procurement officers were charged with maintaining peace and order in the territories the army conquered. A new degree of centralized control entered into the civilian bureaucratic structure and was retained as a feature of continental bureaucracy for many years.

The bureaucratic organization developed by European governments later spread into commercial and industrial enterprises, which grew dramatically in size and complexity as a consequence of the Industrial Revolution. Small family-run shops of artisans were replaced by large factories employing hundreds, even thousands of employees. An efficient administrative structure was necessary to coordinate and plan the activities of these workers, and the bureaucratic model provided the necessary control and coordination. Nearly all large complex organizations currently existing in the United States can be classified as bureaucracies.[24]

The rational bureaucratic model was successfully incorporated into manufacturing operations in the late nineteenth century during a period of fierce competition. Victory in this economic competition was necessary for survival as economic units grew in size and reduced the number of rivals. The notion of social Darwinism allowed manufacturers to justify the costs of competition, including very low wages and poor working conditions for the factory workers. By the turn of the century the leaders of the rising trade union movement, armed with the socialist doctrines of Marx and others, challenged social Darwinism. They asserted that managers must concern themselves with more than the factor of competition outside the factory. Workers' interests and needs must also be accommodated. The prevalence of large, complex bureaucratic institutions in modern society has resulted in an extensive social science literature on the structure, management, and effects of organizations. Several distinct models of the organization and its impact on workers have been developed.[25]

For example, the classical school of organizational theory grew out of the analysis of government bureaucracies in Europe. Max Weber is the original and best known of these theorists. The classical model emphasizes the formal organizational chart and the proper and formal chain of command depicted on such a chart. The chart indicates a division of labor and implies that each worker efficiently performs a specialized task. Communication takes place through the upward hierarchy, permitting the occupant(s) of the apex of the structure, the president or board of directors, to control, direct, and unify the organization's tasks toward a goal. Workers throughout the hierarchy are assumed to be motivated primarily by material rewards, which therefore are to be manipulated to correspond closely to workers' output. Such a reward structure was expected to provide the maximum motivation to productivity. Thus the environmental factors of formal organizational structure and adequate incentives (pay) were thought to be directly linked to worker productivity.

This model was plagued by evidence that informal social networks grow up in organizations and that these networks are important communication channels, bypassing and deliberately avoiding the formal chain of command. The consequences of these informal communication channels clearly have an impact on the control and direction of the organization. Thus the human relations school was born, in reaction to the classical model. The new model emphasized communication among workers, participative decision making, and democratic leadership. In this view informal communication and the informal social environment were more directly related to worker productivity than were formal communication networks, physical conditions of workers, or exact monetary incentives.

Many people have begun to think about the pervasiveness of bureaucratic organizations and the importance of understanding their impact on workers and society. For example, workers at the lower end of an organizational hierarchy may suffer from poorer mental health, less job satisfaction, and less self-esteem and security; in addition, they may develop more dependency and passivity than those at higher levels of the organization. Some evidence suggests that a leadership style based on trust and participation is more effective than an authoritarian style. Chapter 8 reviews some work on the measurement and comparison of large organizations, on their differential impact on workers, and on their susceptibility to change.

The Fifth Trend: Experimental Psychology and Personality Theory.   The idea that environmental factors affect man's behavior, attitudes, and moods is a recurrent one in experimental psychology and personality theory. Sigmund Freud's emphasis on the dynamic and internal motivational causes of human behavior led to a temporary lack of interest in environmental influences on behavior. Personality theorists felt that the basic causes of behavior were the individual's ideas and feelings rather than stimuli from the environment, assuming that individuals have particular traits that vary in amount or degree from person to person. These traits are stable and enduring, and they have a fairly general impact on behavior. As a rule, we assume that people will show reasonable consistency of behavior in different settings. When an individual is described as dominant or aggressive, for example, we assume that he will be relatively dominant or aggressive in a variety of settings. In this view, the underlying personality is reasonably stable regardless of the environmental setting.

Henry Murray broadened this perspective. He developed a complex personality theory that included both the familiar concept of individual needs (e.g., needs for achievement, for affiliation, for autonomy, for order), and the less familiar concept of environmental press. The concept of need represents the significant internal or personal determinants of behavior. The concept of press represents the significant external or environmental determinants of behavior. Murray's main point is self-evident: we are much more likely to understand the behavior of an individual if we have an accurate picture of his environment. Murray was one of the first psychologists to systematically conceive of environmental forces that might affect individual behavior.[26] His basic contribution, the notion of environmental press, led to the development of techniques to measure the social climates of environments (see Chapter 10).

Field Theory and Gestalt Psychology. A related line of development came from gestalt psychology and Kurt Lewin's field theory. Psychological field theory was an outgrowth of the older sciences of physics and chemistry. The field concept of physics, which developed out of work on electromagnetic fields and resulted in Einstein's theory of relativity, had an important impact on psychological field theory. In gestalt psychology "the way in which an object is perceived is determined by the total context or configuration in which the object is embedded. Relationships among components of a perceptual field rather than the fixed characteristics of the individual components determine perception."[27] The gestalt psychologists often demonstrated these principles through the use of reversible perceptual illusions (i.e., figures that took on a different meaning depending on the context in which they were shown).

Lewin formulated his psychological field theory out of his exposure to gestalt psychology and to the field theory of the physical sciences. He believed that behavior was a function of the total field that existed at the time the behavior took place. Lewin conceived of the life space as made up of the person (P) and the psychological environment (E). He felt that environmental facts could influence the person and that personal facts could influence the environment. People have needs and the environment has "valences," which may or may not satisfy these needs. One cannot understand an individual's behavior without information about both his needs and the ways in which the environment can satisfy or frustrate these needs. It thus made no sense to Lewin to analyze behavior without reference to the person and to his psychological environment.[28]

Ecological Psychology. Egon Brunswick was one of the first psychologists to adopt a frankly ecological orientation. He was particularly concerned with the rigid principles of experimental design that dominated laboratory psychology. It was (and often still is) felt that in a laboratory experiment one can systematically and independently vary the important determinants of a particular behavior. Brunswick pointed out that many laboratory situations artificially "tied" certain stimuli (i.e., made them covary in an unnatural or unrepresentative fashion) or artificially "untied" them (i.e., prevented them from covarying together in a natural way). Brunswick felt that stimulus situations should be representatively sampled in relation to how often they actually occurred. He concluded that it was necessary to study the organism in its natural ecological environment to understand how it functioned.

It was through these notions that Brunswick arrived at a position known as "probabilistic functionalism"—functional because it studied the individual's successes and failures in the actual environment, probabilistic because the stimuli and acts in the individual's environment were only probable. The individual can never be absolutely certain that a given act (or stimulus) will allow him to attain his goal.

Hammond has succinctly described functionalism:

> Its tradition stems from Darwin and its main concern is the relation between the organism and its environment—an environment, however, that must be described in terms of distal objects, events and persons. And *probabilistic* functionalism not only recognizes, but advances to full respectability, the uncertain relations among environmental variables—an uncertainty that requires an organism to employ probabilistic means in order to adapt and thus to survive.[29]

Brunswick's own view was that "both historically and systematically psychology has forgotten that it is a science of organism-environment relationships, and has become a science of the organism."[30] He criticized psychologists for being careful about sampling a wide range of people in their experiments but totally neglecting a careful sampling and ecologically representative array of stimulus conditions.

Roger Barker's work on ecological psychology developed out of the intellectual tradition fostered by both Lewin and Brunswick. Barker's theory included elements of Brunswick's emphasis on the ecological setting of behavior and elements of Lewin's concern with the psychological environment. Lewin felt that it was impossible to make predictions about behavior directly from knowledge about the nonpsychological environment (i.e., the perceptual or ecological environment). Therefore he evolved a system of purely psychological constructs. However it is obvious that events that occur in the ecological environment have an important impact on individual behavior. Lewin himself was influenced by events in the ecological environment. He was an Austrian Jew who emigrated from his native land to the United States because of Hitler's rise to power and this fact of the ecological environment influenced the individual's behavior. But Lewin had no adequate conceptual bridge to link the two fields (i.e., psychology and ecology). As Barker puts it, "Who can doubt that changes in our environment ranging from new levels of radiation, to increased numbers of people, to new kinds of medicines, and new kinds of social organizations, schools, and governments are inexorably changing our behavior, and that our new behavior is, in turn, altering our environment?"[31] Barker's lifelong work in developing an "eco-behavioral" approach to this area is discussed in Chapter 7.

Conditioning and Social Learning Theory.   Another method of analyzing the environment is an outgrowth of the development of classical conditioning by the Russian physiologist Ivan Pavlov. Pavlov showed that environmental stimuli could acquire specific meaning through their association with a primary reward (e.g., food). A hungry dog will salivate on seeing and smelling food. This "natural" response develops out of the animal's continuous interaction with its environment. A hungry dog will not "naturally" salivate when it hears the sound of a bell. Pavlov found that if a bell was sounded either just before or during the presentation of food, a dog would learn to salivate when the bell was sounded even in the absence of food. This very simple experiment provided a mechanism by which environmental stimuli could "acquire" new meaning. By extension, any environmental stimulus could acquire specific meaning for an individual, that is, it could be linked to new responses. This process is known as classical conditioning.[32]

A thoroughgoing environmentalism developed in American psychology on the basis of this principle. If a dog can be conditioned to salivate to the sound of a bell, why cannot a human child be conditioned to become fearful, dominant, or aggressive?

It was out of this intellectual tradition that B. F. Skinner projected his theory of operant conditioning. From Skinner's perspective, the social environment is not simply a passive agent that permits strong personalities to alter its qualities. If anything, the reverse is true. People vary their behavior according to the rewards they receive after they have made an appropriate response. Positive reinforcement may take the form of attention, approval, submission, and so on. Behavior may also be altered through negative reinforcers (e.g., disapproval, contempt, ridicule, and insult).

Skinner believes that the social environment importantly influences behavior, and he feels that an individual may increase his power to achieve a reinforcement by joining a group. When many people pull on a rope, for example, each person is reinforced as long as the rope moves. The man marching in a parade is reinforced by the acclaim of the crowd, which would not be forthcoming if he were marching alone. The coward who is part of a shouting mob is reinforced when his victim is terrified, but he would not shout all alone. Thus the reinforcing consequences generated by a social group often exceed the consequences people can achieve by acting alone.

These notions have led to the development of a social learning perspective of human behavior. The social learning theorist assumes that people vary their behavior substantially in different social and physical environments. Variations in behavior occur primarily because the reinforcement consequences for particular behaviors vary. For example, if aggressive behavior is rewarded in school but punished at home, it is likely that a child will be aggressive in school but not at home. This perspective is discussed in Chapter 11, in which Skinner's utopian novel *Walden II* is critically analyzed.

Stimulus Deprivation and Stimulus Enrichment.   A related line of development has come from studies of maternal separation and its effect on the development of young children. René Spitz's classic study of a foundling home versus a nursery gave evidence of a connection between maternal and social deprivation and increased infant mortality, susceptibility to disease, retardation in growth, and failure to achieve normal developmental progress. Spitz studied 130 infants in two institutions with comparable quality of food and levels of hygiene. In the foundling home the infants were cared for by nurses, whereas the mothers provided the care in the nursery. In contrast to nursery children, foundling home children showed extreme susceptibility to disease—almost all had histories of intestinal infection, even though the home maintained excellent conditions of hygiene, including bottle sterilization. Contrary to what would be expected, older children—those who had been in the home longer—were more likely to die during a measles epidemic than younger children. In addition, growth levels, talking, and walking were severely retarded in the foundling home children.[33]

Skeels has presented a remarkable study that supports the findings of Spitz. Eleven mentally retarded children were shown to have experienced the effects of an early intervention, which consisted of a radical shift from one institutional environment to another. The major difference between the two institutions was in the amount of stimulation and the intensity of the relationships between the children and the adult caretakers. These children were eventually placed in adoptive homes. In contrast, a control group of 12 similar children were exposed to a relatively nonstimulating orphanage environment over a prolonged period.

Over a period of 2 years the experimental group showed a substantial gain in functional intelligence, whereas the control group showed a substantial loss. Another follow-up was conducted 2½ years later. The 11 children who had been placed in adoptive homes increased their earlier gains in intelligence. Skeels followed the children into adulthood finding that all 11 children in the experimental group were self-supporting; none was in an institution. In the control group of 12 children, one had died in an institution and seven were still living in institutions.

Strikingly, the experimental group completed an average of 12 years of education and four completed some college work. The children in the control group completed an average of less than the third grade. These remarkable group differences were also evidenced in occupational achievement and income, in marital and family status, and so forth. Skeels concluded that the difference between the two groups was due to the "program of nurturance and cognitive stimulation," which was "followed by placement in adoptive homes that provided love and affection and normal life experiences. . . . It can be postulated that if the children in the contrast group had been placed in suitable adoptive homes, or given some other appropriate equivalent in early infancy, most or all of them would have achieved within the normal range of development . . . ."[34]

Evidence indicates that enriched environmental stimulation may result in more rapid learning and intellectual development[35] and in actual changes in the anatomy and chemistry of the brain.[36] These findings have brought about fresh interest in identifying and promoting the characteristics of growth-enhancing environments (e.g., Project Headstart, antipoverty programs, community self-development programs).

The Sixth Trend: Architecture and Environmental Psychology. The architectural profession's concern with the effects of architectural artifacts on human behavior grew out of the philosophy of functionalism. Functionalism is the central tenet of modern twentieth-century architecture. In reaction to the gingerbread, cornices, and other ornate frills plastered onto the exterior of buildings in the 1800s, the modern school stated that "form follows function." Architects were to concentrate on building efficient, functional offices, factories, and so forth.

One of the most famous early exponents of this philosophy was Walter Gropius, whose distinctive office and public buildings have been copied by many designers. The epitome of the functionalist design used by Gropius is the rectangular office building, supported by a central core of reinforced concrete and surrounded on the exterior by an expanse of glass. In addition to designing many such buildings, Gropius founded a school for architects called the Bauhaus. The Bauhaus emphasized the essential unity between engineers, scientists, and architects. Architects must understand the uses of modern materials and methods and must create efficient, economical factories and offices using these techniques.[37]

Another well-known exponent of functionalism was Le Corbusier, who coined the phrase, "form follows function." His critics have charged that this philosophy was at best an ideal that was not really practiced. For example, some of Le Corbusier's esthetically dramatic designs for houses were completely unworkable from a housekeeping point of view. The problem was that for form to be adequately united with function, the architect had to know all the functions of a building, all the activities to be performed in it. Also, he had to know the physical spaces and devices that would optimize performance of all these functions. Architects in practice found it impossible to anticipate all the activities to be performed in the physical space. Even for the activities that were anticipated, they did not understand the behavioral consequences of designs, furniture arrangements, and other environmental conditions. Thus they could not design the optimum physical space for the anticipated activities and functions.

The beginning of a solution to this problem was to make certain that the design *allowed* for performance of anticipated activities. The proper approach was to draw up a comprehensive list of the activities anticipated in the designed space and to create a design that allowed those activities.[38] The search for optimum functional design could follow from these beginnings, with the aid of social scientists in understanding the behavioral and psychological effects of designs.[39]

A second tradition of concern with the effects of architecture grew from psychiatry. In the nineteenth century Thomas Kirkbride found existing mental hospitals depressing in appearance. He feared that this would adversely affect patients directly, and indirectly too, through their visitors who would also be bothered by the depressing buildings. The following quotation was frequently cited by later authors concerned with psychiatric architecture:

> A hospital for the insane should have a cheerful and comfortable appearance, everything repulsive and prisonlike should be carefully avoided. No one can tell how important this may prove in the treatment of patients nor what good effects may result from first impressions thus made upon an invalid on reaching a hospital. Nor is the influence of these things on the friends and relatives of patients unimportant.[40]

Thus Kirkbride was spurred to design a better mental hospital, and the design he arrived at has been extensively copied in the nation's state mental hospitals. Realization of the importance of psychiatric architecture and its behavioral effects has become much more widespread in the last two decades.

A third strand of interest in architectural effects on behavior is due to the urban renewal–public housing movement in the United States. Crime and physical and mental illnesses in the slums of industrial cities contributed to the growth of a massive public housing program. Rehousing in clean, sanitary, modern, and frequently high-rise facilities cleaned up the slum neighborhoods, making downtown a more viable residential area and providing adequate space and working plumbing to thousands of families.

Yet problems of disease and crime were not alleviated by this program. By the middle of the twentieth century it was becoming clear that many of the continuing difficulties were directly attributable to the poor design of the new public housing projects, particularly the massive high-rise structures. Schorr traces this awareness of the inadequacies of high-rise projects and the links between the architecture, the crowded living conditions, and the behavioral and social consequences.[41] Social scientists became increasingly interested in the consequences of the design of physical spaces when they were asked to evaluate the effects of public housing programs and the sources of the failure of these programs.

Thus three distinct intellectual traditions contribute to the current concern with the behavioral consequences of physical spaces. Architects became interested in the behavioral consequences of design in the search for the optimally functional design. Psychiatrists and psychologists working in mental hospitals sought help from the design professions in finding a better physical space for treating mental illnesses. Social scientists involved in public housing and urban renewal studies became aware of the many negative consequences of the prevalent high-rise housing projects and expanded their interest in physical spaces to more adequate, suburban-type housing. These trends, which enhanced the growth of environmental psychology, are discussed in Chapter 4.

The Seventh Trend: The Ecology Movement. The increased significance attached by the last decade to the physical environment of "Spaceship Earth" is a product of the startling realization of the planet's essential finiteness. Geologists became concerned about running out of sources of important mineral ores and energy deposits. Biologists and meteorologists learned of the limits of tolerance of human and animal populations to man-made pesticide use and air pollution. Demographers were painfully aware that current population growth rates ought not to be sustained. Growing public interest in and awareness of these academic concerns resulted in the conservation movement of the late 1960s and early 1970s.

The possibility that the advanced industrial economies may run out of critical minerals and metals was raised at least a decade ago by a study of the relationship between demands and known supplies of materials such as petroleum, molybdenum, bauxite, uranium, and various other materials vitally necessary in the manufacturing processes of advanced economies.[42] The geographic dispersal of deposits of many of these substances made the supply problem seem more critical. Cobalt, for example, is found in the Congo, diamonds and gold are largely concentrated in South Africa, and so forth. Should the producing nations for economic or political reasons decide to withhold the substances from the world market (as has lately occurred with petroleum), an untenable situation can quickly develop. Recent comprehensive studies of the resource picture of the United States reached similar conclusions.[43] By the year 2050 we may have run out of several economically important substances for which no substitute is known: helium, natural gas, lead, copper, zinc, petroleum.[44]

One of the seminal works to arouse public awareness of the consequences of environmental pollution was Rachel Carson's *Silent Spring*.[45] Carson outlines the spreading use of DDT during the 1950s and 1960s in an attempt to stop the spread of Dutch elm disease, which is carried and spread by a small bark beetle. The disease threatens to kill all our Dutch elms, and the streets of thousands of small towns across the country are lined with this stately tree. Consequently, as the disease spread, thousands of towns, encouraged by the Department of Agriculture, sprayed lavishly and expensively with DDT. The attempt was largely futile for various reasons, but it has had important and insidious effects on animal ecology.

The beetles and earthworms near the trees gradually built up large concentrations of DDT in their bodies. These two organisms are the favorite food of many birds, especially robins, and the DDT was thus transferred to the bird population. The Department of Agriculture had not tested the effects of DDT on birds and was unaware that egg-laying and egg-hatching processes would be checked and interrupted on a large scale. The end result has been "silent springs," devoid of the songs of robins and other species in many communities.

Other forms of environmental pollution of the air in urban areas by the ubiquitous American automobile, of the waterways by industries, of forests by careless campers, of the sea by garbage and oil dumping, have become increasingly evident and have aroused the public consciousness and ire. Ecology days, teach-ins, legislative action, and recycling projects, were instituted because of this public awareness of pollution not only near to each individual's home, but immediately and inescapably inside and outside it.

Population growth in this country and elsewhere has also become the focus of concern for scholars and the public. Ehrlich and Ehrlich point out that from 1940 to 1949 the world population growth rate was 0.9% per year, implying that the human population would double in 77 years. During the decade from 1950 to 1959 the yearly rate increased to 1.8%, with a doubling period of 39 years. The last decade, 1960 to 1969, has witnessed yearly growth rates fluctuating between 1.8 and 2.0%.[46]

A comparison of the resulting projected population levels with the earth's food production capability quickly leads one to conclude that the current rate of population growth cannot be sustained without disastrous consequences. Even with the full benefits of the best agricultural technology, the so-called Green Revolution, food production can not possibly keep ahead of population growth for more than two more decades. Keyfitz points out that voluntary birth control is unlikely to produce the desired results, since many couples want more than the 2 to 3 children necessary to sustain populations at their current levels.[47] Thus to avert natural catastrophes, government-controlled and -enforced birth control appears to be the only available recourse.

Resource depletion, pollution, and population growth problems imply the need is to move toward a stable society to avert worldwide ecological catastrophe.[48] Such a society would be characterized by a strictly controlled and limited human population in which adequate food sustenance and perhaps maintenance of other resource levels would be allowed. The population would be stable in the resource area in that it would avoid final depletion of critical materials before substitutes could be found. It would carefully ration resources to leave a supply for future generations. It would stabilize pollution of the planet. Recycling would be emphasized, and the production of unusable wastes as by-products of manufacturing processes would be minimized and discouraged.

Every student of the environmental-ecological problem concludes that population control is the necessary condition for making the social and scientific, technological adjustments necessary to the survival of the human species. A stable human population will leave a hungry, polluted, and resource-depleting world, as Ehrlich and Ehrlich point out; but a stable population is the essential condition without which planet-wide disaster, overtaking all species, is inevitable.

A Synthesis of Perspectives: A Social Ecological Approach.   We have discussed seven broad trends underlying current interest in the environment. We now attempt to draw concepts from these trends and to integrate them from a particular perspective, "a social ecological approach." Several points of special emphasis distinguish this social ecological approach from the major perspectives discussed previously.

First, a social ecological approach attempts to understand the impact of the environment from the perspective of the individual. In human ecology the unit of study is the entire community, which is seen as an adaptation to nature. In cultural ecology the unit of study is the entire culture. In Toynbee's perspective the unit of study is an entire civilization. In our approach the basic unit of study is the individual. It is finally the individual who reacts to the weather, who must adapt to the physical layout of the city, who must cope with the bureaucratic structure of large organizations, who is influenced by the reward structure of his social environment, and so forth.

For example, we talk of the unlimited capacity of people to change and control their environment. But is this actually the case? The answer depends on the particular perspective taken. Certainly man can build and tear down cities. But you and I cannot change the physical environment of New York City or of San Francisco. We must essentially accept these cities and their environments for what they are. In this very basic sense each individual must adapt to the currently existing environment. From the perspective of a large society, much of the environment can be controlled and changed. But only small "bits and pieces" of the environment are under the personal control of a single individual.[49]

Second, a social ecological approach attempts to synthesize the study of the physical and social environments. Its concern is with the basic unity of the milieu. The impact of one aspect of the physical environment depends on other aspects of the physical environment. Heat affects people more under crowded conditions, and smog always seems more irritating when it is hot. The impact of one dimension of the social environment depends on other aspects of the social environment. Employee absenteeism and sickness are usually higher in larger work groups, but this may not occur under conditions of high cohesiveness and autonomy. Furthermore, the impact of the physical environment (e.g., noise) depends on aspects of the social environment (e.g., whether the noise is relevant to necessary task performance). And the impact of the social environment (e.g., authority and status) depends on such characteristics of the physical environment as the arrangement and spacing of furniture in an office.

Physical and social environments are inextricably related and must be studied together. Our discussion of various aspects of the environment in separate chapters is simply a convenient way of presenting this complex material. It helps to clarify the wide range of environmental variables that must be considered in reviewing the impact of the environment on man.

Third, a social ecological approach emphasizes individual adaptation, adjustment, and coping. How does the individual handle environmental stress? How do people cope with the changing human condition? Our emphasis is on how individuals adapt to the environment rather than on how the human community as a whole adapts. Whereas a social ecological approach is equally concerned with human adaptation and human environments, we stress somewhat more heavily an environmental perspective. We do this because we believe that assessments of environments must precede assessments of the impact of these environments on human functioning. Thus the focus here is more on milieu than on man, although the essential aspects of milieus are their effects on human adaptation.

This concern with human adaptation leads to concern with the mechanisms by which the environment acts on man. How does the environment exert its impact? There are five different, yet related, conceptions of how the environment works in the major trends already discussed. These conceptions vary on a "positive-negative" dimension; that is, they vary from seeing the environment as essentially negative and stressful to seeing it as basically stimulating and challenging.

Environments may be seen as actively *stressful*. A stressful or "bad" environment may cause illness and/or premature death (the disease model), it may stunt physical and personal growth (maternal deprivation), or it may "cause" pathological reactions such as crime and mental illness. In this conception, the environment is active and may have very strong impact. Too much responsibility and pressure may facilitate a heart attack. High population density may result in stress, which in turn facilitates pathology.

The environment may be seen as a limiting, resisting, or inhibiting force (i.e., it delimits what is likely to occur). One cannot sit down in a room without chairs. One cannot easily write when there are not writing spaces. Friendly behavior is inhibited in a hostile environment, and hostility is inhibited in a friendly environment. This way of regarding the environment basically derives from evolution and human ecology. In this view, the environment *limits* and constrains what man can do.

The environment may *select* some living organisms or people by favoring certain characteristics. This notion comes directly from Charles Darwin's idea of natural selection. The environment "selects" or favors stronger or more dominant animals because these animals have reproductive superiority, thus leave more progeny. This is exactly what happens in "social Darwinism." The social environment selects or favors certain people (or civilizations) because their characteristics (e.g., assertiveness or aggressiveness) give them specific adaptive advantages.

Environments select in another way which is more relevant from the individual's perspective. Universities carefully choose incoming students—and incoming faculty members. Industries carefully screen new employees. Professional football and baseball teams select potential players with exceeding care. Many social and recreational organizations (e.g., sororities and fraternities) painstakingly select their new members. Thus the human or social environment acts in at least as highly selective a manner as the natural or physical environment. The environment may be seen as a *"releaser"* of man's capacities. The environment supports or allows behavior to occur. In a sense this is similar to the second view except that it approaches the environment from a more positive perspective. The environment offers opportunities for action. The provision of a chair allows one to sit, and the provision of a table to write. The notion is often carried one step further in the idea that environmental stimuli may "elicit" a particular behavior. An interesting picture or "conversation piece" elicits personal interaction. A cohesive social environment elicits friendly and supportive behavior.

Finally, the environment may be seen as an active and positive force. It may impose demands, but these demands stimulate and *challenge* the individual. It facilitates personal and social growth. This, of course, is Toynbee's view of the role of the environment in the development of civilizations. It is the human relations perspective on personal development in bureaucratic organizations. It is the perspective of community-oriented programs that attempt to facilitate mental health and personal growth by changing important community environments, such as primary and secondary schools. It is the "stimulus enrichment" perspective, which argues that an environment full of novelty and variety actively enhances growth. A social ecological approach attempts to conceptualize these mechanisms to promote better understanding of the ways in which the environment "acts" on man.

Fourth, there is a practical applied orientation to a social ecological approach. Individuals who are aging and/or who have serious crippling illnesses often carefully delimit and restrict the environments they enter. This implies withdrawal and limitation of growth. How can we organize environments in which such people can maximize their functioning and personal growth?

Furthermore, information is necessary to help select "congruent" and satisfying environments. People actively seek information about environments to enhance the probability that these environments will be satisfactory. Students actively select universities; employees actively select work organizations. A social ecological approach is designed to help individuals by providing more accurate and complete information about existing environments and environmental choices. It is also desirable to use this information to enhance constructive change.

Fifth, a social ecological approach has an explicit value orientation: it is not simply an approach for science. It is also a humanistic approach by which to benefit mankind. A social ecological approach is dedicated to increasing the amount of control individuals have over their environments, and to the question of how environmental planners can plan environments and still avoid acting as agents of social control. It is dedicated to increasing individual freedom of choice in selecting environments.

We now have an environmental crisis in human dignity.[50] Certain environments threaten the aged, the ghetto dweller, the mental patient, the handicapped person, and so on. Crowded, noisy, urban milieus devalue individuals. Most physical and social settings are designed without regard for the "human" properties of people. We must recognize that the environment can facilitate or frustrate human behavior and experience. A social ecological approach seeks to identify man's most central needs and to obtain information about how human environments can best satisfy these needs.

We conceive of social ecology as the multidisciplinary study of the impacts of physical and social environments on human beings. Its primary concern is with the enhancement of human environments to improve the quality of human life. It is linked to traditional concerns of human ecology in its emphasis on the measurement of objective physical characteristics of environments and in its emphasis on the short-term evolutionary and adaptive consequences of these environments. It differs from the traditional concerns of human ecology in that its unit of study is the individual rather than the human aggregate or community.

Social ecology is linked to traditional concerns of the behavioral sciences, particularly psychology and sociology, in its emphasis on the importance of the social environment and in its explicit consideration of environmental impacts on psychological variables such as self-esteem and personal development. It is distinct from traditional concerns in the behavioral sciences in its explicit emphasis on the physical environment in interaction with the social environment.

Social ecology is linked to traditional concerns in psychiatry, medicine, and epidemiology in its focus on the identification of dysfunctional or pathological reactions (e.g., illness, accidents, suicide, crime) and their relationships to environmental variables. It is distinct from traditional concerns in these areas in its concentration on the adaptive and growth-enhancing influence of environmental variables.

Thus a social ecological approach relates to areas of continuing concern in existing fields of inquiry. The range and interconnection of environmental variables usually studied in isolation give this approach a diverse, robust, and socially relevant focus. A social ecological approach provides a distinctive "point of entry" by which human environments and their impacts on human functioning can be studied.

The Book in Brief.   The following chapters provide an overview of varying perspectives on man-environment relations. Chapter 2 discusses the theories of historians and geographers on the subject of environmental impact. Part Two presents the major ways in which physical environments have been characterized. Chapter 3 reviews work on the impact of the weather on human behavior. Chapter 4 discusses the role of the man-made architectural environment. Chapter 5 reviews evidence indicating that population density, crowding, and physical space affect behavior. Chapter 6 presents material linking noise and air pollution to behavior.

Part Three takes up the major ways in which social environments have been characterized. Chapter 7 critically analyzes an eco-behavioral approach to understanding the environment. Chapter 8 discusses the impact of organizational structure and change on workers' attitudes and behavior. Chapter 9 presents a somewhat unique approach to this area. Here the "human aggregate" provides a perspective by which the average characteristics of the people in an environment constitute a measure of that environment. Chapter 10 introduces the concept of social climate, which is conceived of as the "personality" of the environment.

Part Four attempts to synthesize the material through two related approaches. Chapter 11 uses the methods of studying environments discussed in Parts Two and Three to critically analyze human conceptions of ideal living environments. Chapter 12 presents relevant conclusions and discusses issues relating to the development of optimum human environments and to the limits of man's ability to shape and transcend environmental impact.

REFERENCES

1. Jordan, P. A real predicament. *Science*, **175:**977–978, 1972.

2. Mumford, L. *The urban prospect*. Harcourt Brace Jovanovich, New York, 1968 (quotation on p. 221).

3. Toynbee, A. *The study of history*, Vol. 1, *The geneses of civilizations*, Part 1. Oxford University Press, New York, 1962, p. 269.

4. Toynbee, A. *The study of history*, Vol. 2, *The geneses of civilizations*, Part 2. Oxford University Press, New York, 1962, p. 31.

5. Toynbee, A. *The study of history*, Vol. 2, *The geneses of civilizations*, Part 2. Oxford University Press, New York, 1962, p. 291.

6. Toynbee, A. *The study of history*, Vol. 2, *The geneses of civilizations*, Part 2. Oxford University Press, New York, 1962, p. 393.

7. Hawley, A. *Human ecology*. Ronald Press, New York, 1950, p. 3.

8. Theodorson, G. (Ed.). *Studies in human ecology*. Row Peterson, Evanston, Ill., 1961.

9. Park, R. Human ecology. In G. Theodorson (Ed.), *Studies in human ecology*. Row Peterson, Evanston, Ill., 1961, p. 25.

10. Alihan, M. *Social ecology*. Columbia University Press, New York, 1938.

11. Hawley, A. *Human ecology*. Ronald Press, New York, 1950.

12. Firey, W. Sentiment and symbolism as ecological variables. *American Sociological Review*, **10:**140–148, 1945.

13. Freilich, M. Ecology and culture. *Anthropological Quarterly*, **40:**26–43, 1967.

14. Steward, J. The concept and method of cultural ecology. In P. English and R. Mayfield (Eds.), *Man, space, and environment*. Oxford University Press, New York, 1972, pp. 120–129 (quotation from pp. 120–122).

15. Macht, D. Psychosomatic allusions in the Book of Proverbs. *Johns Hopkins Institute of the History of Medicine Bulletin*, **18:**301, 1945.

16. Kahldun, I. *The Muqaddimah: An introduction to history*. Translated from the Arabic by Franz Rosenthal, Vol. 2, Pantheon Books, New York, 1958.

17. Rosen, G. The evolution of social medicine. In H. Freeman, S. Levine, and L. Reeder (Eds.), *Handbook of medical sociology*. Prentice-Hall, Englewood Cliffs, N.J., 1963, p. 36.

18. Grotjahn, A. *Soziale Pathologie*, 2nd ed. August Hirschwald Verlag, Berlin, 1915 (as quoted in Rosen, G., *op. cit.*, p. 44).

19. Hinkle, L. and Wolff, H. The nature of man's adaptation to his total environment and the relation of this to illness. *Archives of Internal Medicine*, **99:**442–460, 1957 (quotation on p. 457).

20. Sargent, F. Man-environment: Problems for public health. *American Journal of Public Health,* **62:**628–633, 1972.

21. Dubos, R. and Pines, M. *Health and disease.* Life Science Library, Chicago, 1965, p. 10.

22. Grob, G. *The state and the mentally ill: A history of Worcester State Hospital in Massachusetts 1830–1920.* University of North Carolina Press, Chapel Hill, 1966, p. 66.

23. Bendix, R. Bureaucracy. In D. Sills (Ed.), *International encyclopedia of the social sciences,* Vol. 2. Macmillan and Free Press, New York, 1968, pp. 206–219.

24. Perrow, C. *Complex organizations: A critical essay.* Scott, Foresman, Glenview, Ill., 1972.

25. Etzioni, A. *Modern organizations.* Prentice-Hall, Englewood Cliffs, N.J., 1964.

26. Murray, H. *Explorations in personality.* Oxford University Press, New York, 1938.

27. Hall, C. and Lindzey, G. *Theories of personality,* 2nd ed. Wiley, New York, 1970.

28. Lewin, K. *A dynamic theory of personality: Selected papers.* McGraw-Hill, New York, 1935.

29. Hammond, K. (Ed.). *The psychology of Egon Brunswick.* Holt, Rinehart & Winston, New York, 1966, p. 21.

30. Brunswick, E. Scope and aspects of the cognitive problem. In H. Gruber, R. Jessor, and K. Hammond (Eds.), *Cognition: The Colorado Symposium.* Harvard University Press, Cambridge, Mass., 1957, p. 6.

31. Barker, R. On the nature of the environment. *Journal of Social Issues,* **19**(4):17–38, 1963 (quotation on p. 19).

32. Hilgard, E. *Theories of learning,* 2nd ed. Appleton-Century-Crofts, New York, 1956.

33. Spitz, R. Hospitalism: A follow-up report. *Psychoanalytic Study of the Child,* Vol. 2. International Universities Press, New York, 1947.

34. Skeels, H. Adult status of children with contrasting early life experiences: A follow-up study. *Monograph of the Society for Research in Child Development,* **31,** 1966, p. 56.

35. See, for example, A. Moore, The Responsive Environments Laboratory. In B. Gross and R. Gross (Eds.), *Radical school reform.* Simon & Shuster, New York, 1969.

36. Bennett, E., Diamond, M., Krech, D., and Rosenzweig, M. Chemical and anatomical plasticity of brain. *Science,* **146:**610–619, 1964.

37. Gropius, W. *Bauhaus 1919–1928.* Branford, Boston, 1959.

38. Lipman, A. The architectural belief system and social behavior. *British Journal of Sociology,* **20:**190–204, 1969.

39. Studer, R. and Stea, D. Architectural programming, environmental design, and human behavior. *Journal of Social Issues,* **22:**127–136, 1966.

40. Kirkbride, T. *On the construction, organization and general arrangements of hospitals for the insane.* Lippincott, Philadelphia, 1880, p. 52.

41. Schorr, A. *Slums and social insecurity: An appraisal of the effectiveness of housing policies in helping to eliminate poverty in the United States.* Social Security Administration, Division of Research and Statistics, Research Report No. 1, U.S. Department of Health, Education and Welfare. Government Printing Office, Washington, D.C., 1963.

42. Landsberg, H., Fischman, L., and Fisher, J. *Resources in America's future: Patterns of requirements and availabilities, 1960–2000.* Johns Hopkins University Press, Baltimore, 1963.

43. Study of Critical Environmental Problems (SCEP). *Man's impact on the global environment.* MIT Press, Cambridge, Mass. 1970.

44. Cloud, P. Mineral resources in fact and fancy; and Hubbert, M., Energy resources. In W. Murdoch (Ed.), *Environment: Resources, pollution and society.* Sinauer Associates, Stamford, Conn., 1971, pp. 71–116.

45. Carson, R. *Silent spring.* Houghton Mifflin, Boston, 1962.

46. Ehrlich, P. and Ehrlich A. *Population resources and environment: Issues in human ecology.* Freeman, San Francisco, 1970, pp. 23–24.

47. Keyfitz, N. The numbers and distribution of mankind. In W. Murdoch (Ed.), *Environment: Resources, pollution and society.* Sinauer Associates, Stamford, Conn., 1971, pp. 31–52.

48. Goldsmith, E., Allen, R., Allaby, M., Davoll, J., and Lawrence, S. *Blueprint for survival.* Houghton Mifflin, Boston, 1972.

49. Michelson, W. *Man and his urban environment: A sociological approach.* Addison-Wesley, Redding, Mass., 1970.

50. Proshansky, H. The environmental crisis in human dignity. *Journal of Social Issues,* **29:**1–20, 1973.

CHAPTER TWO

Environment and Man: Perspectives from Geography[a]

Imagine yourself relaxing on a warm, lazy, summer day, reclining on a comfortable hammock, and enjoying an ample supply of food and beverages. Is this situation likely to stimulate you to initiate intense activity or to pursue earth-shaking achievements? If you answer in the negative, you are implicitly agreeing with one long-established theory of the geographic environment's effect on man.

According to this view, human civilization requires adversity, in particular geographic adversity, as a stimulus for its progressive development. For example, the climate of the tropics, much like our hypothetical summer day, is not considered to be conducive to hard work or high levels of culture. In such an environment human needs are meager. Clothing can be skimpy if it is used at all. Housing must only provide shelter from rain and shade from the midday sun. Furthermore, a bountiful nature places ready at hand everything necessary to satisfy these needs. Palm leaves are available for shelter; fruit trees and banana plants abound, requiring no effort at cultivation; fish are teeming in easily accessible lagoons. It is an idyllic picture, but as the theory stipulates, idyllic surroundings encourage idleness. Thus it is easy to understand the failure of tropical areas to produce powerful, advanced societies. No one living there needed to go through the trouble of creating them.

Temperate climates put men in a quite different position. The weather

[a] This chapter is co-authored by Robert Brownstein and Rudolf Moos.

is more severe, and greater effort and industry are required if housing is to provide adequate protection from the elements. Crops can be cultivated only part of the year. Those with foresight, who worked hard and accumulated a surplus during the growing season, would have enough to last through the barren periods. But anyone who adopted the carefree lifestyle of the tropical dweller faced certain disaster. The temperate climate then—through its added adversity—encourages extra effort and planning for the future. These qualities lead to increasing levels of production, to consistent improvement in techniques and institutions, and, over the long run, to the rise of civilizations.

The foregoing thesis is hardly a definitive explanation of the development of human culture. It is, however, an example of the subject matter to be explored in this chapter. The impact on man and on his institutions of the geographic environment has been of interest throughout recorded history. The record of scholarly endeavor indicates its long-standing appeal to men of letters as well as laymen. In fact, as Sorokin recognized, "One's difficulty consists not so much in indicating the thinkers who have pointed out the influence of the geographical environment as it does in indicating those who have not mentioned it."[1]

The details of inquiries on issues that have excited curiosity over millenia cannot be briefly summarized. Hence we focus on only the best known proponents of the major schools of thought, suggesting in particular several central issues intrinsic to the general question of man's relationship to the geographic environment.

Definition of the Environment.   Any analysis of man's relationship to the environment necessitates a precise understanding of the term "environment." For example, what factors are to be included: temperature, natural resources, rainfall, microorganisms, and so on? On what basis can we set the boundaries of the environment? Can we say that a New Yorker's environment includes the weather in Kansas because this factor determines the accessibility of his food supply? Does it ever make sense to speak of an environment in general, or can we only stipulate particular environments for specific types of organisms or specific human cultures? Both people and ants inhabit San Francisco. Do they share the same environment?

Natural Versus Human Environments.   We usually think of the environment, particularly the geographic environment, as a "given" to which man reacts. In our modern age, however, man interacts with and substantially modifies his environment. Are we to consider the results of such interaction as themselves part of the environment? Is it more useful to regard man's efforts to adjust to the smog and noise of urban life as an adaptation to the environment or as a response to the consequences of his own action?

Mediating Forces.   Does the environment affect man directly, or is its influence mediated by some other factor such as technology or social organization? Is the presence of oil in an area an environmental influence if the society living there does not understand the useful potential of that substance? Can the environment be characterized at all independently of culture and technology?

Generalization Among Environments.   One would be hard pressed to discover two areas whose environments were exactly the same. But does the "uniqueness" of each environment preclude general conclusions about environmental influences on man? Are we limited to describing the impact of conditions in the Arabian desert on Bedouin tribes? Or can we make broader statements on the effect of deserts on human culture? And if the latter is possible, which aspects of desert conditions should we emphasize: heat, absence of water, absence of plant life?

Geographic Versus Other Environmental Influences.   Does the geographic environment include the only set of factors that explains human activity, or the major factors, or only one group out of many factors? For example, can we say that civilization appeared in the Tigris-Euphrates Valley exclusively because of climate, primarily because of climate and agricultural technology, or because of climate, technology, and a complex interaction of many other factors? Are geographic features ever necessary and/or sufficient causes of some human event?

Free Will.   For centuries philosophers have debated whether human action is caused by factors external to man's consciousness or is derived from his own initiative and decisions—that is, from his will. This question underlies attempts to show that geographic factors are causal determinants of human activity. Belief in free will prohibits complete acceptance of geographic causation; at the other extreme, complete denial of free will requires some explanation of causality, geographic or otherwise.

   These issues should be kept in mind as questions to be addressed to the theoretical positions that follow. The remainder of this chapter is devoted to an analysis of geographic perspectives regarding man and the environment. These are divided into six subheadings: (1) determinism, (2) possibilism, (3) probabilism, pragmatism, and quantification, (4) neodeterminism, (5) ecology, and (6) new approaches.

Environmental Determinism.   Determinism is a doctrine stipulating that every event or action is caused by some antecedent condition. Geographical determinism is a subcategory of general determinism; it asserts that human activity can be primarily explained by conditions in the geographic environment. This position classically asserted that man is influenced by natural forces he is powerless to control.

Classical Approaches.   To comprehend the theories of the environment of the scholars of ancient Greece, it is necessary to consider the tenets of the physical philosophy that served as a background for the development of their hypotheses. According to this view, physical phenomena were based on a combination of the four elements (earth, air, fire, and water) and the four qualities (dry, cold, hot, and moist). Thus, for example, the humours of the body could be derived in the following fashion: hot + moist = blood, hot + dry = yellow bile, cold + moist = phlegm, and cold + dry = black bile.[2] From this position, a single logical step led to a theory linking climate and physiology. As Franklin Thomas explains,

> It seemed natural that the character of the climate or weather would tend to increase hot, cold, dry, and moist conditions in one case or another, and would thus have a direct influence upon the health of the individual. Hot and dry climates would dry up too much of the bodily moisture and reduce vitality; changes in seasons would have an influence upon the four elements and affect the health, disposition, and temperament of peoples, all of which were determined by the mixture of the elements."[3]

Specific Greek theories reflected this belief that a direct causal connection between environment and man resulted from the interaction of fundamental substances. In his treatises on medicine, Hippocrates considered diseases involving particular body humours to be most prevalent in the season in which climatic attributes were most similar to the humour's physical basis. Thus in winter, phlegm (cold and moist), which originates in the brain, is predominant, and winter is noted for catarrhal and pituitary afflictions. Autumn is linked to black bile (cold and dry). Since that humour was believed to rise from the spleen, diseases of the latter organ could be expected.[4]

Aristotle, who made considerable use of Hippocrates' findings, believed that climate and national character were closely related. In *Politics*, he noted,

> The inhabitants of the colder countries of Europe are brave, but deficient in thought and technical skill, and as a consequence of this they remain free longer than others, but are wanting in political organization and unable to

rule their neighbors. The peoples of Asia on the contrary are thoughtful and skillful but without spirit, whence their permanent condition is one of subjection and slavery.[5]

Interestingly, Aristotle's findings tended to substantiate the superiority of the Greeks over other peoples less well located.

Theorists of ancient Rome continued to employ Greek philosophy as a basis for their conjectures.[6] Their hypotheses were similar to those of Hippocrates and Aristotle. However, one modification of Greek theory is worthy of mention. When Vitruvius argued that a superior race would be located midway between the extreme north and the extreme south, he drew the dividing line slightly north of the area Aristotle had designated. In fact, he selected the territory of his own civilization. The great Arab geographer Ibn Khaldun also extolled the superior characteristics of those inhabiting a moderate, temperate, climate. Unfortunately, Arabia was so far south that it could hardly be considered a midpoint between the regions of extreme hot and extreme cold. Nevertheless, Khaldun managed to discover that the waters of the Arabian peninsula had a cooling effect, which produced a climate equivalent to that of other temperate areas, thus supporting the superiority of his own people.

The obvious chauvinistic bias in these contentions calls into question the objectivity of early theories of environmental impact. Many classical thinkers had a tendency, perhaps reinforced by political or ideological considerations, to regard their geography and their climate as inexorably conducive to human superiority.

Modern Theorists.   The medieval period (at least in Europe) was unproductive of new contributions toward an understanding of the relationship between man and environment. With the turn of the nineteenth century, geography, like so many other disciplines, entered a period marked by revolutionary theoretical developments. Yet the first decades of the 1800s were still principally influenced by the thoughts of an earlier age. In these years Hegelian philosophy dominated Europe. Karl Marx was writing a doctoral dissertation on Epicurus, which he completed in 1841. Preliminary efforts at scientific sociology began to appear, but Darwin's *Origin of Species* was not published until 1859. Thus it is not surprising that theorists of this period were heavily swayed by theological and idealist concepts.

Carl Ritter, one of the founders of modern geography, was such a theorist. A complex scholar whose work developed throughout his lifetime, Ritter approached his geographical studies from a distinct philosophical point of view. Like the German idealists, he believed that the world could be comprehended only as a whole. Ritter linked this position to a teleological vision of the universe; the earth as a totality must have a purpose. Ritter's perspective was highly anthropocentric, and he identified the earth's purpose with the development of its highest life form, man.[7]

Ritter stressed the importance of the configurations of the continents. Compact and uniform land areas, he argued, were most likely to have backward and homogeneous cultures. Africa, being compact, uniform, and backward, was cited as an example. Europe, on the other hand, was neither compact nor uniform. Its large coastline (in comparison to its area), broken by numerous seas and bays, permitted the widespread reception and diffusion of culture. Asia, which possessed uniformity and compactness as well as an irregular coastline, demonstrated a mixture: homogeneity and backwardness in the interior and a high development of civilization along the coast. Ritter did not consider man to be a passive repository for environmental impact. He acknowledged that increases in human knowledge permitted people to control nature and to reduce their vulnerability to geographic influences.[8]

As the century progressed, other scholars elaborated overtly and rigorously deterministic analyses. One such school of thought, which came to have considerable impact on the progress of geography in France and Britain, was initiated by the French mining engineer turned social theorist, Frédéric Le Play.[9] An excellent illustration of the determinist application of Le Play's method is provided by one of his students, Edmond Demolins. To account for the diversity of the peoples on the earth's surface, Demolins argued that the geographic features of the regions people pass through when they migrate, as well as the conditions in the places from which they start and in which they finally settle, shape their character and social institutions.[10]

For example, Demolins discussed the original inhabitants of the steppes, large tracts of level grasslands in southeast Europe and Asia. Because the principal vegetation on the steppes is grass, the region is ideal for the pastoral life style of nomadic shepherds. Pastoralism requires a dependence on animals, especially the horse, which allows the herdsman sufficient mobility to follow his flocks as they seek new pasture. Demolins observed that horses flourish on the steppes. Thus an environmental law is revealed; the steppe is essentially adapted to the horse, and it is the horse that adapts the steppe to man.

Pastoralism as a mode of work determines other aspects of the steppe-dweller's culture. His food and the material for his crafts are limited to the by-products of his herds. Since the nomad is always on the move, his dwellings and tools must be rugged and easily transportable. There is no room for large complex machinery, long-lasting buildings, or luxury goods. In addition, the limited scale of production does not require any economic organization more complicated than handcraftsmanship. Thus the steppe peoples have little or no division of labor, wage rates, or unemployment; work is communal, centered in the family workshop.

Geographic factors also affect property relationships. Grass demands no cultivation, yet once the grass cover has been consumed, the land loses all value to the herdsman and he moves on. Thus no motivation exists for the institution of private property in land.

Furthermore, since land and work are communal, and the family is the only basis of social organization, patriarchal structures appear, featuring common property and common subordination to a single father-leader. This mode of family life can be credited with affecting the personal characteristics of its members. Patriarchy suppresses individual initiative and promotes traditionalism and conservative attitudes.[11]

Once nomads leave the steppes, they are subject to the environmental influences of the regions they cross (the route). For example, the Huron, Iroquois, and Algonquin Indian tribes are said to have entered North America through Alaska, traveling eastward to the Great Lakes. This route carried them across terrain crowded with numerous small lakes, and they evolved the technique of making birchbark canoes—light enough to be portaged. Women, children, and old men, who would be encumbrances on portages, were temporarily left behind. To secure sustenance, this group turned to agriculture, which was essentially practiced by the women. Several social consequences followed from this separation. First, the society became a matriarchy. Second, marriage became a partnership between a producer of maize and a hunter of game, with the relative abundance of each food source determining its particular structure. Where game was plentiful but the soil infertile, one man could afford to feed several women who would not be able to support themselves, and polygamy became the norm.[12]

Another determinist thesis, this one linking the scientific study of history with man's relationship to the environment, is Buckle's *History of Civilization in England*. Buckle specifies four aspects of nature that have significantly influenced mankind: climate, food, soil, and the general aspect of nature. Buckle is innovative in the way in which he links these to the social dynamics of societies, particularly the accumulation and distribution of wealth. He argues that as food supplies increase, population will likewise increase, and as a consequence wages will fall. He assumes that an increase in population means an increase in labor supply; the law of supply and demand will trigger a response to the increase in the number of potential workers—namely, lowering the workers' market price (their wages).

How is this relationship connected to geographic factors? In cold areas more food is required to maintain body temperature. At the same time the rigorous climate limits cultivation. Clearly with food scarce and much in demand, population and labor force will fall; as a consequence, wages will rise. The converse is true for hot areas. In addition, one can draw political implications from this thesis. In warm countries that possess fertile soil, a dual process occurs. The abundance of food results in a large work force and low wages, but the richness of the soil permits the production of vast wealth. Hence a small part of the population will be extremely wealthy and powerful; the masses, however, will remain destitute and starving. The unequal division of economic power will be reflected in a similar distribution of political power.[13]

Although the factors already noted affected economic distribution, the fourth factor, "aspects of nature," influenced the patterns of human thought. Where natural phenomena are massive and powerful, men see themselves as insignificant and inferior. But where nature appears feeble, men are tempted to reason, to experiment, and to control natural processes. Applying this thesis on a global scale, Buckle discovers that "In the civilizations exterior to Europe all nature conspired to increase the authority of the imaginative faculties, and weaken the authority of the reasoning ones." In Europe, on the other hand, natural phenomena tended to "embolden the understanding, thus inspiring man with confidence in his own resources, and facilitating the increase of his knowledge, by encouraging that bold, inquisitive and scientific spirit . . . on which all future progress must depend."[14]

Considering his findings on distribution of wealth and directions of thought, Buckle chauvinistically concludes that "looking at the history of the world as a whole, the tendency has been, in Europe to subordinate Nature to man; out of Europe to subordinate man to Nature."[15] Here he encounters a paradox resulting from his efforts to embrace both the determining power of nature and man's potential for emancipation from that power. It was, after all, nature—the cold climate, the less imposing phenomena—that accounted for European man's capacity to "subordinate" it. Thus, to paraphrase Minshull, it was determined that man should not be determined.[16]

As the nineteenth century progressed, attempts to apply new developments in the natural sciences to the study of man proliferated. Darwin revolutionized the social and several of the natural sciences with his theory of natural selection. Marx launched frontal assaults against prevailing economic and philosophical traditions, arguing for dialectical materialism as the science of history. Comte and Durkheim were advancing sociology as an independent discipline employing empirical theory. The study of man's relationship to the geographic environment could hardly remain unaffected.

One of the best known and most controversial of the post-Darwinian nineteenth-century geographers was Frederich Ratzel, who proposed several hypotheses relating to climatic influences on civilizations. Ratzel held that the most invigorating temperate climate was one in which isothermal lines group together, producing a region of varying and contrasting climates. Even winds were considered significant, either as factors in trade during the era of sailing vessels or as causes of destruction, thus intensifying the struggle for existence and stimulating progress.[17] He also emphasized geographic location as a factor in national development.

Ratzel's thought reached the United States through the work of his disciple Ellen Semple, whose *Influences of the Geographic Environment* was published in 1911. Although Semple rejected the organic theory of the state, she retained a basically determinist point of view. Consider her opening paragraph:

> Man is a product of the earth's surface. This means not merely that he is a child of the earth, dust of her dust; but that the earth has mothered him, fed him, set him tasks, directed his thoughts, confronted him with difficulties that have strengthened his body and sharpened his wits, given him his problems of navigation or irrigation, and at the same time whispered hints for their solution. She has entered into his bone and tissue, into his mind and soul.[18]

To develop her argument, Semple identified four fundamental classes of environmental effects—direct physical effects, psychical effects, economic and social effects, and movements of peoples. She produced substantial evidence to illustrate each category. Perhaps the tenor of Semple's evidence and her literary style can be gleaned from the following selection discussing the psychological impact of the environment.

> The physical effects are reflected in man's religion and his literature, in his modes of thought and figures of speech. . . . The whole mythology of the Polynesians is an echo of the encompassing ocean. The cosmography of every primitive people, their first crude effort in the science of the universe, bears the impress of their habitat. The Eskimo's hell is a place of darkness, storm, and intense cold; the Jew's is a place of eternal fire. Buddha, born in the steaming Himalayan piedmont, fighting the lassitude induced by heat and humidity, pictured his heaven as Nirvana, the cessation of all activity and individual life.[19]

One cannot hope to summarize the work of Ellsworth Huntington, the final determinist we discuss. His scholarly production totaled some 29 volumes (author or coauthor), chapters in 28 other books, and some 180 articles.[20] However, we can note his essential objective and illustrate his methods of analysis. In his discussion of religions Huntington attempts to demonstrate that animism is most likely to occur in jungle areas and monotheism in deserts. Part of his explanation follows.

> One of the chief elements in animism is fear of the unknown. Such fear is encouraged by life in a tropical jungle. An ignorant savage, let us say, is walking in the jungle, when a stick falls on his head. He can detect no cause. No leaves stir in the branches above him; no monkey or bird moves away. It seems as if someone had deliberately thrown the stick, but no one is visible. The easiest supposition is that some creature like a man, but more ill-tempered and quite invisible, must have done it. The same line of reasoning suggests that an invisible spirit is at work when the man stumbles on a hidden root, hears a frightening sound in the dark, or is afflicted with some strange illness.
>
> Consider the difference between a five-mile walk at night in the desert and in the jungle. Instead of clouds, rain, darkness, wet branches, soggy leaves, and mudholes, the desert walker encounters clear skies, dry air, bright starlight or moonlight, dry ground, and practically no vegetation. . . . If he becomes tired, he can lie down safely almost anywhere. He can listen to the vast stillness, watch the stars and the moon, and then sleep without fear of insect, beast, man, or storm. Because of all this he also sleeps with little fear of evil spirits. Nevertheless, the sun smites him by day and the cold by night. The wind, also, is to be feared. It fills the air with blinding dust which chokes his lungs, hides landmarks, and sometimes moves the desert sand so rapidly that when the dust disappears, the traveller cannot recognize the dunes which formerly marked the way to the spring where he must drink. The desert dwellers also fear drought which may lead to the starvation of the flocks. . . . The desert man is as free as the jungle man to believe in spirits that inhabit stones, bushes, lizards and beasts of prey, but there is less incentive to do so. Even if he does believe in them, they are unimportant compared with big things like sun, wind, and drought. Hence it is natural for the primitive desert man to pin his faith to a few powerful gods who rule large areas. This does not compel him to believe in a single God, but it makes the transition to that belief easy and natural.[21]

Huntington believed climate to be enormously significant in its effect on human health, behavior, and institutions (see Chapter 3). Neverthe-less, he maintained that he was not endorsing a single-factor theory of climatic determinism, citing heredity and cultural endowment as other relevant factors.[22] Despite the qualification, he is usually categorized as a thorough-going environmental determinist.

Criticisms of Determinism. The determinist position has been the target of substantial criticism. Some have suggested alternative theories of human-environment relationships, and these are discussed subsequently. At this point we briefly examine arguments asserting that the determinists have failed to prove their case.

Several critics charged that the evidence offered by determinists was too vague, inconclusive, or limited in scope to support their theories. Clarkson argued that "The strongest statements of direct determination of social effect from environmental cause were reserved for those instances in which the factual data were skimpiest, frequently instances from very early historical periods."[23] Sorokin maintained that the evidence used to prove particular determinist theories was often contradicted by data available in other sources.

Sorokin also criticized the determinists' tendency to cite simple correlations as proof of causation. Huntington, for example, argued that seasonal variations in crime rates indicated that criminal behavior was determined by climate. Even if the statistical correlation of crime and season is accurate, however, climatic causality is very much in doubt. For example, crime rates also fluctuate, perhaps to higher degrees, according to nationality, social stratum, and occupation; climate is thus at best one of several relevant factors. Second, climatic influences may have only indirect influence on criminal acts. Men may become more or less criminal "not because the temperature is higher or the humidity is lower or the sunlight is less bright, but because the direct factors of criminality such as poor crops or out-of-doors social life are partly influenced by climatic conditions."[24]

Once it was argued that a given geographical factor determined some human activity, critics insisted that the same factor elsewhere on earth should produce an identical human response. The evidence, however, conclusively demonstrated that this was not the case. Thus Sorokin, considering the view that environment determines forms of human habitation, points out that the Hopi and Navaho Indians, who occupied the same parts of northwestern Arizona for long periods of time, produced substantially different dwellings. The former created terraced sandstone houses with rectangular rooms, and the latter dwelt in conical, earth-covered huts.

Although the environment changes, it rarely does so to a significant degree over the time span relevant to recorded history. Critics of determinism wished to know how major changes in social and political organization could take place in a context of geographical stability if the latter phenomena determined the structure of the former.

Many critics granted that the environment had some influence on human activity, but even these did not believe that environment was the major influence. Numerous cases were advanced of situations in which other nongeographical factors had predominant causal impact. Thus Sorokin questioned the relationship between environment and food consumption patterns by noting that the differences in consumption between social classes within a given geographical area are often greater than the differences between residents of differing areas.

Critics also objected to the practice of speaking of the environment as an autonomous variable without considering the nature of the organism whose environment is in question. This fallacy is obvious for discussions of different animal species. An evaluation of the earth's environment from the perspective of fishes would be the precise opposite of an evaluation from the perspective of humanity—at least in terms of the percentage of the earth's surface that was habitable. However exactly the same argument applies to different human groups. In evaluating the claim that soil and climate affect a society's accumulation of wealth, Sorokin indicated that the wealth-producing capacities of a geographic area are not simply a function of its physical attributes but also of the culture that inhabits it. Fertile soil is of limited value to a people who have not yet discovered agriculture; likewise, coal and oil represent wealth only when a certain level of technological capability has been attained.

Possibilism.   As a reaction against determinism, there appeared a new theory, possibilism, emphasizing the role of man in the unfolding of history. Lucien Febvre wrote the single sentence that best encapsulates its central thesis: "There are no necessities, but everywhere possibilities; and man, as master of the possibilities, is the judge of their use."[25]

According to this view, man is not a passive creature, helpless before environmental pressures. Rather, man is "in the first place." The environment of each locality offers a set of opportunities (possibilities), but it is man who evaluates the options and selects those to be pursued. Opportunities define what can be done, not what will be done; they may be rejected as well as capitalized on.

Possibilists note that a given geographical area may offer different sets of possibilities at different times. Three factors explain this. First, certain environments are variable, and when they change, they restructure man's options. As the Sprouts note, "Some of the changes in the earth's structure result from physical processes of nature: earth slipping, volcanoes erupting, rocks falling, water flowing and freezing, wind blowing, plants, animals, and micro-organisms proliferating, etc. Sometimes these natural processes cause human catastrophes: earthquakes, floods, famines, epidemics, and the like."[26] Second, developments in technology open new possibilities. For example, prior to the invention of the ship, a river may have been an obstacle to trade and communication, imposing a limit on the possibilities in a region. But once man discovers how to travel on the water, the river's role is reversed; it becomes a means of expanding the available opportunities.

Third, as human needs vary, previously unnoticed or undesired aspects of the environment provide possibilities for satisfying new aspirations. One hundred years ago, Death Valley, in the desert of southern California, was thought to be a nightmarish environment; people either tried to avoid it or moved through as quickly as possible. Yet today, solitude, quiet, and undisturbed natural surroundings are deemed highly desirable, and for at least part of the year many tourists trek into Death Valley for the express purpose of staying there and enjoying the environment.

Another theoretical tenet of possibilism is the recognition that the options for human action in any geographic area are always limited; man cannot do whatever he pleases in regard to human nature. This point is perhaps best illustrated in the writings of the French geographer, Jean Brunhes. Brunhes believed that human beings enjoyed enormous latitude in the kinds of activities they could initiate. Nevertheless, he consistently stressed that there did exist limits that must be taken seriously. Everyone has unavoidable needs for food, clothing, and shelter. Somehow, man's relationship to nature has to meet these needs.

Nor did Brunhes assume that man's increased technological capacities had removed him from natural limitations. To Brunhes, the attempt to press beyond natural limits involved grave risks, and "the penalty exacted for acting contrary to physical facts is all the more cruel as man's victory over them is great and glorious." There was ample evidence to prove his point.

> When man succeeds in building dikes to hold back the waters of a Po or a Hoang-ho, or manages to drive the North Sea back and win the Dutch polders, the risks he runs are proportional to the fruitfulness of his efforts. An invasion of the sea or an abnormal flooding of these rivers is destructive to the very extent that the natural forces were victoriously tamed.[27]

The possibilists were aware of economic and social limits on the environmental possibilities that could be realized. Human time and resources are, of course, quite finite; everything feasible cannot be accomplished, and there is a consequent opportunity cost associated with the projects that do take place. As Bowman quipped, men can move mountains, but not without first floating a bond issue. The Sprouts have noted that the question of selecting the most advantageous environmental option links possibilism, a geographic theory, to the other social sciences. It is very much in the domain of economics, sociology, and political science to compare the social costs and benefits of various projects.

An examination of the possibilists' approach to particular substantive problems may clarify their understanding of the relationship between man and nature. Clark Wissler, an American anthropologist, considered the problem of the impact of nature on the development of human inventions. Far from maintaining that inventions simply appeared in the human mind, that the environment was irrelevant, Wissler agreed that "it is undoubtedly due to the presence of snow that the Eskimo invented the snow house and to experience with birchbark that the Eastern Woodland Indians devised the bark-covered tipi."[28] However the mere presence of snow or birchbark is not a sufficient explanation. These materials have no intrinsic quality that requires men to use them in their dwellings. Snow and birchbark are possibilities, not causal forces, and men must have the understanding and the will to make use of them before the construction of igloos or teepees can proceed.

Or consider the question of the effect of the environment on the stagnation or decline of civilizations. A determinist might argue that such phenomena can be understood as an effect of the limited supply of natural resources (see the discussion of B. Meggers' thesis, p. 54). Yet the possibilist geographer Isaiah Bowman insists that human institutions are the primary causal factors. "It may be shown that there has never been a civilization that declined because it exhausted the possibilities of the land. No nation has ever fully developed its frontier! The earth has never gone back on man, but man has found himself entangled in the unpredictable effects of his own system."[29]

According to Bowman, a declining civilization is not one that faces an absence of geographic possibilities; rather it has failed to take advantage of possibilities. Thus he makes the following argument about China during the 1920s:

> The prevailing type of her culture makes it impossible for her people to occupy semiarid regions that are suited to extensive machine cultivation, like the western fringe of settlement in the United States. It has been estimated that if China were to employ such lands they would add more than 500 million acres to the present total. . . . But the required change in type of farm practice would be as revolutionary to the Chinese as migration to a new land. Moreover, it would demand a beginning with capital for machine equipment, and this cannot be got from either private sources or government at this time. So the population stays bound to the crop and land cultivation system created through the ages—in its present intense form a product of the last century or two.[30]

No doubt Bowman would consider the new environmental possibilities opened up by the revolutionary political and social forces of the People's Republic of China as contemporary proof of his point.

Probabilism and Pragmatism.   For several decades possibilism and determinism defined the parameters within which geographers debated the relationship between man and environment. However the basis of the dispute became extremely confused. One problem concerned the difficulty of deciding whether factual evidence should be interpreted as proof of determinism or possibilism. Consider a hypothetical case in which a human activity is consistently correlated with a geographic factor—for example, all humans living in subfreezing climates live in tribes. Would this finding support determinism or possibilism? One cannot automatically assume the former, and W. E. Wallis provides an intriguing argument to the contrary.

> The correlation between man's economic life and his geographical environment is not evidence of the influence of physical environment. The correlation shows the extent to which man has adapted himself to the environment, the extent to which he has compelled it to minister to his needs, to serve his purposes, to respond to his will. . . . If "being influenced" by the environment means making the most of it, then it is the part of wisdom to be influenced.[31]

The same issue appears in an analysis of a technological response to the environment, such as the use of air conditioning in the tropics. Does this example demonstrate that the environment has determined the direction of man's technological development, or does it indicate that man has mastered the environment by managing to escape its unpleasant characteristics? The evidence can be used in either way. A simple correlation between human action and an environmental condition is insufficient to indicate whether an act represents determinism or the free selection of an advantageous possibility.

A second problem in the debate between determinist and possibilist involved the degree of difference between the two positions. If natural regions encompass definite systems of possibilities, and if these possibilities can be ranked in their ability to satisfy human needs, how much difference is there between the designation of the most likely possibility and modified determinism? What distinguishes the argument that the desert requires a nomadic life style from the position that although other social patterns could exist in the desert, nomadism is by far the most common, practical, and probable alternative? In such a context, the possibilists could only insist that their point of view included a belief in free will. Yet that response removes the issue from the domain of the geographer and transfers it to philosophy.[32]

Dissatisfaction with these ambiguities led post-World War II geographers to reexamine the usefulness of the determinism-possibilism dichotomy. One alternative was to eliminate the debate by suggesting a new perspective that bridged the gap between environmental causality and free will. O. H. K. Spate proposed such a theory, which he titled "probabilism." Spate never developed his notion with any rigor. He used the term simply to refer to a literal recognition that some possibilities were more likely to be attempted than others, and something could be learned about the probability that a given project would be carried out by examining environmental factors.[33]

Subsequently others have elaborated on the probabilist thesis. The Sprouts in particular emphasize the linkages between probabilism and a theory of human decision making. Such a focus is based on three assumptions: that human beings make choices (decisions), that all possible choices are not equally probable, and that the choice made will determine the action taken. Hence if we wish to know the probability that people will initiate one of several possible actions, we have to understand how they reach decisions.

Probabilistic theories of decision making may involve complex mathematical and statistical models. Let us examine the situation of a farmer who has the option of planting a variety of different crops. What factors must be considered to predict the probability of his selecting a particular pattern of cultivation? First we must ascertain the farmer's motivation and goals. He may desire to make as much money as he can during the year; he may be interested in ensuring production of at least some minimal yield; or he may wish to preserve the fertility of the soil for subsequent years. Each of these objectives may lead to a different strategy. Determining such motivations can be a serious research problem —especially if one wants to learn how a large population will behave. Several methods can be employed. An analyst can rely on people's adherence to cultural norms (i.e., certain groups may be known to value security), or he can employ an assumed model of human nature (such as the economist's hypothetical rational man) or carry out survey research. But he must understand what the subjects are attempting to achieve; otherwise he cannot predict how they will evaluate different environmental options.

Second, the quantity and quality of information a farmer has about his environment must be discovered. It is of limited value to examine the possibilities of an area objectively, for the farmer will not base his decision on the conditions that actually exist but rather on those he perceives to exist. Thus there may be insects in the area which would devastate a cotton crop. Yet if the farmer is unaware of their presence he may consider cotton to be a feasible alternative.

Finally, one must know something about how the farmer utilizes information. He may indeed rationally select the pattern of cultivation that seems most likely to satisfy his goals, but he also may not. Cultural prescriptions may prevent him from implementing an otherwise optimal strategy (perhaps certain crops are believed to be sacred and cannot be harvested). Or he may be part of a broader decision-making unit (e.g., a producer's cooperative). In that case, the structure and rules of the larger organization must be considered in predicting a decision. If these or other factors affect the way in which the farmer makes up his mind, they are relevant to our analysis.[34]

Few geographers are formal adherents of probabilism. The approach of most of those seeking to move beyond the determinism-possibilism controversy can best be referred to as pragmatic. Pragmatists do not know whether the universe is organized according to determinism or free will, and they do not know how to find out. Moreover they are unwilling to delay substantive research until they are capable of resolving what they perceive as philosophical questions. Instead they accept as a working hypothesis a qualified determinism, the assumption that natural and human processes of sufficient regularity do exist. This pragmatic attitude is squarely in the mainstream of contemporary practice in the social sciences.[35]

An example may clarify this perspective. Wooldridge and East studied the distribution of population in Sweden and learned that it broadly correlated with the distribution of economic resources. Such a finding does not imply that every Swede lives near an economic resource, nor does it imply that the Swedish people do not employ free will in deciding where they wish to live. It merely indicates that at least for the period under consideration, the existence of economic resources can be linked with some regularity to population distribution. One can infer only that economic motivation affected the decision to select a place to live. The data do not support or reject either determinism or possibilism. We have simply a potentially useful, pragmatic, geographic observation.

Neodeterminism.   In the preceding discussion we explained the probabilist argument that human beings are more likely to select one geographic possibility than others. In some situations, however, the probable alternative is not merely more likely to occur, it is virtually certain. When probabilities reach such levels, one can reasonably argue that in essence the environment is determining human action.

Griffith Taylor, a modern determinist who basically supports the position just outlined, argues that nature has prescribed a master plan for the world in which environmental costs and benefits are so distributed that it would be sheer folly for mankind to follow any but a single, obviously beneficial path. Projects not included in the plan would be possible, but they would be foolhardy, wasteful, and usually doomed to failure in the long run. In particular, Taylor emphasizes the importance of the plan in shaping man's response to naturally inhospitable regions (the Sahara, Antarctica, northern Canada, and central Australia). He insists that "centuries hence the deserts of the world will still be deserts; and man will have shown that he has had the good sense to use the better areas, which nature has determined shall be worth his attention."[36]

Although the master plan clearly designates the most advantageous activities relating to the environment, it does not require that man exploit these potentials at any definite rate. In fact, Taylor refers to his viewpoint as Stop-and-Go determinism, which he illustrates as follows.

> In any large city we see traffic moving along established routes, i.e., the main roads. The directions are completely established, but what is the function of the police officer at the crossing-places? He can block all traffic, he can accelerate the movement, or decelerate it at his wish, but he does not turn it out of the established routes. In nine-tenths of the world (and I am willing to agree the analogy is not too close in highly-endowed areas) man is like the traffic controller. Nature says, "This land is too dry, or too cold, or too wet, or too rugged; there is very little choice as to what can be done with it." Man can ignore the region, as in the case of Antarctica, or he can struggle along in a sparse pastoral occupation as in half of Australia, etc. He definitely has very little choice. . . . It is absurd to say that man can choose which he pleases among many possible directions.[37]

Thus nature sets the direction of human advancement. Societies may stagnate, or develop rapidly or slowly, but they can only progress in the manner determined by the environment.

Other geographers have criticized Taylor's theory. Tatham, citing the possibilist position, argues that man is free to make unwise or suboptimal decisions if he so chooses. In addition, regions that offer difficulties may still include substantial benefits, perhaps enough to be worth the effort of exploitation. There is no reason to assume that mankind will always select the path of least resistance. "If the nations of the world believed that their continued existence depended on growing bananas at the Pole," Tatham remarks, "who can doubt that cost would be ignored, an artificial environment created and bananas grown?"[38] To this specific point, Taylor replies that "it is a modified form of such foolish action which the modern 'determinist' is trained to prevent."[39] Of course such a reply presupposes the conviction that there exists an objective means of evaluating environmental potentials and that some group of persons are competent to make the evaluations.

Betty Meggers, an anthropologist, has stated a second neodeterminist theory of the environment. Meggers observed that empirical efforts to demonstrate specific relationships between environment and culture have generally yielded negative results. She believes that the source of the problem is not the absence of a relationship but rather the failure to discern the fundamental factors involved in the relationship. In particular, efforts to correlate culture and environment classified the latter according to categories employed by geographers. What results would follow if a different classificatory standard were used? Since the primary contact between culture and environment is through subsistence activity, Meggers defines four types of environment in terms of agricultural potential: no potential, limited potential, improvable potential, and unlimited potential. Her field studies, particularly in South American rain forests, provided evidence of the following patterns. Tropical rain forests (limited potential) precluded certain levels of cultural complexity (large concentration of population, stable settlements, etc.). In addition, advanced cultural traits did not diffuse into these regions from adjacent areas. Finally, when advanced cultures migrated into the limited potential area, they were unable to preserve their former level of development and declined.

Studies of other areas that exhibited similar patterns led Meggers to offer the following thesis: "The level to which a culture can develop is dependent upon the agricultural potentiality of the environment it occupies. As this potentiality is improved, culture will advance. If it cannot be improved, the culture will become stabilized at a level compatible with the food resources."[40] Meggers is arguing that the environment limits what man can do; it does not ordain what he will do within those limits. For example, many societies fail to develop to a level as high as their agricultural potential would permit. Nor is Meggers citing the environment as the only cause of civilization's decline. Finally, Meggers' law, unlike Taylor's plan, does not imply that higher civilizations can never transfer their culture to regions of low potential. She maintains only that such civilizations could not indigenously appear in those areas, nor could they survive if restricted to the resources available there. As long as other areas of high agricultural potential provide sufficient products and services to "underwrite" the low potential region, a civilization can encompass both.

Human Ecology. Through the late nineteenth and early twentieth centuries, as geographers struggled to comprehend the interaction between man and his environment, a kindred discipline was emerging that would focus on similar questions. Ecology, a term derived from the Greek *oikos* (a house or place to live in), first appeared in German biologist Ernst Haeckel's studies of plant life published in 1868. Since that time, the field has broadened to include both animals and human beings.[41] We cannot fully discuss all the subsequent developments in ecology, but we do examine the distinct qualities of ecological analysis, the potential of ecology as a perspective for research on man's relationship to the geographic environment.

From its inception ecology was overtly Darwinian, focusing on the "web of life,"—the interactions through which organisms adapted to one another and to the world around them in a struggle for existence. In addition, it developed a holistic approach to these phenomena and processes.[42] This perspective permitted a definition of the environment broader than that employed in much of the previous geographic literature. Ecology encompassed the full spectrum of organic life (plants, animals, microbes) as well as all the physical resources relevant to the existence of living organisms. There was no need to limit inquiry to surface features or climate. Ecology emphasized the totality of relationships among organisms and between them and their physical environment. It included the complete analysis of food chains, energy flows, and other complex and dynamic cycles.

Recently geographers have begun to consider seriously the potential benefits of employing ecological concepts or methods in their own studies. D. R. Stoddart particularly stresses the usefulness of the concept of ecosystem. As defined by Fossberg, this term refers to

> a functioning interacting system composed of one or more living organisms and their effective environment, both physical and biological. . . . The description of an ecosystem may include its spatial relations; inventories of its physical features, its habitats and ecological niches, its organisms, and its basic reserves of matter and energy; its patterns of circulation of matter and energy; the nature of its income (or input) of matter and energy; and the behavior or trend of its entropy level.[43]

According to Stoddard, such a framework has properties of significant value to geographic analysis of the environment. First, it includes within a common rubric man, the physical environment, animals, and plants. Many previous geographic approaches have employed an arbitrary dualism, a dichotomy between man and nature. Also they tended to exaggerate a single relationship, the environment's impact on human activity. However the ecosystem concept directs attention to the unity of its member elements in interlocking and ongoing processes; for example, it calls attention to man's impact on the environment. Second, the relationship between the parts of an ecosystem exhibit a "more or less orderly, ratonal, and comprehensible" structure, which can be identified and studied. An analysis of the feeding habits of more than 200 species of fish in coral reefs of the Marshall Islands in the Pacific revealed a complex but consistent pattern through which primary producers (algae and phytoplankton), secondary consumers (herbivores and carnivores), tertiary consumers (carnivores), and quaternary consumers (roving carnivores) provided nutrition for one another.

Third, ecosystems function. There is a continuous flow of matter and energy between component elements, and at least in simple ecosystems this entire process can be examined quantitatively. Fourth, as a form of general system, ecosystems can be examined from the vantage point of general systems theory (formally the ecosystem is an open system tending toward a steady state and obeying the laws of open system thermodynamics). Depending on the complexity of the specific problem and the relevant level of analysis, a variety of forms of model construction then become possible. "Systems may be built at the framework level (e.g., settlement hierarchies or transport nets) or as simple cybernetic systems (e.g., the mechanism of supply and demand, and of Malthus' doctrine), or at the more complex level of social systems and living organisms."[44]

Stoddart recognized that the analysis of ecosystems had been applied primarily to the nonhuman world. However some efforts have been made to examine ecosystems that include man, often on islands, which serve as natural laboratories for ecological research. Roy Rappaport, for example, has discussed the interaction between prehuman Pacific island ecosystems and migrating human populations that first arrived there.

Although historical data are limited, Rappaport manages to suggest the manner in which island ecosystems may serve as a barrier to human invasion. Several islands were visited by pre-European wanderers who attempted but failed to establish successful settlements; that is, the island ecosystem proved capable of rejecting man entirely. In most cases the crucial obstacle was the island's size or the lack of fresh water supplies. But some areas posed unique survival problems. On Sidney Island in the Gilberts, the sea channel to the island's lagoon dried up, resulting in a level of salinity too high to maintain marine life. At the same time the configuration of the shoreline did not afford an adequate base for the deep-sea fisherman. Thus the attempt to colonize Sidney was abandoned after a 20-year struggle to maintain adequate food resources. Even where man was able to establish a foothold, the island's ecosystem could still restrict the living species and the artifacts he might bring with him. Sweet potatoes and kava, cultivated in much of Polynesia, could not be success-fully transferred to several atolls. Likewise, stone tools and dugout canoes could be used, but not replaced, on islands lacking the requisite materials.

In addition to an island ecosystem's capacity to regulate the admission of human newcomers, it could also affect their social development. Rap-paport cites the following evidence. On atolls, where success in the acqui-sition of food was influenced to an extreme degree by unpredictable and uncontrollable natural events (typhoons and droughts), the human popu-lation never organized their economic activities to any appreciable extent. However on high islands the situation was quite different; food supplies were potentially stable as long as man did not upset or degrade the functioning of the existing ecosystem. Such a disturbance might be caused, for example, by the indiscriminate burning of forests as a means of clearing land, or by hunting, with consequent impact on the island's water supply and pattern of soil erosion. Yet men could successfully avoid damaging the ecosystem that sustained them by carefully regulating their impact on the environment, particularly their food-producing activities. In fact it is on the high islands that large-scale economic organization amenable to such regulation can be found. Thus Rappaport suggests the following tentative hypothesis: where man is helpless before the envi-ronment, economic organization can do no good and never develops; where organization can assist man in meeting his needs through the environment, on the other hand, it does appear.[45]

In recent decades, scholars in various disciplines have employed an ecological perspective in the analysis of a broad spectrum of substantive issues relevant to man's relationship with his environment. The three cases discussed below illustrate the added insights available through this point of view.

A study by British geographer S. R. Eyre indicates how a thorough ecological analysis can correct an oversimplified determinist generaliza-tion about the connection between physiographic factors and the site of human settlements. In rural Britain Eyre observed a row of villages located in close proximity to the point at which a series of springs emerged from a cliff's base. For 2 or 3 miles both east and west of the villages, settlement was extremely sparse. The availability of water from the springs was offered as the reason for the selection of that settlement site.

Eyre argues that location of water supply is an insufficient basis for explaining the placement of the villages. First, other ecological factors in the area, such as particularly rich soil, grazing areas, and abundant supplies of firewood and timber, made the site desirable even in the absence of a spring line. Second, an ecological analysis views technology as a means of interaction between man and environment. Inhabitants of this region had had the technical capacity to construct wells since Neolithic times. Also, it is highly unlikely that the founders of the village had sufficient understanding of biology to appreciate the hygienic reasons for preferring a spring source to an open water supply further downstream. Both factors indicate that the first residents were not tied to the spring line as the only source of water.[46] One should carefully note the implications of Eyre's argument. By disputing a single-factor determinist thesis, he is not denying the importance of man's interaction with the environment. On the contrary, he stresses that a relationship exists in complex and indirect forms, requiring in-depth ecological analysis.

An ecological analysis can provide a common framework through which different disciplines can concentrate on a problem of mutual interest. For example, sociologist Otis D. Duncan has considered the question of Los Angeles smog. Duncan suggests four ecological categories: population, organization, environment, technology (P, O, E, T); he argues that an understanding of the causes of, and possible solutions for, urban smog require an analysis broad enough to encompass each of these variables.

A brief discussion of the history of Los Angeles smog and early efforts to control it verify the complexity of the phenomenon. Smog was first noticed when it began to irritate human eyes and respiratory organs (E–P), damage growing plants (E–E), and crack rubber, thereby accelerating the deterioration of automobile tires (E–T). Civic groups attempted an initial response through a model control ordinance; eventually the state assembly formed the Los Angeles County Air Pollution Control District (E–0). Soon abatement devices were developed and installed on industrial plants (O–T).

Further research demonstrated the impact of automobile exhaust on smog (T–E) as well as the susceptibility of the Los Angeles Basin to temperature inversions, which keep polluted air within the city (E–E). Meanwhile population increases brought more automobiles into the area, aggravating the problem (P–E). A number of diverse organizations sought to respond (E–O). Through a complicated interplay between private groups and government agencies (O–O), large-scale programs of public health research were instituted and efforts were begun to discover a means of reducing the pollutant components of auto exhaust (O–T).

Although recognizing that this examination of the smog problem is brief and superficial, Duncan nevertheless concludes, "Even the barest account of that situation . . . can leave no doubt that social change and environmental modification occurred in the closest interdependence—so close, in fact, that the two 'levels' of change were systematically interrelated." Duncan's presentation demonstrates that P, O, E, and T are all closely related in the smog problem, and it is probably impossible to comprehend the situation without considering all four factors. However it is something else to document a systematic relationship among these factors. For example, among the many relationships noted was the effect of smog on plants (E–E) and the activities of private and government agencies attempting to devise a solution (O–O). The methodologies necessary to explain these two relationships are utterly dissimilar. In addition Duncan states, "A number of diverse organizational responses (E–O) to the smog problem have occurred." This relationship poses an enormous methodological difficulty, the transition from environmental factor to human response.[47]

In our final example, historian James Malin argues that ecology can be of assistance in disputing a well-known determinist hypothesis within his own discipline. At the end of the nineteenth century, Frederick Jackson Turner presented what was to become a classic work of historiography, his paper on "The Significance of the American Frontier," to the American Historical Association. According to Turner, the Western frontier exerted a profound impact on American life, having strongly influenced the American national character, particularly by encouraging individualism, which allegedly promoted democratic values. The frontier also served as a safety valve providing the restless, dissatisfied, and unemployed elements in urban areas with an outlet for their energies, thus reducing pressures toward social conflict. However, Turner went on to argue that this beneficial frontier had closed; it ceased to exist when American civilization spanned the continent. A corollary of his thesis is that aspects of American culture produced by the frontier may be lost unless some other social force or institution is found to sustain them.[48]

Malin directs his criticism toward the assertion that the frontier no longer exists. From an ecological point of view, he maintains, a frontier is not an absolute boundary but rather the limit within which a culture with a given technology can successfully interact with the environment. As long as technological innovation takes place, that limit and the frontier can expand. Areas once thought useless may become of value, or through improved technology, regions that have been exhausted in one resource may be discovered to have potential in others. In fact, Malin envisions a frontier whose only limit is man's technical creativity.

> There can be no such thing as the exhaustion of the natural resources of any area of the earth unless positive proof can be adduced that no possible technological "discovery" can ever bring to the horizon of utilization any remaining property of the area. An attempt to prove such an exhaustion is meaningless, because there is no possibility of implementing such a test.

Historical experience points to an indeterminate release to man of such "new resources" as he becomes technologically capable of their utilization.[49]

Current Approaches. In recent years geographers have produced some innovative approaches to the relationship of man to his environment. Two examples are given here.

In a study of the Chiapas Highlands of southeastern Mexico, A. D. Hill illustrates how two cultures, the Ladino and the Indian, interact in fundamentally different ways with the same environment. He also describes how these contrasting relationships with the environment affect the pattern of intercultural contact. Hill believes that each culture perceives its habitat through a "cultural lens," which structures reality according to its particular tradition and heritage. Culture determines what people consider their needs to be, what natural resources they consider useful to satisfy those needs, and what equipment, tools, and institutions they have available with which to attempt resource exploitation.

An examination of Ladino and Indian cultures reveals substantial differences in basic attitudes toward the environment. The Indian's relationship to nature is tightly integrated into the fabric of his entire culture. Continuity in one requires continuity in the other. For example, the growing of maize not only provides the bulk of an Indian's diet, it is also essential to the maintenance of his identity and prestige. It is culturally defined as man's work, and even those who can support their families by some other means "invariably choose to work also in the maize." In addition, Indian culture "imbues the physical environment with a mystical quality so powerful and compelling as to discourage the individual from conceiving of tampering with it beyond the bounds which tradition ascribes."[50] Thus it makes no sense to manipulate technologies to affect the environment, for the latter is under mystical control, and the best way to cope with such supernatural forces is adherence to the age-old way of life.

The perspective of the Ladino is just the opposite. He does not stand in awe of nature; rather he feels capable of manipulating it to produce wealth, power, and prestige. He sees no reason to be wary of innovative technology. Availability of capital and labor and market conditions are the factors on which the Ladino bases his decisions. Where they are favorable, the physical milieu is open to exploitation. One scholar expresses the distinction between the two cultures as follows.

The principal and fundamental goal of Indian culture is to effect a peaceful adjustment or adaption of men to the universe. In contrast, the main goal of

> Ladino culture is to effect the control of the universe by man. The Indian wishes to come to terms with the universe, the Ladino wishes to dominate it.[51]

Differences in culture produce differences in practice. The Indian lives close to nature, using many natural features and exhibiting a deep knowledge of his habitat. He accepts his environment and does not attempt to change it. Indian behavior is fundamentally conservative, demonstrating strong continuity over time. Ladinos are more distant from their immediate environment or, if one prefers, closer to the larger environment that surrounds the highlands. They often rely on materials fabricated elsewhere and import technology to transform the local geography in a fashion commensurate with their interests. They are flexible, susceptible to change, and responsible for the introduction of modern artificial features (roads, etc.) into the region.

When these two cultures come into contact, conflict between them works to the detriment of the Indian. In a sense, he is better adjusted to an environment the Ladino is transforming. As Hill notes, in the modern (Ladino) system that is appearing, the Indian

> is a "defensive participant"—he only moves here and there to defend himself. He never takes the initiative, the offensive, because he does not understand the new system. . . . He cannot compete with the ladino because he does not know "the rules of the game." He merely goes through the motions without knowing why the game is being played. The spirits of the Indian Meitatiles, fly over the town to guard the Indian community. But they do not watch the new road—it is the ladino's road and not a part of the Indian system.[52]

In brief, the Indians seek to maintain a once stable culture (adapted to a once stable environment) in a changing world. They are not oriented to employ the environment in a competitive struggle for wealth and power. Ladinos, however, are well adjusted to modern grain markets, capital and credit systems, and technical processes. When combined with an aggressive life style, their knowledge presents an impressive potential for domination.

Our second study is Peter Gould's application of game theory to the problems of farmers in the Barren Middle Zone of Ghana. Game theory attempts to show how rational decisions can be made under conditions of uncertainty, to outwit an opponent or at least to maintain a superior position. To employ such a perspective in an analysis of man-environment relationships, Gould must make several assumptions. First, it is possible for men to make rational choices. Second, different choices relating to interaction with the environment (whether or not to expand cultivation) will have different utilities (size of harvest) depending on how environmental processes operate (whether there is enough rain). Third, from the human point of view, the environment is unpredictable; no one knows whether next year will provide sufficient rain. Fourth, the environment is a game player. This is not a pantheist notion—we are all well aware that nature does not consciously decide whether there will be rain. For the purposes of this model, however, man and nature are opposing players in a competitive game, and man remains uncertain of what the environment's move will be.

In Gould's analysis, Ghanaian farmers are playing a two-person, five-strategy, zero-sum game against nature. In other words, there are two players (the farmers and nature), five strategies (the five crops the farmers may plant in any year—yams, maize, cassava, millet, and hill rice), and the contest is zero sum (what one side wins, the other side loses, the loss of a crop being considered a win for nature). For the purposes of simplicity, nature only gets two moves: dry years and wet years (inadequate rainfall and adequate rainfall). Consider a sample round in the game: farmer plays a crop of half maize and half millet, nature plays a dry year, and the harvest is the payoff.

The objective of the analysis is to devise the best moves for the farmers. If we know how much of a given crop a farmer can produce in dry and wet years, we can create a payoff matrix that indicates the returns for each of the five possible crop strategies. If a farmer plants only yams, his return might be 82 (a hypothetical caloric measurement of yield) in a wet year but only 11 in a dry year. Of course planting only yams may not be the optimal strategy. The payoff matrix can be solved graphically or algebraically to indicate the mixture of crops that ought to produce the maximum harvest.

Game theory predicts how to produce a maximum yield under conditions of uncertainty. If one knows how to predict future rainfall, if it is possible to reduce uncertainty by estimating probabilities of future rainfall, different strategies are called for. Furthermore, a winning strategy may offer no more than the best of a bad situation. The environment limits the maximum yield, whatever the crop mixture, and if the terrain is bleak even the maximum return may not provide more than bare subsistence.[53]

Issues and Answers.   Diligent readers are at this point entitled to query, "Have all those scholars developing all those theories of the environment over centuries actually resolved anything?" The answer may be unsatisfying and sobering. Conclusions are tentative, theory supplants theory, and as the human species changes its needs and its interests, it changes its understanding of itself. But tentative and incomplete solutions are still functional. Without resolving all the theoretical issues involved, ecologists may still be capable of helping to reduce air pollution. In that spirit, let us consider the issues suggested as foci for attention in the introduction.

Definition of the Environment. Our discussions have repeatedly revealed that the way in which the environment is defined has enormous impact on the way in which the environment is understood to affect mankind. Thus we find Eyre bringing additional factors into his ecological analysis of the English countryside to refute a determinist thesis and Meggers advocating a new method of classifying environments to support determinism.

Also we recall critics of determinism who emphasized that an environment could not be defined at all without considering the culture of those who inhabit it. Hill's study of Ladinos and Indians supports this contention; the same physical features have different potentials for those who perceive them from different cultural perspectives.

Our position on this issue is relativistic. How we define an environment depends on what we want to know about it. If we wish to understand how a human group will function in a given geographical region, we must define the environment in terms of the culture and technology of that group. Although the presence of uranium may be irrelevant to an aboriginal population, the supply of firewood is crucial. If we are interested in the kind of food an area can produce, we might focus on a set of factors similar to Meggers' concepts of agricultural potential. But if we are concerned with the environmental basis of religion, we should perhaps, like Huntington, consider the power of the wind and the stillness of the night.

Natural Versus Human Environments. Many studies demonstrate how men have transformed the environment in which they live. Brunhes notes the reclamation of marshland through drainage, Rappaport cites the impact of man on island ecosystems, and Duncan records the changes in air quality over Los Angeles. Should these products of human action be considered part of the environment? We think they should. The new conditions constitute a new milieu in which men must plant, harvest, and breathe. They become part of the environment to which man must adapt if he is to survive.

However we must also point out that what men have changed once, they may be able to change again. Designating phenomena as part of the environment in no way guarantees their permanence. Rather, aspects of

the environment produced by human action (e.g., air pollution) are prime
candidates for correction by human action.

Mediating Forces.   There is a historical trend toward recognition that
many factors mediate the environment's impact. Ancient theorists suggested direct relationships between environmental factors and human
physical and psychological attributes. The societies in which they lived
were technologically less capable of mediating environmental forces than
are modern ones. By the time of the Industrial Revolution, even determinists were acknowledging the indirect processes through which environment affected behavior. Thus Demolins might argue that the steppe
causes pastoralism, which in turn causes patriarchal families, which in
turn causes conservative personality types; but he would not maintain that
environment directly determines personality. Possibilism and its succes-
sors, as well as ecological analyses, continued this trend. For example, one
must understand both man's level of knowledge and his objectives before
predicting how he will respond to nature. Our conclusion is that culture
and technology, at even the most primitive levels, are integral parts of
man's relationship to nature. As these factors increase in complexity, their
mediating role expands.

Generalization among Environments.   Many of the authors cited in this
chapter have considered the basis on which relationships between man
and the environment might be generalized. This is not surprising, since
all scientific theory is based to some degree on the existence of generalizations. Theorists of man's relationship to the environment are already
committed to the search for generalizable findings.

Those who agree that generalization is possible still find much to
disagree about. Points of dispute fall into several broad categories. First
there are questions about the validity of specific generalizations. For
example, Sorokin criticized the determinist generalization that environment determined forms of dwellings by noting the counterexample of the
Hopi and the Navaho. Second, geographers disagree about which
definition of the environment permits accurate generalization. Here
again, we recall Meggers' advocacy of a general relationship between
cultural development and environment, provided the latter is defined
according to a specific concept of agricultural potential. Third, it is unclear which environmental factors must be taken into consideration before valid generalizations can be made. In his critique of Turner's thesis,
Malin argues that generalizations of direct relationships between environment and human behavior (such as linkages between some geographic
factor and a mode of social organization) are susceptible to error unless

they include an understanding of the technological capacities of the population under analysis.

Finally, geographers differ regarding the degree to which generalizations are valid. Early determinists saw the relationships they discovered as eternal natural laws. Possibilists, believing in free will, were reluctant to endorse any lawlike relationships other than the admission that certain activities were environmentally possible at certain levels of technological development. Probabilists preferred to generalize about what was likely rather than what was certain. Neodeterminists believed that extraordinarily likely relationships were so close to certainty that the distinction between the two could be disregarded. Pragmatists took the position that certain regularities—limited in terms of the variables included and the time period of applicability—could legitimately be established and might supply information useful to human endeavor.

Considering these approaches, our conclusion is twofold. Science always generalizes about phenomena that are not precisely (certainly not in time and space) identical. Nevertheless such generalizations may be close enough to serve the purposes of the analysis. Thus different positions on the degree of generalization may be acceptable, depending on the objective of study.

On the other hand, the problem of discovering the definition of the environment and the set of environmental factors most suitable for broad and accurate generalization remains open. Progress here will depend on the extent to which suggested models fit the available data. Those seeking to understand the relationship between environment and levels of cultural development will rapidly discover that defining the former variable in terms of topographical features (hills and valleys) yields few if any generalizations. However, both Malin's and Meggers' definitions provide numerous findings that may be generalized, thereby indicating the value and potential of those frameworks.

Geographic Versus Other Environmental Influences.   Early determinists argued that the geographic environment alone could essentially explain how societies developed. More modern determinists recognized the importance of other environmental factors, even as they continued to emphasize the geographic environment's dominant status. As possibilism, probabilism, and ecology developed, the balance of opinion tipped away from a reliance on geographic causality; cultural factors, and particularly technology, were credited with primary significance in affecting patterns of human action. In fact, the new approaches maintained that much of the impact of the geographic environment was mediated by other variables.

We do not wish to exaggerate this trend by concluding that the geographic environment can explain little or nothing. At the least, an understanding of natural environmental processes may be useful in specifying the full costs and limits of various human endeavors. However if one's objective is to comprehend the basis of social phenomena such as cultural norms, demographic patterns, or economic or political behavior, it is quite evident that knowledge of the geographic environment alone will be insufficient.

Free Will.   Students of the environment have taken every conceivable position on the issue of free will. In general, the viewpoints of geographers can be roughly divided among several schools of thought. Pure determinists such as Demolins argue that the environment *causes* human behavior patterns; a given milieu produces a specific social type, and will is irrelevant to the process. Critiques of determinism may dispute the belief in geographic causality without necessarily advocating free will. They may, for example, accept an equally determinist but nongeographic explanation of human action (i.e., economic determinism). Possibilists, however, believe in free will. In fact they emphasize that conviction as a factor distinguishing their own position from a qualified determinism.

Many geographers choose to avoid the issue. They make no claim about the existence of human freedom or the lack thereof. They are content simply to note the regularities in man-environment relationships that are sufficiently consistent to serve the purposes of their investigations.

We divide the problem into two parts. First there is the basic question of whether man directs his own destiny. We refrain from judgment on this point and refer the reader to experts in philosophical inquiry. Second there is the question of whether modern man sees himself as capable of exercising his will in relation to the environment. Without doubt, the belief that technological progress will permit humanity to transform nature according to its needs *has* been an attribute of industrial civilization. However it is also true that ecologists are arguing with increasing frequency that such an attitude is illusory, that modifications of natural processes can have unforeseen and deleterious effects on human welfare. As Brunhes noted decades ago, the very actions men think serve to demonstrate their power over nature may ultimately prove their heightened vulnerability.

REFERENCES

1. Sorokin, P. A. *Contemporary sociological theories.* Harper & Row, New York, 1928 (quotations from p. 99).

2. Garrison, F. H. *An introduction to the history of medicine*. Saunders, Philadelphia, 1924.
3. Thomas, F. *The environmental basis of society*. Century, New York, 1925 (quotation from p. 19).
4. Moon, R. O. *Hippocrates*. Longman's, Green, New York, 1923.
5. Kristof, L. K. D. The origins and evolution of geopolitics. *Journal of Conflict Resolution*, **4:**15–51, 1960 (quotation from p. 17).
6. Thomas, *op. cit.*, pp. 33–40.
7. Tatham, G. Geography in the nineteenth century. In G. Taylor (Ed.), *Geography in the twentieth century*. Philosophical Library, New York, 1957.
8. Thomas, *op. cit.*, pp. 127–128.
9. Sorokin, *op. cit.*, pp. 83–86.
10. Tatham, G. Environmentalism and possibilism. In G. Taylor (Ed.), *Geography in the twentieth century*. Philosophical Library, New York, 1957.
11. Sorokin, *op. cit.*, pp. 73–79.
12. Tatham, Environmentalism and possibilism, *op. cit.*, p. 143.
13. *Ibid.*, p. 136.
14. *Ibid.*, pp. 136–137.
15. *Ibid.*, p. 136.
16. Minshull, R. *The changing nature of geography*. Hutchinson, London, 1970.
17. Thomas, *op. cit.*, pp. 78–79.
18. Semple, E. *Influences of the geographic environment*. Holt, Rinehart & Winston, New York, 1911 (quotation from p. 1).
19. *Ibid.*, pp. 40–41.
20. Konigsberg, C. Climate and society: A review of the literature. *Journal of Conflict Resolution*, **4:**67–82, 1960.
21. Huntington, E. *Mainsprings of civilization*. Wiley, New York, 1945 (quotations from pp. 287, 293).
22. Konigsberg, C. *op. cit.*, pp. 75–76.
23. Clarkson, J. Ecology and spatial analysis. *Annals of the Association of American Geographers*, **60:**700–716, 1970 (quotations from pp. 703–704).
24. Sorokin, *op. cit.*, pp. 163–164.
25. Febvre, L. *A geographical introduction to history*. Knopf, New York, 1925 (quotation from p. 236).
26. Sprout, H. and Sprout, M. *The ecological perspective on human affairs*. Princeton University Press, Princeton, N.J., 1965 (quotation from p. 90).
27. Brunhes, J. *Human geography*. Rand McNally, Skokie, Ill., 1920 (quotation from p. 227).
28. Wissler, C. *Man and culture*. Crowell, New York, 1923 (quotation from p. 318).
29. Bowman, I. *The pioneer fringe*. The American Geographical Society, Worcester, Mass., 1931 (quotation from p. 42).

30. *Ibid.*, pp. 42–44.

31. Wallis, W. Geographical environment and culture. *Social Forces,* **4:**702–708, 1926 (quotation from pp. 707–708).

32. For discussions of possibilism, determinism, and free will, see: Febvre, *op. cit.,* pp. 181–182, 238–240; Brunhes, *op. cit.,* pp. 225–226; Sprout and Sprout, *op. cit.,* pp. 94–97.

33. Spate, O.H.K. Toynbee and Huntington: A study in determinism. *Geographic Journal,* **118:**406–428, 1953, especially pp. 419–420.

34. Sprout, H. and Sprout, M. Probabilistic models of behavior. In H. Sprout and M. Sprout, *op. cit.,* pp. 99–116.

35. See the distinction between tactical determinism and strategic determinism in G.R. Lewthwaite, Environmentalism and determinism: A search for clarification, *Annals of the Association of American Geographers,* **56:**1–23, 1966, especially pp. 12–15.

36. Taylor, G. Geography in the twentieth century. Philosophical Library, New York, 1951 (quotation from p. 16).

37. *Ibid.*, p. 11.

38. Tatham, Environmentalism and possibilism, *op. cit.,* p. 161.

39. *Ibid.*, p. 161, footnote 2.

40. Meggers, B. Environmental limitations on the development of culture. *American Anthropologist,* **56:**801–824, 1954 (quotation from p. 815).

41. Hawley, A. H. *Human ecology.* Ronald Press, New York, 1950, pp. 3–10.

42. Stoddart, D. R. Darwin's impact on geography. In W. Davies (Ed.), *The conceptual revolution in geography.* University of London Press, London, 1970, pp. 57–61.

43. Stoddart, D. R. Geography and the ecological approach. In P. W. English and R. C. Mayfield (Eds.), *Man, space, and environment.* Oxford University Press, New York, 1972 (quotation from p. 157).

44. *Ibid.*, pp. 157–161 (quotation from p. 161).

45. Rappaport, R. Aspects of man's influence upon island ecosystems: Alteration and control. In P. W. English and R. C. Mayfield (Eds.), *Man, space and environment.* Oxford University Press, New York, 1972, pp. 180–193.

46. Eyre, S. Y. Determinism and the ecological approach. *Geography,* **49:**369–376, 1964 (quotation from pp. 373–374).

47. Duncan, O. D. From social system to ecosystem. *Sociological Inquiry,* **31:**140–149, 1961.

48. Taylor, G. R. (Ed.). *The Turner thesis.* Heath, Boston, 1956.

49. Malin, J. C. Ecology and history. *Scientific Monthly,* **70:**295–298, 1950 (quotation from pp. 295–296).

50. Hill, D. A. The process of landscape change: Bicultural implications. In P. W. English and R. C. Mayfield (Eds.), *Man, space, and environment.* Oxford University Press, New York, 1972, pp. 44–46.

51. *Ibid.*, p. 48.

52. *Ibid.*, pp. 40–49.

53. Gould, P. R. Man against his environment: A game theoretic framework. In P. W. English and R. C. Mayfield (Eds.), *Man, space, and environment.* Oxford University Press, New York, 1972, pp. 147–151.

PART TWO

Physical Environments:
Natural and Man-Made

CHAPTER THREE

The Weather and Human Behavior[a]

Most people probably agree with the ancient belief that the weather has important effects on human behavior. W. F. Petersen reviews the writing of Hippocrates and cites the following example of the Greek physician's belief in the influence of weather:

> Whoever wishes to pursue properly the science of medicine must proceed thus: First, he ought to consider what effects each season of the year can produce; for the seasons are not at all alike, but differ widely both in themselves and at their changes. The next point is the hot winds and the cold, especially those that are universal, but also those that are peculiar to each particular region. . . . For knowing the changes of the seasons, and the risings and settings of the stars, he will have full knowledge of each particular case, will succeed best in securing health, and will achieve the greatest triumphs in the practice of this art.[1]

Hippocrates was concerned with effects of weather requiring treatment by a physician; more recent writers have emphasized psychological and behavioral effects. Ellsworth Huntington found climatic factors to be important in explaining the vigorous, bustling American national character. Selective migration of more robust and active individuals, and the abundant opportunities and resources found on the American continent, are usually offered as explanations of the American national character. Huntington felt that an additional explanatory factor was necessary, since

[a] This chapter is co-authored by Paul Sommers and Rudolf Moos.

similar migration and opportunity are found in South America, Australia, and New Zealand. He thought the factor was climatic, specifically the contrast of the seasons and the frequent passage of storms, which both can provide a direct physiological stimulus to the human organism, thereby tending to make Americans more active and energetic than their presumably less stimulated neighbors to the south.[2]

This chapter reviews attempts to explain man's behavior by the state or changes of the weather. We first examine theories about the effects of overall climatic conditions. We then deal with more specific studies of particular weather variables. Variables like barometric pressure, temperature, wind, and humidity are reviewed with respect to their impact on mood and comfort, performance of mental tasks, and social or actuarial indices such as homicides and suicide rates. The next section examines a single variable, heat, in more detail. The impact of the moon is briefly discussed; and the attempts of men to control the weather are touched on. Finally, we treat some generally recurring issues in this literature.

Climate and Culture.   Huntington thought that advanced civilizations were more likely to develop in certain climates. He collected statistics on monthly variations in library circulation, participation in engineering society meetings, riots in India, mental hospital admissions, suicides, sexual offenses, factory employees' productivity, military cadets' academic test scores, and so forth. Using these data Huntington arrived at a description of the ideal climate for human performance. This climate has a moderately stimulating but not exhausting contrast of seasons, and it features the frequent passage of storm fronts to provide additional short-term climatic stimulation.[3]

Huntington prepared a map showing the geographic distribution of his ideal climate and compared this map to another map of the distribution of the world's major centers of civilization. The close correspondence between these maps led Huntington to conclude that the ideal climate he defined was a primary prerequisite to the development of an advanced civilization. Major civilizations such as those in the Tigris-Euphrates Valley, in Egypt, and even in the Western hemisphere developed in what were the climatically optimum areas of the past, according to Huntington. For example, he cites studies of tree rings as evidence of climatic changes at the appropriate times and places to account for the difference between the supposedly ideal climate on the Yucatan peninsula at the time the Mayan culture flourished and the presently unpleasant tropical conditions of that region. The current centers of civilization (i.e., the advanced industrialized areas) are located in the currently ideal climatic zones.

Mills used data on the daily mean temperature and temperature range from 107 weather stations around the world to develop an index of climatic stimulation. He assumed that 38 to 60°F was the optimum range for the daily mean temperature for humans; his index incorporated yearly mean, seasonal range, and daily variability of temperature. The results show, for example, that the climate of Cincinnati, Ohio, is 5.68 times as stimulating as that of Key West, Florida. When the index values are plotted on maps, generally moderate but stormy climates are depicted as more stimulating than very hot, very cold, or invariant climates.[4] Although Mills' quantitative methods are fancy, they have nothing to recommend them over Huntington's. Both are dependent on initial assumptions of doubtful validity, and both stand or fall on the intuitive reasonableness of the results. Both methods result in a portrayal of the climate of Western Europe and northeastern and midwestern United States as the best in the world. It is no accident that Mills and Huntington were residents of these respective regions.

Whereas Huntington and Mills believed in the importance of the outdoor climate, Markham observed that man has mediated the effects of climate by controlling the temperature in the interior of his dwelling places. Markham finds that all the world's great civilizations, from the Euphrates Valley cultures on, were located in regions without excessive heat, in which the primary climatic problem was to keep sufficiently warm during the cold periods. The grate or open fire was a fairly effective means of controlling the indoor climate for the Babylonian and Egyptian civilizations, which were located in relatively warm areas needing only minimal heating systems.

The Romans took a step forward in a cooler climate by inventing one of the world's first central heating systems. They used hot smoke conducted through terra cotta pipes in the walls and floors of public buildings, especially the numerous bath houses. Markham is delighted to find that the degeneration of these heating systems antedated the final fall of Rome. He concludes that the abandonment of indoor climate control was the primary factor in the downfall of this civilization. He notes that when advanced heating systems were abandoned by the Romans, the locus of dominant world power passed back into the warmer regions of Persia and Arabia, which could make do with less sophisticated grates and open fires.[5]

Markham has the distinction of being one of the first writers to emphasize the importance of indoor climatic control, and he is the only writer to offer such a broad historical theory based on indoor climate. However, the decline of Rome was a slow, gradual process. One cannot designate the abandonment of piping and heating technology as the cause of the downfall just because the loss of these arts preceded the final and abrupt end of Roman government.

National character or temperament has also been attributed to the prevailing climate. Lynn finds that four social indices—suicide, psychosis, alcoholism, and caloric intake—are highly intercorrelated. By rank ordering 18 countries on each of the four factors, adding the four ranks together for each country, and reranking the totals, Lynn obtains an index to a common factor, which he believes is a national personality characteristic. Lynn argues that this characteristic is anxiety, and that national anxiety is high where high alcoholism and suicide rates are coupled with low rates of hospitalized psychosis and caloric intake. He cites extensive evidence linking each of his social indices to anxiety to buttress his empirical finding of a common factor.[6] If Lynn's interpretation of a common factor linking suicide, psychosis, alcoholism, and caloric intake is correct, the anxiety level in Ireland and the United Kingdom should be higher than in Japan and West Germany, and the United States should fall somewhere in between. Similarly, the anxiety level in the northeastern United States should be higher than in the rural South.

Having ruled out several alternate explanations of the anxiety factor, Lynn concludes that climatic variations may be the primary cause. He finds that summer heat, storminess, and solar radiation correlate fairly well with the anxiety factor. Lynn favors storminess as the best explanation, or perhaps some correlate of storms, such as electromagnetic long waves or ozone concentrations. Thus Lynn points to the same climatic variables as Mills and Huntington. Like the two earlier authors, Lynn thinks that storms have a beneficial impact on mankind. In Lynn's case the effect is mediated by the anxiety factor. A moderate number of storms results in a moderate level of anxiety, which is good for the mental and physical well-being of most people. Storms may have negative effects on some people (suicides, alcoholics), but this social cost is presumably outweighed by beneficial effects on economic growth.

The broad scope offered by the authors discussed thus far is intriguing, but it is impossible to accept unquestioningly or to test statistically. Since whole civilizations are used as the dependent variables, no true replication is possible. Laboratory experiments are out of the question. Studies of more restricted scope, offering experimental tests of some of their conclusions, may present more definitive results.

Weather and Man.

Health, Performance and Accident Rates.

Physically, weather can give you a headache or a heart palpitation; it can send you to the hospital with appendicitis. On the mental side, weather can interfere with your speed in adding up income tax returns; it can set off a crime wave, major or minor; it can raise or lower your I.Q.[7]

Everyone is aware of the marked changes in mental state that come with . . . storms. With a center of low pressure approaching—the pressure falling and the temperature rising—we are afflicted with a feeling of futility, an inability to reach the usual mental efficiency, or to accomplish difficult tasks. In children this takes the form of an increased irritability, a restlessness and petulance that parents find most trying. Adults on such days are also more quarrelsome and fault finding, with a tendency to a pessimistic viewpoint toward all matters that arise. Such weather provides the most perfect background for marital outburst of temper.[8]

These quotations illustrate some effects commonly attributed to weather—in particular, to heat and barometric pressure. Very little empirical evidence has been collected to demonstrate the subjective but interesting effects on mood and domestic behavior referred to in the second excerpt. Somewhat more work has been done on objective and more easily collected measures of weather effects such as accidents, suicides, and crimes.

There are a few studies of effects of naturally occurring weather states on health-related variables, particularly pain. Trabert had 17 men report on their health each day over a 10–20 week period. He found correspondences between reports of good health and high or rising barometric pressure, and between reports of bad health and low or falling pressure. He reported similar correspondences between high or rising pressure and good performance of secondary school students, and between low or falling pressure and poor performance.[9] A local wind condition, the *Foehn,* famous in Innsbruck and the surrounding Alpine area for its deleterious psychological impact, mediated these effects. When the Foehn blew, subjects were less likely to report being in good health and teachers were less likely to rate their classes' performance as good.*

One method of reducing the complexity found in studies of naturally occuring weather effects is to control and manipulate the weather variables. Although meteorologists are not yet capable of large-scale weather control, Hollander and his associates at the University of Pennsylvania have worked with a sophisticated instrument for controlling temperature,

---

*Several studies referring to the Foehn are reviewed below. The Foehn is a warm, dry, descending wind found in several regions near the Alps in Europe. It results from a combination of an ordinary storm and the effects of the Alpine topography. Winds in other countries to which behavioral and psychological effects have been attributed are the Bora, the Mistral, and the Sirrocco in Europe, the Sharav and the Chamsin in the Near East, the Pomponio in Argentina, the Chinook in Colorado, and the Santa Ana in southern California. Among the effects attributed to these winds are irritation, nervousness, depression, pain sensations, traffic accidents, and increased deaths from lung and heart disease.

humidity, rate of air flow, ion concentration, and ion charge. The "Climatron" is a controlled climate chamber consisting of a 15-foot-square room with attached bathroom, in which two patients can live comfortably in a hotellike setting for long periods of time. Entrance and exit to and from the chamber is accomplished via a space age air lock. Thus patients can remain in the chamber for days or weeks while doctors, nurses, food, and entertainment come and go through the air lock.[10]

Hollander and Yeostros studied the pain sensations of arthritics using the Climatron. Patients with obvious physical symptoms of arthritis lived in the chamber in pairs for periods of at least 2 weeks. Twelve of these patients claimed to be weather sensitive (i.e., changes in the weather were said to affect their symptoms). The patients were exposed to single variations of pressure, then humidity; finally variations of pressure and humidity were produced simultaneously with pressure falling as humidity rose. Subjective worsening of the arthritis was found within minutes of the onset of rising humidity with falling pressure. An objective clinical index showed significant worsening of arthritic symptoms, compared with the initial control period and with the single variations of pressure and humidity. Successive occurrence of the stormlike pressure-and-humidity variation had a cumulative deteriorating effect on the patients. When the variation was stopped at the point of lowest pressure and highest humidity, most patients improved slightly.[11] Thus stable weather conditions, whether fair or foul, may be better for arthritics than changing conditions typical of a storm.

Turning to somewhat more objective measures of weather effects, the classroom behavior of students has been the subject of several studies beginning with Dexter at the turn of the century.[12] Dexter reported that abnormal winds, very low barometric pressure, and excessive humidity were associated with increased use of corporal punishment in the Denver public schools.[13] From a compilation of the daily deportment records of 250 grade school pupils in New York City over approximately 500 school days, Dexter found that low barometric pressure was related to poor deportment, whereas high pressure was related to good behavior. Moderate winds were related to an excess of bad deportment, and either high winds or calm conditions were associated with good behavior.[14]

Auliciems studied English school children in their normal classrooms performing exercises in arithmetic and taking general intelligence tests. Indoor temperatures slightly below the optimum level for comfort were found conducive to maximum performance; low relative humidity and moderate air movement within the room were also related to good scores. The external environment also had important effects. Low outdoor temperatures, relatively low wind speeds, low relative humidity, and lack of sunshine were related to good performance.[15] Auliciems indicates that more significant effects are found on more difficult test instruments, which suggests that the impact of naturally occurring atmospheric conditions on the performance of school children may be quite important.

Weather variables have been related to health, pain sensations, student behavior, and student performance. These studies are associative or correlative; no causality is implied. All the behavior variables studied are "soft" variables, rather difficult to quantify. Yet the variety of results reported suggests that ordinary day-to-day weather variations do indeed affect people's sensations and behavior in important ways. Certain types of pain and sensations may be aggravated by falling barometric pressure, particularly when this condition is accompanied by rising humidity. Cool days with little wind and precipitation appear to be favorable to good behavior and academic performance in classrooms.

Muecher and Ungeheuer found a relationship between certain weather phases and accident occurrence and visits to a dispensary. Most accidents and dispensary visits occurred during phases of deteriorating or stormy weather or on days of Foehnlike weather. Two experimental studies are also reported. Reaction time of 20,000 visitors to a public exhibition in Munich was measured on a simple motor response test. Perceptual sensitivity was also evaluated in 96 subjects who had just completed a difficult arithmetic test. In both experiments performance fell significantly during the deteriorating-stormy and Foehnlike weather phases. Muecher and Ungeheuer conclude that excessive variation of the usual diurnal weather patterns must be regarded as stresses that cannot be fully compensated by humans and thus lead to a decrement in performance.[16]

Moos focuses explicitly on Foehn conditions. The folklore surrounding the Foehn includes the belief that biological and perhaps behavioral effects of the Foehn precede the actual occurrence of the wind by 6–8 hours. For example, arthritics claim that they can predict the onset of a Foehn by the sensations in their afflicted joints. Moos tests for this anticipatory effect by classifying accident data from Zurich, Switzerland, during 1958–1961 into 4-hour periods ranging from 8 hours prior to the onset of a Foehn to 4 hours after the cessation of the wind.[17] Accident rates were significantly higher during the 4 hours just preceding the Foehn. Somewhat greater accident proneness was shown during the actual Foehn. Other investigators have also found evidence of more accidents during Foehn days.[18]

Moos notes that more Foehn winds begin during the afternoon or evening than during the remainder of the day, and more accidents occur during the afternoon rush hour than at any other period of the day. Thus the data could show a relationship between Foehn and accidents for reasons not necessarily indicative of a causal connection between the two. However, Krueger[19] suggests that the positive ionization of the air, which may occur several hours prior to the onset of the wind, may cause physiological effects that in turn result in "anticipatory" symptoms and mood and behavioral changes. Muecher and Ungeheuer's stress hypothesis suggests that rush hour drivers, who face an additional stress from Foehn weather conditions, may show slower reaction time and reduced perceptual clarity, thus leading to more accidents.

Another approach to the study of weather effects is to use data from social and actuarial indices (i.e., police records, coroners' records, and records from various institutions that record the date or time of use by the public). Heller and Markland report that higher temperatures are associated with increased police activity. They used two weather variables, average daily hours of sunlight and average daily temperature, to predict the number of citizen calls for service. In general the model predicts more calls as temperature or hours of sunlight increase. Heller and Markland suggest that their model can help plan for manpower deployment within a city and for vacation scheduling for police officers.[20]

Two studies relating police activity to weather variables have been completed by Sells and Will.[21] Weather patterns were correlated with police variables such as number of assaults or auto accidents from 6 p.m. to midnight each day over a period of one year. Two major weather factors were found in each study. One of these factors was composed of high temperature and low atmospheric pressure (i.e., blue skies and sunny, pleasant weather). The police activities most highly correlated with this factor were Meet Complainant, Information, Investigation, and Vacation Check of Residence. These correlations were consistently high, indicating that fair weather is associated with increased police activity. More people are away on vacation, resulting in increased Vacation Checks, and those remaining in the city are more likely to request or receive police attention.

The other major factor was composed of precipitation and fog. Rainy, foggy weather was associated with increased police dispatches for dealing with accidents and for assisting another officer. However the total number of police calls may decrease during rainy-foggy weather because of reduced dispatches for traffic violations and several other categories of minor incidents.

Taken together, this work suggests a widespread effect of fair weather and increased hours of daylight on police activity. This effect may be partly attributable to institutional schedules—schools and industries allow a high proportion of their students and workers to vacation during the warmer months of the year. Other empirically demonstrable effects of weather may vary from region to region because of very different weather patterns, as suggested by Dexter's work in New York and Denver classrooms.

Thus there are several investigations of weather effects on automobile accidents and other police-reported incidents. The type of weather affecting police reports varies from one region to another; for example, the Foehn is a problem in Germany and Switzerland, but high temperature and precipitation are of more concern in Texas. Some of the possible explanations for these phenomena stem from common sense. Fog or precipitation is related to accidents because of decreased effectiveness of automobile brakes and reduced driver visibility. Heat may increase the aggressiveness of persons under experimental conditions, and this might account for some of the accidents during hot periods, whereas other events occur during warm weather because increased numbers of people are vacationing. However the Moos study suggests that there may be anticipatory effects of some weather phenomena, and the relationship between anticipation of an event and accidents is much more complex and elusive. Mediating variables such as reduced reaction times due to stressful weather events need to be further investigated.

Social Indices: Psychiatric Hospital Admissions and Suicide Rates.   Several investigators have suggested that climatic variables may be related to the pattern of admissions to mental hospitals. Reviewing studies done in Japan, Australia, North and South America, and Europe, Abe finds a consistent pattern in both the Northern and Southern hemispheres: admissions begin to increase during the local spring season and reach a peak either in spring or summer. Additional evidence for this pattern is reported for seven prefectures of Japan, in which admissions increase during spring and summer. The more southerly prefectures, in which spring arrives earlier, show an earlier rise in the curve of monthly admissions and an earlier peak in the summer.[22]

Similar seasonal patterns are reported by several other investigators. For example, Stewart and Wildman found a summer peak at a southern state hospital and comment that uncomfortable summer weather may be so stressful to some people that it is the "straw that breaks the camel's back," resulting in increased mental hospital admissions.[23] James and Griffin found a rise of admissions during the warmer months and a fall during the cooler months for admissions to the entire state hospital system in Texas. They point out that a significant climatic effect of this magnitude—an increase from 3000 winter admissions to around 3400 summer admissions—is of considerable practical importance to hospital administrators in planning budgets and expenditures.[24] The only dissenter in this body of literature is Pantleo, who observed a seasonal pattern that conformed to the patterns reported by other investigators but was not statistically significant.[25]

The evidence suggests a consistent seasonal pattern of admissions to public mental hospitals in industrialized countries in both the Northern and Southern hemispheres, and in the various regions of the United States. Nearly all studies have discovered a peak in spring or summer, generally an increase through spring to a peak in summer, followed by a decline through the fall and winter months. This pattern reaches levels of statistical significance in most studies. In addition, a relationship between admissions and specific temperature measures emerged from two investigations, confirming the idea that the general climatic condition expressed by the season is the important variable. Most workers have named rising average temperatures and increased hours of daylight as the weather variables responsible for the typical seasonal pattern of admissions. These weather variables must then be interpreted as additional stresses in the existing strain and turmoil of modern life. Some persons are less able to compensate for the additional climatic stress and end up in mental hospitals. Some events associated with the seasons may also be important in this context; for example, children on vacation during the summer may increase "seasonal" stress. Hauck has suggested that the low rate of hospital admissions in the fall and winter months may be due to the elation of fall colors, the bountiful harvest, the fact that children have been sent off to school, and the family emphasis of the Christmas season.[26]

Investigation of the relationship between suicides and climatic factors began with the French sociologist Emile Durkheim in the late nineteenth century. Durkheim found a seasonal pattern of suicide in European countries, with the greatest number of suicides occurring during the three summer months in most of the countries studied. Durkheim felt that the length of the daylight period was the primary seasonal variable involved, since the overall climate differences between the northern and southern European countries did not correspond well with the suicide rates.[27] He specifically rejected seasonal temperature variations as a direct explanatory variable on the grounds that they were not drastic enough.

Durkheim pointed to social factors causing more interaction among people during the daytime and during the warmer months of the year. Increased interaction may produce the increased stress that leads some persons to suicide. Durkheim is not denying seasonal effects, nor is he saying that a very hot day might not drive one or two deranged persons to take their lives. He simply emphasizes the importance of social factors that mediate and transmit the effects of the weather, thus resulting in a faster social pace during the spring and summer in European countries.

Barometric pressure has been examined as a specific causal variable by two investigators.[28] C. A. Mills found relationships between falling pressure and high suicide rates, and between rising pressure and low rates. In addition, Mills states that the regions of the United States with the highest suicide rates are those regions over which many cyclonic storms pass (i.e., regions with the greatest variability of barometric pressure). Sanborn et al. found that suicides in the state of New Hampshire rise when barometric pressure is low. Since the pressure and suicide data were averaged over 3-month intervals before they were correlated, however, it would appear that these investigators are using barometric pressure as an indicator of overall seasonal effects.

Digon and Bock estimated the range of suicide-free days that might occur by chance in an urban area the size of Philadelphia and compared this range to the actual occurrence of suicide-free intervals over 3 years. They found that the occurrence of suicide-free intervals was not outside the realm of chance and concluded that the timing of suicides may be purely a chance phenomenon. Yet they report that the number of suicides was significantly less when barometric pressure and humidity were high and that the number of suicides increased when barometric pressure fell by a large amount.[29] However this finding was not replicated by Pokorny in a similar study in Houston, Texas.[30]

Pokorny and his associates question the extent of seasonal or weather influences on suicides. They found that 11 weather variables studied were not significantly related to the time of suicide occurrence. The methodology selected for this study differs from that of the other investigators mentioned in that the relationship of the overall seasonal patterns of suicides and weather variables was ignored on the grounds that the variation of the suicide data may have corresponded by chance to the variation of the weather variables over the year. Thus Pokorny et al. partialed out the portion of the correlation that was due to the uneven distribution of a given weather variable over the year.[31] In so doing, they may have partialed out precisely the effect every other investigator is talking about, claiming that everyone else's results simply occurred by chance!

The question of weather effects on social indices such as mental hospital admissions and suicides is more controversial than the question of weather effects on moods, arthritic symptoms, and police dispatcher calls. The latter indicators of human behavior are regarded as "soft" and less objective than an impersonal social statistic such as suicide. But there are many alternate interpretations of a country- or statewide social index, particularly because complex procedures and many sources of error may be involved in compiling an overall index. On the other hand, searching for weather effects on suicide rate variations is not an unreasonable idea. If weather variations can become significant stressors for some people some of the time, it is precisely persons who are already highly stressed (e.g., persons who are thinking vaguely about suicide) who are likely to exhibit behavior affected by added meteorological stress.

Two suggestions for resolving these issues come to mind. First, variables such as the number of daylight hours are seasonal indicators more than they are weather variables. Use of alternate variables could clear up some of the difficulties inherent in using a weather variable that is highly correlated with seasons. The weather phase or the Sells and Will factor analytic weather pattern methodologies may be quite useful in studying social indices. Second, smaller case studies of individuals might help to relate behavior and mood directly to weather. Admittedly, distinguishing weather effects from the effects of personality and environmental setting might be very difficult.

Heat and Human Behavior.   Heat, perhaps the most extensively studied weather variable, has been investigated under both experimental and naturally occurring conditions. In this section we examine work on heat in isolation from other weather variables. Literature on comfort standards, attitudes, interpersonal relations, and behavioral and social indices is reviewed.

Thermal Comfort Standards.   Many investigators have studied the comfort sensations of workers and school children in attempts to find the optimal temperature-humidity range for comfort and performance. Hickish asked factory workers to report their thermal sensations on a 7-point scale, from much too warm to much too cool. He derived comfort standards by assigning an arbitrary upper limit to the comfort zone, excluding all temperatures at which more than 20% of the workers reported being too warm.[32] The standard Hickish suggests for summer months is 69–74°F. This is the basic methodology of the thermal comfort literature. A decision must be made about coding the scale the subjects vote on; that is, which votes are in the comfortable range and which are to be considered uncomfortable. Second, a decision must be made about the proportion of uncomfortable votes that will be acceptable in the Comfort Zone. Some people will be uncomfortable at nearly any temperature, and others will be comfortable throughout the range of temperatures employed in a given study. Some control must be used for sex differences. The type of

clothing worn by subjects must be taken into account. Given these decisions, one is left with a fascinating variety of studies, as the following
examples illustrate.

Rohles and Nevins learned that buildings occupied for only short
periods (auditoriums, lecture halls, stores) should not use the same standards as structures occupied for longer periods (e.g., homes and offices)
because activity levels and clothing differences typically varied in the two
types of structure.[33] McNall and his colleagues found no seasonal variations and no sex differences in the comfort votes of male and female
college students who were all dressed in identical shirts and trousers.[34]
They also found that as the activity level increased, metabolic rates increased and the most comfortable temperature fell. Data on sex differences indicated that at any given activity level, males tend to burn up more
calories than females. However males also preferred a lower comfort
standard than females, metabolic rate being held constant.[35]

Auliciems discovered that the outdoor weather affected the comfort of
children inside the classroom. Children desired a warmer room on warm
days, a cooler room on cold days. Clothing differences or seasonal acclimatization may have been responsible for these differences.[36] Rohles
and Johnson concluded that under experimental conditions the comfort
votes of elderly persons correspond closely to those of college students,
popular belief notwithstanding.[37]

Gagge et al. studied the differences between moving from a comfortable environment to an uncomfortably warm or cool one, as opposed to
moving from an uncomfortable environment to a comfortable or neutral
one. Three male subjects, 22 to 24 years old, clad only in their shorts, were
exposed to various thermal conditions in experimental "hot rooms." They
spent at least an hour in each thermal condition before moving to a room
with a different condition. In the case of moving from comfortable to
uncomfortable conditions, sensations of discomfort resulted when body
temperatures changed from the normal 36.5°C, a change that lags considerably behind the environmental change. In the case of moving from
uncomfortable to comfortable conditions, the sensation of comfort preceded the physiological change.[38]

The study implies that real-world comfort conditions can never be
optimized while people move around from inside to outside, or from a
building with one standard for sedentary work to another with standards
for more arduous work. The real-world "second-best" standard would
have to be a compromise between the correct standard for persons constantly in a given environment (a high school teacher) and persons in
transit (the students). It is possible that clothing may provide sufficient
mediation between the standard for persons constantly in an environ-

ment and persons in transit, particularly if a compromise temperature standard is used.

Bedford reviews his own and other researchers' studies of thermal comfort and points out several problems in setting thermal comfort standards.[39] Different comfort effects result from using floor heating or outlets in the ceiling. Cold walls or an excessive gradient of temperature from floor to ceiling may make people very uncomfortable despite a reasonable air temperature. Thus designers must allow for the radiant properties of floors and walls rather than simply measuring the temperature of the air. Bedford points out that thermal comfort is not the complete goal of heating and ventilating engineers. In the thermal comfort literature humidity and air movement are generally fixed at some level to allow variation of temperature only, this variable being sufficiently complex in itself. In the real world of offices, factories, and schoolrooms, humidity and air movement must be controlled as well for truly pleasant conditions.

Performance Indices.   Another body of literature has considered man's performance on a variety of physical and mental tasks in relation to heat and comfort. The central assumption behind this research is that it is not the subjective comfort of workers or students that really matters, but what they produce under various environmental conditions. We review three studies on this issue: one considers physical work tasks, and the others analyze real-life situations involving mental tasks.

Wyndham varied the heat, air movement, and quality of supervision in a simulated work setting in an African gold mine. The basic goals of the study were to identify beforehand the workers most likely to experience heat stroke under typical mine conditions and to find ways to maintain the productivity of the remaining workers under severe thermal stress.[40] Randomly selected Bantu workers performed a typical gold mine work task: shoveling rocks into a 1-ton mine car for a continuous 5-hour shift under the direct supervision of a foreman. The total quantity of rock moved and the rectal temperatures of the workers were recorded. The workers shoveled rocks with no breaks other than for frequent temperature readings to identify potential stroke victims.

The type of supervision provided had distinct effects. One Bantu, known to be a "good" supervisor (i.e., a hard driver with a good production record) was compared with an "inefficient" supervisor who for some reason had not yet been fired and with a control condition of no direct supervision. The quality of supervision had the expected effects under relatively cool conditions (86°F or below); the good supervisor got more rock moved than either the inefficient supervisor or the control condition.

However at very hot temperatures (92°F or above) the quality of supervision had no effects on productivity; the laborers worked very slowly in all conditions.

Separate studies reported by Wyndham investigated racial differences in adaptation to heat. Experiments were performed using a simulated hot, humid climate at 90°F and a work rate of 5 calories per minute, a standard Wyndham considers normal for men engaged in physical work in heavy industry in Europe. Rectal temperatures and heart and sweat rates were measured for 20 young adult males from each of the following groups: Caucasians from Johannesburg, from tropical parts of Australia, and from the Sahara Desert; Bantus from Johannesburg and from other countries near South Africa; Bushmen from the Kalahari Desert region and from the Okvango Swamps; Australian aborigines; and Chaamba Arabs from the Sahara. Despite formidable difficulties involved in assuming that these were matched samples (sic!) and in testing each group in both acclimatized and unacclimatized states, Wyndham concluded that reactions to heat stress do not relate to body size but to the climate from which the subject comes. If subjects were well acclimatized to their respective home regions, and if the experimental conditions resembled those prevailing in the home territories, they exhibited less heat stress than if the experimental conditions were unfamiliar. The season in which tests were conducted had some effect, indicating that acclimatization varies by season.

R. D. Pepler and his colleagues conducted an extensive field study on thermal comfort and performance at two grade schools, two junior high schools, and two senior high schools in suburban areas near Portland, Oregon. In each category of school, one school was climate-controlled (i.e., air conditioned) and the other was not.[41] Since the schools were located in similar geographical areas with respect to both natural climate and social factors, the primary differences between them were the level and variability of classroom temperature and the level of air movement. Two test scores were obtained each week for selected classes at each school. Spelling classes were selected at the grade schools, social studies and Spanish classes at the junior high, and Latin and math classes at the high school.

Students in the non-climate-controlled schools showed more variability of performance when temperatures inside and outside were high. A similar association was found at the climate-controlled schools except for six warm days when student's performance was less variable. Thus on the average comfort and performance show a simple relationship at the non-climate-controlled schools. There was less variability in student performance on more comfortable days. The same relationship held at the climate-controlled schools, except that performance benefited from air conditioning on very warm days even though students felt that the classrooms were too cool on those days.[42]

Wyon reports the results of earlier work conducted in Sweden by himself and associates. In one study 13-year-old children were given routine reading speed and comprehension tests in a language laboratory under temperatures varying from 68 to 86°F. Both speed and comprehension deteriorated by more than 30% when temperature was raised from 68 to 81°F, but performance was slightly improved at 86°F. Other experiments showed performance to be affected more in the afternoon than in the morning, and it appeared that less able students were affected more than bright students.[43]

Wyon points to the importance of mediatory or intervening variables in explaining these results. Three categories of intervening variables are postulated as mediating environmental stress and performance. Time-invariant factors linked to stress and strain include the subjective calibration and subjective information contents of a stimulus. Time-invariant factors not linked to stress include intelligence and personality. Time-variant factors linked to strain include arousal, attention, and effort. Wyon's listing of different categories of mediatory variables is an important step toward explaining inconsistent results from related studies (e.g., the question of sex differences in the thermal comfort literature, the differences between young and old people, or the complex performance vs. temperature curve in Wyon's own study). One must of course directly measure and further specify these categories of intervening variables; otherwise they represent purely circular arguments.

Provins offers an alternate conceptualization of the variables mediating between comfort and performance. Performance levels can be understood only if one knows both the general skill level required by the task and the level of arousal or activation of the individual subject.[44] A graph mapping arousal against a wide range of air temperatures would result in a U-shaped curve. For any given task some range of air temperatures could be varied such that as the temperatures increase, a subject's performance would first increase, then decrease, as he approached an optimally aroused state and then became overaroused at higher temperatures. An easier task would result in a lower level of arousal at any one temperature. More work along these lines is needed. Despite the difficulties of directly measuring intervening or mediating variables, Provins and Wyons are correct in asserting that there is no simple, direct relationship between the meteorological environment and human behavior. Some combination of person- and setting-related variables may mediate, transmit, modify, or resist the variations of weather and climate as they affect behavior.

Mortality Rates.   Mortality rates have been extensively studied in relation to heat. Gover presents data indicating that high mortality was
associated with hot spells in 86 cities in the United States during the
1930s.[45] Another study using data from New York City for 9½ years
concludes that excess mortality is directly related to maximum temperature readings of the day before death occurred.[46]

Oechsli and Buechley found unusually high mortality rates, particularly among older people, during three September hot spells in the Los
Angeles Basin. The three September hot spells with temperatures over
100°F were compared with the remaining, not-so-hot days of a 42-day
period surrounding the hot spell. Total mortality rates exceeded the
number expected by more than 200%. Rates for persons older than 85
exceed the expected rate by 810% in 1955. The actual number of "excess"
deaths ranged from 546 deaths in 1939 to 946 in 1955. The third hot spell
selected for study, September 1963, did not fit the pattern of the two
earlier periods. The authors speculate that the lower mortality during
1963 may have resulted from the widespread application of air-
conditioning equipment. As evidence in support of this view, they offer
the comment that a September peak of electricity usage occurred during
this year, whereas in all previous years, including ones with September
hot spells, the monthly peak occurred during the winter.[47]

Buechley et al. found a coinciding heat island and region of excess
mortality for a July hot spell in the New York metropolitan area. Consistently higher temperatures were recorded in the central core of the city, as
compared with the suburbs. A region of high mortality during the heat
wave corresponded closely with the high-temperature region. The calculations of these investigators indicate that 150–200 fewer deaths might
have occurred in the central city if suburban heat levels and living conditions had prevailed.[48] The authors attribute the excess of deaths over the
expected number to heat effects on the basis of the geographical similarity
of the death and heat "islands."

Schuman found excess mortality associated with the June–July 1966
heat waves in New York, St. Louis, Los Angeles, Detroit, and Madison–St.
Clair. Mortality increased overall from 17 to 56% in these cities. The poor,
the elderly, the physically handicapped, and those with circulatory problems had even higher rates, up to 140% for nonwhite females in St. Louis.
Persons with higher income, better medical care, fewer handicapping
physical conditions, and access to air conditioning or to the cooler suburbs
were less likely to fall into the excess mortality group.[49] Additional data
for New York City show homicides and diabetes to be most strongly
affected, with 138 and 117% increases, respectively. In contrast, cancer,
certain heart diseases, and infant deaths were much less affected; increases in these categories ranged from 15 to 20%.

Morbidity rates have also been correlated with weather variables. Brezowsky reviews several studies of human biotropy in relation to weather phases. He uses a 10-phase typology for the area of West Germany in which his own work was conducted. His warm-humid phase is the most biotropic; that is the most pathogenic effects are concentrated in this phase. Brezowsky correlated 43,347 deaths in Munich over a 4-year period with the weather phase in which death occurred. More deaths were found in the two most biotropic phases. In fact Brezowsky asserts that if the weather was restricted to the least biotropic phase, which is characterized by cool, mild, and dry weather, there would have been only 37,587 deaths in Munich over the years in question, instead of 43,347! These figures are based on a naive extrapolation of the number of deaths occurring on phase 1 days to the entire 4-year period. It is not reasonable to assume that the phase 1 death rate would have remained unchanged if the entire year suddenly had been blessed with phase 1 weather. However, it is quite clear that the observed distribution of deaths is highly related to weather conditions.[50]

All these studies are based on the methodology of excess mortality. Rather than investigating each individual case and making a determination of the specific relationship of that case to heat, this methodology examines periods when mortality takes a short-term leap upward and returns to its normal level soon afterward. The extra or "excess" deaths above the normal level that occurred during a heat wave are then attributed to the unusual phenomenon without any direct examination of specific cases of mortality or specific diseases or types of persons, except in the manner these items happen to be defined and recorded in public coroners' reports. Given that the magnitude of excess deaths is very substantial, the methodology seems reasonable. However it would be interesting to know the life expectancies for some of the disease categories reported by Schuman. Would these people have died anyway in the next 2 or 3 months, or could they have survived many months or years in the absence of a major environmental stress? The answer to this question makes a big difference in terms of social policy toward deaths from environmental stress.

Behavioral and Attitudinal Effects.   A small body of literature exists on the behavioral effects of heat on individual human beings. Two studies have considered violent riots in relation to heat. Lombroso studied riots in India over 22 years. Most of the uprisings took place during the hot months of the year when the temperature was probably between 80 and 90°F. During excessively hot periods, closer to 100°F, no riots occurred, indicating that very high temperatures can be inhibiting to mass disruptions.[51]

More recent evidence comes from the *Report of the National Advisory Commission on Civil Disorders.*[52] Temperature data were available for 18 disorders in 1967 in the United States. For these 18 cases, the temperature on the day the riot broke out was 79° or above. In half the cases the temperature was above 90°F. The report does not tell how these 18 cases were selected from the total number of civil disturbances in 1967, nor why temperature data were available for only this relatively small sample of the total number of civil disturbances. Also, the report does not state that these riot days were among the hottest of the month, or that they were unusually high for the particular city during the summer. Thus the strength of the association between heat and riots is difficult to ascertain.

More carefully designed experimental studies clearly demonstrate that personal behavior changes under very hot conditions. Griffitt designed an experiment in which 40 college students participated under either hot (90°F) or comfortable (78°F) conditions. An attitude questionnaire filled out by each subject was used to generate responses to a bogus questionnaire, purportedly that of a "stranger." The stranger's responses were chosen to agree with those of the subject either 75 or 25% of the time. Subjects rated strangers who agreed with their own views 75% of the time as more attractive than strangers who did not agree as often. In addition, attractiveness ratings were lower under uncomfortably hot conditions, regardless of the extent of agreement between subject and stranger. Use of a subjective mood scale showed an association between subjective discomfort and lower attraction ratings. The author concludes that the temperature manipulation resulted in subjective discomfort, which in turn resulted in lower attractiveness rating of the "stranger." The results imply that important evaluative decisions (jury votes, employee hiring or firing) should not be made in very hot temperatures.[53]

Baron chose two temperature levels and two levels of anger arousal in 40 college-age subjects to investigate the relationships between heat and aggression. After exposure to either a comfortable or a hot experimental room, anger arousal was manipulated by an apparent subject, who was really an accomplice of the experimenter. The accomplice read some evaluative writing by the subject and made complimentary or very insulting remarks to the subject. Next, subjects were instructed to teach the accomplice-subject a set of nonsense syllables. An electric shock device was used to punish the learner-accomplice for failure to learn the syllables. The results for anger arousal were exactly as expected (i.e., angered subjects administered longer and more painful shocks to the learner). However subjects in the hot condition delivered shorter shocks to the learner than did the subjects in the cool condition.[54] Thus either the heat did not result in aggressive tendencies, the experimental conditions were so hot that the subject's pity for a fellow-sufferer was aroused, or the subject was so uncomfortable that he sought to escape the experimental conditions by being lenient. A variety of temperature levels would have to be studied to clarify this issue.

Baron and Lawton followed the experimental conditions just outlined but added a modeling dimension to the situation. Half the experimental subjects were exposed to an aggressive model teacher before performing the teacher role in the experiment. The aggressive model administered frequent and lengthy shocks to the learner. The rest of the subjects were exposed to the aggressive model only after they had completed the teacher-role portion of the experiment. The manipulation of hot and cool room temperatures and of the subjects' anger arousal produced exactly the same results in the no-model condition as in the earlier study of Baron. However the subjects who were provided with an aggressive model were more aggressive in the hot conditions than they were under comfortable conditions.[55] The importance of an aggressive model is perhaps the most significant finding of this study. If heat is a factor in the development of a riot, it is possibly through the model effects of an initial violent incident that the widespread violence is started. If riot development at all resembles the experimental conditions (heat, anger arousal, aggression opportunity), one should expect reduced probability of mass violent disruption if no initial violent model is presented to the potential rioters.

An analogous seasonal design was used by Michelson to study the interpersonal interactions of Toronto housewives during a winter month and a summer month. In February, one of the coldest months in Toronto, 173 married women living in suburban homes and with children at home were interviewed; 130 of the women were reinterviewed in June of the same year, a period of quite warm weather. The interviews concentrated on current rates of participation in selected activities (shopping for groceries, attending parties in homes, attending church, taking educational courses, etc.)

There were large changes in participation rates between February and June. Many activities showed net decreases in participation; some showed net increases. For example, attendance or participation in sports activities increased 28%, telephoning decreased 15%, but movie attendance showed no changes. Decreasing participation from winter to summer was entirely in indoor activity categories. The biggest increase was for sports activities. More people saw nearby friends or relatives at least once a week in the summer. In general Michelson finds that the transition from winter to summer brings about a decline in use of the indoor and immediate outdoor environment and an increased use of the larger neighborhood and total urban environment.[56]

This study links the concerns of this chapter to two other approaches to studying human behavior covered in this book. Chapter 4 discusses the effects of architectural environments. The Michelson study indicates that the possible influences of building design or urban planning on behavior vary by season because people are likely to engage in different activities in different seasons. Chapter 7 reviews Roger Barker's work on behavior settings. The activities studied by Michelson could be fruitfully discussed in a behavior setting context. One useful dimension of behavior settings might relate to the seasonal use of the setting.

Studies of civic attitudes, environmental use, thermal comfort, performance, social indices, and specific behaviors have been reviewed here in relation to heat. Experimentally produced or naturally occurring high-temperature environmental conditions have been convincingly related to human behavior in many of these studies. The broad range of effects and methodologies used sometimes makes it difficult to attribute human behavior directly to the effects of higher temperatures. The importance and the nature of intervening or mediatory variables have been stressed. Nonetheless, the evidence indicates that high temperature results in reduced performance levels, subjective discomfort, and certain specific behavior changes. The relationship between small and specific effects such as these and larger seasonal variations in social indices is not yet specifically known, although this is certainly an intriguing issue.

The Phases of the Moon.   Next we examine the issue of lunar influences on human behavior. Popular belief in the association of insanity and epilepsy with exposure to the moon dates from ancient times. The Talmud states that epilepsy is caused by standing nude before the full moon.[57] Hippocrates wrote: "As often as one is seized with terror and fright and madness during the night, he is said to be suffering from the visitation of Hecate (the moon goddess)."[58] Shakespeare mentions the popularly held belief in the influence of the moon in *Othello:*

It is the very error of the moon,
She comes more near the earth than she was wont
and makes men mad.

Benjamin Rush was one of the first people to offer a common-sense explanation of the effects of the full moon on patients in mental hospitals. In 1807 Rush speculated that the light from the moon, coming through unshuttered windows, would keep some of the patients awake, and these few by their restlessness might waken other patients, thus contributing to the belief of the staff in the influence of the moon on madness. Clevenger provided some evidence to support the common-sense position assumed by Rush. He reported that dropping the curtain on the window of the room in which a patient affected by the moon slept frequently sufficed to eliminate the supposed lunar influence. Rush and Clevenger did not manage to counteract centuries of popular belief in lunar influences. Investigations into possible lunar effects in psychiatric patients have continued to the present day.

Osborn presents data indicating an association between psychiatric hospital admission and moon phases. Admissions to a 125-bed psychiatric hospital over a one-year period were tabulated by the phase of the moon in which they occurred. The theoretical range of admission frequencies for each phase of the moon, given a hypothesis of no lunar effect on admission, was compared against the observed frequencies. The full moon phase showed significantly more admissions than could have occurred by chance. Osborn does not attempt to explain his results but simply suggests that replication attempts be carried out before any causal hypotheses are explored.[59]

Lieber and Sherin also report a significant statistical relationship between phases of the moon and human behavior. They report a significant periodicity in the occurrence of homicides in Dade County, Florida, and a similar but nonsignificant periodicity in homicides reported in Cuyahoga County, Ohio. In both regions homicides peaked around both the full moon and the new moon.[60] In presenting a tidal theory as a tentative explanation of their results, the authors note that there may be biological "tides" within the human body which are correlated with lunar tides. These biological tides occur in the water flow between the fluid compartments of the body (intra- and extracellular, intravascular). The authors speculate that these biological tides, along with associated changes in hormones and electrolytes, may affect neuromuscular irritability, thus resulting in significant emotional changes. These emotional changes might result in increased occurrence of homicides during periods of greater lunar gravitational influence (i.e., full and new moon phases).

Other recent authors have attempted to discredit the theories of lunar influences on human behavior.[61] For example, Pokorny used suicide and homicide data from Texas during the years 1959 to 1961. These data were tabulated by moon phase and by quarter of the year coded in relation to the perigee–apogee cycle of the moon. No significant difference was found in the number of suicides or of homicides occurring in any of the four lunar phases, nor between the two quarters surrounding apogee compared with the two quarters surrounding perigee.[62] This result fails to replicate the findings of Lieber and Sherin.

Pokorny followed the statistical procedure of Osborn, using data from a 400-bed psychiatric unit in a Texas Veterans Administration hospital between 1959 and 1961. Each day was coded by lunar phase as in the Osborn study. An analogous procedure was followed for perigee–apogee quarters of the year. Each of the 3 years and each of the 3-year totals were then examined for differences between the observed and expected number of admissions for each phase and quarter. The extent of difference for each of the years considered separately was quite substantial; however the pattern of relationships between observed and expected numbers of admissions varied across the entire period. Thus when the yearly figures were summed, there was no significant difference between the observed and expected frequencies for any phase or any quarter. Pokorny speculates that some weekly cycling phenomenon not related to the moon's phases is being picked up by the procedure of comparing the numbers of admissions to lunar quarters and phases.[63]

From the limited number of studies reviewed here, it is apparent that the literature lacks a solid theory to explain lunar influences on human behavior and that most observed relationships that have been subjected to statistical tests of significance have produced tentative results at best. The extent and perseverance of folklore about the moon suggests that more precise measures of possible lunar influences should be used in place of, or in addition to, gross social indicators such as suicide and hospital admission rates. Measures of patient and staff behavior within hospital settings, measures of subjective affect, or simple performance and reaction time tests could be used. Alternative explanations of any associations with lunar phases or quarters must of course be actively pursued.

Changing and Controlling the Weather.   Man's interest in the harmful effects of the naturally occurring physical environment has led to attempts to control and change that environment. Many efforts have been impelled by economic reasons—to secure rain for the crops or to ward off a frost that could kill sensitive plants. In this section we briefly review attempts to control or intentionally modify the weather.

Loud noises produced by cannon were popular tools for inducing rainfall and diverting damaging hailstorms in eighteenth-century Europe. The practice of diverting hailstorms was still popular in 1896, when the mayor of an Austrian town set up a network of 36 particularly noisy cannons around his district to protect his constituency from hailstorms. In 1902 the Austrian government became concerned about the large number of deaths and injuries resulting from "hail cannon" accidents (11 killed and 60 injured in 1900), and it was decided to set up an experiment to test the efficacy of hail cannon. Selected areas in Austria and Italy were surrounded with hail cannon and similar nearby areas were left unprotected. Damaging hail storms during the next 2 years on both the protected and unprotected fields led the Austrian government to conclude that hail cannon were useless, and the machines were outlawed. However Italian farmers today purchase hail rockets in large numbers and claim that exploding rockets in hail clouds stops hail.[64]

In 1850 James Espy was aware that water in the atmosphere could condense into clouds and produce rainfall if the evaporated water could be raised by upward currents of air. Espy proposed to Congress that large quantities of timber in the western states be used to modify the weather by simultaneously lighting 40 acres of timber every 20 miles, every seven days, along a north–south line 600–700 miles long. Espy calculated that a line of rain-shedding cumulus clouds would be generated which would move eastward to the Atlantic, drenching the nation. Espy's proposal was not approved by Congress, which, then as now, was not especially interested in funding scientific projects.[65]

Most recent efforts at inducing rain and preventing hail have been predicated on the contributions of Vincent Schaefer, who in 1946 accidentally discovered how to seed clouds and cause them to shed rain. Schaefer used a home freezer unit lined with black velvet to study these properties of supercooled water droplets (i.e., water droplets suspended in air in liquid form at air temperatures below 32°F). A beam of light was shined into the box, and the investigator simply breathed into it producing a miniature cloud. Schaefer tried unsuccessfully to turn the droplets into ice crystals by dusting them with various particles, to give the droplets a condensation nucleus to form on. He decided to reduce the air temperature of the box well below the capacity of the freezing unit, and he procured some dry ice as the easiest means of lowering the temperature. As soon as dry ice was placed in the box, the water droplets froze and precipitated onto the bottom of the box.

Subsequent field experiments on naturally occurring supercooled cumulus clouds demonstrated that Schaefer had accidentally discovered a key to rain-making. Supercooled water droplets were seeded with dry ice particles, and the droplets were converted into ice crystals and precipitated as rain. After Schaefer's work became known, cloud seeding with dry ice or silver iodide was undertaken extensively by scientists and by commercial operators who sold their services to farmers. Commercial operators have given glowing reports about the efficacy of seeding as a means of causing rain to fall, but many scientists have remained skeptical. The great variability of cloud systems makes it impossible to predict whether a given cloud will produce rain, especially if the prediction is limited to a small area. If a cloud that is seeded subsequently produces rain, one cannot really determine whether the seeding caused the rain or whether the cloud would have precipitated anyway.[66]

The limited number of rigorously designed and evaluated scientific projects prompted a very cautious statement from the National Academy of Sciences, which conducted a review of weather and climate modification projects. "There is increasing but still somewhat ambiguous statistical evidence that precipitation from some types of cloud and storm systems can be modestly increased or redistributed by seeding techniques."[67]

Hobbs and Radke present a case study of artificial seeding that should clear up some of the ambiguity mentioned in the National Academy of Sciences statement. Using an airplane equipped with particle-sampling devices, thermometers, and seeding equipment, University of Washington meteorologists measured the physical properties of a cloud system over the western slope of the Cascade mountains. Precipitation rate and ice crystal structures were measured, and the cloud was seeded with silver iodide. When seeding was completed the airplane proceeded to a downwind target area over the eastern slope of the mountain range. More measurements of crystalline structure, precipitation rate, and temperature were obtained. The cloud temperature fell rapidly, as much as 2°C in 30 seconds. New crystal types were found that could have formed only in a cloud with the characteristics of the seeded cloud. Optical effects due to ice crystals were observed in the former rain-droplet cloud. On the ground, observers on the western slope under the seeding area reported reduced precipitation, whereas downwind in the target area on the eastern slope, increased precipitation was found during the period predicted by the meteorologists. Thus the net effect of the seeding was a redistribution of precipitation from the western side of the Cascades over the peaks to the eastern slopes, accompanied by observable changes in the clouds' physical properties.[68]

In additon to rain-making, silver iodide and dry ice seeding is used in attempts to suppress hail and to disperse fog. Hail suppression has been most widely practiced in the Soviet Union. Silver iodide particles were launched by cannon and rockets, into hail clouds, supposedly converting the hail to rain or altogether preventing precipitation. No randomized experiments have been conducted, however, which makes it difficult to evaluate the success claimed for these operations. Dispersal of cold fogs (i.e., supercooled ground clouds) using silver iodide is widely and successfully practiced in the United States at all major airports. Little progress has been made with warm fogs except by the extremely expensive FIDO method used during World War II, in which the fog was temporarily burned off to allow aircraft to take off or land. This technique works but is so expensive that it has not been used except during the wartime situation.

Much larger-scale man-made alterations of the overall climate of geographical regions have been suggested. One proposed method of converting Greenland into productive agricultural land is to coat the area with coal dust, thereby increasing the amount of heat absorbed from the sun and melting the ice. Someone calculated the amount of coal dust that would be required and concluded that the project would be prohibitively expensive and difficult tactically—transportation of the dust to Greenland during one summer period before the snow began to fall again might not be possible! Another suggestion was to build a dam across the Bering Straits between Siberia and Alaska. The very cold water of the Arctic Ocean could then be pumped into the Pacific, and warmer water would flow into the Arctic from the Atlantic, gradually warming the ice cap and causing it to melt. Blackening a large strip of land, thereby increasing upward convection currents, has also been suggested for increasing rainfall in desert areas. The convection currents could theoretically lead to cloud formation and perhaps rainfall downwind of the blackened area.

Unfortunately, the results of such climate modification projects are not predictable. For example, it is not certain that removal of the Arctic ice cap would be permanent; Fleagle cites one expert who thinks that once removed, the ice cap could not regenerate itself, and another who thinks that the removal would be a very short-term phenomenon, perhaps lasting only until the subsequent winter.[69] It is also possible that removal of the ice cap would set off a long-term oscillation of the earth's climate comparable to an ice age. The immediate effects on the rest of the world are also uncertain.

Sagan, Toon, and Gierasch suggest a means of reducing the uncertainty associated with possible intentional climate modification experiments on Earth. Using data obtained from Mariner 9, they show that the climate of Mars is similar to that of the Earth in that two basic planetary conditions are possible—an ice age (current on Mars), and more clement conditions with higher atmospheric pressure and considerable surface water. Therefore the planet Mars could be used as an experimental laboratory, a large model of the Earth.[70] Something analogous to coating Greenland with coal dust could be tried on Mars. The Martian polar caps could be coated with a black substance, increasing surface albedo significantly. Presumably, scientists could observe the resulting climatic oscillation from the safety and comfort of this planet or satellite-based telescope observatories. It is apparent that the natural environment of the entire solar system may soon be no more "natural" than that of the Earth.

Reduction of storminess in the middle latitudes would be harmful to the inhabitants of these areas, according to Mills and Huntington (with whose research this chapter began). Mills and Huntington would say that since the energy or stimulation provided by the current climate would be reduced, work productivity would inevitably suffer. Their conclusions can hardly be accepted as the definitive statement on the psychological and behavioral effects of changing weather; yet the technology necessary to drastically modify the Earth's climate currently exists, reminding us that almost no one since Huntington and Mills has seriously attempted to predict what effects climate modification might have on the general state of civilization.

Even if the meteorological and psychological effects of intentional climate modifications were known, the economic, legal, and social effects would still need to be considered. Weather or climate modification has costs as well as benefits, and both must be calculated and mutually weighed. Suppose a rancher hires a cloud seeder to increase precipitation over his property. The seeding operations may increase rainfall over the target ranch, but they will have side effects. Rainfall may decrease over the seeding area, slightly upwind of the target ranch, and it may increase downwind of the target ranch. Thus the upwind farmer may sue the target rancher because of reduction of rainfall upwind, and the target rancher may sue the downwind farmer to recover some of the costs of seeding. Government regulation of weather modification efforts may be required to protect public interests.[71] More complex legal issues are discussed by Hunt.[72]

The dangers of pursuing large-scale climate control projects include crop failures and famines, wars over water rights, and unintentional floods. For example, some experts believe that cloud-seeding experiments may have contributed to the damage caused by the June 1972 flood in Rapid City, South Dakota. Kellog and Schneider point out that "we cannot escape the fact that the atmosphere is a resource that is shared by all the world's people, and is a tightly coupled system that cannot be pushed very hard in one place without making a bulge somewhere else."[73]

General Issues: Weather and the Social Scientist.   Many weather variables and a variety of behavioral effects have been reported in the literature reviewed in this chapter. Daily and seasonal climatic contrasts, including passage of storm fronts, have been associated with vigorous and advanced civilizations. High or rising barometric pressure may result in subjective feelings of good health, whereas falling pressure with rising humidity or a warm-season cold front may produce increased pain sensations among arthritics and patients recovering from surgery. Cool days with little wind and precipitation, and days with high or rising barometric pressure, have been associated with good pupil behavior in classrooms and good academic performance. On warm days greater variability of academic performance has been found. Stormy and Foehnlike weather phases have been associated with increased reaction times and with increases in automobile and industrial accidents. Rising average temperatures during the spring and summer months have been coupled with increased suicide and mental hospital admission rates. Very high, uncomfortable temperatures have been linked to reduced work output, poor visual acuity, unfavorable evaluations of strangers, increased mortality rates, and civil disorders.

Perhaps the most general conclusion to be drawn from this body of literature is that scientific work in the area of weather effects on human behavior is relatively sparse. We have at least alluded to the bulk of the research done in the last 70 years. Solco Tromp is one of the few recent scientists to take a systematic and wide-ranging look at the effects of climate and weather. Coming from the German biometeorology school, he emphasizes physiological effects rather than psychological or broader social problems. In opening his discussion he states:

> The growing concern of modern society about the scientific and social consequences and political implications of our environment . . . should be a stimulus to the atmospheric scientist not to concentrate solely on basic scientific research. Once in a while he should consider the many physical, sociological, and political consequences of minor changes in our atmosphere and hydrosphere.[74]

Part of the reason for the neglect of weather effects on human behavior is that the methodological problems are formidable. Rohles refers to the field of environmental psychology as "a bucket of worms." He lists a total of 18 physical, organismic, and interactive variables that must be taken into account in any study of thermal comfort, his particular emphasis within the field.[75] Each of these variables is an independent or semi-independent variable and must be explicitly controlled or measured. The "bucket of worms" is even more entangled in the literature reviewed previously on social indices such as suicide and mortality.

To make sense of different approaches to defining the relevant measurable and controllable variables, it is helpful to have underlying conceptions of the overall environment and of the specific ways in which the atmospheric environment, weather, can affect behavior. One common conceptualization is that of larger and smaller environments. In the terms of Marston Bates, three levels of atmospheric environments can be distinguished: microclimate, ecoclimate, and geoclimate.[76] Microclimate refers to the conditions immediately surrounding a given organism; in the case of humans, it is the environment underneath their clothing. This is the climate focused on by the thermal comfort literature. Ecoclimate is the climate of the habitat, the buildings or fields in which humans work or live (e.g., the classrooms in which performance is studied in relation to classroom temperature). The geoclimate, the climate measured by the weather station in a particular region, has been the subject of meteorologists and of Huntington and Mills. Bates points out that human variables and climate variables interact to such an extent that it is helpful to think in terms of the human ecosystem, which can be broken down by climatic level. A three-level model of environments or ecosystems should be of great utility in identifying appropriate statistical techniques in empirical studies. One cannot measure the environment experienced by students inside a classroom using weather station data.

Two theories about how weather can affect behavior are apparent in the literature. The first interprets weather changes or weather extremes as stresses. The psychological literature on stress suggests that some persons feel more stressed than others at any given time. Thus if an additional stress is applied uniformly to everyone by a weather change, those who are already highly stressed are more likely to exhibit behavioral or mood changes. A change may be simply a performance decrement or an increase in reaction time, or it may be "the last straw," which results in a more drastic alteration of behavior.

Given the stress-based approach, it is reasonable to look for weather effects in indices of pathogenic behavior such as suicide or homicide or mental hospital admissions data. However both the difficulty of interpreting these data and the underlying conceptualization suggest that smaller performance and reaction time effects should be studied in the same "overstressed" populations. This important step has not been taken. Performance and reaction time studies have been conducted using "normal" populations (all automobile drivers in Munich, randomly selected gold mine laborers, etc.).

Weather has also been conceptualized as a simple stimulus to the human organism. A stimulus can have physiological effects (e.g., warm temperatures raise the body temperatures of subjects), and it can have psychological effects, such as the enervated feeling so often experienced by Mills as a cyclonic storm passed over Ohio. The psychological effects may result from an environmentally induced physiological change, from nonphysiological but environmentally induced attention or arousal changes, from personality-related likes or dislikes for certain environmental conditions, or from socially learned definitions of certain weather phenomena as significant and important.

Many investigators have noted that the nature and interactions of these mediating variables are quite complex. Provins feels that if the level of skill required by a task and the level of arousal of the subject are known, the subject's performance can be predicted. Wyon breaks down arousal into three independent categories of intervening variables, thereby illustrating the extreme variability of mediation between the stimulus provided by the weather and the resulting performance level.

If certain weather states and/or weather changes are general stimuli rather than just stresses, indeed human behavioral effects might be identified in areas other than performance decrements and indices of socially maladaptive behavior. Test performance of school children, subjective affect, and the work productivity measures favored by Ellsworth Huntington are all reasonable areas in which to search for weather effects.

The role of compensatory or adaptive behavior in masking weather effects is seldom dealt with. People clearly become physiologically and psychologically acclimatized or adapted to unusual environments; hence their performance in such an environment generally improves over time. Wyndham's study of gold mine laborers demonstrates the adaptive ability of humans under very severe thermal stress. Pepler shows that teachers adapt to air conditioning by reporting a narrower range of neutral or not uncomfortable temperatures.

Thus a researcher is faced with a very difficult methodological problem. He can try to find effects in subjects already adapted to a given weather situation, or he can introduce unacclimatized subjects into an unfamiliar environment and face the objection that he is measuring the very unfamiliarity, and the individual's mechanisms for coping with the unknown, rather than weather effects. One solution to this problem is to carefully identify the similarity of one's experimental design to real-world conditions. The range of levels of acclimatization existing in the real world are certainly sufficient to justify almost any experimental design.

One final issue deserves consideration. Man's increasing control over the environment, especially at the micro- and ecoclimate levels, may slowly reduce his biological, psychological, and social capability to adapt to new environmental conditions. Man's emphasis always seems to be on modifying the environment rather than on modifying or controlling the human organism to give it the innate capability to cope with the environment. As a long-run strategy, the human species may find itself reducing its capability to cope with the effects of unintentional climate modifications by way of carbon dioxide pollution of the atmosphere, increasing the surface albedo of the planet through prodigious construction projects, and rerouting rivers and streams to satisfy agricultural and urban needs. Our cultural and technological resources may or may not provide sufficient flexibility to cope with our climate modification projects, intended or otherwise.

REFERENCES

1. Petersen, W. *The patient and the weather.* Edwards Brothers, Ann Arbor, Mich., 1934.

2. Huntington, E. *Mainsprings of civilization.* Wiley, New York, 1945.

3. Huntington, E. *Civilization and climate.* Yale University Press, New Haven, Conn., 1915.

4. Mills, C. *Living with the weather.* Caxton Press, Cincinnati, Ohio, 1934.

5. Markham, S. *Climate and the energy of nations.* Oxford University Press, New York, 1947.

6. Lynn, R. *Personality and national character.* Pergamon Press, Oxford, 1971.

7. Berke, J. and Wilson, V. *Watch out for the weather.* Viking, New York, 1951 (quotation from p. 3).

8. Mills, C. *Medical climatology: Climatic and weather influences in health and disease.* Charles C. Thomas, Baltimore, 1939 (quotation from p. 177).

9. Trabert, W. Innsbrucker Foehnstudien III: Der physiologische Einfluss von Foehn und Foehnlosem Wetter. Kaiserlich-Koeniglichen Hof- und Staatsdruckerei, Vienna, 1907.

10. Hollander, J. and Erdman, W. The controlled-climate chamber. In S. Licht (Ed.), *Medical climatology.* Waverly Press, Baltimore, 1964.

11. Hollander, J. and Yeostros, S. The effect of simultaneous variations of humidity and barometric pressure on arthritis. *Bulletin of the American Meteorological Society,* **44:**489–494, 1963.

12. Dexter, E. *Weather influences.* Macmillan, New York, 1904.

13. Dexter, E. The child and the weather. *Pedagogical Seminary,* **5:**512–522, 1897.

14. Dexter, E. School deportment and the weather. *Educational Review,* **19:**160–168, 1900.

15. Auliciems, A. Some observed relationships between the atmospheric environment and mental work. *Environmental Research,* **5:**217–240, 1972.

16. Muecher, H. and Ungeheuer, H. Meteorological influence on reaction time, flicker fusion frequency, job accidents and use of medical treatment. *Perceptual and Motor Skills,* **12:**163–168, 1961.

17. Moos, W. S. The effects of "Foehn" weather on accident rates in the city of Zurich (Switzerland). *Aerospace Medicine,* **35:**643–645, 1964.

18. Buettner, K. Present knowledge on correlations between weather changes, sferics and air electric space charges, and human health and behavior, *Federation Proceedings,* **16:**631–637, 1957.

19. Krueger, A. Are negative ions good for you? *New Scientist*, 668–670, June 1973.

20. Heller, N. and Markland, R. A climatological model for forecasting the demand for police service. *Journal of Research in Crime and Delinquency*, **7**:167–176, 1970.

21. Sells, S. B. and Will, D. P. Accidents, police incidents, and weather: A further study of the city of Fort Worth, Texas, 1968. Technical Report No. 15, Group Psychology Branch, Office of Naval Research and Institute of Behavioral Research, Texas Christian University, Fort Worth, 1971.

    Will, D. P. and Sells, S. B. Prediction of police incidents and accidents by meteorological variables. Technical Report No. 14, Group Psychology Branch, Office of Naval Research and Institute of Behavioral Research, Texas Christian University, Fort Worth, 1969.

22. Abe, K. Seasonal fluctuation of psychiatric admissions based on the data for 7 prefectures of Japan for 7-year period 1955–61 with a review of literature. In *Proceedings of the Joint Meeting of the Japanese Society of Psychiatry and Neurology and the American Psychiatric Association*, The Japanese Society of Psychiatry and Neurology, 1964, pp. 173–176.

23. Stewart, B. and Wildman, R. Climatic conditions and southern hospital admission rates. *Journal of Clinical Psychology*, **23**:397–398, 1967.

24. James, R. and Griffin, A. Seasonal admission rates in Texas mental hospitals. *Journal of Clinical Psychology*, **24**:190, 1968.

25. Pantleo, P. Climatic temperature and psychiatric admissions. *Journal of Clinical Psychology*, **26**:308–310, 1970.

26. Hauck, P. Seasonal changes in admission rates of a state hospital. *Journal of Clinical Psychology*, **13**:305–307, 1957.

27. Durkheim, E. *Suicide: A study in sociology*. Translated by J. Spaulding and G. Simpson. Free Press, New York, 1951. (Original French edition, 1897.)

28. Mills, C. Suicides and homicides in their relation to weather changes. *American Journal of Psychiatry*, **91**:669–677, 1934.

    Sanborn, D., Casey, T., and Niswander, G. Suicide: Seasonal patterns and related variables. *Diseases of the Nervous System*, **31**:702–704, 1970.

29. Digon, E. and Bock, H. Suicides and climatology. *Archives of Environmental Health*, **12**:279–286, 1966.

30. Pokorny, A. Sunspots, suicide, and homicide. *Diseases of the Nervous System*, **27**:347–348, 1966.

31. Pokorny, A., Davis, F., and Harberson, W. Suicide, suicide attempts, and weather. *American Journal of Psychiatry*, **120**:377–381, 1963.

32. Hickish, D. Thermal sensations of workers in light industry in Southern England. *Journal of Hygiene*, **53**:112–123, 1955.

33. Rohles, F. and Nevins, R. Short duration adaptation to comfortable temperatures. *ASHRAE Transactions*, **74**:IV.1.1–IV.1.4, 1968.

34. McNall, P., Ryan, P., and Jaax, J. Seasonal variation in comfort conditions for

college-age persons in the Middle West. *ASHRAE Transactions*, **74:**IV.2.1–IV.2.9, 1968.

35. McNall, P., Ryan, P., Rohles, F., Nevins, R., and Springer, W. Metabolic rates at four activity levels and their relationship to thermal comfort. *ASHRAE Transactions*, **74:**IV.3.1–IV.3.20, 1968.

36. Auliciems, A. Effects of weather on indoor thermal comfort. *International Journal of Biometeorology*, **13:**147–162, 1969.

37. Rohles, F. H. and Johnson, M. A. Thermal comfort in the elderly. *ASHRAE Transactions*, **78**(Pt. 1):131–137, 1972.

38. Gagge, A., Stolwijk, A., and Hardy, J. Comfort and thermal sensations and associated physiological responses at various ambient temperatures. *Environmental Research*, **1:**1–20, 1967.

39. Bedford, T. Research on heating and ventilation in relation to human comfort. *Heating, Piping and Air Conditioning*. 127–134, December 1958.

40. Wyndham, C. Adaptation to heat and cold. *Environmental Research*, **2:**442–469, 1969.

41. Pepler, R. The thermal comfort of students in climate controlled and non-climate controlled schools. *ASHRAE Transactions*, **78** (Pt. 1):97–109, 1972.

42. Pepler, R. Variations in students' test performances and in classroom temperatures in climate controlled and non-climate controlled schools. *ASHRAE Transactions*, **77:** (Pt. 2):35–42, 1971.

43. Wyon, D. P. Studies of children under imposed noise and heat stress. *Ergonomics*, **13:**598–612, 1970.

44. Provins, K. Environmental heat, body temperature and behavior: An hypothesis. *Australian Journal of Psychology*, **18:**118–129, 1966.

45. Gover, M. Mortality during periods of excessive temperature. *Public Health Reports*, **53:**1122–1143, 1938.

46. Kutschenreuter, P. H. A study of the effect of weather on mortality in New York City. M. S. thesis, Rutgers University, New Jersey, 1960.

47. Oechsli, F. and Buechley, R. Excess mortality associated with three Los Angeles September hot spells. *Environmental Research*, **3:**277–284, 1970.

48. Buechley, R., Van Bruggen, J., and Truppi, L. Heat Island = Death Island? *Environmental Research*, **5:**85–92, 1972.

49. Schuman, S. Patterns of urban heat-wave deaths and implications for prevention: Data from New York and St. Louis during July, 1966. *Environmental Research*, **5:**59–75, 1972.

50. Brezowsky, H. Morbidity and weather. In S. Licht (Ed.), *Medical climatology*. Waverly Press, Baltimore, 1964.

51. Berke, J. and Wilson, V. *Watch out for the weather*. Viking, New York, 1951, p. 19.

52. *Report of the National Advisory Commission on Civil Disorders*. Bantam, New York, 1968.

53. Griffitt, W. Environmental effects on interpersonal affective behavior: Am-

bient effective temperature and attraction. *Journal of Personality and Social Psychology,* **15:**240–244, 1970.

54. Baron, R. Aggression as a function of ambient temperature and prior anger arousal. *Journal of Personality and Social Psychology,* **21:**183–189, 1972.

55. Baron, R. and Lawton, S. Environmental influences on aggression: The facilitation of modeling effects by high ambient temperatures. *Psychonomic Science,* **26:**80–82, 1972.

56. Michelson, W. Some like it hot: Social participation and environmental use as functions of the season. *American Journal of Sociology,* **76:**1072–1083, 1971.

57. Kelley, D. Mania and the moon. *Psychoanalytic Review,* **29:**406–426, 1942, p. 407.

58. Oliven, J. Moonlight and nervous disorders: A historical study. *American Journal of Psychiatry,* **99:**579–584, 1943 (quotation from p. 580).

59. Osborn, R. The moon and the mental hospital: An investigation of one area of folklore. *Journal of Psychiatric Nursing and Mental Health Services,* 88–93, March–April 1968.

60. Lieber, A. and Sherin, C. Homicides and the lunar cycle: Toward a theory of lunar influence on human emotional disturbance. *American Journal of Psychiatry,* **129:**101–106, 1972.

61. Shapiro, J., Streiner, D., Gray, A., Williams, N., and Soble, C. The moon and mental illness: A failure to confirm the Transylvania effect. *Perceptual and Motor Skills,* **30:**827–830, 1970.

62. Pokorny, A. Moon phases, suicide, and homicide. *American Journal of Psychiatry,* **121:**66–67, 1964.

63. Pokorny, A. Moon phases and mental hospital admissions. *Journal of Psychiatric Nursing,* 325–327, November–December 1968.

64. Battan, L. J. *Harvesting the clouds: Advances in weather modification.* Doubleday, Garden City, N.Y., 1969, pp. 17–19.

65. Fleagle, R. G. (Ed.), *Weather modification: Science and public policy.* University of Washington Press, Seattle, 1968, pp. 6–7.

66. Battan, *op. cit.,* pp. 62–70.

67. *Weather and climate modification: Problems and prospects.* V. 1., *Summary and recommendations.* Final report of the Panel on Weather and Climate Modification to the Committee on Atmospheric Sciences, National Academy of Sciences, National Research Council, Washington, D.C., 1966 (quotation from p. 4).

68. Hobbs, P. V. and Radke, L. F. Redistribution of snowfall across a mountain range by artificial seeding: A case study. *Science,* **181:**1043–1045, 1973.

69. Fleagle, *op. cit.,* p. 4.

70. Sagan, C., Toon, O., and Gierasch, P. Climatic change on Mars. *Science,* **181:**1045–1049, 1973.

71. Malone, T. F. Weather modification: Implications of the new horizons in research. *Science,* **156:**897–901, 1967.

72. Hunt, R. S. Weather modification and the law. In R. G. Fleagle (Ed.), *Weather modification: Science and public policy.* University of Washington Press, Seattle, 1968, pp. 118–137.

73. Kellog, W. and Schneider, S. Climate stabilization: For better or for worse? *Science,* **186**:1163–1172, 1974 (quotation on p. 1170).

74. Tromp, S. Future scientific developments in human biometeorology. *Annals of the New York Academy of Sciences,* **184**:43–61, 1971 (quotation from p. 43).

75. Rohles, F. H. Environmental psychology: A bucket of worms. *Psychology Today,* **1**:54–63, 1967.

76. Bates, M. The role of weather in human behavior. In W. Sewall (Ed.), *Human dimensions of weather modification.* University of Chicago Press, Chicago, 1966.

CHAPTER FOUR

The Architectural Environment: Physical Space and Building Design[a]

The design of buildings and cities has an effect on the behavior of the people who live and work in them. The arrangement of apartments, hallways, and exits in a housing complex can encourage the formation of friendships among neighbors and discourage the occurrence of crime. The pattern of streets may promote their use as playgrounds in one neighborhood and thoroughfares in another. The placement of chairs in a classroom can facilitate or inhibit class discussion. The behavioral impact of architectural designs has received varying amounts of consideration from planners and users, as illustrated by three examples of different environmental settings.

A group foster home for high-school-age delinquent girls was located in three different settings in northern California during a 2-year period. A researcher described the first location as follows:

> The first group home . . . was in an older residential neighborhood, fairly close to the downtown area and centrally located to business offices, the Court House, and other civic services. The home was an older, twelve bedroom, five bathroom structure with approximately 4000 square feet of living space. Each girl had her own individual room. This insured some privacy and allowed each girl to choose her own decor and furnishings. The living room, den and library on the first floor enabled girls to have visitors and to feel fairly comfortable about entertaining relatives and friends. The

[a] This chapter is co-authored by Rudolf Moos and Paul Sommers.

large dining room table made it possible and convenient for them to talk about problems around the dinner table, and it seemed to help them feel part of a family unit as well. A large kitchen and service area allowed them to do their own washing and drying, to experiment in cooking, and to help in preparation of meals. Several sewing machines were available so that they might learn to sew if they wished.

This home was an ideal setting for a girls' home insofar as it possessed a warm atmosphere and contained a great deal of room.[1]

The group home was forced to move to a less desirable and much smaller facility located in a college neighborhood. The second house seemed to cause feelings of insecurity among the girls because of over-crowding and because they were stared at by curious students. Space and privacy were lacking, and there was an increase in unauthorized borrowing and outright theft of personal possessions among the girls. The girls felt and acted much better on completion of a move to a larger house located in a stable residential area. The third home provided the necessary sense of security and privacy that had been absent in the second location.

The spatial layout of the furnishings in a room can tell us a great deal about the behavior typical of that setting:

Walk into an empty courtroom and look around. The furniture arrangement will tell you at a glance who has what authority. In nearly every country, judges now look down on their courtrooms from a raised platform. . . . [The judge's] dignity is enhanced not only by his elevated chair but by the attendant's cry, "All stand," as he . . . file[s] into the room. . . . The judge's commanding seat catches first attention, but the eye soon wanders to the other furniture. In a British or American courtroom, the jury box stands out to the right of the enclosure behind the "bar." Between it and the judge's bench on a raised platform somewhat lower than that of the judge stands the chair waiting for the witness, facing outward into the room so that all can hear, including the press for whom a gallery or at least a bench is often reserved to give meaning to the concept of "publicity" characteristic of the common law concept of "due process." . . . Both prosecutor and defense counsels are placed on the same level, without benefit of elevation above the courtroom's floor. . . . This location of equality with that of the defense is suited to the prosecutor's standing in a legal system that reveres the adversary procedure. . . . The humble location of the state's attorney's chair indicates to the jury that his word is no more weighty than that of counsel for the defense. . . . Last, but not inconsequential among the participants in the trial, is the court secretary, for on him falls the task of preparing the record. . . . He takes his place just under the judge's nose at a table placed where everything from the bench, the witness stand, and the tables for state's attorney and defense can be heard. He is expected to record every word spoken by any participant, and to reproduce it during the night in neatly typed pages. . . .[2]

In this case, the behavior of the participants and the architecture of the room are mutually reinforcing. The roles of the different courtroom participants are reflected in the design and layout of the furnishings, and these in turn elicit expected courtroom behavior, such as deference toward the judge and a sense of equality between prosecution and defense.

Robert Sommer provides a final example in which builders have incorporated certain designs in their creations to elicit specific kinds of behavior. In certain situations, he observes, the intention may be to make people feel less comfortable and at ease:

> In most [airline] terminals it is virtually impossible for two people sitting down to converse comfortably for any length of time. The chairs are either bolted together and arranged in rows theater-style facing the ticket counters, or arranged back-to-back, and even if they face one another they are at such distances that comfortable conversation is impossible. The motive . . . appears the same as that in hotels and other commercial places—to drive people out of the waiting areas into cafes, bars and shops where they will spend money.[3]

These examples illustrate the complexity of interpreting the effects of an environment on people's behavior. How can we be sure that behavior is due to a specific environmental variable? Were the girls in the group home affected more by the socially unsuitable neighborhood of the second house or by the "architectural" problem of insufficient space and the crowded living conditions thus induced? Was the warm atmosphere of the first house attributable to its physical characteristics or to the house parents' feelings of security and satisfaction before they were forced to relocate the home?

Environments may also exert differential effects on people of different ages, cultures, and personalities. For example, the courtroom design may elicit feelings of respect and fairness with regard to the judicial system among white, middle-class participants, but the effect may be very different among lower-class blacks. Placed in such an environment, they may view the courtroom as the domain of the rich, white power structure, hardly a place where they can expect to receive a fair judgment by their peers.

Finally, there is the question of the extent to which architecture determines behavior. Two close friends can say their intimate farewells even while uncomfortably seated in an airline terminal. Clearly, the goals and preferences of individuals are important mediators of architectural impact.

The Concept of Congruence. A useful model in exploring the effect of the man-made physical environment on human behavior is the "intersystems congruence" approach developed by Michelson. Environments are viewed not as determining behavior in themselves but as setting broad limits on the phenomena that can occur in a given setting. Within these limits, an environment may make some phenomena "either easier or more difficult to maintain, so that, all else equal, these phenomena will tend to be found successfully maintaining themselves more in some types of settings than in others."[4] Instead of simply giving environmental factors a dominant role over other variables, Michelson's model adds the environment as another system acting interdependently with the social, cultural, and personality systems. It provides a setting in which phenomena in other systems are more or less likely to occur.

The examples mentioned in the previous section can be viewed in this framework. Interactions supportive of socially acceptable behavior can be seen as congruent with the first location of the girls' boarding house, but not the second. The furnishings and layout of a courtroom are congruent with the view of a judicial system based on due process and respect for the judge. The placement of chairs in an airline terminal is incongruent with the comfortable carrying on of intimate conversations. Yet in all these cases, social, cultural, and personality variables may intervene, resulting in behavior that would not be expected based on the environmental variables alone. In this chapter we use the intersystems congruence approach to examine the effect of different architectural settings on human behavior.

The Effect of Architectural Design on Specific Behaviors. In the last 20 years research has focused on the effects of different man-made environments on specific types of behaviors. We consider three components of architectural design, beginning with distance and its impact on friendship formation and the utilization of facilities. We then study the effect of different spatial arrangements, including both the arrangement of furniture and walls within a building, and the design of the building itself. Finally, we discuss the impact of various amenities, such as carpets and wall color.

Distance. The effect of distance on social interaction, especially on the formation of friendships, has been studied extensively. Researchers have collected most of their data from student dormitories, new housing projects, and suburban neighborhoods. Since these settings are often occupied by highly homogeneous groups of people, the pattern of social interaction can more confidently be attributed to architectural design than to such variables as age, occupation, education, and social class. Because they are more likely to be at home when researchers are at work, unemployed housewives have been the most common source of data in these studies.

Festinger, Schachter, and Back studied friendships and social group formation in two student housing complexes at the Massachusetts Institute of Technology.[5] One complex consisted of 100 prefabricated two- or four-room single-family houses (Westgate); the other was a group of former Navy barracks, each converted into 10 four-room apartments (Westgate West). The residents of the two complexes were married veteran students and their wives and children. A highly homogeneous group, virtually all the students were engineering or natural science majors aged 20–35, who had previously resided in urban areas in upper-middle-class homes.

The authors made a distinction between physical distance, the measured linear distance traversed in walking between two apartments, and functional distance, which includes the variables of design and relative position as they affect the number of involuntary, casual contacts between people. Both physical and functional distances can affect the number of casual meetings on stair landings, in front of doorways, or on the way to the garbage can. Functional distance can vary between units in two sets of apartments even when the individual units are separated by the same physical distances. In one building the route resident A must take to reach his apartment might cause him to pass by three or four apartment entrances, but in another nearly identical building an extra corridor for two of the intervening apartments would result in passing by just one or two intervening apartments.

In both complexes physical distance was very important in determining friendship choices. Next-door neighbors were chosen as friends most often, and the number of choices declined rapidly with increasing physical distance. As for functional distance, the people in the four end houses in Westgate, which faced the street rather than the courtyard, received fewer choices than people living in any other position, including two end houses facing the courtyard. At Westgate West the lower-floor residents whose apartment entrances were closest to the stair landing gave more choices to upper-floor residents than to other lower-floor residents. Whether individuals had to pass their neighbors' apartments to reach the stairs affected the likelihood that they would form friendships with residents living directly overhead. Thus functional distance had an important effect on friendship choices.

The distinction between physical and functional distance is evident in a study by Leo Kuper of postwar housing in the Braydon Road residential area in Coventry, England.[6] The houses in Braydon Road were semidetached units with pairs of houses sharing a common wall. Insulation was scant, and residents were constantly aware of the activities of their adjoining neighbors. Nevertheless Kuper observed that when asked to name a familiar neighbor, residents cited individuals who lived in apartments to the side of theirs but did not share a common wall. Side neighbors did share walkways, which gave access to the side doors of the housing units. The side doors, which were used much more frequently than the front doors, faced each other on opposite sides of the walkway, thereby encouraging contact between side neighbors. Residents who shared a common wall had a greater distance separating their doors. Thus side neighbors, although certainly at a greater physical distance than wall neighbors, were more apt to form friendships because the functional distances were not so great.

Suburban Settings. Whyte's book, *The Organization Man,* contains some material on the effects of architectural variables on suburban residents, particularly housewives. Whyte notes that:

> In suburbia friendship has become almost predictable. Despite the fact that a person can pick and choose from a vast number of people to make friends with, such things as the placement of a stoop or the direction of a street often have more to do with determining who is friends with whom. . . . This may be conformity, but it is not unwitting conformity. . . . Give a suburban housewife a map of the area, and she is likely to show herself a very shrewd social analyst. After a few remarks about what a bunch of cows we all are, she will cheerfully explain how funny it is she doesn't pal around with the Clarks any more because she is using the new supermarket now and doesn't stop by Eleanor Clark's for coffee like she used to.[7]

Whyte's view of the effects of suburbia is not overly sympathetic; however he has some evidence gathered in the suburban community of Park Forest to back up his sarcasm.

For a period of 3½ years Whyte read all the social notes of Park Forest newspapers (a feat of endurance worthy of note), and plotted the locations and type of social event on a map of the area. He found great regularity and stability over time in the pattern of partying. Social groups formed along and across streets. Over the backyard neighbors were rarely invited. Guests at any one event came from a rather circumscribed area, except for one atypical group, the Gourmet Society, which drew its membership from all areas of the community. Thus dedicated adherents of a particular activity may go to some trouble to get to the facilities or persons that make the activity possible. Except for such atypical groups, short physical distance and direct face-to-face orientation of home entrances were characteristic of party groups in Park Forest.

Similar results were found in Levittown, near Philadelphia. Housewives' reports of visiting among neighbors showed that across the street neighbors were visited often, with side neighbors visited slightly less often and across the backyard neighbors visited rarely. In this case both physical distance and functional distance are involved. All main entrances, driveways, and many windows faced the street in Levittown. Visual contact with side and across the street neighbors was roughly similar, but the side neighbors were further away functionally. Thus it is not surprising that across the street neighbors were favored in terms of visiting.[8]

A recent study reinforces these conclusions about physical distance. Three hundred wives in a cooperative townhouse development were asked about their socioeconomic status and friendship patterns. As in other neighboring studies, more friendships were found in the area immediately surrounding each person's residence. Most friendships were made within a range of 100 feet or about five dwelling units. The percentage of friends seen nearly every day declined quickly with distance. Next-door neighbors were chosen as close friends by 46% of the sample, neighbors two doors away were chosen by 24% of the sample, and neighbors three or four doors away were chosen by 13%. Thus closeness is an important factor in explaining friendships among women whose only similarity may be life cycle stage. Friendships formed at greater distances usually involve some additional similarities in social class.[9]

The findings in this area are unusually consistent. They point to two main factors related to architecture and site plan. The first is the physical distance between doorways—that is, the distance the housewife so frequently traverses in walking to her friend's portal. As distance increases beyond two or three home entrances, the number of friends mutually chosen is extremely small and probably depends on contact in a community organization or some other social, nonarchitectural influence. Some studies of physical distance have confounded physical and functional distance (e.g., the number of intervening doorways passed on the way to the friend's doorway). Increased functional distance is also associated with reduced interaction. The second major factor is the relative orientation of doorways or "fronts" of houses. The more indirect the orientation of two doorways, the less interaction is likely to occur.

Life cycle characteristics are an important factor in these results. A higher proportion of young married families are found in suburban communities as compared to central city areas. It is precisely among young married couples with small children that friendships with persons close at hand are likely to be emphasized, simply because taking children on crosstown trips involves logistic difficulties, and hiring a baby sitter is expensive. A high proportion of women of childbearing age in the subject population will increase the strength of an architectural effect on neighboring behavior.

Several studies have suggested that the site plan or relative orientation of, and distance between, doorways affect behavior by fostering or discouraging passive, casual contacts between neighbors engaged in their everyday household tasks (hanging out the laundry, supervising small children, mowing the lawn, etc.). These casual contacts may frequently develop into close friendships not because of the discovered similarity of neighbors but because of the lack of offensive dissimilarity and the continued passive, casual, and unavoidable contacts. It takes real effort to avoid friendship under such circumstances, and the price of obtaining privacy may be social ostracism. Close physical and functional distance is congruent with the formation of friendships and incongruent with social isolation.

The effect of distance in residential communities is not limited to the formation of friendships. Lansing, Marans, and Zehner compared six planned communities in terms of residents' satisfaction, compatibility, use of recreational facilities, and vehicular travel.[10] Interviews were conducted with residents of single-family houses and townhouses in each of the communities, which encompassed a range of levels of site planning. The distance to the nearest recreational facilities had striking effects on use rates. Moreover, residents were willing to travel different distances to different facilities, depending on the sport involved. For swimming, boating, tennis, and picnicking, the participation rate declined rapidly as distances increased from 0 to ½ mile. With other activities such as hiking and bicycling, facilities were rather less sensitive to distance. The participation rate for golf did not decline much up to 5 miles from home. Thus, although proximity is congruent with the utilization of facilities, the relationship is mediated by the type of recreation involved and the corresponding desire by residents to pursue certain activities regardless of the distance to the appropriate area.

Design and Spatial Arrangement.   Another important area of architectural design is the arrangement of spaces within the interior of a building. Such spaces may be determined by the placement of walls or partitions to divide up large rooms, the arrangement of furniture inside a room, and the overall architectural design of the building itself.

Often residents of military barracks and college dormitories must live in settings over which they have little control and to which there may be no alternatives. Such environments probably maximize the influence of architectural design. Furthermore, these settings house institutions that are organized around specific goals—military preparedness and academic learning. These factors have encouraged the examination of how the design of the residences affects the achievement of the intended objectives of the organizations of which they are a part.

One study examined Air Force barracks to determine whether friendship choices of the recruits reflected the type of dormitory the individuals occupied.[11] Bunks were segregated into units of six in two types of barrack. A closed design consisted of walls but not doors between each group; an open design had no interior obstructions other than furniture. Each of three open and three closed barracks housed approximately 60 recruits. The recruits were given a map of their barrack and asked to identify the person assigned to each bunk, the extent of interaction with each man during free periods, and the identity of the three men with whom each preferred to buddy. Men assigned to open cubicle barracks correctly identified the occupants of more bunk locations than men assigned to closed cubicle barracks. For free time interaction, men in closed cubicle barracks were more likely to choose men from within their own cubicle. These men were also more likely to name individuals within their own cubicle as buddies. Restriction of sensory contact (visual, auditory, and in a military barrack setting, presumably olfactory as well) thus is associated with less social interaction with persons physically located farther away.

The implications of these findings depend on organizational goals and values. By enhancing the development of small, cohesive, within-cubicle friendship groups, the closed cubicle design may build up the morale and personal security of group members. However closed cubicles may also result in more social isolates, since some men will not be compatible with the others in their particular cubicle. Personal animosities resulting from crowded living conditions may be less easy to handle within the small closed cubicles. A clear statement about the Air Force's training goals is necessary in choosing between the two barrack designs.

The effects of assigning individuals to share a small living space has also been examined in a review of the impact of dormitory architecture on student behavior.[12] Student desires for privacy are seriously compromised by the ubiquitous double room. The lack of private areas other than the room, and the large public bathrooms and long corridors found on the typical dormitory floor, force students into more social interaction than they may desire. Roommates must schedule study, recreation, and sleeping to avoid conflicts. University regulations make it difficult for students to express and develop their individuality through alteration and decoration of their rooms. Clusters could ameliorate these problems by converting corridor space into lounges surrounded by study-sleeping rooms, without sacrificing the large house lounge. In such designs the additional privacy would use little additional total space, and thus should not be more expensive than traditional designs.

Office Settings.   People spend a considerable amount of time in office settings over which they seldom have much control, although the setting can have marked effects on their performance. As in the previous examples, attention has been focused on the effects of arranging walls and partitions to place people in close contact with one another.

One sociologist observed interactions between twelve file clerks who sat in three 4-person rows. The filing area was part of a large office within which a total of 29 women and 8 men worked. The data on the file clerks were arranged by seating row in a matrix, showing that there was more interaction within rows than between rows. Many of these interactions did not concern business matters, and the filing cabinets did not inhibit visual or auditory contact between women in different rows. Thus distance may be the primary factor.[13] Judging from the results obtained in other settings, the relative orientation of the clerks, who sat facing their filing cabinets and looking at the backs of the women in the rows ahead of them, may also have been a significant factor.

Partial walls have also been shown to restrict friendship formation. The friendship choices of 295 clerks from a single floor of an English insurance office were recorded. There were no complete walls subdividing the floor, but there were two small partially enclosed areas in which 81 workers were seated. The workers faced an outside window when seated at their desks; thus their visual contact with clerks in the larger, open area was somewhat restricted.

The number of choices made declined steadily as distance between desks increased, especially for younger clerks. Men had a slightly higher tendency to choose persons far away than did women, perhaps because men, being the minority in this office, were more isolated from one another. Clerks in the smaller enclosed area were more cohesive and less likely to choose persons outside their own area than were clerks in the larger open area. More social isolates were found in the small enclosed areas. This may be a result of the higher proportion of workers physically isolated beside a wall or in a corner.

The practical implications of this study depend on management goals and values. The more cohesive groups found in smaller areas might be more effective small work groups within the large department than the less cohesive small groups in the large area. On the other hand, clerks in the larger area had more ties with persons farther away from their own desks, and this might contribute to a more effective department-wide work force. Thus organizations could encourage either small group effectiveness or communication within large departments by appropriately altering spatial seating arrangements.[14]

An example of recent efforts to design offices to facilitate certain goals is the "office landscape," or *Bürolandschaft,* which originated in West Germany in the early 1960s. The aim was to replace the traditional rectilinear layout of desks and the cubicle arrangement of private offices with a plan that would reflect the pattern of work groups and the organizational processes to be accomplished within the setting. The innovators wanted to encourage the formation of tightly knit work groups who perceived themselves as united in striving to achieve a common goal. All levels of staff would work in the office landscape. Boundaries between work groups and a sense of privacy would be provided by low, movable barriers that could be easily adapted to new work arrangements. Vistas of the entire office would discourage the feeling of isolation common in cubicle arrangements and would enable workers to see their position in relation to the rest of the organization. Recent research has indicated that even though the office landscape may increase group sociability, it may also result in increased noise levels, loss of privacy, and more visual distractions. Nevertheless, it serves to illustrate the developing interest in the relationship of spatial design to behavior.[15]

Hospital Settings.   Much of the research on the effects of different arrangements of furniture has been conducted on psychiatric wards. Psychiatric patients tend to be passive and dependent, usually accepting their environment as given and unchangeable. The placement of a chair or table, often viewed as fixed, can have a substantial impact on individuals who must spend considerable amounts of time in these settings. Staff have been interested in ways of manipulating furniture to improve the therapeutic environment.

Good, Siegel, and Bay worked out a refurbishing-refurnishing proposal for a traditional "Kirkbride" or linear-plan psychiatric ward. Inexpensive and relatively portable modular furniture systems were designed. Furniture arrangements were developed which would promote interaction in some areas of the ward and distinctly discourage interaction in other areas. Staff could then vary treatment simply by dispatching a patient to another area within the ward. A long list of desirable and usual patient behaviors was drawn up to ensure that the new design would allow easy and adequate performance of these behaviors. The visual, acoustic, and general esthetic qualities of the ward would drastically change and would vary within the ward in accordance with the plan for more interaction in certain areas. The design project was never carried out, but it has stimulated a great deal of discussion and experimentation regarding the effects of psychiatric architecture on patients.[16]

For example, one experiment in encouraging social interaction was initiated by rearranging the chairs on a ward around small square tables. After a 2-week settling-in period during which the women patients were occasionally talked out of pushing the chairs back to their old positions near the walls, systematic observations of verbal interactions were resumed. Both brief and sustained interactions had increased in number, although almost all interactions continued to be between just two people. Although some social changes obviously had occurred in connection with the architectural manipulation (staff enforcing the new arrangement), the furniture rearrangement was clearly accompanied by observable behavior changes which would have been difficult to achieve with the former "railroad station" setting.[17]

Patient behavior in the lounges of traditional and modern design psychiatric wards at a state mental hospital has been compared. Preselected locations in the lounges of each ward were observed six times a day. The observers recorded who was in the area and what each person was doing. It was discovered that patients in the modern design wards were more often engaged in interaction with other patients than were patients in traditional wards. The lounges of the modern design wards had more seating arrangements consisting of light chairs clustered about tables. The lounges of the traditional design wards typically had long lines of heavy chairs placed side by side. This was in part because of the provision of internal structural differentiation in the modern wards by planters and partial walls. These structures broke up the large open spaces and made it virtually impossible to have long lines of side-by-side chairs.[18]

In one study a solarium at one end of a psychiatric ward was equipped with comfortable and attractive furniture, placed to encourage conversation and attract patients to the area. Patient behavior was observed on the ward before and after the change. The distribution of activities in all the ward's public places was affected by the change. The solarium's share of all public room activities rose from 25 to 42%, while the percentages occurring in the corridor and dayroom areas dropped. Social behavior (e.g., talking and card playing) and active behavior (e.g., walking around) decreased in the corridor and dayroom, whereas both increased in the solarium. Isolated passive behavior (e.g., staring off into space) increased in the solarium and the dayroom but decreased markedly in the corridor. These changes were attributed to the architectural change, although the authors note that important, nonrelated social changes were also taking place on the ward.[19]

An early discussion of psychiatric architecture by Osmond offered a basic bipolar dimension along which architectural environments vary. At one end of the continuum are sociofugal environments, which discourage social contacts and the formation of interpersonal relationships. Railway stations, hotels, and most mental hospitals are examples of this type of design. At the other pole are sociopetal environments, such as tepees, igloos, and small seminar rooms, which encourage contacts and the development of interpersonal relationships. Osmond favors circular or radial designs for mental hospital wards; with this approach interaction would be facilitated by placing bedrooms at the outer circumference of the structure and common recreation and meeting areas in the center, thus eliminating all hallways. Patients going from bedroom to bedroom, or into the lounge to read a magazine, would be put into frequent contact with other patients and staff. These unavoidable contacts would provide patients with realistic opportunities to practice "normal" and acceptable social behaviors.[20]

Holahan has tested the actual behavioral effects of designs presumed to be sociopetal or sociofugal.[21] One hundred twenty psychiatric patients were randomly assigned to six-person groups. Each group was observed for a 45-minute period in an experimental dayroom. The patients were provided with snacks and game equipment and instructed to do as they pleased, as long as they did not rearrange the furniture. Two tables and eight chairs were prearranged in the room. When a group of six patients entered, they found one of four arrangements: sociofugal, consisting of chairs along the walls and tables in the center of the room; sociopetal, featuring chairs clustered around the tables in the center of the room; mixed, with some chairs near the walls and some near the tables; and free, with the chairs stacked in a corner, the patients being told to arrange them as they pleased.

Less social interaction was found in the groups placed in the sociofugal setting than in the sociopetal or mixed setting groups. The patients in the free setting interacted less than the patients in the sociopetal and mixed settings, and only slightly more than the patients in the sociofugal setting. Also, more cigarettes and coffee were consumed in the sociopetal and mixed settings than in the sociofugal settings. (This consumption effect may be desirable only as an indicator of increased social interaction, since the products consumed may have adverse effects on patients' health.)

Single-corridor, double-corridor, and radial designs for nursing units have been studied in a specially constructed general hospital building. Factors such as nursing station design, basic support facilities, and administration were kept constant. Using observational data collected from each of the three nursing shifts on each of the 12 nursing units, the authors showed that the radial design is generally preferable to the other two types. Nurses spent more time directly caring for their patients and less time walking from one part of the unit to another in the radial design units. Comparing radial and double-corridor units, each staff member on the four radial units spent 9 minutes less per day walking back and forth within her unit. Slightly larger differences were found for comparisons of radial and single-corridor designs, showing the single-corridor to be the worst design in terms of direct patient care. These activity differences were accompanied by higher staff satisfaction and better morale in the radial units.[22]

At least one ward-remodeling project has been carried out and its effects on patients' behavior have been evaluated. Holahan and Saegert started with a U-shaped, poorly furnished ward featuring a nurses' station, a dining room and dayroom in the middle section, and male and female bedrooms in opposite wings. The remodeling consisted of introducing partitions and new furniture in the bedrooms to increase privacy and provide more behavior options in these rooms, more small group table-and-chair arrangements in the dayroom, and the creation of a second dayroom for TV watching and game playing. A second ward, identical to the original condition of the remodeled ward, was used as a control.

Twenty-five randomly selected patients were observed in each ward 6 months after the remodeling. Patients were observed and interviewed at selected times of the day during the first week after their admission. More socializing and less isolated, noninteracting behavior was found on the remodeled ward. These patients also had more positive attitudes toward their ward than the control ward patients had toward theirs. Even the most disturbed patients on the remodeled ward were conscious of the pleasant physical surroundings. On the control ward, the patients most satisfied with their physical surroundings were those who slept the most![23]

The design of a hospital may affect behavior in other ways than encouraging social interaction. Mayer Spivack has discussed the effects of the design of large hospitals, which are often marked by long, undifferentiated corridors, either windowless or containing windows that overlook boring and depressing scenes. He describes his feelings in walking through an above-ground passageway 2,970 feet long in a VA hospital:

> Here one walks and walks—endlessly. If the infinitesimal vanishing point of the linear perspective is to be trusted, there is indeed no end in sight. Because of the extreme length and uniformity of the passageway, one feels no sense of progress. Without this cognitive and sensory feedback, one's sense of time and distance becomes distorted. It is a frustrating experience. . . . The total effect is that of looking down a gun barrel.[24]

The auditory characteristics of the tunnel were even more unsettling, with echoes making normal conversation impossible and magnifying ominous-sounding footsteps. Such settings, which can adversely affect even undisturbed persons, are all too common in supposedly therapeutic milieus. Patients whose perceptions are often distorted or uncertain to begin with cannot find much comfort there.

Educational Settings.   The overall design concept of a school may affect informal interactions between students and teachers. Myrick and Marx collected questionnaire and interview data from more than 1300 high school students in three architecturally different high schools.[25] Two of the facilities were housed in one or two main classroom buildings; the third had a campus design with several separate buildings. At the campus design school 5 to 10% more interactions occurred in the halls, stairs, and lobbies, and 7 to 10% fewer interactions occurred in classrooms than at the other two schools. Students and teachers spent more time traveling to and from isolated rooms and had less time to interact informally in classrooms before and after instructional sessions. There was 20% less student-teacher interaction in the classroom at the campus design school. This implies that the instructional program may suffer if a campus design is chosen, because teachers and students do not have as much opportunity to interact concerning academic matters before and after class.

Myrick and Marx propose that school designs can be categorized as cohesive or isolating. A cohesive building encourages interaction and hopefully cohesion, through its compact layout and the provision of central areas in which students can gather in large groups between classes. The isolating building discourages large group interactions and cohesion with its extended layout, lengthy corridors, and many alternative routes for getting from one classroom to another. The concept of "cohesive buildings" is analogous to that of "sociopetality" developed by Osmond in his work on psychiatric wards.

Getzels has pointed out that different architectural arrangements of classrooms imply different images of the student. The rectangular classroom, in which pupils' chairs are bolted to the floor in straight rows and the teacher's desk is front and center, is congruent with the image of the "empty organism," which learns only from the teacher. The square classroom, in which pupils' chairs are movable and the teacher's desk is in a corner, is congruent with the image of the "active organism" participating in the learning process. Classrooms without a teacher's desk, in which the pupils' desks are trapezoidal, making a circle when placed next to one another, are congruent with the image of the "social organism," learning primarily from his peers. The open classroom, featuring several activity and resource centers and no desks at all, is congruent with the image of the "stimulus-seeking organism" searching for novel, challenging experiences through which learning takes place. Thus the physical organization of the classroom is shaped by values about the learning process, and, in turn, it shapes the way in which students learn.[26]

The effects of building design are not limited to institutional settings. Oscar Newman has studied residential housing to determine the relationship between architectural design and criminal activity.[27] He noted that the crime rate in housing projects increases with the project's size and height. He attributes this to a lack in the large projects of "defensible space," a term he uses for the mechanisms that improve surveillance and bring an area of a building under the control of its residents. Newman advocates constructing three-story walk-up buildings for low-income families, who are most plagued by crime problems. Entries and corridors should be designed so that a minimum number of families share a common lobby, and the public spaces should provide ample opportunities for visual surveillance. The limit on the number of people who share the common space clearly identifies those who are to be its users and instills in them a feeling of responsibility for the defense of the space. Thus residents would be encouraged both to recognize intruders in their space and to feel obliged to call the authorities if necessary.

Amenities. Aspects of the environment much more subtle than distance or spatial layout can affect behavior. The color of the walls in a room, whether the room is perceived as "beautiful" or "ugly," and whether it is provided with such amenities as comfortable chairs or carpeting, may all be important. Research in this area has been conducted in both laboratory and real-life settings.

For example, Maslow and Mintz asked college students to rate the "energy" and "well-being" of several individuals from a series of photographs of their faces. Rating sessions were conducted in a "beautiful" room, in an "ugly" room, and in an "average" room. The beautiful room had two large windows, beige walls, indirect overhead lighting, comfortable furnishings, and several art objects. It was supposed to resemble a study in a home. The ugly room had small windows, "battleship gray" walls, a single light bulb with a dirty and torn shade, and furnishings chosen to give the impression of a janitor's storeroom in disheveled condition (complete with real dust and garbage). The average room was a professor's office with three windows, more battleship gray on the walls, two mahogany desks, a metal filing cabinet, a cot, several bookcases, and assorted chairs. Noise level, odor, time of day, and seating arrangements were the same in all three rooms to control for possible bias in the rating procedure.

The subjects in the beautiful room rated the photographs as higher on "energy" and "well-being" than did the subjects in either the average or ugly rooms. These conclusions held regardless of the sex of the subject and for both the examiners involved. The effect of the ugly room was decidedly more negative than that of the average room.[28]

The two examiners also provided ratings of the photographs during each of the six rating sessions, ostensibly as a check on the reliability of the rating procedure. They were unaware that they were themselves subjects in the experiment. The effects of the beautiful and ugly rooms were not limited to initial exposure to these rooms. The photographs of faces were rated higher on "energy" and "well-being" by both examiners in the beautiful room during all six rating sessions.[29]

Kasmar developed the Environmental Description Scale (EDS) and used it to investigate patient perceptions of a beautiful room and an ugly room in a psychiatric institute. Two windowless offices of the same size were identically painted and equipped with the same basic furniture. To achieve an "ugly" effect in one room, work papers were scattered all over the desk and stuffed into the metal wastebasket; the asphalt tile floor was left uncovered. The beautiful room was enhanced by a burnt-yellow carpet, an abstract picture, a large artificial plant, and a desk lamp. The wooden wastebasket and the desk were kept neat and tidy. The subjects, male and female applicants for outpatient treatment in the institute, were interviewed in one of the two rooms by one of two psychiatric residents. The ugly room was rated as less appealing, more poorly organized, smaller, and more directly and harshly lighted than the beautiful room. The room characteristics did not have an overall effect on patient ratings of the therapist, or on patient mood.

Thus people do not necessarily rate other persons less favorably when they are sitting in an ugly room. The influence of beautiful or ugly rooms may also depend on what therapist behavior is being considered and on the age and sex of the patient. Certain patients may be affected by characteristics of rooms, especially if the therapist behaves in an authoritarian or critical manner.[30]

Three environmental conditions were varied in experimental rooms in another study. Each subject was taken into one of two identically sized experimental rooms; one had a window and the other was windowless. The subject was asked to sit in a chair, padded or wooden. The room was either embellished (i.e., carpeted, with pictures on the walls) or unembellished. A 10-minute videotape consisting of the reading of passages from a nineteenth-century sex manual was shown to the subject, followed by a 10-item questionnaire concerning factual material in the videotape presentation. Finally, the subject filled out a questionnaire in which he rated the room with respect to its interest, pleasantness, distractingness, and comfort.

Subjects found the embellished room more interesting than the nonembellished room. If the room was embellished and/or had a window, it was rated as more pleasant. A soft chair combined with a windowless and unembellished room was rated as uncomfortable, but a wooden chair in an embellished room with a window was rated as comfortable. Thus the effect of furniture depends on the context in which it appears. The comfort ratings for the wooden chair and the padded chair can only be understood in relation to the other two architectural conditions. Apparently a wooden chair, located in an otherwise pleasant and interesting room, may be rated as more comfortable than a soft chair located in an unpleasant, windowless room.[31]

The impact of providing amenities has been studied by introducing carpets in psychiatric wards and general hospitals. In one study involving two nursing divisions of a general hospital, one carpeted and the other tiled, sound meters established that carpets reduced noise levels. Accident records for the carpeted division showed reduced on-premises injuries from falls. Patient and staff reactions to the carpet were sampled by in-hospital interviews and mailed questionnaires. Patients reported that the carpet gave the hospital a spacious and warm appearance and that the carpeted division was quieter. Nursing staff who customarily wore thick, rubber-cushioned shoes reported feeling more tired at the end of the day; this problem was corrected by use of hard-soled shoes.[32]

Patient and staff behavior was altered when carpets were laid in two units of a state mental hospital. Unit A was a locked ward for male and female geriatric patients, housed in a one-story building. An inexpensive felt carpet was installed in the lobbies, corridors, and dayrooms of the building; "Galleon Gold" was used in the men's wing, and the women were treated to "Alice Blue." Unit B, an acute treatment unit for elderly patients, offered short-term care in a new two-story building that was locked only at night. When unit B first opened, beige carpets had already been installed everywhere except the upstairs lobby, where a blue tweed was featured.

Staff in Unit A had not been enthusiastic about installation of the carpet, which was an innovation pushed through by the administration. After installation staff agreed that the general appearance of the unit had improved, but they felt that the carpet was inappropriate for their patients and that it resulted in many maintenance problems. Patients were much more positive; they liked the carpet's appearance and thought walking on the carpet was more comfortable. Both patients and staff reported that some of the men stopped being incontinent in lobbies and corridors after installation of the carpet.

In unit B staff had been permitted more input in obtaining the carpet and were able to pretest carpet samples so as to avoid future cleaning problems. Patients and staff generally approved of the carpet, although some patients who had been transferred from a tiled building had become accustomed to sliding their feet along the floor. When they attempted to walk in this manner on the carpet, they tended to fall down. As in the case of unit A, some of the men were less often incontinent in public places.[33]

The effect of carpet installation on incontinence of mental hospital patients was replicated in another study of two adjacent wards for disturbed women, both located on the fifth floor of a state mental hospital building. One ward was carpeted; the other had asphalt tile. Patients and staff in the carpeted ward modulated their voices more, and the patients were less irritable and excitable. Some normally incontinent patients requested bathroom privileges after installation of the carpet. One patient tried to roll up the corner of the carpet to avoid soiling it with her usual behavior.[34]

It is apparent that introducing a carpet into a ward is a complex social process, not just a straightforward environmental manipulation. Patients and staff tend to associate carpets with previously experienced noninstitutional environments. Patient behavior, particularly with respect to incontinence, may change because of the association of carpets with homes or other community environments in which incontinence of adults is not appropriate. Staff may react to the introduction of carpets as a symbol of their relationship to administrators rather than as a purely physical change to be evaluated only as it affects life on the ward. The interrelation of significant social changes with architectural innovations is of great importance in evaluating the impact of design or architectural changes.

Modifying an Incongruent Environment.   We have discussed how three aspects of the environment—distance, spatial arrangement, and amenities—can make a setting more or less congruent with various kinds of behavior, ranging from friendship formation and social interaction to better job performance and the curtailment of crime in housing projects. We have been assuming that an environment that is incongruent with certain behavior will render less likely the occurrence of that behavior. Of course if people really want to act in a certain way, the lack of environmental support can often be overcome. Another alternative is often selected by individuals—they modify an incongruent environment to make it more congruent with the behavior they wish to enact.

An example of such an adaptation is provided by L. E. White. He observed the outdoor play of children who lived in a four- and five-story block of flats in a city-developed estate in South London. The open courtyard area, which was not intended for children's play activities, was used extensively for a variety of types of play: hide and seek, riding tricycles and other wheeled vehicles, ball games, and so on. A circular toddlers' enclosure served primarily as a football field. Covered porch areas became "club houses" in rainy weather, and an automatic elevator in one building became an extremely popular toy for children. Nearly every feature of the estate chosen by children in their play activities was used in a manner not intended by the designers of the estate. The primary reason for this adaptation of facilities was that since very little in the way of play areas and facilities was provided by the designers, the children were forced to adapt other facilities.[35]

Similar examples of people changing an incongruent environment, especially through simple modifications such as the rearrangement of furniture or the introduction of amenities like wall-hangings or plants, are common everyday experiences. When faced with an environment that is fixed because of practical considerations, the desired modifications may be made only in the minds of the participants. An illustration of such an adaptation is provided by Louis Karmel. He instructed students at two different high schools, one with and one without windows, to draw a picture of a school. A significantly higher proportion of students at the windowless school drew windows in their pictures. The study suggests that when placed in a setting that could not be changed physically, the children coped by modifying their mental picture of the environment.[36]

Sometimes it is possible to change to a new environment. For example, one class of boys 17–18 years old was uncooperative and noisy. The class was held in a small room so crowded with desks that no rearrangement of the furniture was possible. The teacher moved the class to an unused staff common room that had two large tables. He seated his class around these tables separating the two most troublesome students. As the term proceeded the misbehavior of the two troublemakers was controlled by the other students seated around them.[37]

Environments congruent with certain behaviors may make these behaviors more likely to occur. But one of the characteristics that distinguish man from other animals is his ability to adapt to hostile environments and to change them to meet his needs. Thus people will attempt to modify incongruent environments. If they cannot, as is often the case, they may cope by changing their behavior, by changing their mental images of the environment, or by "dropping out" and selecting a more suitable setting.

Congruence with Cultural and Social Characteristics. We have concentrated thus far on the ways in which aspects of the physical setting can be congruent with certain specific kinds of behavior. Environments can have an even wider impact by affecting the lifestyles and values of the people who live in them. Examples of such changes are provided by studies of people who have been relocated into housing projects when their neighborhoods were leveled in the course of urban renewal.

Anecdotal evidence has been presented on the effects of the London County Council's slum resident rehousing program. East London slum residents, with widespread social networks based on their extended families and nearby neighbors, were offered single-family detached housing in an outlying suburban area. Only those with young children typically made the move. The higher cost of the housing plus commuting costs made frequent visiting with those who remained behind in the slum impossible.

Extended families were often broken up by the rehousing program. Adults visited their elderly parents back in East London once a month instead of nearly every day, and other relatives and friends were visited much less often. Young and Willmott poignantly portray the feelings of those who made the move to the suburbs. One woman said: "I don't even go to my Mum now. I haven't got the fare money. But you've got to put up with things if you want a place for your children. Your children come first I say." Another woman noted: "Mum likes me to go and see her. I used to be with her a lot. She missed me a lot at the beginning. But we had to think of the kiddies, didn't we?"[38]

The researchers note two changes in values among the new suburban residents. The setting encouraged people to try to "keep up with the Joneses," emphasizing the importance of money and jobs. Putting a high value on "things," people became more object-oriented and less people-oriented. This attitude was coupled with an emphasis on future time and planning ahead. Life was not as spontaneous as it had been in the old neighborhood.

Such a change was resisted by many of the residents of Boston's West End who were forced to relocate during the early 1960s. The setting they had lived in encouraged frequent spontaneous and informal contacts. Buildings were close together, with windows near enough to enable adjacent neighbors to carry on conversations while in their respective apartments. Many residents spent substantial amounts of time sitting on the front steps, where they would engage passersby in conversation. Shops, which often occupied the ground floor of the buildings, encouraged additional street activity. Had these residents moved to the suburbs, their entire life style would have been difficult, if not impossible, to maintain. Such low-density areas, with distinct separations between residential and business uses, and between housing lots themselves, are incongruent with the numerous spontaneous interactions that were such a key element in the social life of the West Enders. Unwilling to make such a change, most residents relocated to areas of greater Boston marked by high densities and mixed land use.[39]

The motivation for building public housing comes from a realization that pervasive negative effects may result from extremely poor housing in slum areas. A comprehensive government review states that "desperately inadequate" housing is implicated in negative self-images, poor health, cynical attitudes toward the people and organizations outside the slum, a high degree of sexual arousal without legitimate outlets, difficulties in managing children, and social relationships that tend to deemphasize family relations in favor of widespread neighbor relationships.[40] A more recent review agrees that health may be endangered if poor housing includes the presence of rodents or lead-based paint and that satisfaction with housing is low in slum areas.[41]

Wilner and his colleagues compared 300 families scheduled to move into a public housing project with 300 control families, slum dwellers from the same areas as the project population. Project residents were conscious of improvements in their living circumstances, thought that their children played in safer areas, and reported increased privacy, fewer physical barriers to sociability, and reduction of psychological discomfort related to inadequate space in the home.

Project parents were less likely than control parents to argue with their children about spending too much time away from home. This implies that project children spent more time at home, possibly because of increased personal space and more comfortable physical surroundings. Project families established somewhat better neighbor relations than they had had in the slum and better relationships than the control group. More helpful, mutually supportive behavior and more friendly interaction were reported in the project. Interest in and use of the immediate community environment were greater for project families, but these attitudes did not generalize to the larger urban or national settings, in which both control and project families showed little interest.[42]

Public housing is not a panacea for social problems. Residents in the Pruitt-Igoe housing project in St. Louis were more satisfied with their apartments, but less satisfied with the surrounding neighborhood, than were slum dwellers in the same area. There was very little public open space within the project. This architectural defect made it difficult for people to continue neighborhood visiting patterns of the type they had practiced in slum neighborhoods, and it also made them easy prey to muggers, burglars, and rapists. Seldom-used staircases, apartment entrances visible from only one other apartment entrance, and elevators became frequent sites for crimes of all kinds.[43]

Public housing has the potential of eliminating the physical conditions responsible for these negative consequences of slum life, and there has been recent concern because public housing often fails to provide a better physical environment. In addition, the possible benefits of rehousing projects must be weighed against the primary social cost of disrupting widespread social networks in the slum area. Several authors have documented the existence and the disruption of these networks, whose existence does not necessarily imply a deemphasis on the family.[38, 44] The neighbor networks very often involve members of the extended family to an extent that no current alternative to high-density, low-cost (slum) housing can offer. The disruption of these networks may be the single largest impact of the move to public housing.[44]

Another aspect of suburban life that has received considerable attention is the possibility that it discourages individuality. In his Park Forest study Whyte discusses the consequences of a neighborhood design that tends to encourage interaction and make isolation and privacy impossible: "The court, like the double bed, enforces intimacy, and self-imposed isolation becomes psychologically untenable."[45] A leveling, homogenizing process may take place, with both positive and negative consequences. An intellectual may become ashamed to admit that she reads Plato, and the former rural Republican may revise his political opinions, admitting that not all Democrats are Communists. The wives are probably constrained to conversing about children, and the men naturally must spend most of their weekends manicuring the front lawn. One further consequence of intense interaction and group cohesion in small neighborhood areas was little participation in civic or cultural affairs. People active in the overall community came from less socially active, less cohesive courts in Park Forest; conversely, the courts where interaction was most intense contributed few civic leaders.

The picture of the suburbs as a great homogenizer is not shared by all researchers. Based on his findings in Levittown, Gans refutes the charges of Whyte and others who have severely criticized suburban life styles. Whyte sees as harmful most of the effects of the frequent interaction fostered by suburban site plans (e.g., no privacy, forced homogenization, little civic activity). Gans found that morale and cohesion within families was high in Levittown, that the residents reported good adaptation to the suburb, and that organizational participation was rather high. Homogeneity in Levittowners, measured by several family background characteristics, did not seem greater than in other residential areas near Philadelphia, not did it seem to increase over time.[46]

The environment can also affect individual role behavior. Peter Marris studied the changes brought on by the relocation of families in Lagos, Nigeria, from large square-shaped compounds to a series of row houses.

Women in the old settings were accustomed to being traders of goods, which they sold to government employees on their way to work. Such behavior was facilitated by the open areas of the compound, obvious encouragements to frequent interactions. The women objected to their new houses, which they associated with women in the undesirable role of housewife, whose only concern is to keep her house in neat order.[47]

Anthony Wallace has argued that apartment housing has affected the ease with which American men can assume the role of "pioneer" and "doer of great deeds" in the eyes of their wives and children. The era in which a man could demonstrate his strength by splitting a stack of logs has long passed. Even the physical chores of maintaining a garden or performing household repairs are unavailable to the apartment dweller. The American male is thus forced into a new role of "star boarder," since his traditional role, glorified in folklore and the media, is incongruent with his present residential setting.[48]

Congruence and Its Relation to Background Characteristics. The same environment may affect different people in quite different ways. The age, social class, cultural background, and personality characteristics of the users of a setting may determine the degree to which the setting will be congruent with the behaviors its users wish to perform. A few examples serve to illustrate the importance of examining both the setting and the individuals in it when investigating the impact of a particular environment.

One of the principal attractions of suburban living has been its image as an ideal place to raise young children. There are yards and space where children can play safely without close supervision. The distance separating residential areas from busy commercial districts is comforting. But such separation is a drawback when the children become teenagers. Suburbia becomes a place where there is "nothing to do," especially for those who lack access to an automobile. There are few neighborhood stores around which to congregate, and the houses, built with bedrooms designed for small children, do not provide enough space to entertain friends. Thus as Gans observed in his study of Levittown, a community designed for parents and young children can be "Endsville" for adolescents.[49]

The lack of congruence in the preceding example results from the different needs of people at different points in the life cycle. Incongruence can also be rooted in the outlook and values held by individuals. For example, Fried and Gleicher have pointed out that people of different social classes can perceive and use the same environment in different ways.[50] Middle-class persons use a street as a corridor to get from one place to another. In contrast, working-class individuals view it as a congregating and living space. Similarly, cultural differences affect perception. When residents of Lagos were relocated from open compound housing to row houses, the older residents were dissatisfied with the accommodations. The self-contained dwellings, which lacked open yards, were not suited to their customary communal way of living. However Nigerians who had worked or studied abroad had shed some of their traditional values and felt comfortable in the new setting.[51]

Ethnic and personality differences are related to the distances people prefer to place between themselves. Baxter, in observing people visiting a zoo, noted that Mexican-Americans tended to keep the least distance between each other when interacting in pairs. Black Americans were most often separated by the greatest distances, and Anglo-Americans fell into the middle category[52] (see Chapter 5). Mehrabian and Diamond conducted related research in a laboratory setting. After noting that the orientation of furniture in a room affected the social interaction of participants, they discovered that the personalities of the subjects had important mediating effects. Persons more uncomfortable about associating with strangers were more relaxed at greater distances. They also tended to make use of a sculpture conversation piece to set themselves at ease.[53] These differences based on cultural or personality variables are important to note. An arrangement of furniture that promotes intimacy with one pair of persons may make another quite uncomfortable.

Mental Congruence.   Thus far we have been concerned with how well different environments actually accommodate the characteristics and behavior of people who use them. This is what Michelson has termed "experiential congruence."[54] But there can also exist a state of "mental congruence," in which individuals think that certain environments will accommodate their personal values, needs, and lifestyles. Such beliefs are important considerations, regardless of whether they can be empirically substantiated. Michelson cites the example of the large number of people who believe that the suburbs are a good place to raise families. This state of mental congruence between "familism" and "suburbanism" can exist even though a state of experiential congruence between the two may not. Often people's perceptions of their environments are more important than the realities of the environments themselves.

Research in one aspect of mental congruence, concerned with how people perceive their own neighborhood, has been pursued through the concept of cognitive mapping, as outlined by Downs and Stea.[55] They suggest that spatial behavior is dependent on each person's subjective or cognitive map of the physical environment. To get to work in the morning or to find his way to a store, each person must have some information available if he is to turn at the appropriate corners, get off the bus at the proper stop, take the correct stairway to the second floor, and so forth. The process of acquiring, coding, recalling, and decoding such information about the "whereness" and other physical attributes of various features of the environment is called *cognitive mapping*.

Cognitive maps of neighborhoods and of the downtown area of Los Angeles vary greatly among groups of people who live in different parts of the city. In one study black residents from an area near Watts had very restricted conceptions of the city. Internal streets and buildings were noted only for the downtown area; surrounding areas were indicated as undifferentiated blocks. Spanish-speaking Boyles Heights residents had even more restricted maps, generally including only a few city blocks in their immediate neighborhood. Residents of a white upper-class district gave detailed images of the entire Los Angeles Basin. Residents of a middle-class suburban area gave considerable detail for the San Fernando Valley area but little detail of the downtown area. Residents of a Jewish neighborhood in the San Fernando Valley also supplied restricted maps of downtown.[56]

Social class, ethnic, and intellectual characteristics influence cognitive maps. Residence location also strongly affects a person's cognitive map of a given urban area. The areas a person seldom enters will be quite undifferentiated. The map is thus initially determined by behavior; once formed, however, cognitive maps may themselves affect subsequent behavior. Suburbanites may not go downtown because they do not have accurate cognitive maps of the area and therefore do not know how to find the facilities and services they would be seeking.

The effect of cognitive maps on behavior has been demonstrated by interviewing housewives in Cambridge, England. Each housewife was given a map and asked to draw a line around the limits of her neighborhood. The neighborhood maps were called "schemata," since each was rather unique in size and shape. The schemata were analyzed in relation to each woman's locality (i.e., a half-mile radius in any direction from a respondent's house). Schemata and locality generally overlapped but did not exactly correspond, and schemata tended to be skewed toward the downtown area of Cambridge.

The skewing of schemata toward downtown related to the shopping behavior of the housewives, who preferred to use not-too-distant shops in the direction of downtown over closer shops in the opposite direction. In addition, the larger the schemata, measured by the number of houses included, the more local friends and club memberships were mentioned, indicating greater social involvement.[57] The direction of causation is not clear. The choice of local friends may be due to relatively small schemata, or the small schemata may be in part determined by an initial choice of friends. In either case it is clear that perception and social behavior are linked.

The cognitive mapping literature offers clues about how people manage to find their way around from place to place in cities. The shape and detail of a person's cognitive map of an area may affect the frequency and type of use he makes of that area. In investigating why people form the cognitive maps that they do, researchers have tried to find out what aspects of a city make it memorable. Residents of Boston, Jersey City, and Los Angeles were asked for descriptions of their city, the location of buildings or areas, and directions for getting to some point in the city. People's images of cities had five distinct elements: paths, edges, districts, nodes, and landmarks. Paths are the street, subway, foot or canal routes people use to travel through the city. Edges are boundaries between distinct areas of the city, such as shorelines, streets, or walls. Districts are two-dimensional areas with identifying boundaries and characteristics. Nodes are the foci between which urbanites travel, such as junctions, places of transfer from one form of transportation to another, or the core or epitome of a district. Landmarks are buildings, signs, and hills used in finding one's way around in a city. The investigator, Kevin Lynch, concluded that intelligent manipulation of these five elements can contribute to residents' mobility within cities by "forming our new city world into an imageable landscape: visible, coherent, and clear."[58]

In Ciudad Guayana, a growing industrial city in Venezuela, the city's planners gave explicit consideration to Lynch's thesis that high imageability can aid resident mobility within a city. Thus Ciudad Guayana provides an interesting setting for the replication of Lynch's findings. Seventy-five randomly selected householders were interviewed in each of four areas: an American-style suburban area, a squatter community, a low-density planned community, and a colonial-style small town. The subjects were asked to recall physical features of specific areas of the city. The most frequently mentioned features of the city included a prominent viewpoint that many people passed each day; locations near decision points, such as intersections, bus stops, and ferry crossings; and centrally located and easily visible places. Frequent use by the person, uniqueness of the facility to the particular person, and symbolic features (e.g., a dam that was important to the local economy but visually blended into the landscape) also contributed to recall.[59]

Every city has a distinctive atmosphere or flavor that differentiates it subjectively from other cities. One study, comparing New York and Boston, found that New York was described as high-class, alive, happy, exciting, entertaining, full of tourists, but also as cheap and vulgar, foreign and dangerous. Boston was more often described as old and quaint, different, filthy, unvaried, not depressing, and very fast-paced. The degree of consensus varied greatly among cities. The most commonly used clusters of words comprised less than 10% of all descriptions in all the cities studied. Thus there are large individual differences in people's reactions to urban environments.[60]

This work suggests the possibility of checklists and rating scales to differentiate among cities and regions within cities. These descriptive terms could be used to develop a scale that would measure people's preferences for urban settings. Urban designers might benefit greatly from the information obtained by such a scale. The distinctiveness dimensions mentioned in the two previous studies could be used to generate a scale to rate the "imageability" of urban features. This might help planners design urban settings in which the mobility of residents would be aided by the strategic location of highly distinctive features.

Conclusions.   In this chapter we have discussed how human behavior is affected by the man-made physical environments that people occupy. Studies in real-life and laboratory settings have demonstrated how environments encourage behaviors with which they are congruent. Having this understanding, the next task is to develop ways in which designers and architects can work with the people who will use their creations, ensuring that the results will be congruent with the users' goals.

To accomplish this objective people must become more aware of their environments and, moreover, willing to do something about creating settings that suit their needs. Thomas G. David has called for the development of "environmental literacy." Such a process involves transforming environmental awareness into a "critical, probing, problem-seeking attitude towards one's surroundings. It entails the active definition of choices and a willingness to experiment with a variety of spatial alternatives and challenge the environmental status quo."[61]

The tendency of the "environmental status quo" to discourage innovations in design and the rearrangement of existing settings cannot be overemphasized. People become used to the settings they occupy and treat them as fixed, even though often they can be changed. Once positioned, even though easily movable, tables and chairs frequently remain in place. In designing new structures, solutions are often limited to traditional forms. For those accustomed to living and working in rectangular-shaped spaces, it is hard to imagine that very different kinds of spaces can be just as functional. David has pointed out that people usually conceptualize their environmental needs in terms of specifiable products, not generic performances. If the task at hand is to design a space where children can learn, we must not limit ourselves to preconceived images of what constitutes a classroom. Instead, we must ask what kind of behavior we want in the setting we create, and how can it be encouraged.

To answer such questions designers have increasingly sought to involve users in the planning process. This task has been made more difficult by the growth of nonuser clients such as government agencies and corporation boards. Architects must go beyond simply questioning those who employ them, inquiring about the needs of all those who are affected by their designs. James Holt has concluded that the user population of a new school includes the entire community—both those who are directly involved, such as teachers, students, and administrators, and members of the community at large who pay taxes for the building and send their children there to learn. Holt advocates the formation of charrettes, or intensive group planning efforts, to involve a wide range of people in the planning process. Community members encompassing the entire spectrum of users, together with professional educators, architects, engineers, planners, psychologists, business representatives, and local public officials, brainstorm for a concentrated period to develop a clear conception of their design needs and solutions. Where the charrette technique has been used to plan facilities, the result has not been limited to innovative designs. There has also been a drastic reduction in the distance between people and their institutions, and a more involved and cohesive community environment has been created.[62]

Sommer has pointed out that user input should not end with the process of designing a structure. He calls for the institutionalization of an evaluation process of buildings after they have been constructed, through the efforts of environmental consultants and the creation of a data bank for user information. Just as doctors and dentists see their patients periodically for checkups, architects and designers should reexamine their creations to see if they are "healthy." Users, who would receive instructions on how their environments were intended to be used, would supply their own feedback on how well such environments served their needs. The cost of evaluations could be borne by the clients, professional associations, manufacturers' trade associations, and consumer groups. Copies of the designs and the results of the evaluations would be collected and stored on microfilm or in computers, to facilitate retrieval. Designers working on a specific problem could easily assess the effectiveness of past solutions in meeting similar needs.[63]

The physical environment we create affects our behavior. By recognizing this relationship, and by closely examining both our objectives and the ways in which our designs function, we can create environments that are more congruent with our goals.

REFERENCES

1. Turner, E. A girls' group home: An approach to treating delinquent girls in the community. Community Treatment Project, Research Report No. 1, Department of the Youth Authority, Sacramento, Calif., 1969 (quotation from pp. 27–28).

2. Hazard, J. N. Furniture arrangement as a symbol of judicial roles. *ETC: Review of General Semantics*, **19**:181–189, 1962 (quotation from pp. 181–186).

3. Sommer, R. *Personal space.* Prentice-Hall, Englewood Cliffs, N. J., 1969.

4. Michelson, W. *Man and his urban environment: A sociological approach.* Addison-Wesley, Reading, Mass., 1970, p. 25.

5. Festinger, L., Schachter, S., and Back, K. *Social pressures in informal groups.* Harper & Row, New York, 1950.

6. Kuper, L. "Blueprint for living together." In L. Kuper (Ed.), *Living in towns.* Cresset Press, London, 1953, pp. 11–97.

7. Whyte, W. H. *The organization man.* Simon & Schuster, New York, 1956 (quotation from pp. 330–331).

8. Gans, H. J. *The Levittowners: Ways of life and politics in a new suburban community.* Pantheon, New York, 1967.

9. Athanasiou, R. and Yoshioka, G. The spatial character of friendship formation. *Environment and Behavior,* **5**:43–65, 1973.

10. Lansing, J. B., Marans, R. W. and Zehner, R. B. *Planned residential environments.* Survey Research Center, Institute for Social Research, University of Michigan, Ann Arbor, 1970.

11. Blake, R., Rhead, C. C., Wedge, B., and Mouton, J. S. Housing architecture and social interaction. *Sociometry,* **19**:133–139, 1956.

12. Heilweill, M. The influence of dormitory architecture on resident behavior. *Environment and Behavior,* **5**:377–412, 1973.

13. Gullahorn, J. T. Distance and friendship as factors in the gross interaction matrix. *Sociometry,* **15**:123–124, 1952.

14. Wells, B. W. P. The psycho-social influence of building environment: Sociometric findings in large and small office spaces. *Building Sciences,* **1**:153–165, 1965.

15. Brookes, M. and Kaplan, A. The office environment: Space planning and affective behavior. *Human Factors,* **14**:373–391, 1972.

16. Good, L. R., Siegel, S. M., and Bay, A. P. *Therapy in design: Implications of architecture for human behavior.* Charles C. Thomas, Springfield, Ill., 1965.

17. Sommer, R. and Ross, H. Social interaction on a geriatric ward. *International Journal of Social Psychiatry*, **4:**128–133, 1958.

18. Gump, P. V. and James, E. V. Patient behavior in wards of traditional and modern design. Midwest Psychological Field Station, University of Kansas, Lawrence, 1970.

19. Ittelson, W. H., Proshansky, H. M., and Rivlin, L. G. The environmental psychology of the psychiatric ward. In H. Proshansky, W. Ittelson, and L. Rivlin (Eds.), *Environmental psychology: Man and his physical setting.* Holt, Rinehart & Winston, New York, 1970, pp. 419–439.

20. Osmond, H. Function as the basis of psychiatric ward design. *Mental Hospitals*, **8** (Arch. Suppl.):23–29, 1957.

21. Holahan, C. J. Seating patterns and patient behavior in an experimental dayroom. *Journal of Abnormal Psychology*, **80:**115–124, 1972.

22. Trites, D. K., Galbraith, F. D., Sturdavant, M., and Leckwart, J. F. Influence of nursing-unit design on the activities and subjective feelings of nursing personnel. *Environment and Behavior*, **2:**303–333, 1970.

23. Holahan, C. J. and Saegert, S. Behavioral and attitudinal effects of large-scale variation in the physical environment of psychiatric wards. *Journal of Abnormal Psychology*, **82:**454–462, 1973.

24. Spivack, M. Sensory distortions in tunnels and corridors. *Hospital and Community Psychiatry*, **18:**12–18, 1967.

25. Myrick, R. and Marx, B. S. An exploratory study of the relationship between high school building design and student learning. U.S. Department of Health, Education, and Welfare, Office of Education, Bureau of Research Washington, D.C., 1968.

26. Getzels, J. Images of the classroom and visions of the learner. *School Review*, **82:**527–540, 1974.

27. Newman, O. *Defensible space: Crime prevention through urban design.* Macmillan, New York, 1973.

28. Maslow, A. H. and Mintz, N. L. Effects of esthetic surroundings: I. Initial effects of three esthetic conditions upon perceiving "energy" and "well-being" in faces. *Journal of Psychology*, **41:**247–254, 1956.

29. Mintz, N. L. Effects of esthetic surroundings: II. Prolonged and repeated experiences in a "beautiful" and an "ugly" room. *Journal of Psychology*, **41:**459–466, 1956.

30. Kasmar, J. V., Griffin, W. V., and Mauritzen, J. H. The effect of environmental surroundings on outpatients' mood and perception of psychiatrists. *Journal of Consulting and Clinical Psychology*, **32:**223–226, 1968.

31. Tognolli, J. The effect of windowless rooms and unembellished surroundings on attitudes and retention. *Environment and Behavior*, **5:**191–201, 1973.

32. Greco, J. T. Carpeting vs. resilient flooring: A comparative study in a metropolitan hospital. *Hospitals*, **39:**55–58, 1965.

33. Cheek, F. E., Maxwell, R. and Weisman, R. Carpeting the ward: An exploratory study in environmental psychiatry. *Mental Hygiene*, **55:**109–118, 1971.

34. Lee, R. The advantages of carpets in mental hospitals. *Mental Hospitals,* **16:**324–325, 1965.

35. White, L. E. The outdoor play of children living in flats: An enquiry into the use of courtyards as playgrounds. In L. Kuper (Ed.), *Living in towns.* Cresset Press, London, 1953, pp. 235–258.

36. Karmel, L. J. Effects of windowless classroom environment on high school students. *Perceptual and Motor Skills,* **20:**277–278, 1965. See also *The effect of windowless classrooms on elementary school children.* Architectural Research Laboratory, Department of Architecture, University of Michigan, Ann Arbor, 1965.

37. Richardson, E. The physical setting and its influence on learning. In H. Proshansky, W. Ittleson, and L. Rivlin (Eds.), *Environmental psychology: Man and his physical setting.* Holt, Rinehart & Winston, New York, 1970, pp. 386–397.

38. Young, M. and Willmott, P. *Family and kinship in East London.* Free Press, New York, 1957.

    Young, M. and Willmott, P. From Bethnal Green to Greenleigh. In S. Friedman and J. Juhasz (Eds.), *Environments: Notes and selections on objects, spaces, and behavior.* Brooks/Cole, Monterey, Calif., 1974 (quotations from p. 240).

39. Gans, H. *The urban villagers.* Free Press, New York, 1962.

40. Schorr, A. L. Slums and social insecurity. U.S. Department of Health, Education and Welfare, Social Security Administration, Division of Research and Statistics, Research Report No. 1, Washington, D.C., 1963.

41. Kasl, S. V. Effects of housing on mental and physical health. Department of Epidemiology and Public Health, School of Medicine, Yale University, New Haven, Conn., 1973.

42. Wilner, D. M., Walkley, R., Pinkerton, T., and Tayback, M. *The housing environment and family life: A longitudinal study of the effects of housing on morbidity and mental illness.* Johns Hopkins Press, Baltimore, 1962.

43. Yancey, W. L. Architecture, interaction, and social control: The case of a large-scale public housing project. *Environment and Behavior,* **2:**3–21, 1971.

44. Fried, M. Grieving for a lost home. In L. Duhl (Ed.), *The urban condition.* Basic Books, New York, 1963, pp. 151–171.

45. Whyte, *The organization man, op. cit.,* p. 351.

46. Gans, *The Levittowners, op. cit.*

47. Marris, P. *Family and social class in an African city.* Northwestern University Press, Evanston, Ill., 1962.

48. Wallace, A. F. C. Housing and social structure: A preliminary survey with particular reference to multi-storey, low-rent public housing projects. Philadelphia Housing Authority (mimeo), 1952, from Michelson, *Man and his urban environment, op. cit.,* p. 81.

49. Gans, *The Levittowners, op. cit.*

50. Fried, M. and Gleicher, P. Some sources of residential satisfaction in an urban slum. *Journal of the American Institute of Planners,* **27:**305–315, 1961.

51. Marris, *op. cit.*

52. Baxter, J. Interpersonal spacing in natural settings. *Sociometry*, **33**:444–456, 1970.

53. Mehrabian, A. and Diamond, S. Effects of furniture arrangement, props, and personality on social interaction. *Journal of Personality and Social Psychology*, **20**:18–30, 1971.

54. Michelson, *Man and his urban environment, op. cit.*, pp. 30–31.

55. Downs, R. M. and Stea, D. Cognitive maps and spatial behavior: Process and products. In R. M. Downs and D. Stea (Eds.), *Image and environment: Cognitive mapping and spatial behavior.* Aldine Press, Chicago, 1973.

56. Orleans, P. Differential cognition of urban residents: Effects of social scale on mapping. In R. M. Downs and D. Stea (Eds.), *Image and environment: Cognitive mapping and spatial behavior.* Aldine Press, Chicago, 1973.

57. Lee, T. Urban neighborhood as a socio-spatial schema. *Human Relations*, **21**:241–268, 1968.

58. Lynch, K. *The image of the city.* MIT Press, Cambridge, Mass., 1960 (quotation from p. 103).

59. Appleyard, D. Why buildings are known: A predictive tool for architects and planners. *Environment and Behavior*, **1**:131–156, 1969.

60. Lowenthal, D. Environmental assessment: A comparative analysis of four cities. Publications in Environmental Perception, No. 5, American Geographical Society, New York, 1972.

61. David, T. G. On environmental literacy. *School Review*, **82**:687–705, 1974.

62. Holt, J. Involving the users in school planning. *School Review*, **82**:706–730, 1974.

63. Sommer, R. *Design awareness.* Rinehart Press, San Francisco, 1972.

CHAPTER FIVE

Population Density, Crowding, and the Use of Space[a]

People who live in sparsely populated areas and therefore feel detached from the pressures of population problems may soon see the day when they feel overcrowded. The population of the world was 1.25 billion at the turn of the century, 2.5 billion in 1950, and is expected to reach 6–7 billion by the year 2000; this means that world population is increasing by more than 100,000 persons a day![1] As population increases, already populous areas become more crowded, and areas previously considered undesirable residential locations are developed and inhabited; in other words, the population moves up *and* out.

In *My Petition for More Space*,[2] John Hersey gives a futuristic account of what life may be like if the population continues to grow at the present rate: the world has grown so crowded that society is completely totalitarian, dissent is inconceivable, and "acquiescence the law of survival." Hersey's story concerns the experiences of Sam Poynter as he tries to cope in the petition "waitline" of thousands so densely packed that motion is almost impossible. There are also library waitlines, state park waitlines, and so on. The longest lines are at the museum of openness called the "Green," where people may wait all day for a glimpse through windows that look onto a space of empty grass.

Poynter gradually learns that the petitions of the people pressed against him include requests for a protein allotment, for cigars, to conduct

[a] This chapter is co-authored by Rudolf Moos and James Kulik.

141

a lottery, and to change jobs. A woman whose grandson is one of only 400 students chosen to learn to read that year is petitioning to prevent her grandson from learning to read so that he may be taught a "useful skill," instead. A young man and his wife want a permit to have a child. It took Poynter three years and 17 written requests to obtain a permit for a child. Only one child has been allowed per couple for the last two generations.

Poynter's own petition is for the maximum amount of single-person space permitted by law, 8 feet by 12 feet. A person's space is defined by lines painted on the sleeping-hall floor. Poynter has already made the most of his 7 by 11 allotment; except for his chest-bed, his space is completely barren. Guests find his space intoxicating because so much of it *is* space.

However the notion of asking for more space is so outrageous that pandemonium erupts when others learn the nature of Poynter's petition. Soon a shrill, metallic shrieking is heard above the uproar as a young man succumbs to "line-sickness," a feeling of being "frozen for eternity in a condition of waiting." Line-sickness is very contagious under crowded conditions, and though the crowd is now hushed and rigidly "holding on," a woman near Poynter also succumbs. Only a mass effort of singing by the crowd eventually silences the shriekers.

At the petition bureau window, after more than 5 hours in the waitline, Poynter quickly realizes that the mechanical voice from behind the window has access to all the facts of his life from a computerized biobank. Through a series of abrupt shifts and subtle misdirections in questioning, each petitioner's belief in the moral base of his petition is artfully undermined, and each petition is rejected. Poynter's request is no exception, and as he starts his 2-hour walk to work through the crowds, he is already beginning to construct his next petition.

Line-sickness and related phenomena are products of Hersey's imagination, but popularized writings by everyone from ecologists to politicians have postulated equally deleterious social and psychological effects of crowding.[3] Hypothesized social effects of crowding include deterioration of education and service systems, higher crime rates, economic stress, more controls by "Big Brother," riots, and wars; presumed negative interpersonal and psychological effects are mental illness, increased drug addiction and alcoholism, family disorganization, loss of freedom, withdrawal, aggression, and reduction in the quality of life. Separating crowding "facts" from "fictions" will be an increasingly important problem in the years to come as world population escalates.

Brief presentation of a conceptual model of crowding may help illustrate the parameters of the human crowding phenomenon. One of the most complete conceptual frameworks of crowding is the stress model proposed by Stokols.[4] The model presented here is an extension of the

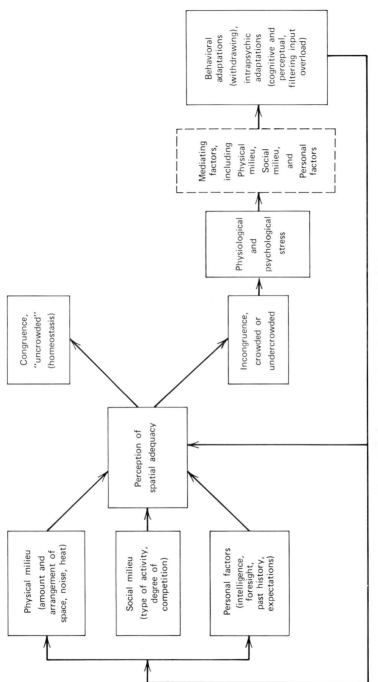

Figure 5.1 A conceptual model of crowding phenomena.

Stokols model (see Figure 5.1). Stokols suggests that a state of crowding exists, and is perceived as such by an individual, when his or her demand for space exceeds the available supply. This definition distinguishes between "density" and "crowding." Density denotes a physical condition involving limited space, whereas crowding has the additional requirement of *perceived* spatial inadequacy.

The crowding phenomenon may be conceptualized as a continuum that ranges from perceptions of spatial inadequacy (crowded) to perceptions of spatial adequacy (uncrowded) to perceptions of spatial excess (undercrowded or isolated). Cognizance of spatial inadequacy or spatial excess evokes psychological and physiological stress in the individual. Although the present model primarily concerns crowding stress, there is evidence that isolation (undercrowding stress) may be associated with various symptoms, including mental illness.[5] The perception of space as inadequate, adequate, or excessive is mediated by the interaction of the physical milieu, social milieu, and personal factors.

The most important qualities of the physical environment are the amount and arrangement of space. As space becomes scarce, the individual is behaviorally constricted; however various arrangements of available space can allay or heighten the feeling of constriction (e.g., surrounding a small room with mirrored walls and/or careful arrangement of furniture may make the room appear larger).

Stokols has also proposed that the salience of reduced space may be intensified by physical stress factors such as noise, heat, and temporal duration. If these assumptions are valid, people living in Hong Kong tenement slums should be certain to experience crowding stress. The median square feet per person in some Hong Kong dwellings is only 43, and many families must share their living space with nonkinsmen.[6] The tenants are thus subjected to very restricted space with little opportunity for more efficient spatial arrangements. Compounding the situation are the physical stressors of excessive heat and odors emanating from cohabitators, as well as the noise produced by the teeming urban ambience.

Social factors, such as the type of activity the individual is engaged in, affect the salience of spatial restriction. For example, crowded spectators may completely forget about the limited space while a football game is in progress. Once the game is over, however, spatial restrictions are soon perceived as people attempt to exit. Stokols suggests that the individual may view other people as "in competition" for scarce resources (e.g., a direct path to the exit gate), and such feelings may increase perceived crowdedness.[7] Similarly, to the extent that the Hong Kong resident construes his or her situation as primarily one of competition for the limited resource of space, he or she may have increased feelings of spatial restriction.

Finally, Stokols proposes that personal factors also mediate the perception of crowding. Individuals who possess foresight, high intelligence, strength, and other "superior" personal qualities may be less apt to experience crowding stress. For example, persons with realistic foresight should be more successful in avoiding crowded situations, and persons of high intelligence may be more likely to find creative solutions to problems of crowding. Similarly, physically strong individuals may be able to cope with crowded situations by exerting control over weaker persons.

Another relevant personal factor is the extent to which the individual believes that his or her experiences are personally or environmentally controlled (internal-external locus of control).[8] "Internal" individuals may be able to function more efficiently than "external" individuals in crowded situations, especially when behavioral responses to crowding are possible. In situations of prolonged and unremitting crowding, however, "externals" may experience less stress than "internals," who are unaccustomed to feeling that they cannot influence the situation.

The past history of the individual in relation to the availability of space may also mediate the experience of crowding.[9,10] An individual who is accustomed to large amounts of space would probably expect more space in any given setting than a person who is used to less space. As a result, the former might find spatial constraints more discrepant with his expectations, thus more stressful.

The conceptual model proposed by Stokols emphasizes the need to consider the interaction of the physical milieu, the social milieu, and personal factors when attempting to predict whether different groups of people will perceive a situation as congruent or incongruent with their expectations of space. Similarly, physical variables interact with social and personal variables to dictate the type of stress-reducing or adaptive response that a crowded individual will select. Thus although behavioral responses are often adopted when spatial variables can be easily altered, the specific mode of response is dictated by the overall situation. An individual may choose perceptual and cognitive modes of reducing crowding stress, especially if behavioral adaptations to the crowded situation are impossible. For example, an individual who is faced with a crowded room may leave the room in search of more personal space. However if the social situation (e.g., the boss' party) and/or personal factors (e.g., physical incapacity) make escape impossible, the person may become deeply engrossed in conversation and forget about the spatial restrictions, or attempt to withdraw from social interaction, thereby increasing his privacy.[11]

The latter coping mechanism is related to the concept of overload put forth by Milgram.[12] According to Milgram, a state of overload exists when a person is unable to process all the inputs from the environment, either because there are too many inputs to cope with or because successive inputs come so fast that input A cannot be processed by the time input B is presented. Furthermore, when the system does become overloaded, adaptations occur (e.g., less time per input, disregard of low-priority inputs, filtering and weakening of input intensity). Milgram construes urban life as a perpetual set of encounters with overload—too many people and stimuli, and resultant adaptations. Urbanites who are unable to leave the crowded situation (city) must adopt coping patterns that include withdrawing from much potential interaction.

In summary, we have presented a conceptual model of crowding that is multidimensional in that social and personality factors interact with the physical milieu to facilitate or inhibit psychological and physiological stress in the individual. Spatial variables alone do not allow accurate predictions of whether a given person will perceive a situation as crowded and, therefore, stressful. The mode of coping response selected by an individual in a crowded situation (or an undercrowded situation) will depend on whether behavioral or cognitive adjustments are appropriate. Finally, the coping response may alter the individual's perception of spatial adequacy and/or change the conditions that initially made the individual feel crowded.

Demographic Studies of Crowding.   Studies of the pattern of crime and mental illness in and around urban areas have produced startling findings. The rate of major crimes in the most populous cities is five times greater than in smaller cities, eight times greater than in the suburbs, and eleven times greater than in rural areas. Of all violent crime reported, 30% occur in the six cities with 10% of the nation's population. Similarly, mental illness rates are higher in urban than in rural areas and highest in downtown sections of cities[13] (see Chapter 9). With the promise of further population and urban growth, investigators have turned to demographic studies to examine the effects of crowding on human behavior.

Investigators have employed differing measures of population density and differing degrees of methodological sophistication. Demographic studies have generally used the number of people per unit of space both as a definition of density and as a measure of crowding.[14] However the conceptual model indicates the spatial limitation (density) is only one aspect of the crowding phenomenon and does not necessarily lead to perceived crowding. Since demographic studies deal with complex urban situations involving large numbers of people, precise delineation of the elements of crowding is very difficult.

Schmitt has distinguished between "inside" density, or the number of people per unit of living space, and "outside" density, the number of people in a larger community (e.g., a census tract).[15] Jane Jacobs makes a similar distinction between overcrowding and high population density. She considers the number of dwellings per acre as a measure of density, whereas crowding is measured by the relation of the number of people in a dwelling to the number of rooms available; the definition of overcrowding is 1.5 or more persons per room.[16]

The distinction between inside and outside density is useful for categorizing living situations. For example, suburban living typically involves a relatively small number of people both inside and outside residences. Conversely, the urban ghetto usually has a high concentration of people both inside and outside dwellings. Rural areas often have high inside but low outside densities, whereas luxury areas in New York often have low inside densities but a large number of people in the surrounding neighborhood.[17] Each of these living situations presents a different combination of density factors and may have differential influences on human behavior.

Galle, Gove, and McPherson distinguish between density factors at the personal or individual level, which they refer to as "interpersonal press," and "structural" factors of density. Interpersonal press is defined as the number of persons per room and the number of persons per housing unit; structural factors include the number of housing units per structure and the number of residential structures per acre.[18] Thus the level of overall population density (persons per acre) in a community area may consist of different combinations of at least four components of density. It is therefore important to clarify exactly which measure(s) or component(s) of population density are associated with the particular dependent variables featured in each study.

The importance of specificity and delineation of the components of population density is illustrated in an early study by Schmitt.[19] Schmitt assessed the relationship between five measures of population density and the juvenile delinquency and adult crime rates in Honolulu. The five measures of population density included (1) population per acre; (2) average household size; (3) proportion of married couples without their own household; (4) proportion of dwelling units in structures with five or more living units; and (5) percentage of occupied dwelling units with 1.51 or more persons per room. Twenty-nine Honolulu census tracts were grouped into three categories on the basis of their respective densities.

Two of the five density measures (population per net acre and the percentage of units with 1.51 or more persons per room) showed strong positive correlations with juvenile and adult crime rates. That is, the more people per acre and/or the more units with 1.51 or more persons per room, the higher the crime rate in that area. For example, the delinquency rate per 1000 persons was 15.8 in tracts with fewer than 20 persons per acre, 18.2 in tracts with 20 to 59.9 persons per acre, and 25.5 in the eight tracts with 60 or more persons per acre. The adult crime rates in the same tract categories were 0.66, 0.68, and 1.72 per thousand persons, respectively.

More recent demographic studies have tried to determine which measures of density—for example, population or housing per net acre (outside density) or persons per room (inside density)—are most closely associated with measures of social disorganization. Schmitt reported another study done in Honolulu in which population density (as measured by population per acre) was found to be highly associated with the following factors: death rate from all causes, venereal disease rate, rate of hospitalization for mental illness, rate of juvenile delinquency, tuberculosis rate, and rate of imprisonment.[20] These relationships held even when overcrowding (inside density), as measured by the percentage of occupied units with 1.01 or more persons per room, was held constant. However the reverse was not true; that is, the correlation between overcrowding and the various measures of social disorganization fell from .37 to .17 when net density (persons per acre) was kept constant.

Schmitt also attempted to control for two social background variables known to be associated with social disorganization: (1) the proportion of people 25 years of age or older who had 12 or more years of schooling, and (2) the proportion of families and unrelated individuals with 1949 incomes of $3000 or more. These two variables were used as indicators of education and income, respectively. When education and income were held constant, the associations between persons per acre and the above-mentioned measures of social disorganization were still relatively high (median correlation of .56). However there were no significant relationships between the percentage of occupied units with 1.01 or more persons per room and the social disorganization variables (median correlation of .17).

Schmitt concluded that although overcrowding may be relevant, density must be the more important variable in Honolulu. Yet the results of Schmitt's study have been repeatedly challenged. For example, there is some question that the percentage of dwelling units with 1.01 persons or more per room is a valid measure of overcrowding. Jacobs considered at least 1.51 persons per room to be necessary for overcrowding. Freedman has argued that Schmitt's measures for education and income were inadequate, and median education and median income would have been more sensitive measures.[21] Freedman believes that adequate controls might have further reduced the associations between the number of persons per acre and the indices of social disorganization.

Another challenge to Schmitt's results came from a study done in Chicago, in which the net population density (persons per acre) was first related to the following five indices of social pathology: (1) the standard mortality ratio (the age-adjusted death rate of a given community area, expressed as a ratio to the death rate for the 1960 total population of Chicago), (2) the general fertility rate, (3) the public assistance rate, (4) the juvenile delinquency rate, and (5) the rate of admissions to mental hospitals.[22] There was a significant association between persons per acre and the five indices of social pathology; that is, as the population density increased, each index of social pathology increased. When the authors controlled for social class (as measured by the percentage of employed white collar males, median years of schooling, and median income) and ethnic status (as measured by percentages of blacks, Puerto Ricans, and foreign-born), the associations no longer differed significantly from zero.

Rather than conclude, however, that population density (persons per acre) is unrelated to social breakdown once social class and ethnicity are taken into account, the authors divided population density into four component parts: (1) the number of persons per room, (2) the number of rooms per housing unit, (3) the number of housing units per structure, and (4) the number of residential structures per acre. Galle and his colleagues then examined the combined influences of the four components of density (multiple correlation) and found a relationship with each pathology that remained significant even when class and ethnicity were controlled. They also considered the combined influences of the social class and ethnicity variables on each pathology, uncovering significant relationships; however these relationships were markedly reduced when the four components of density were controlled, indicating that density components were significantly influencing each relationship.

Finally, analysis of the relative importance of each of the four components of density revealed that the number of persons per room was strongly associated with all indices of pathology except the rate of mental hospital admissions. The most important correlate of mental hospital admissions was the number of rooms per housing unit. In addition, the percentage of persons living alone was highly related to admissions to mental hospitals ($r = .72$), even after class and ethnicity were controlled ($r = .59$).

A study done in Hong Kong focused on the relationship of inside density to measures of stress, entertainment patterns, emotional health, and parental supervision.[23] Urbanized areas in Hong Kong have a median dwelling size of 400 square feet and a median living space of only 43 square feet per person. By comparison, the lower limit of floor space per person in Europe is set at 170 square feet, and the desirable standard set by the U.S. Public Health Service is twice that figure. Among Mitchell's respondents, 39% shared their dwelling unit with nonkinsmen, 28% slept three or more to a bed, and 13% slept four or more to a bed!

Using self-ratings of "happiness" and "worry" as measures of stress, Mitchell learned that people in higher density dwelling units (fewer square feet per person) rated themselves as less happy and more worried than people in lower density units. Furthermore, low-income families in high-density dwellings showed more stress than low-income families in low-density dwellings. High dwelling unit density also discouraged friendship practices among neighbors and friends. Mitchell found that the higher the dwelling density, the less likely a family was to entertain nonfamily members. Indeed, 49% of the Hong Kong married couples sampled reported that they never invited people to their home.

Mitchell also found that two social features of housing—the number of households sharing the same dwelling unit and the number of people in that unit—may have particularly adverse effects when individuals are located on the upper floors of buildings. Only multiple-family dwellings on upper floors were associated with emotional symptoms (e.g., headaches, nervousness, insomnia). Crowded interaction with nonrelatives (i.e., strangers) is probably more stressful than crowded interaction with family members. The available adaptive (behavioral) response of going out into the street for more space allows lower floor dwellers to cope better with the crowded multifamily conditions inside.

This notion of behaviorally escaping crowded conditions gains some support from Mitchell's finding that higher inside density is associated with decreased supervision of children by parents. Galle and his colleagues suggested that parental irritability, social obligations, and the need to inhibit personal desires, increase as the number of persons per dwelling increase. Children in crowded dwellings are thus more likely to escape what they perceive as a relatively unattractive and stressful setting that is filled with noise, has no privacy or place to study, and has other undesirable features.[24] Mitchell has further suggested that anyone's leaving the apartment or room, even temporarily, may be welcomed by the adults because this action reduces the density (and crowding).

In a recent study Levy and Herzog[25] used a multivariate regression analysis to estimate the independent effects of density and crowding, adjusted for social class and the heterogeneity of the population, in 125 geographic areas in the Netherlands. They found that population density had an independent effect on indices of social pathology such as delinquency, particularly offenses against property and sexual crimes, and illegitimacy and divorce rates. Crowding was not highly related to social pathology (in fact some of the relationships were negative); however the authors point out that there is little or no crowding in the Netherlands (mean number of persons per room for the country as a whole is 0.66).

Summary of Demographic Studies.   Given the suggestiveness of correlational statements about crowding, only tentative conclusions can be drawn from the demographic studies presented. First, three of the studies reviewed indicate an association between inside (dwelling unit) density and juvenile delinquency and/or adult crime. The work of Mitchell provides a clue to the manner in which crowded home conditions may indirectly influence juvenile delinquency. Children from dwelling units of greater density, Mitchell discovered, were more often outside their homes, thus outside adult supervision.

Second, there appears to be a U-shaped relationship between inside density (persons per room) and mental illness. Schmitt found a moderate association between the percentage of occupied units with 1.01 or more persons per room and the rate of hospitalization for mental illness. Mitchell reported that higher density (fewer square feet per person) was associated with more emotional symptoms only *if* the unit was composed of more than one family and *if* the unit was situated on an upper floor. Galle and his colleagues found that the proportion of people living alone was significantly related to the rate of mental hospital admissions. This finding was corroborated by Hare, who reported that areas in Bristol, England, which had higher rates of first admissions to mental hospitals, also had larger proportions of persons living alone.[26] Kahn and Perlin learned that the probability of outpatient contact with a mental health facility increased as dwelling unit density increased.[27]

In terms of our conceptual model, high levels of multifamily dwelling unit density may evoke sufficient stress to increase tension and irritability and to give rise to mental and physical symptoms, particularly when physical withdrawal from the situation is difficult. For example, there is probably a minimum amount of space necessary for optimal health and social adaptation. On the other hand, persons living alone may experience feelings of alienation and isolation that may adversely affect their emotional state. Thus both overcrowding and undercrowding stresses may be related to mental illness, although for quite different reasons.

Third, the conflicting results of studies that have related the number of persons per *acre* to indices of social disorganization corroborate our belief that high density per acre logically exerts a less direct effect on the individual. Since the impact that a large number of people per acre has on an individual is mediated by many variables, it is less direct than the impact of a large number of people in a room (inside density). For example, downtown urban areas often have high-rise buildings composed largely of single living units. Thus residents in these high density per acre areas may rarely see one another, therefore feeling perhaps more isolated than crowded.

There may be yet other reasons for the conflicting results: cross-cultural differences in the extent of population density or crowding, differences in attitudes or expectations regarding optimum space needs, and/or the degree to which mediating variables are controlled. There is considerable controversy over the influence of mediating variables in this area. Some investigators maintain that social class, education, race and similar variables, must be controlled before any effect of density can be determined. Yet other investigators maintain that these mediating variables are inextricably linked to density, and any attempt to separate them by statistical techniques results in artificial findings.

In this connection, Galle and his colleagues found that by first relating their four components of density to four indices of pathology, an average of more than 75% of the variance of the pathologies could be explained. Social class and ethnicity variables then accounted for slight additional variance, indicating that they had little or no added effect on the pathologies. When social class and ethnicity variables were *first* related to the four indices of pathology, however, they accounted for an average of more than 75% of the variance, and the density components then added little to the explained variance of the pathologies. This indicates that density, social class, and ethnicity are closely interwoven and possibly inextricably related variables, at least in currently existing urban slums.

Consider a concrete example provided by a poor girl who lived in crowded conditions:

> As I grew older, I became more aware of the restrictions one had to put up with when a whole family lived in a single room. In my case, because I lived in fantasy and liked to daydream, I was especially annoyed by having my dreams interrupted. . . . We all had to go to bed at the same time, when my father told us to. . . . This might be as early as eight or nine o'clock, when we weren't at all sleepy, but because my father had to get up early the next morning, the light had to be put out. Many times I wanted to draw or read in the evening, but no sooner did I get started when "To bed! Lights out!" and I was left with my drawing in my head or the story unfinished.[28]

It is unlikely that the environment of this girl will facilitate the type of education that she might use to extricate herself from poverty. The result is often perpetual poverty and/or criminal behavior. In other words, not only can poverty influence density (the poor can only afford crowded and subpoor housing), but density may influence poverty (and education).

The continued existence of cities is living testimony that most humans can effectively adapt to environments composed of large numbers of persons per acre. However it is possible that the cost of adapting to crowded environments may be subtly reducing the quality of life in those areas. As noted previously, Milgram feels that urbanites encounter so many people that they must filter out those who are unimportant, thus withdrawing from many potential social interactions. One unfortunate result of such coping responses is a restriction of moral social involvement with persons classified as "strangers."[29] The murder of Catherine Genovese in 1964 in full view of 38 New York City "neighbors," none of whom intervened, dramatically corroborates the notion of deficient social involvement. Altman and his colleagues found that people in more heavily populated areas were less helpful to strangers in need of a telephone than were strangers in less heavily populated towns.[30]

Many other studies also suggest that people from high-density areas develop norms of noninvolvement, perhaps as a means of coping with stimulus overload. It is worth wondering whether "successful" adaptation to crowded environments is altogether beneficial. Dubos has suggested that man's malleability enables him to adapt to conditions and habits that may eventually destroy the values most characteristic of human life.[31] Dubos cites man's physical adaptability to polluted cities and his social adaptability to the emotional stresses caused by crowding and competition. He warns us that present coping responses to such unhealthy conditions may be concealing psychological and physiological damage that may accumulate over time.

Experimental Studies of Crowding. Experimental studies on the effect of density on human behavior are mainly an outgrowth of the dramatic results of earlier experimental work on animals. John Calhoun, who conducted what is probably the most famous animal laboratory study of crowding,[32] simply allowed a small population of Norway rats to breed freely within an enclosed area that contained ample food and water. He observed that the population soon became abnormally large, and social organization gave way to social pathology. Calhoun reported that many females were unable to carry a pregnancy to full term or to survive delivery if they did. Females who did give birth constructed inadequate nests and gave insufficient care to their young. Some males became hyperaggressive; others grew abnormally passive and withdrawn from social interaction. Attacks on pregnant females, cannibalism, and infant mortality were prevalent, and large groups of animals crowded together abnormally at feeding times, a phenomenon Calhoun aptly referred to as a "behavioral sink."

A study by Alexander and Roth revealed that a troop of Japanese monkeys placed in a situation of short-term acute crowding exhibited more mild (squabbling) and severe (mobbing) forms of aggression than had been evidenced under spacious conditions.[33] Severe aggression was attributed to removal from a familiar habitat, and mild aggression was construed as a result of density per se.

Naturalistic observations by Christian, Flyger, and Davis found that a population of Sika deer that was confined to a small island experienced mass mortality and decreased reproductivity after the population density had reached a maximum of approximately one deer per acre.[34] The mass mortality was attributed to shock resulting from the prolonged adrenocortical hyperactivity caused by high density.

These and similar nonhuman studies have generally supported the belief that high population density has very negative effects on certain species of animals. Some investigators have cited these studies as evidence that mankind will experience comparable social disorganization as a result of increasing population density. However such macabre predictions, based on extrapolation of animal studies to humans, may be inappropriate. Most animal studies have involved experimentally induced situations of high density that ordinarily do not occur in natural habitats. When animals are able to propagate without check under natural conditions (e.g., when a predator has been eliminated), the animals exhaust their food supply, lose weight, and bear fewer young.[35] Thus the population size is constantly adjusting to the available food supply. Furthermore, René Dubos has pointed out that "The readiness with which man adapts to potentially dangerous situations makes it unwise to apply directly to human life the results of experiments designed to test the acute effects of crowding on animals."[36]

Several investigators have recently recognized the importance of using human subjects to experimentally determine the effects of crowding on complex behaviors. These workers often conduct either "spatial density" research, which compares the behavior of same-sized groups in rooms of different sizes, or "social density" research, which compares the behavior of groups of different sizes in same-sized rooms.[37] Social density manipulations are complex because any differences between groups of different numbers in same-sized rooms are necessarily confounded by different amounts of space per person (spatial density). A group of ten persons in a given room is a larger group *and* offers less space per person than a group of five people in a room of the same size. Thus to test whether spatial density and social density have differential effects on human behavior, it is necessary to equalize the space per person in the high- and low-density settings.[38] The dependent variables most commonly studied in experimental work on human crowding include task performance, interpersonal attraction, and personal comfort and aggressiveness.

Experimental Studies of Task Performance.   Freedman, Klevansky, and Ehrlich conducted a series of three experiments in which subjects performed simple tasks (e.g., crossing out a certain number from a page of random numbers) and complex tasks (e.g., creatively devising alternative uses for a common object) under varying degrees of crowdedness.[39] Groups of five or nine same-sex subjects worked in rooms of 160, 80, or 35 square feet for 4 hours at a time on successive days.

Six tasks were performed during the daily 4-hour testing periods by the high school students who served as subjects for experiment I. Experiment II likewise used high school students, but only three tasks were required, in an attempt to foster boredom, reduce motivation, and maximize any effects of stress associated with crowding. Experiment III was identical to experiment II except that women between the ages of 25 and 60 served as subjects.

All three studies showed negative results (i.e., there were no differences either between the five-person and nine-person groups or between the different sized rooms). Groups in high spatial density and social density situations did as well as groups in low spatial density and low social density situations. There was no indication of greater effects over time. Negative results are difficult to interpret, since lack of differences may be attributable to methodological problems such as insensitive measures. However the crucial issue in evaluating these studies is the experimental situation itself. The situation was rather formal and structured and did not involve any physical movement that might have interfered with the work of others and/or represented competition for limited space.

Sherrod recently used a slightly less structured paradigm to corroborate and expand the task performance findings of Freedman et al. Eight groups of eight and one group of seven female high school students first performed simple and complex tasks for one hour while sitting on the floor in conditions that were either noncrowded, crowded, or crowded-with-perceived-control (i.e., the subjects were told that they could leave the experimental room at any time). Subjects were then taken to a normal, noncrowded room where they spent an hour working on a proofreading task and a puzzle-solving measure of frustration tolerance. There were no differences in either simple or complex task performance in any of the three conditions of crowding, but *post*crowding measures of frustration tolerance (as measured by the number of attempts the subject made at solving two insoluble puzzles) were adversely affected by crowding. Frustration tolerance was least for persons who had been in the crowded condition, intermediate for those who had been in the crowded-with-perceived-control condition, and greatest for those who had been in the noncrowded condition. Thus crowding may have deleterious behavioral after-effects that may be reduced if the individual has a perception of control over the conditions of the crowding.[40]

Interpersonal Attraction and Personal Comfort. Ross and his colleagues manipulated spatial density by putting groups of eight male or female subjects into either small or large rooms for either 5 or 20 minutes. Temperature, physical discomfort, and extraneous noise were controlled in an effort to study density per se. During the 5- or 20-minute experimental period, subjects discussed several "choice dilemma" problems. Subjects were then asked to complete a series of questionnaires; one of these required a self-evaluation and an evaluation of the other group members in terms of likability, warmth, goodness, and so on.[41]

Males and females perceived the degree of crowding similarly, and the differences in the length of the discussions (i.e., 5 or 20 minutes) had no effect. However males in the small room rated themselves and the other members of the group as less likable, less good, and so on, than did males in the larger room. Conversely, females rated themselves and the other group members more positively in the small than in the large room. Thus, although males and females construed the degree of crowding equally, they apparently differed in their expectations of optimal interpersonal spacing. Males felt that the small room was too intimate for interaction with the same sex, but females found it comfortable. The large room apparently produced comfortable interpersonal spacing for males but too distant spacing for females.

Griffitt and Veitch studied the effect of high density on affective behavior and personal comfort.[42] However they also manipulated room temperature, a physical stress factor that may intensify feelings of spatial restriction. Griffitt and Veitch kept room size (63 square feet) constant and ran subjects in either small (3 to 5 persons) or large (12 to 16 persons) same-sex groups. Room temperature was either normal (73.4° F) or hot (93.5° F). Each group was kept inside the experimental room for one hour. The first 45 minutes were devoted primarily to ratings of the subjects' feelings toward the situation with regard to its pleasantness, comfort, and other features. The remaining time was used to gather affective ratings toward an anonymous stranger, based on inspection of a specious attitude questionnaire allegedly filled out by the stranger.

Subjects in the high-temperature and high-density conditions experienced more negative feelings about the experiment and toward the stranger than did subjects in the normal-temperature and low-density conditions. No sex differences were reported. Freedman has argued that because Griffitt and Veitch manipulated social density, their effects may have been attributable to the number of people in the room (i.e., group size), not to limited amounts of space per person (crowding).

Sommer and Becker found that higher social densities in a college classroom were associated with more negative student ratings of comfort and satisfaction.[43] Students in 32 separate classes that used the *same* classroom provided ratings of all aspects of the classroom environment. Classes ranged in size from 5 to 22, with a mean of 13 students. There were approximately twice as many complaints about ventilation, room size, and overall satisfaction in the large as in the small classes. The correlations between class size and the percentage of complaints about ventilation, room size, and overall satisfaction were all statistically significant. Only one classroom was studied, and generalizations must be tempered by this limitation; yet there does appear to be an association between (social) density and user satisfaction.

Aggressiveness.   Freedman and his colleagues conducted a series of studies that dealt not only with interpersonal attraction and personal comfort but also with aggressiveness,[44] the third and final dependent variable to be discussed. In the first experiment they manipulated spatial density by placing groups of four male or four female high school students in either small or large rooms for 4 hours. During the first 3 hours group members discussed various topics and engaged in a game requiring cooperation. During the last hour subjects played a modified version of the Prisoner's Dilemma game which allowed each player to choose either cooperative or competitive (aggressive) responses over trials. Males made more aggressive (competitive) responses in the small than in the large room, whereas females were somewhat more aggressive in the large than in the small room. As a result of these sex differences, the overall effects of density were "masked," with only slightly more overall aggressive responses made in the small than in the large room.

The second experiment used a completely different setting and different measures, but it produced consistent results. The sample consisted of males and females between the ages of 18 and 80 years, representing many ethnic groups and socioeconomic levels. Once again spatial density was the independent variable, with male or female groups of at least seven placed in either small or large rooms for 4 hours. Subjects first became acquainted with one another, then each person listened to tape recordings of five mock jury situations and gave his or her verdict and a proposed sentence for each case. Some cases were discussed openly by the "jury" and others were not, but in each case the juror voted privately. In addition, subjects completed a questionnaire designed to determine interpersonal attraction and personal comfort.

Relative to the males in the large room, the males in the small room enjoyed the experiment less, liked the other members of the group less, considered the other members less friendly, and sentenced somewhat more severely. Conversely, females in the small room liked the situation more, thought the other women in the group were more likable and friendly, and sentenced significantly more leniently than females in the large room. Again there were no overall effects of density for either interpersonal affective measures or aggressiveness indices. Importantly, when Freedman and his colleagues conducted the same experiment using mixed-sex groups, all effects on all aggressive and interpersonal affective measures disappeared. This suggests that the room density by sex interaction may be specific to groups consisting of all males or all females, but the reason for this phenomenon is not entirely clear.

Stokols and his colleagues studied 64 same-sex male and female groups of eight college students each. The groups first participated in a "question and answer" quiz game in either large or small rooms. After approximately 70 minutes the game was terminated, and each subject was given a questionnaire to rate how he or she had felt during the game. There were no differences between male and female perceptions of the degree of crowding in the small room. However males perceived themselves as significantly more aggressive in the small room, whereas females felt more aggressive in the large room. Furthermore, females perceived the small room to be cozier and quieter than the large room, whereas males perceived the large room as cozier and quieter.[45]

Several possible reasons have been suggested for the differential reactions of males and females to large and small rooms, including: (1) innate sex differences in responding to limited personal space, (2) different activity levels (i.e., males are more active, therefore need and want more space), (3) learned differences of personal contact expectations, and (4) differing expectations concerning the likely pleasantness of a situation.[46]

The latter two possibilities seem especially cogent. The notion is that American society views close physical contact much more positively between women than between men. As a result, males regard close physical contact with other males rather negatively, whereas females expect situations of close contact with other females to be positive. Crowding may intensify the learned space expectations for a given situation, with the result that males react more negatively to a crowded room of males, whereas women react more positively to greater numbers of women in a room. For crowded mixed-sex groups, males and females may share common expectations toward the situation, therefore reacting similarly.

Hutt and Vaizey observed the effects of crowding on aggressive behavior in five autistic children, five brain-damaged children, and five "normal" children all between the ages of 3 and 8.[47] Social density was the independent variable, and the investigators studied the behavior of small (6 or less), medium (7–11), and large (12 or more) groups during "free play."

Aggressive behavior (e.g., fighting, snatching or breaking toys) of brain-damaged children increased as social density increased, whereas normal children became significantly more aggressive only in the largest group. Autistic children showed negligible aggressive behavior. Furthermore, normals engaged in progressively less social interaction as group size increased. Brain-damaged subjects interacted more in the medium-sized group, whereas autistic children showed significantly less interaction in the medium size group than in small or large groups. The significance of the results are unclear because the sample size was quite small and only one setting was used. Also, group size may be confounding the effects of high density.

Finally, a study by Chalsa Loo examined the effect of spatial density manipulations on the aggressive behavior and social interaction of 60 normal children aged 4 and 5.[48] Ten groups, each consisting of three boys and three girls, participated in 48-minute sessions of free play with no adults present in both a small room (90 square feet) and a large room (265.1 square feet). Surprisingly, boys were more aggressive in the low- than in the high-density situation, whereas aggression in girls did not differ between densities. The children also interacted with significantly fewer children in the high- than in the low-density condition.

Overview of Experimental Studies.   Although experimental studies of crowding allow greater control over extraneous variables, they pose other problems that make generalizations tenuous. Subjects in experimental crowding studies are typically volunteers who are placed in high-density situations for short periods of time and are aware of the limit on time, and thus the stress. Brief and longer exposures to high density may have quite dissimilar effects. Furthermore, the situation itself is sometimes quite "unnatural" and is usually highly structured, involving specific tasks to be performed and little physical activity or competition for space among subjects. These variables could exert a limiting influence on the generalization of existing experimental studies to natural situations of crowding (see Chapter 7 for further discussion of naturalistic studies).

Several studies have demonstrated sex differences in reaction to spatial constriction, perhaps because of differential learned expectations toward close contact with the same sex. Subjects in all-male groups like one another less when they are more than when they are less crowded, whereas members of female groups generally like one another more in high than in low (spatial) density conditions. Males seem to be more competitive and aggressive in higher density situations, whereas females react with greater cooperation and leniency in more densely populated rooms.

Density studies of children have produced conflicting results. Hutt and Vaizey found that high social density was positively related to aggression, whereas Loo reported less aggression in high than in low spatial density settings. Loo has suggested several reasons for the incongruence of the reported results of density studies.[49] First, social density and spatial density may simply have differential effects on individuals. We have already noted that social density may confound group size and density (space per person), whereas spatial density manipulations vary density independently of the size of the groups.

Second, the degree of structure of the experimental environment may influence perceptions of crowding. Studies on children typically have little environmental structure in that fixed structures (e.g., chairs and desks) are absent, and primarily portable toys are used. In contrast, studies on adults generally provide a chair or desk for each individual, and this piece of furniture serves to delineate boundaries, thus to reduce conflict, anxiety, and feelings of crowding.

A third possible reason for the conflicting results concerns the degree to which the experimental activities are structured. Most of the adult studies included experimental activities that were formally structured, although verbal interaction among group members was usually encouraged. This may be why interpersonal attraction and hostility show changes with density, whereas task performance does not.

Studies on children have been much more unstructured, involving observations of free play situations. The mobility, excitability, and general emotional level of the subjects should be higher when activities are more unstructured. However the density of Loo's crowded condition was so great that motor activity in the unstructured environment was difficult and uncomfortable. Thus this high-density situation may have reduced aggressiveness by providing insufficient space for the use of aggressive toys, by reducing the level of excitement generally present when children play together, and by generally inhibiting the children from interacting.

Finally, the age and individual characteristics of experimental subjects may affect the results of crowding studies. No research compared the effects of density on individuals of various ages, yet children and adults may react to density differently. Similarly, although the personal factors that mediate an individual's reaction to density have not been explored in depth, individuals undoubtedly differ in their reactions to density situations. It is thus possible that differences in selection factors, especially among volunteer subjects, may produce different groups whose constellations of personalities lead to conflicting results. There is evidence that each individual has a "body-buffer zone" or "personal space" surrounding him or her, and if this zone is invaded, feelings of stress appear. The discovery that expectations for personal space differ individually, situationally, and culturally may prove important in future experimental studies of crowding.

The Human Use of Space.   The concept of "territoriality" is usually defined as a set of behaviors by which an organism claims an area, demarcates it, and defends it against members of its own species.[50] Observations of territorial behavior in animals have shown that various species stake out a territory that they will defend against intruders to protect their young, to obtain food, to carry out mating patterns, and to preserve the species by establishing appropriate ecological balances.[51]

Human territoriality has only recently begun to be examined. Lyman and Scott have proposed a taxonomy of four human territorial forms: public territories, to which most persons have access; home territories, or areas that allow freedom of behavior and a sense of control and intimacy; interaction territories, where social gatherings may occur; and body territory, or anatomical space and the immediate surroundings.[52] Three types of encroachment were also identified: violation (unwarranted use of a territory), invasion (unsolicited crossing of a boundary), and contamination (making the territory impure). Reactions to encroachments may take the form of turf defense (aggressive defense), insulation (barrier erection), or linguistic collusion (communal isolation by way of idiosyncratic communications).

Intimately related to notions of human territoriality are studies of "proxemics," the human use of space in everyday life. Studies of the use of space represent a third approach to crowding issues, because spatial restriction is construed as an antecedent condition for the experience of crowding. Information concerning man's perceived need for space, and his reactions to invasions of that space, may facilitate the development of a more adequate conceptual model of crowding phenomena.

Pioneer work in proxemics by Hall has measured the spacing between interacting Americans in terms of intimate, personal, social, and public distances.[53] Intimate distance ranges from 0 to 18 inches, personal from

18 to 48 inches, social from 48 to 144 inches, and public over 144 inches. The specific distance chosen depends on the nature of the transaction (i.e., the relationship of the interacting individuals, how they feel and what they are doing).

Also influencing human space usage is the concept of "personal space." Personal space is described by Sommer as an area into which intruders may not come. Personal space has also been described as a "portable territory" in that it accompanies the individual wherever he or she goes, although it does seem to shrink under crowded conditions.[54] An invasion of personal space is construed as an intrusion on an individual's self-boundary, which may elicit stress reactions and adaptive responses designed to reduce that stress.

Violations of Personal Space.   How do individuals react when their personal space is violated? Personal space invasion should be related to crowding in that an individual who perceives another person as too close (i.e., as invading his or her personal space) will presumably feel spatially constricted, therefore crowded. Baxter and Deanovich used a projective method to demonstrate that inappropriate intrusions into another individual's personal space engendered anxiety and stress.[55] Forty-eight college coeds were assigned to either a "crowded condition" (the female experimenter sat within 6 inches of the subject) or a "spatial condition" (the female experimenter sat approximately 4 feet from the subject). Each subject was presented with eight different affective situations involving a female doll and a male doll and was asked to rate the anxiety that the female doll experienced in each situation. The dolls were crowded together in four of the settings, whereas they were spaced apart in the other four situations. It was expected that each subject would project her feelings onto the stimulus doll.

Crowded subjects projected significantly more anxiety in their ratings of the figures than did uncrowded subjects. The crowding effect became more pronounced during the latter half of the experimental period, supporting the notion that inappropriate invasion of personal space or crowding may engender greater anxiety and stress with time. The authors proposed that the time relationship may be a result of the obligatory inability of the crowded subjects to flee the experimental situation or to change their seating position. This idea is consistent with studies that have indicated that the prepotent reaction of victims of personal space invasion is to reestablish personal space (by interposing barriers between themselves and the invader, by asking the invader to move, etc.), or, if necessary, to withdraw from the situation.

Felipe and Sommer have conducted a series of investigations to observe people's reactions to personal space invasions.[56] In the first experiment a male experimenter approached and sat within 6 inches of male mental hospital patients who were sitting alone on a bench on the hospital grounds. If the victim attempted to reestablish his personal space by moving down the bench, the experimenter moved to maintain the 6-inch spacing. Control subjects were male patients, sitting alone within eyesight of the experimenter.

The results were quite dramatic. Within 2 minutes 36% of the experimental subjects had left the situation, but none of the control subjects had moved. Within 9 minutes only 8% of the controls had left, versus a 50% withdrawal rate by the invaded group. The latter figure eventually rose to 64% by the 20-minute limit, although only 33% of the control subjects had departed by then. Interestingly, only two patients asked the experimenter to give them more room; instead, patients typically tried to reestablish their personal space by turning away, pulling in their shoulders, and placing their elbows at their sides.

A second study took place at tables in a study room of a university library. The distance a female experimenter established between herself and a solitary female victim was varied from 1 to about 5 feet. Controls were nonapproached females who were sitting alone within sight of the experimenter. Victims who had the least space (1 foot) between themselves and the experimenter withdrew from the situation significantly more than did the subjects who had more appropriate spacing. By the end of the 30-minute sessions, 87% of the controls remained seated, but only 30% of the females who were originally closest to the experimenter were still present. Only one of the 80 students vocally expressed a desire for the experimenter to move over, although many subjects initially manifested attempts to regain personal space (drawing in the arms and head, turning away from the experimenter, using books, purses, and coats as barriers, etc.). When these attempted adaptive responses failed to reduce the apparent stress and discomfort caused by the intrusion, withdrawal from the situation occurred.

Barash demonstrated the importance of the status or dominance of the invader in eliciting reactions from the victim.[57] He used the same paradigm just described, but established two conditions—the faculty condition, in which he wore a sport jacket and tie to identify himself as a professor, and the student condition, in which he wore typical college student attire of bluejeans and a "casual" shirt. Since ethological studies have indicated that dominant animals usually possess more personal space than subordinates,[58] Barash reasoned that subordinates might experience more distress at the close approach of a dominant (faculty member) than at a similar approach by a relatively subordinate (student) intruder.

Barash only sat beside male students who were sitting alone and reading or writing, and only when a control subject within sight was available. Approaches were made at "close" (chair spacing of only about 3 to 6 inches) and "medium" (about 12 to 27 inches) distances, and the experimental sessions lasted a maximum of 30 minutes. Student departure was highly associated with approach proximity, and there were significant differences between all respective combinations of control and experimental conditions. Furthermore, student attire was shown to be less effective in precipitating departures than was faculty attire at the same distance. Only 5 of the 50 males who were subjected to close faculty approaches asked for more room, whereas 11 of 50 close student approaches resulted in oral requests for additional space. Barash suggested that vocalizations may be construed as relatively aggressive responses, which are somewhat inhibited by the presence of a dominant person (i.e., a faculty member).

It is apparent that sitting "too" close to a person may cause that person to become uncomfortable and perhaps withdraw from the situation. Yet it is equally apparent that an individual's personal space requirements shrink in certain settings, and people do not always feel anxious when strangers sit very close (e.g., at a crowded football game). How can these conflicting reactions to personal space encroachment be reconciled? Barash suggests that the answer probably lies in the person's perception of whether his or her personal space has been violated. Such a determination is guided by the overall appropriateness of the spatial arrangement, given the amount of space available and the status, sex, relationship, and intentions of the invader. In other words, people have certain "expectations" of appropriate personal space in different settings, and a violation of a given expectation may evoke negative affect, discomfort, and possibly active withdrawal.

Individual Differences in the Use of Space.   There are important sex differences with regard to personal space expectations. For example, Hartnett, Bailey, and Gibson had subjects approach either a male or female experimenter until the subject wanted to stop his or her approach.[59] Each of the 32 male and 32 female subjects was also approached by the male or female experimenter until the point at which the subject wanted the experimenter's approach to stop. Both males and females allowed the experimenter to come closer to them than they came to the experimenter. Furthermore, the female subjects allowed both male and female experimenters to approach more closely than did the male subjects, suggesting that female expectations of personal space in the experimental situation were smaller than those of the males.

Pellegrini and Empey found that females chose to interact more proximally with other females than did males with other males.[60] Each of 30 male and 30 female subjects were first led into a room in which a same-sex "listener" was seated. Subjects were instructed to "pull up a chair" (the only chair in the room was about 18 feet away) and to describe themselves for 3 minutes to the listener. Females seated themselves significantly closer to the female listener than did male subjects to the male listener. These sex differences in personal space corroborate the experimental studies in which females reacted more favorably to other females in higher density rooms, whereas males were more positive toward other males in rooms in which more personal space was available.

Physical abnormalities also influence the personal space requirements of ill or handicapped people and the normals with whom they interact. Spinetta, Rigler, and Karon found that a group of 25 leukemic children aged 5 to 10 desired greater personal space than a matched control group of chronically but not fatally ill hospitalized children.[61] The leukemic children preferred that four significant figures (nurse, doctor, mother, father) in a hospital-room replica be placed at a greater distance from an ill child figure than did the control children. When asked to place the figures in their "usual" place in the hospital-room replica, the leukemic children placed them at a greater distance from the sick child than did the controls. Furthermore, in subsequent admissions to the hospital, the leukemic children increased the distance significantly more than did the controls, perhaps reflecting that the dying children's significant others had become more distant from them.

Worthington corroborated the notion that people increase their personal space requirements when interacting with physically ill or handicapped persons.[62] Randomly selected subjects in an airport who were asked directions by an experimenter seated in a wheel chair with a tube running from the left nostril to under the lapel approached significantly less closely than did subjects who approached an experimenter who was seated in the airport lobby and looked normal.

Several studies have suggested that people with personality abnormalities may have larger needs for personal space than do "normals." For example, Horowitz, Duff, and Stratton found that a group of schizophrenic patients reported larger personal space needs and expectations than did a control group of normals.[63] Each of 25 schizophrenic and 25 nonschizophrenic males was asked to draw lines around mimeographed silhouettes of male figures to demarcate the distance the subject liked to maintain between himself and others during social interaction. The schizophrenic patients drew a significantly greater area around each silhouette than did the normal group, presumably an indication of the desire for more personal space or a larger "body-buffer zone."

There is also some evidence that individuals with a history of violent behavior may be more sensitive to the physical closeness of other people.[64] Kinzel compared the respective body-buffer zones of eight prison inmates with histories of violent behavior with those of six inmates who had no history of violent behavior. Each inmate stood in the middle of a room while the experimenter slowly approached from 8 feet away. When the inmate felt that the experimenter was "too close," he was instructed to say "Stop." Eight approaches from different directions were made toward each inmate, with the area within the closest distances tolerated by the subject demarcating that subject's body-buffer zone.

The violent prisoners had a body-buffer zone almost four times larger than the nonviolent group. Importantly, the body-buffer zones had decreased by approximately 50% for both groups by the end of the experiment. Furthermore, violent inmates had larger rear zones than frontal zones; that is, they allowed the experimenter to approach them more closely from the front than from the back. On the basis of these results, Kinzel suggested that many chronically violent persons may have abnormalities in body image that cause them to perceive an invasion of their personal space as an intrusion on their bodies.

This study had some methodological difficulties, such as the smallness of the sample, the nonrandomness of the sampling, and the lack of double-blind techniques. However a study done by Hildreth, Derogatis, and McCusker rectified some of these methodological shortcomings and still produced generally corroborative results.[65] Thirty-six newly imprisoned inmates were selected at random, and the body-buffer zone of each inmate was determined in a procedure similar to that used by Kinzel. Measures of aggression, which were based on interviews and case records, were determined 3 to 4 weeks later by an experimenter who was unfamiliar with the body-buffer zone data.

Body-buffer zones were significantly larger for more than for less violent inmates. Furthermore, rear zone areas were larger than front zone areas in both groups, supporting the possibility that crowding from the rear may engender relatively more anxiety and stress, at least among males.

These studies demonstrate the necessity of considering personal and background factors in future experimental paradigms of crowding. We have seen that groups differ in their personal space expectations according to their sex, their physical health, their mental health, and their tendencies toward violence. Personal differences with regard to introversion-extroversion, autonomy, dominance, affiliation, and so on, may also prove to be associated with differential personal space expectations. Differential needs for space are relevant because a person with an expectation of greater personal space may have a lower crowding threshold, therefore being more apt to perceive a situation as crowded. Future studies of crowding also need to consider the finding that personal space expectations may change as an individual becomes more familiar with other people in the setting. Thus crowding studies that use the same subjects on successive trials may produce results dissimilar to those that use subjects for single trials.

Cross-Cultural Differences in the Use of Space. We have reviewed evidence indicating that personal space requirements or expectations are situation-specific (i.e., individual space expectations expand and contract, depending on the overall situation) and individual-specific (i.e., individuals in identical situations will differ in the amount of space they expect). As if the issue were not already sufficiently complex, cross-cultural and subcultural studies have indicated that space requirements are also culture-specific (i.e., cultures and subcultures differ in their spatial expectations for similar situations).

Hall observed that Germans generally expected more personal space than Americans, whereas Latin Americans, French, and especially Arabs, generally interacted more proximally and had smaller personal space expectations than Americans.[66] In fact, there did not appear to be any such thing as personal space intrusion in public places within the Arab culture. Watson and Graves rated four groups of Arab college males and four groups of American college males on five proxemic variables while the respective groups were conversing in an observational room.[67] The results dramatically supported Hall's original impressions. The Arab students not only faced each other more directly, they sat closer together, touched each other more, looked more directly into the eyes of their conversational partner, and spoke louder than the American students.

Little also found that social interaction distances for people of northern European cultures were significantly larger than for people of Mediterranean cultures.[68] Native-born male and female college students of the United States, Sweden, Greece, southern Italy, and Scotland served as subjects. Each subject was asked to position a pair of same-sex dolls so that the dolls "looked natural" in each of 19 different situations (e.g., good friends discussing a pleasant topic). Greek students expected the most proximal interaction, followed by Italians and Americans, Swedes, and finally the Scots. The validity of the doll placement paradigm was recently supported in a study by Haase and Markey, in which doll placement was seen to be a relatively accurate predictor of an individual's actual behavior in a proxemic situation.[69]

Most recent research has shown that spatial expectations also differ among subcultures *within* the United States. For example, Baxter went to the Houston Zoo to unobtrusively observe the natural interpersonal spacing of 859 ethnic pairs, each of which was classified as either Anglo-, black-, or Mexican-American.[70] There was a highly significant difference among ethnic groups, with Mexican pairs of all ages and both sexes standing the closest together, Anglos intermediate, and blacks the least proximal. An interaction between ethnic group and sex group was also noteworthy; for both Anglo and black groups, respectively, male-female pairs stood closest together, and male-male pairs stood the most distant from each other. Within Mexican groups, however, the female-female groups stood the closest to each other and male-male groups interacted from the greatest distance.

It is apparent that cross-cultural and subcultural differences in interpersonal space usage have important applications to crowding phenomena. For example, future crowding studies will not be able to treat "Americans" as a homogeneous group but will need to specify which American subculture is under study. Customs that lead to differential expectations for personal space under similar circumstances must be considered in further work, for they may also lead to differential perceptions of situations as crowded and stressful.

Research and Policy Considerations.   The United States has a relatively low overall population density (57 persons per square mile, vs. 611 persons per square mile in Great Britain[71]); nevertheless it is a crowded nation because of its population distribution. Approximately 70% of our population is concentrated in less than 2% of the total land area.[72] However advocating a population redistribution policy to avoid deleterious effects of crowding may be both premature and unrealistic. Much remains to be learned about crowding phenomena before effective social policies can be implemented. Furthermore, nations may differ in the need and type of policies to be implemented because of cultural variations in space usage. Zlutnick and Altman have suggested that future research focus on three areas: the effect of density as a determinant of behavior, the historical antecedents of responses to crowding, and coping and adaptive responses to crowding.[73]

Many of the studies cited in this chapter have sought to determine the effects of density—that is, whether differential degrees of density result in differential experiences or behaviors. Since perceived crowding may cause both psychological and physiological stress, studies that also use physiological dependent variables would be valuable. The physiological cost of crowding, as well as the association between physiological stress and self-reported discomfort, could then be determined.

Future studies must also more carefully consider the mediating effects of the physical and social structure of high-density settings. For example, Desor found that people are less likely to feel overcrowded in rooms to which partitions are added, in which there are fewer doors, and in which the area is rectangular rather than square.[74] Furthermore, the nature of the activity significantly affects the optimal amount of space allocated per person. Thus it may be possible to relieve feelings of crowding in high-density housing projects by methods other than increasing space. One alternative may be architectural designs featuring numerous partitions, few doorways, and rectangular rooms. Factors such as the interior quality of the apartment and the quality of the neighborhood environment might influence policy decisions if they could be shown to mediate perceptions of crowding.

Wicker has suggested investigating the effects of high density or "overmanning" by means of behavior settings.[75] He stresses the need to consider not only the number of persons in a setting but how that number relates to the personnel requirements of the setting (i.e., the number of people required to maintain the setting), and to the maximum number of people the setting can accommodate. Studying the maintenance minima and capacities of settings enables one to consider policies that may alleviate perceptions of crowding by means other than increasing the physical capacity of the setting. Possible strategies may include scheduling an additional performance of the setting or altering the setting program so that more people can be accommodated. An example of the latter is a chamber music group that reorganizes to become an orchestra (see Chapter 7).

It is often assumed that crowding has deleterious effects on human functioning, yet the positive influences of high density must also be considered. Humans have a need for stimulation and novelty, which if unsatisfied (understimulation), may result in anxiety, hallucinations, and impaired perceptual and cognitive functioning.[76] The varied amount of sensory input provided by high-density settings may thus be desirable, especially to individuals who have a high optimal level of stimulation. For example, many individuals who have lived in densely populated college dormitories refer to the experience as worthwhile.[77] Le Corbusier has written, "The virtue of the big city is that it becomes a magnetic pole of attraction from which emanates the spiritual achievement resulting from intense concentration."[78] Jane Jacobs has extolled the excitement and vitality associated with the exuberant diversity of people and places in big city life and has stated that a concentrated area of humanity may be an asset rather than a liability. The optimum human situation may be one of access to a variety of densities, rather than simple high or low density as such.[79]

Another important goal is to determine the long-term environmental histories influencing differential patterns of responding to high-density situations. In other words, what leads some individuals to react positively to high densities, while others react negatively? The history of the individual in relation to the availability of space may prove to be especially important; that is, persons who are used to more space may develop reaction patterns to density different from those of persons who are accustomed to less space.

Finally the issue of coping and adaptive mechanisms to crowding must be examined in greater detail. The long-term psychological (e.g., norms of noninvolvement) and physiological (e.g., changes in hormone secretion patterns) costs of adaptation need to be determined. This might be accomplished by tracking and correlating various styles of coping with concomitant psychological and physiological processes.[80]

Research on adaptive mechanisms may also clarify the reasons for the stressfulness of crowding. It may be that crowding stress is due to the individual's perceived restricted freedom of choice caused by the presence of others,[81] and perhaps adaptive mechanisms are aimed at regaining a measure of control over the situation. The identification of adaptive methods that enable people to better control interaction with others in crowded settings, to thus minimize psychological and physiological stress, may be especially useful. Even though we may never find ourselves gazing at a museum of space from a "waitline" alongside Sam Poynter, John Hersey's protagonist, it is apparent that we need to enhance our knowledge of adaptive mechanisms to successfully cope with crowded conditions.

REFERENCES

1. Dubos, R. *Man adapting.* Yale University Press, New Haven, Conn., 1965.
2. Hersey, J. *My petition for more space.* Knopf, New York, 1974.
3. Zlutnick, S. and Altman, I. Crowding and human behavior. In J. F. Wohlwill and D. H. Carson (Eds.), *Environment and the social sciences: Perspectives and applications,* American Psychological Association, Washington, D.C., 1972.

4. Stokols, D. A social-psychological model of human crowding phenomena. *Journal of the American Institute of Planners*, **38:**72–83, 1972.

5. Mitchell, R. E. Some implications of high density housing. *American Sociological Review*, **36:**18–29, 1971.

6. Mitchell, *op. cit.*, p. 21.

7. Stokols, *op. cit.*, p. 78.

8. Rotter, J. B. Generalized expectancies of internal versus external control of reinforcement. *Psychological Monograph*, **80:**(whole #609), 1966.

9. Stokols, *op. cit.*, p. 80.

10. Zlutnick and Altman, *op. cit.*, p. 53.

11. Stokols, *op. cit.*, p. 80.

12. Milgram, S. The experience of living in cities. *Science*, **167:**1461–1468, 1970.

13. Freedman, J. L. The effects of population density on humans. In J. T. Fawcett (Ed.), *Psychological perspectives on population*. Basic Books, New York, 1973.

14. Zlutnick and Altman, *op. cit.*, p. 50.

15. Schmitt, R. C. Density, health, and social disorganization. *Journal of American Institute of Planners*, **32:**38–40, 1966.

16. Jacobs, J. *The death and life of great American cities*. Random House, New York, 1961.

17. Zlutnick and Altman, *op. cit.*, p. 51.

18. Galle, O. R., Gove, W. R., and McPherson, J. M. Population density and pathology: What are the implications for man? *Science*, **176:** 23–30, 1972.

19. Schmitt, R. C. Density, delinquency, and crime in Honolulu. *Sociology and Social Research*, **41:**274–276, 1957.

20. Schmitt, Density, health, and social disorganization, *op. cit.*

21. Freedman, *op. cit.*, p. 221.

22. Galle, Gove, and McPherson, *op. cit.*

23. Mitchell, *op. cit.*

24. Galle, Gove, and McPherson, *op. cit.*, p. 29.

25. Levy, L. and Herzog, A. Effects of population density and crowding on health and social adaptation in the Netherlands. *Journal of Health and Social Behavior*, **15:**228–240, 1974.

26. Hare, E. H. Mental illness and social conditions in Bristol. *Journal of Mental Science*, **102:**349–357, 1956.

27. Kahn, R. and Perlin, S. Dwelling unit density and the use of mental health services. *Proceedings of the 75th Annual Convention of the American Psychological Association*, 175–176, 1967.

28. Lewis, O. Privacy and crowding in poverty. In H. M. Proshansky, W. H. Ittelson, and L. G. Rivlin (Eds.), *Environmental psychology: Man and his physical setting*. Holt, Rinehart, & Winston, New York, 1970.

29. Milgram, The experience of living in cities, *op. cit.*, p. 1462.

30. Altman, D., Levine, M., Nadien, M., and Villena, J. (Graduate Center, The City University of New York), unpublished research. In Milgram, *op. cit.*, p. 1463.

31. Dubos, *Man adapting, op. cit.*, p. 278.

32. Calhoun, J. B. Population density and social pathology. *Scientific American,* **206:**139–148, 1962.

33. Alexander, B. K. and Roth, E. M. The effects of acute crowding on aggressive behavior of Japanese monkeys. *Behavior,* **39:**73–90, 1971.

34. Christian, J. J., Flyger, V., and Davis, D. C. Factors in the mass mortality of a herd of Sika deer *Cervus nippon. Chesapeake Science,* **1:**79–95, 1960.

35. Dubos, *op. cit.*, p. 102.

36. *Ibid.*, p. 108.

37. Loo, C. Important issues in researching the effects of crowding on humans. *Representative Research in Social Psychology,* **4:**219–226, 1973.

38. *Ibid.*

39. Freedman, J. L., Klevansky, S., and Ehrlich, P. R. The effect of crowding on human task performance. *Journal of Applied Social Psychology,* **1:**7–25, 1971.

40. Sherrod, D. R. Crowding, perceived control, and behavioral aftereffects. *Journal of Applied Social Psychology,* **4:**171–186, 1974.

41. Ross, M., Layton, B., Erickson, B., and Schopler, J. Affect, facial regard, and reactions to crowding. *Journal of Personality and Social Psychology,* **28:**69–76, 1973.

42. Griffitt, W. and Veitch, R. Hot and crowded: Influences of population density and temperature on interpersonal affective behavior. *Journal of Personality and Social Psychology,* **17:**92–99, 1971.

43. Sommer, R. and Becker, F. D. Room density and user satisfaction. *Environment and Behavior,* **3:**412–417, 1971.

44. Freedman, J. L., Levy, A. S., Buchanan, R. W., and Price, J. Crowding and human aggressiveness. *Journal of Experimental Social Psychology,* **8:**528–548, 1972.

45. Stokols, D., Rall, M., Pinner, B., and Schopler, J. Physical, social and personal determinants of the perception of crowding. *Environment and Behavior,* **5:**87–115, 1973.

46. Freedman, Levy, Buchanan, and Price, *op. cit.*, p. 545.

47. Hutt, C. and Vaizey, M. J. Differential effects of group density on social behavior. *Nature,* **209:**1371–1372, 1966.

48. Loo, C. The effects of spatial density on the social behavior of children. *Journal of Applied Social Psychology,* **2:**372–381, 1972.

49. Loo, Important issues in researching the effects of crowding on humans, *op. cit.*

50. Fried, M. L. and DeFazio, V. J. Territoriality and boundary conflicts in the subway. *Psychiatry,* **37:**47–59, 1974.

51. Proshansky, H. M., Ittelson, W. H., and Rivlin, L. G. Freedom of choice and behavior in a physical setting. In H. M. Proshansky, W. H. Ittelson, and L. G. Rivlin (Eds.), *Environmental psychology: Man and his physical setting.* Holt, Rinehart & Winston, New York, 1970.

52. Lyman, S. M. and Scott, M. B. Territoriality: A neglected sociological dimension. *Social Problems,* **15**:236–249, 1967.

53. Hall, E. T. *The hidden dimension.* Doubleday, Garden City, N.Y., 1966.

54. Sommer, R. *Personal space: The behavioral basis of design.* Prentice-Hall, Englewood Cliffs, N.J., 1969.

55. Baxter, J. C. and Deanovich, B. F. Anxiety arousing effects of inappropriate crowding. *Journal of Consulting and Clinical Psychology,* **35**:174–178, 1970.

56. Felipe, N. J. and Sommer, R. Invasions of personal space. *Social Problems,* **14**:206–214, 1966.

57. Barash, D. P. Human ethology: Personal space reiterated. *Environment and Behavior,* **5**:67–72, 1973.

58. McBride, G. *A general theory of social organization.* University of Queensland Press, St. Lucia (Australia), 1964.

59. Hartnett, J. J., Bailey, K. G., and Gibson, F. W., Jr. Personal space as influenced by sex and type of movement. *Journal of Psychology,* **76**:139–144, 1970.

60. Pellegrini, R. J. and Empey, J. Interpersonal spatial orientation in dyads. *Journal of Psychology,* **76**:67–70, 1970.

61. Spinetta, J. J., Rigler, D., and Karon, M. Personal space as a measure of a dying child's sense of isolation. *Journal of Consulting and Clinical Psychology,* **42**:751–756, 1974.

62. Worthington, M. E. Personal space as a function of the stigma effect. *Environment and Behavior,* **6**:289–294, 1974.

63. Horowitz, M. J., Duff, D. F., and Stratton, L. O. Personal space and the body-buffer zone. In H. M. Proshansky, W. H. Ittelson and L. G. Rivlin (Eds.), *Environmental psychology: Man and his physical setting.* Holt, Rinehart & Winston, New York, 1970.

64. Kinzel, A. F. Body-buffer zone in violent prisoners. *American Journal of Psychiatry,* **127**:99–104, 1970.

65. Hildreth, A. M., Derogatis, L. R., and McCusker, K. Body-buffer zone and violence: A reassessment and confirmation. *American Journal of Psychiatry,* **127**:77–81, 1971.

66. Hall, *The hidden dimension, op. cit.*

67. Watson, O. M. and Graves, T. Quantitative research in proxemic behavior. *American Anthropologist,* **68**:971–985, 1966.

68. Little, K. B. Cultural variations in social schemata. *Journal of Personality and Social Psychology,* **10**:1–7, 1968.

69. Haase, R. F. and Markey, M. J. A methodological note on the study of personal space. *Journal of Consulting and Clinical Psychology,* **40**:122–125, 1973.

70. Baxter, J. C. Interpersonal spacing in natural settings. *Sociometry*, **33**:444–456, 1970.

71. Day, A. T., and Day, L. H. Cross-national comparisons of population density. *Science*, **181**:1016–1023, 1973.

72. Kirk, D. The misunderstood challenge of population change. In C. Loo (Ed.), *Crowding and behavior*. MSS Information Corporation, New York, 1974.

73. Zlutnick and Altman, Crowding and human behavior, *op. cit.*, pp. 54–55.

74. Desor, J. A. Toward a psychological theory of crowding. *Journal of Personality and Social Psychology*, **21**:79–83, 1972.

75. Wicker, A. W. Undermanning theory and research: Implications for the study of psychological and behavioral effects of excess populations. *Representative Research in Social Psychology*, **4**:185–206, 1973.

76. Zubek, J. P. *Sensory deprivation, fifteen years of research.* Appleton-Century-Crofts, New York, 1969.

77. Lawrence, J. E. Crowding and human behavior. *Psychological Bulletin*, **81**:712–720, 1974.

78. Le Corbusier. *The radiant city.* Orion, New York, 1933.

79. Jacobs, *The death and life of great American cities, op. cit.*

80. Zlutnick and Altman, *op. cit.*, p. 55.

81. Proshansky, Ittelson, and Rivlin, Freedom of choice and behavior in a physical setting, *op. cit.*, p. 182.

CHAPTER SIX

Noise and Air Pollution[a]

The Reaction to Noise Pollution.

It was 6:00 a.m. on a balmy April day in 1964. The place was a six-block stretch of Manhattan's Sixth Avenue between Radio City Music Hall and Central Park, in the heart of New York City. Thousands of New Yorkers and transients slept in the cosmopolitan neighborhood of apartments, hotels, and schools. . . . "Slattery's Army" was moving into position, a position it was to hold for three years, from 1964 to 1967. It was a highly mechanized contractor's army, equipped with eighty-pound-class pneumatic paving breakers, track-mounted high-impact rock drills, giant cranes and bulldozers. . . . Workers with scarred eardrums were preparing to launch an open-cut subway extension project for the New York City Transit Authority. . . .

The operating engineer started the battery of air compressors. Jackhammer and rock drill operators hunched forward, waiting for the compressed air to feed their vibrating pneumatic tools.

Suddenly, all hell broke loose. What someone later termed "a symphony of insanity" had begun. The overture to a three-year concert combined the sounds of air compressors, jackhammers, rock drills, chain saws, and dynamite blasts, with additional instrumentation by cement mixers, vibrators, cranes, and portable generators.[1]

During 1964–1967 there was more noise in the neighborhood surrounding the subway cut than city ordinances permitted in factory areas. Telephone conversation was not possible except during the workers' half-

[a] This chapter is co-authored by Paul Sommers, Bernice Van Dort, and Rudolf Moos.

hour lunch break. Office workers in nearby buildings suffered from headaches and short tempers. Apartment residents seemed to become more absentminded, forgetting to take off clothes and eyeglasses before stepping into the shower, and reporting sleeplessness, ringing in the ears, and headaches. To counteract these effects, "Tranquilizers and aspirins were eaten like popcorn. I didn't mind taking sedatives, but I did hate to share them with my two-year old, whose first sentence was 'Noisy street, Daddy, stop the noisy street.' "[2] Sales of earplugs and acoustic earmuffs rose sharply in the corner drug store; theaters and hotels experienced business declines, and apartment houses noted a much higher vacancy rate.

The assault on the ears of Robert Baron and his neighbors is perhaps unusual for the intensity and length of the annoyance and for the refusal of the city government to intervene. Now nearly every suburb and municipality in the nation seems to have a noise ordinance on the books, limiting factory noises, aircraft runups, and motorcycle and truck engine noises. The increasing public concern is just one indication of the ever-increasing urban din, which affects nearly every American at home or at work.

Noise may be defined as a subjectively annoying sound. Intensity and duration of the sound do not matter in this definition. If a person says that a sound is annoying or disrupting, it can be considered a noise. Sound energy travels through the air in waves that alternately compress and rarefy the air at any one point. The number of waves passing by in a unit of time determines the pitch of a sound (i.e., whether it is a "low" rumble or a "high" shriek). The number of waves or cycles that pass by in a second is called a hertz (Hz). Human ears can detect sounds varying in pitch from 15 (a low bass voice) to 20,000 Hz (a high whistle). Sounds pitched lower than 15 Hz may be detected as physical vibrations but not as sounds. Sounds pitched higher than 20,000 Hz can pass undetected by humans.[3]

Sound and noise levels vary with the physical pressure exerted by the sound waves. The unit for measuring noise levels is the decibel (dB). A decibel is a logarithmic ratio of a sound's physical pressure relative to a standard reference pressure. People judge high-pitched sounds to be more intense than low-pitched sounds at the same decibel level. Hence weighting systems have been developed that more closely resemble human subjective responses to noise than do the unweighted or "flat response" decibels. The widely used "A" weighting system is designated dB(A). Leaves rustling in the wind may have a noise level of 20 dB(A), ordinary conversation would create a 60 dB(A) level, an alarm clock ringing 2 feet from your ear might have an 80 dB(A) level, and a jet aircraft passing 500 feet overhead would have a level of about 115 dB(A).[4]

There is another weighting system for rating the annoying quality of

certain environmental noises. The Perceived Noise Level rating was cali-
brated using aircraft noises, but the rating can be used for other annoying
noises (e.g., traffic noise). Decibels weighted in this manner are designated PNdB.[5] Other weighting systems and environmental noise rating
scales exist, but only three forms of the decibel level are discussed here.

We review three types of effects noise exposure may have on people.
Noise is annoying, and extensive work has been done to identify the types
and intensities of sounds that are irritating. People's behavior may change
during and after exposure to noise; laboratory and real world studies
have been conducted to determine whether noise by and of itself can
affect human behavior. Finally, noise can be detrimental to health. Annoyance reactions may include mild psychosomatic complaints
(headache, irritability, insomnia, etc.). These health effects of noise exposure are discussed below. We do not consider the problem of noise-
induced deafness. The federal Environmental Protection Agency (EPA)
has published an excellent review of this area.[6]

Noise in the Community.   Noise level surveys have been carried out in a
variety of community settings to discover what noises annoy people, what
noises disturb their work, and what noises may actually be harmful.
Homes, offices, schools, and streets have been studied. The effects of
specific noisemakers such as factories, airplanes, vehicular traffic, and
even cocktail parties have been analyzed.

If traffic noises or noises from other people talking make it difficult for
you to hear someone speaking to you, you might ask the speaker to talk a
little louder. If you and your partner are the only ones in the room, that
solution would be feasible, but what if there are a hundred or more people
in a single room, all faced with the same hearing problem? What if you are
an acoustical engineer, socially compelled to attend many cocktail parties
with scores of your business and professional colleagues? Two communications engineers who repeatedly found themselves in this situation decided to carry out noise surveys to ascertain whether the average cocktail
party is loud enough to damage the hearing mechanism. They surveyed
seven parties and found that the noise levels did not exceed 80–85 dB(A),
which is not high enough to permanently damage hearing. The authors
noted that the type of beverage served may not affect the results very
much, since one kaffee klatsch surveyed was just as noisy as the cocktail
parties. Also their data suggested that all-male social functions may be
quieter than mixed-sex parties, a finding that is bound to be
controversial.[7]

Noise surveys in office settings have attempted to find the maximum noise level that is consistent with good job performance and minimal disruption of communication. The rationale for this approach is that environmental noise is often directly related to the work process and cannot be completely eliminated. For example, one study was carried out at an Air Force base, at which many office workers worked in buildings near runways and aircraft runup areas. The workers became habituated to whatever noise environment they happened to be working in. They tolerated a range of louder noises temporarily without showing annoyance. If an aircraft runup remained within this range of about 20 dB, no complaints about communication difficulties were reported. When noises higher than the prevailing noise level were experienced for longer periods of time (several minutes), annoyance reactions became apparent. For example, an executive with a private office might become accustomed to a level of 25–30 dB. The typists in the next office might create a level of 55–60 dB, and if the executive walked into the room to talk to one of the typists, he would be annoyed by the typing sound and would experience difficulty in communicating in his normal tone of voice.[8]

Appleyard and Lintell considered the effects of traffic noise generated on three San Francisco streets. One had light traffic, the second moderate traffic, and the third heavy traffic. All were moderate-income residential streets in an Italian neighborhood. The nighttime noise on the heavy traffic street was so intense that one elderly couple reported trying to sleep during the day to make up for sleep lost at night. Other residents on this street called the noise "unbearable" and "too much." Exceptionally noisy vehicles sometimes rattled the windows of apartments and screeched their brakes in last-minute stops, which were especially unnerving events for residents. These conditions caused residents to petition the city government for a sign that would prohibit trucks and buses on their street.

Much more casual social interaction was observed on the light traffic street than on the other two. People congregated on front steps and at the corner drugstore. Virtually no sidewalk activity was observed on the heavy traffic street, other than people scurrying to and from the apartment entrances. People on the noisy street also reported that the street was a rather lonely place to live, in contrast to the light traffic street, which was perceived by its residents as a very friendly, sociable area. These patterns of social interaction might have been affected by the type of people who lived on the three streets as much as by the prevailing noise levels.[9]

McKennell and Hunt undertook a survey of noise levels and public reaction to noise in London. Nearly 1400 adults living in the central area were interviewed at their residences. When asked about things they disliked in their area, one-fifth of the residents interviewed spontaneously mentioned noises of various kinds. Annoyance with noise was partially due to disruption of activities: 26% of the sample said that noise sometimes interfered with their sleep, 32% said that their rest or relaxation was disturbed, and 24% said that noise sometimes interfered with TV or radio listening. Noises heard inside the home were much more annoying than noises heard outdoors or at work. The most frequent and most annoying noise heard at home was road traffic. A comparison with a survey undertaken in London 20 years previously showed that the proportion of the population annoyed by outdoor sound heard at home had increased from 23 to 50%, and the proportion noticing traffic noises had risen from 22 to 77%.[10]

The EPA has conducted a review of community noise survey studies. They list nine qualities of noises that contribute to annoyance:

1.   High-intensity and/or high-frequency sounds.
2.   Lengthy duration of the noise level.
3.   The presence of discrete frequency components.
4.   The presence of impulses.
5.   The abruptness of onset or cessation of the noise event.
6.   Harshness or roughness of the noise.
7.   Intermittency in loudness, pitch, or rhythm.
8.   Lack of information content (for a particular listener).
9.   Interference with activities.[11]

The EPA review concludes that average noise annoyance levels in a community are highly related to the degree of noise exposure. Large individual variations in reactions to noise, which appeared in most studies, have been linked to personal attitudes toward noise. The salient difference between people bothered by noise and people not bothered is not extrasensitive ears or a quiet, rural place of origin but simply the presence or absence of an expressed dislike of noise. The number of complaints about noise registered with authorities in a community is related to the number of people who express high noise annoyance in a comprehensive survey of the population. However the number of citizens actually annoyed is much larger than the number of official complaints.

Several important effects of noise have been mentioned in the four studies of community noise described here and in the EPA review. Noise may adversely affect subjective moods, producing anxiety and irritation. Residents on noisy streets may interact with their neighbors less often than residents on quiet streets. Various domestic activities, including sleep, may be disturbed on noisy streets. However many people expect and/or tolerate a great deal of noise. People in Central London were bothered more by shoddy physical conditions in their homes than by noises. Noise at work is tolerated to a much greater extent than noise at home. The number of complaints to the authorities is much smaller than the number of people in a community who are highly annoyed by noises.

Part of the explanation for this tolerance may be that noise levels increase rather gradually over a period of years as traffic volume increases and more industries are constructed. Homeowners and apartment dwellers may become slowly habituated to the increased noise levels, just as office workers may become accustomed to aircraft noises and noises from typists. However a sudden increase in noise level or incidence may not be easily tolerated, as, for example, when a subway construction crew moves into the neighborhood. Increased annoyance, a variety of subjective and behavioral effects, and a sharp increase in the number of complaints to authorities may be expected in response to a sudden increase in noise level in a community.

Aircraft Noise.   With these findings in mind we now examine a particular type of community noise that has become increasingly frequent in the last few years. As communities grow in population, housing is often constructed under the landing and takeoff ranges of airports, and new airports are built near older residential areas. As larger and louder jet aircraft have begun to use these urban airports, the extent of noise annoyance from aircraft has become an important social problem. Sound level monitoring equipment and noise level regulations are commonplace in American airports as airport managers attempt to reduce noise levels to acceptable ranges. Several studies have been made of community reactions to aircraft noise, the conditions under which people are annoyed, and the conditions under which they will actually complain.

One study compared the noise survey responses of Central London residents with those of people living in an area surrounding Heathrow Airport in London. The airport survey reported results for a high noise area (defined on the basis of actual noise measurements) and for the entire area 10 miles in any direction from the airport. When people were asked what they disliked about the area they lived in, aircraft noises were mentioned by just 1% of the Central London respondents, although 22% of this sample mentioned some kind of noise. In the overall airport area, 10% of the residents interviewed mentioned aircraft noise, and 20% mentioned noises of some kind. For the high noise airport region, 55% of the sample mentioned aircraft noise and 64% mentioned noises of some kind. In addition, 16% of these respondents mentioned that they would like to move to get away from the noise. Sleep and TV viewing and listening were disturbed much more often in the high noise airport area than in the other two regions.

Thus noise is a significant irritant in residential areas near airports, and it is an overwhelming concern for a majority of residents who live very near the airport, where the perceived noise levels reach extremely high peaks. Noise of all kinds is a significant problem in terms of annoyance, activities, and the general desirability of one's home mainly for people living in the region closest to the landing and takeoff routes of aircraft. Other areas within 10 miles of the airport differed very little from Central London in terms of perceived noisiness and subjective and behavioral reactions.[12]

Burrows and Zamarin found that a substantial proportion of the population living near the Los Angeles International Airport was aware of aircraft noise, and many considered noise to be a problem in that it disturbed their domestic activities and sleep. However their behavior showed no attempt to alleviate the annoyance. Only 4% of the sample had ever made a complaint to the authorities. More than 40% had been aware of aircraft noise when they moved into the area. Most respondents who owned their homes reported that their property's value had increased as much as property in other areas of Los Angeles. Sixty percent were unwilling to make any kind of money payment to alleviate the noise problem. Perhaps only people who are relatively tolerant of noise move into neighborhoods near airports, whereas persons bothered by noise may move away or avoid coming into such areas.[13]

A much different noise survey was conducted in West Philadelphia and neighboring Tinicum Township. The entire Tinicum Township lies within a mile of the runways of Philadelphia International Airport, and West Philadelphia is within 2–3 miles. Tinicum lies directly under the corridor of the jet aircrafts' final approach to the runway, making the noise exposure particularly severe. Rather than interviewing a random sample of community residents, as other surveys have done. Bragdon established noise monitoring stations in locations near known noise sources (e.g., airport runway, elevated train tracks, commuter train tracks, a busy street, and a factory). He then interviewed approximately 20 residents in the area closest to each monitoring station. This procedure elicited responses from the residents most exposed to noise in these communities, and it ensured a relatively constant noise exposure for every respondent from a given monitoring region.

About two-thirds of the total sample (West Philadelphia and Tinicum) were quite satisfied with their residential area, calling it an excellent or good place to live. Aircraft noise was mentioned by 55% of the Tinicum residents as the thing they liked least in their area, but by only 1% of West Philadelphia residents. Living directly under the approach pattern in Tinicum exposed residents to much more noise than residents of noisy areas (e.g., near elevated railway) in West Philadelphia, and noise was a more significant irritant to the Tinicum residents. However Tinicum residents felt that their area was a good place to live in spite of the annoying aircraft noise.

Two questions were asked about general health effects of noise. In Tinicum 58% of the respondents felt that noise was harmful to health and well-being, but only 18% of West Philadelphia respondents shared this opinion. In both Tinicum and West Philadelphia, respondents believed that noise could adversely affect their health by angering them and by making them irritable or nervous. Some residents reported sleeping difficulties, including one totally deaf man in Tinicum who was frequently disturbed by vibrations of his house as aircraft passed overhead.[14]

The aircraft noise surveys support the conclusions of general community noise surveys. People notice aircraft sounds and are often irritated by them. One study found that such irritation can endanger people's health, and another reported an association between mental hospital admissions and aircraft noises.[15] Graeven found that awareness of aircraft noise was more closely related to reported health problems than was level of exposure to the noise.[16] These effects are found only very close to aircraft takeoff and landing areas, generally within 2 miles of the runway. Overt behavioral responses are seldom reported in these surveys. Most people do not move away from the noisy areas near airports. Indeed many residents of these areas are well aware of the extent of aircraft noise when they move in. People are not willing to pay money to get rid of aircraft noise. Complaints to airport and city authorities are rare. Other aspects of the physical environment of urban areas seem to bother people more than aircraft noise (e.g., air pollution or very poor housing are mentioned in some areas, traffic congestion and traffic noise are salient issues in others).

By and large, people who live in noisy areas tolerate or adapt to noise. One mechanism of adaptation is to concentrate on the positive aspects of one's residential area. Impressions of good housing, friendly neighbors, or excellent public services may be uppermost in people's minds when they are asked to describe their neighborhood. Noise complaints emerge only when a person is asked a question about bad features of the neighborhood or prompted by a specific question about noise.

Another mechanism of adaptation may be to leave the area. Community surveys obviously must interview the self-selected population that has not (yet) moved out of the area. Demographic characteristics may differentiate between noisy and not-so-noisy neighborhoods, and noise tolerance may be related to the severity of noise exposure.[17] Thus the people interviewed in a community survey may well be a self-selected population that is, on the whole, more tolerant of noise than people who have already moved to quieter neighborhoods.

An Experimental Field Study.   Ward and Suedfeld conducted an innovative field experiment to evaluate the psychological and behavioral consequences of a proposed highway extension that was to pass by classroom and dormitory buildings at Rutgers University. The authors went to the existing highway and recorded the traffic noise generated there at peak traffic periods in the morning and late afternoon, during the night, and during other daytime periods. Sound playback equipment was set up at the university outside a classroom building and in a dormitory, using very large speakers to capture some of the low-frequency rumble associated with large trucks. Students could then be exposed to a very realistic 24-hour-a-day noise environment, comparable to what the proposed highway extension would produce. Selected dormitory residents were exposed to this environment for an entire week. Classrooms were observed for 3 days with noise, and a week later for 3 days without noise, as a control condition. Behavior under both conditions was observed and student reactions were sampled by questionnaires.

Observers found less participation, less attentiveness, and greater difficulty in hearing the comments of instructors and students under noisy conditions. There was a trend toward more use of lecture than discussion formats on the noisy days. The student questionnaires indicated that it was more difficult to take notes, harder to hear speakers, and less enjoyable; moreover, there was less discussion under noisy conditions. Some students were so annoyed by the noise that on two occasions the electrical cable providing power to the sound equipment was cut, and some students threatened to destroy the sound equipment.

The dormitory subjects were divided into three groups so that noise exposure could be varied. One group received high (loudest) exposure to the traffic noise. A second group received a moderate, slightly quieter level of exposure. The third group heard no induced traffic noises at all. The traffic noise clearly affected interpersonal relations in the high noise group relative to the no-noise group, and relative to the high noise group before the traffic noise was broadcast. Group discussions in the high noise group lasted longer, with more statements being made per unit of time, more expressions of disagreement, and more general indications of tension. The high noise and moderate noise groups reported more adverse changes in sleep, studying, social relations, judgment, alertness, and nervousness than the no-noise group. Emotional reactions were extremely negative in the former two groups. Some effects were found on cognitive tests, but they were not reliably related to noise exposure. Arousal as measured by heart rate was not raised by the noise exposure.[18]

The changes in interpersonal relations during noise exposure appear to be related to the annoyance reactions found in community noise surveys. Ward and Suedfeld have presented a more detailed picture of the actual behaviors that culminate in expressions of annoyance. Tension, disagreements, difficulty in hearing, and negative affect toward noise and noisemakers were found in a population exposed to suddenly increased levels of traffic noise. One can be confident that the expression of annoyance due to noise is more than just a complaint. Annoyance is accompanied by observable behavior changes and considerable negative affect.

The long-term effects of noise may of course differ from the short-term effects of a sharp increase in noise level. Behavioral changes and negative affect may gradually change over time to become the general complaining and lack of overt behavioral change found in community noise surveys. Students suddenly exposed to artificially induced noise may attempt to cut the power cable, but if the highway had been built it is unlikely that they would have attempted to block the traffic. They would probably not perceive the real highway as being potentially under their control, and they would probably learn to "put up" with the noise as residents near airports do. In fact, some of the comments on the classroom questionnaire collected in Ward and Suedfeld's study indicate the potential for this type of adaptation to noise. Some students commented that they could get used to the noise; others said that they had expected it to be worse than it actually was.

The significance of this study is that it clarifies some of the connections between annoyance and behavior. Close observation of an annoyed population revealed actual behavior changes, at least in the short run. Use of this type of observation in airport areas, in residential areas bordering on busy urban streets, and in industrial areas, would undoubtedly reveal behavioral and psychological changes of some importance. Large-scale community noise studies cannot provide such data. For this reason less evidence of behavioral response to noise has been found in community surveys.

Noise and Performance: Industrial and Laboratory Findings.   Noise occurs as a by-product of many work processes. Machinery in factories can produce very high noise levels capable of damaging hearing over long periods of exposure. Typewriters in offices can produce irritating and possibly distracting noise levels. The negative effects of noise on worker productivity have been studied in work settings for several decades, and laboratory experiments are an important complement to work in industrial settings.

Perhaps the earliest study to demonstrate that reduced noise levels can raise productivity was conducted in the 1930s in an English cotton weaving factory. Each worker supervised the operation of several very noisy semiautomatic looms. When a thread broke the worker was expected to quickly detect and correct the problem. On the hypothesis that reducing the noise level might improve the workers' average response time, management provided the workers with earplugs that attenuated the 96-dB loom noise by 10–15 dB. Ten weavers wore the earplugs on alternate weeks for 6 months. The gain in total output was just 1% for those wearing earplugs, but the increase in worker efficiency in detecting broken threads was 12%.[19]

The Aetna Life Insurance Company conducted a series of studies on noise levels in its own offices. In one room, sound-absorbent wallboard was installed, which reduced the ambient noise level from 41 to 35 dB. Records from a year before and a year after the installation were compared, showing that calculator operators' errors were reduced 52%, typists' errors by 29%, and employee turnover 47%. Obviously during the 2 years between observations the typists and calculator operators may have simply learned to do a better job, management may have changed its relationship to the workers, or the less efficient workers may have departed. Aetna conducted another experiment to check out such possibilities. The sound-absorbent wallboard was covered with gypsum board, thereby raising the sound level back to 41 dB. Error rates increased slightly for a brief period, although not to their original levels, then dropped again to the same level as the quiet year. Thus noise level was clearly not the only factor involved in achieving the low level of errors during the quiet year, but one cannot rule out the possibility that a quieter environment contributed to the improvement in the workers' performance.[20]

Studies reviewed elsewhere show a great variety of findings, some supporting and some contradicting the hypothesis that high noise levels are associated with reduced productivity in work situations. Some of the studies found that high noise could have an arousing or stimulating effect that is beneficial in securing good performance of work tasks. Other studies reported no difference in worker performance when noise levels were reduced.[21] This variety of findings in the literature, and the difficulties of achieving satisfactory experimental controls over both noise and extraneous environmental and social factors in actual work situations, have led to an interest in laboratory studies of noise. Although it is difficult to generalize from the laboratory to actual work situations, clear-cut laboratory findings may suggest what types of effect to look for in work settings.

In laboratories significant deleterious effects of noise have appeared with tasks involving continuous visual monitoring of gauges or light displays.[22] Woodhead presented a one-second burst of noise at 100 dB to subjects who were performing arithmetic computations mentally and writing down only the answer. The noise was presented either while the subject was memorizing a number to be used in the calculation or while he was performing a subtraction using the memorized number. Relative to no-noise control subjects, subjects who were exposed to noise bursts during the memorizing period were less accurate in their subsequent calculation, and subjects exposed during the calculation took longer to complete the calculation.[23]

Azrin demonstrated that even in a laboratory, supposed noise effects may be the result of the more general condition of stimulus change. Subjects were seated in front of a meter in a darkened, sound-attenuated booth. The needle on the meter could be seen only if the subject pressed a button that illuminated the meter for 0.1 second. The needle was deflected every 3 minutes by the experimenter, whereupon the subject was supposed to push a second button that returned the needle to its original position. Each subject's responses during a period of quiet were compared to his performance during the presentation of noise coming through loudspeakers.

The established pattern of observing the meter consisted of a period of no observation for about 2 minutes followed by rapid and repeated observation up to the deflection of the needle. The needle was then returned to its original position by the subject and a period of no observation resumed. This pattern was disrupted completely by the introduction of noise. Subjects repeatedly and rapidly observed the meter for two or three complete cycles of meter deflection, after which the original pattern of observation was gradually reestablished. However when the noise was stopped, the pattern was again disrupted with rapid and repeated observations. Subsequent resumptions and stoppages of the noise had little or no effect on observation patterns. Azrin concludes that the change of stimulus resulted in a change in observation patterns.[24]

These findings could be interpreted in the following way. With the introduction of the noise, a marked change occurred in the subjects' rather stimulus-deprived environment. Naturally they tried to ascertain whether the change was accompanied by a modification of the needle deflection pattern. Discovering that it was not, they resumed the original pattern of observation of the needle. A similar procedure occurred when the noise stopped. After this the subjects had learned that the noise and no-noise conditions had no meaning in this particular environment, and subsequent noise changes were ignored.

That the stimulus change consisted of the starting or cessation of noise was irrelevant to the experiment. The change might equally well have consisted of flashing lights or a poke in the ribs. The stimulus change factor, and a search for the meaning of the change, may be important in evaluating real-world effects of noise. Hospital patients who are exposed to a variety of noises from machines on which their lives depend may become quite anxious about some alteration of these noises. Office workers may be more concerned about the meaning of a sudden noise change in the neighboring office than they are bothered by the noise.

Glass and Singer conducted a series of experiments relating performance of simple mental tasks to noise exposures. One experiment required subjects to perform two tasks simultaneously while being exposed to either predictable or unpredictable noise. The predictable noise condition consisted of 9-second noise bursts occurring 1 minute apart; the unpredictable condition consisted of noise bursts of randomly chosen duration (3–15 seconds) with a silent interval of randomly chosen duration (0–73 seconds) between noise bursts. The noise burst consisted of superimposed recordings of two people speaking Spanish and one person speaking Armenian with a background of mimeograph, desk calculator, and typewriter noises. The primary task consisted of tracking a moving vertical line on an oscilloscope screen, using an arrow moved back and forth by a car steering wheel. In the subsidiary task randomly chosen digits were announced to the subject, one every 2 seconds. When the subject heard a digit being announced, he was supposed to repeat the previously announced digit. No significant difference was found on the primary task when performed alone or in conjunction with the subsidiary task, in either predictable or unpredictable noise conditions. However when the subjects simultaneously performed both tasks, performance on the subsidiary task was poorer during unpredictable noise exposure. Thus only unpredictable noises disrupted performance, and performance of mental tasks was disrupted only if the subject was busy trying to do two tasks simultaneously.

Glass and Singer also demonstrated that behavioral aftereffects may occur in subjects who have been exposed to noise. When the subject had completed some addition and number and work comparison tests in predictably noisy, unpredictably noisy, or no-noise conditions, the experimenter reentered the room and announced that the first phase of the experiment was over. Two additional tasks followed in the second phase, during which no noises were introduced. The first task was a series of four line-drawing puzzles, two of them soluble and two insoluble. The number of times a subject attempted to solve the nonsoluble puzzles was used as a measure of his tolerance for frustration in the postnoise period. Quality of performance was then tested using a seven-page text containing typographical errors. The number of errors not detected after 15 minutes gave a quality of performance index.

Unpredictable noise exposure clearly reduced the subjects' tolerance for frustration in the postnoise period. For both loud and soft unpredictable noises, fewer attempts were made on the unsoluble puzzles relative to subjects exposed to no noise. Quality of performance also deteriorated markedly on the proofreading task. Again the physical intensity of the noise was not important; only the predictability or nonpredictability of the noise made a difference in the postnoise period.[25]

Several laboratory experiments have measured the effects of noise exposures on mental and vigilance tasks. Performance was found to be worse if the subject could not predict the occurrence or stoppage of noises. People may adapt even to unpredictable noise if they learn that the noise has no meaning to them, as Azrin has shown. Performance decrements are likely to occur only if the subject is greatly challenged by the task he is performing. Behavioral aftereffects may follow noise exposure. Glass and Singer showed that people are less tolerant of frustrating tasks and make more errors after exposure to unpredictable noises.

The relevance of these experimental studies to the world outside the psychological laboratory is questionable. Many laboratory experimenters use nonsensical noises or "white" noises, noises with no meaning to the subject and with an equal physical intensity in several frequency bands. Real-world noises may be sufficiently unlike these laboratory noises to have different effects on behavior. Real-world noises are more complex auditory experiences and usually have a message or meaning for the hearer that can affect his response. Second, the tasks subjects have been asked to perform, and the conditions of performance, often bear little or no relationship to ordinary life situations. One's performance on a vigilance task when sitting in a dark booth with extraordinary noises blasting from behind may not relate to performance on a similar task in an actual work situation—for example, a boilerman in an industrial plant. Even though actual industrial noises are unpredictable in occurrence, the boilerman would know the meaning of the noises and therefore might not be disturbed by them. Tracking a line on an oscilloscope screen while repeating numbers heard on a loudspeaker does not closely resemble the process of driving a car, despite the use of a steering wheel in both cases. "Real" noises and "real" tasks would lend credibility to experimental results.

Overview of the Impact of Noise.   People living in noisy residential areas are clearly annoyed by aircraft, vehicles, neighbors, and other noise sources. Noise is a significant irritant in neighborhoods exposed to severe noise levels from jet aircraft. Noises from traffic, factories, and neighbors are less likely to be extremely irritating. The physical intensity of such noises (decibel rating) is unlikely to be as high as that of an aircraft passing directly overhead on its final approach to the runway. However noise annoyance is less reliably related to noise intensity than to the individual's tolerance for noise. Less intense traffic noises and noises from neighbors are important irritants to some people. If the noise level in a community is suddenly increased, a rash of complaints and behavioral alterations is likely to ensue. However long-term exposures to noise may have effects quite different from short-term exposures, and behavioral effects of long-term exposures are more difficult to demonstrate empirically.

Very loud noises from any source in the community can disrupt activities. TV watching during "prime time" evening viewing hours is often disturbed in noisy areas. Telephoning and conversation may also be affected. Sleep may be disrupted. The full costs of these seemingly minor annoyances and disruptions in terms of irritability toward family members, tenseness, headaches, insomnia, job performance, and so on, is not known. Large-scale community surveys cannot provide the detailed observations of people that are needed to answer questions of this nature. Naturalistic studies are called for, perhaps initially in institutional settings, where there is an opportunity for direct observation and the requisite observational and analytical technology already exist.

The control and predictability of noise timing have important effects on a person's responses. Unpredictable noises have greater detrimental effects on performance than do predictable ones. Annoyance in residential areas near airports is closely linked to and reinforced by the residents' perceptions of their inability to change the decisions of the authorities responsible for the airport's location and traffic patterns. Sounds that one controls in one's home (e.g., one's own stereo) are not considered noise, but a sound from a neighbor (the same record played equally loudly) is considered noise. Individual differences in reactions to the "same" noise must also be taken into account. Variables such as socioeconomic status, hearing ability, and level of arousal and anxiety or tension have been related to people's reactions to noise.

The relationship between expressed annoyance and more overt behavioral reactions to noise exposure is unclear. Glass and Singer note that annoyance seems to be a function of the physical intensity of noise, whereas performance decrements are related to predictability but not to intensity. Laboratory studies have found behavior changes associated with noises that were clearly annoying. One field study found behavior changes following the sudden introduction of traffic noise on a previously quiet university campus. But community noise surveys in very noisy neighborhoods near heavily traveled streets and airports have revealed little or no evidence of behavioral reactions. People adapt or endure; they complain, but do not move out, become neurotic, go to the authorities, or sabotage the aircraft with sufficient frequency that such behavior is noted in community surveys. The experimental field study reviewed previously indicates that a clearer picture of the annoyance-behavior relationship could be obtained by closer observation of noisy residential areas. A particularly interesting study would involve careful observation over a period of time following a sudden increase in noise level due to a drastic environmental change. Adaptation effects could be closely followed and the annoyance-behavior relationship monitored over time.

Adaptation to noise is a major problem underlying community surveys of reactions to noise. Both laboratory and community studies indicate that in most situations most people can adapt to noise and perform their usual tasks quite satisfactorily. The full extent of the psychic cost of this adaptation is unknown. A tentative list compiled by the EPA of psychosomatic complaints possibly resulting from noise exposure includes headaches, irritability, insomnia, reduction in sexual drive, and loss of appetite. These general health effects may be the real cost of adaptation at more overt levels, underscoring the importance of further work on noise effects. For example, exposure to noise may have adverse aftereffects even when no immediate performance effects are revealed. Frankenhaeuser and Lundberg learned that feelings of discomfort and annoyance declined soon after noise exposure stopped, whereas endocrine arousal continued to rise during the subsequent period.[26] These findings further emphasize the risk of underestimating the harmful consequences of noise.

Finally, noise may have positive effects even though it is subjectively annoying. Screeching brakes warn drivers of emergency situations. Bursts of sound can keep people in a state of awareness much longer than they would remain alert in a quiet environment. High environmental noise levels may even be helpful in the treatment of hospitalized schizophrenic patients. Ozerengin and Cowen[27] placed 15 withdrawn and 15 active schizophrenic patients into a quiet (40–60 dB noise level) and into a noisy environment (80–90 dB noise level).

The active schizophrenic patients showed greater conceptual disorganization, more anxiety and restlessness, and poorer performance in the noisy than in the quiet environment. Their need for medication sharply increased. The withdrawn patients, on the other hand, showed better motor and verbal performance, greater perceptual organization, and more regular sleep patterns in the noisy than in the quiet environment. Their need for medication decreased. Clearly further work on the effects of noise must consider possible adaptive as well as maladaptive effects.

Air Pollution, Behavior, and Health.   The problem of air pollution has recently become a topic of grave public concern. Although noise may have beneficial effects under certain circumstances—alerting and arousing drivers, warning workers of dangers, and masking undesirable sounds emanating from the next-door apartment—no one argues that air pollution is beneficial, aesthetically pleasing, or otherwise of socially redeeming value. Air pollution is associated with chronic bronchitis in British cities, nose and eye irritation in Los Angeles, and lung cancer in many metropolitan areas.[28]

The particulates, gases, and liquid droplets that make up air pollution are often divided into primary and secondary classes. Primary pollutants are emitted directly from identifiable sources. Among the common primary pollutants are carbon monoxide, sulfur dioxide, nitrogen dioxide, particulates, and hydrocarbons. These pollutants usually have two daily peaks, one at about 7 a.m. and the other about 8 p.m. In many areas there is a yearly peak during the winter months, when increased space heating releases more combustion by-products into the air. Secondary pollutants are the products of reactions between two or more primary pollutants and other components of the atmosphere. Photochemical pollutants (e.g., the Los Angeles type of smog) are the most common secondary pollutants, typically reaching a daily peak in the early afternoon. An annual peak of pollution levels is usually reached in late summer or autumn, when high temperatures combine with atmospheric stagnation to result in frequent temperature inversions. A cold air mass lying on top of warmer air near the ground prevents the pollutants released at ground level from dispersing. Cities in valleys surrounded by mountains are prone to inversions, particularly if there are no prevailing winds or frequent and large temperature changes to break up the inversion.[29]

The primary pollutant carbon monoxide is the most common air pollutant. Although high concentrations of carbon monoxide are toxic, the gas is colorless, odorless, and tasteless, thus giving no clue to its presence. Performance may be impaired before poisoning symptoms become present. Most of the carbon monoxide in the atmosphere results from incomplete combustion of carbonaceous materials. There are 76 million tons of carbon monoxide emitted in the United States each year from transportation sources. Forest fires may contribute another 7 million tons yearly.[30]

Measurements of the actual carbon monoxide concentrations in community air spaces usually show concentrations lower than 100 parts per million (ppm). A 100-ppm concentration means that 0.01% of the air is carbon monoxide. Average carbon monoxide concentrations on the Los Angeles freeways are about 34 ppm, but peak levels of up to 120 ppm have been observed during rush hour periods.[31] Underground parking garages in Paris had concentrations of about 75 ppm carbon monoxide.[32] Downtown, shopping, and residential areas in Detroit usually have concentrations lower than 10 ppm.[33]

Carbon monoxide's toxic effects are due to its interference with the delivery of oxygen to the tissues, especially the brain, heart, and lungs.[34] Normally the hemoglobin in the blood picks up oxygen in the lungs and carries it as oxyhemoglobin to the tissues. However hemoglobin has a higher affinity for carbon monoxide than for oxygen and will pick up carbon monoxide first if there is relatively more carbon monoxide in the inhaled air than in the blood. The carbon monoxide reacts with hemoglobin to form carboxyhemoglobin. In addition to directly reducing the amount of oxyhemoglobin in the bloodstream, the presence of substantial amounts of carboxyhemoglobin increases the tenacity of hemoglobin for oxygen in the oxyhemoglobin molecule at the tissues, thus making even less oxygen available to the tissues.

Carboxyhemoglobin does not have this toxic effect at the tissues at the levels people reach under normal community conditions. Lengthy exposures to carbon monoxide at concentrations greater than 100 ppm are usually necessary; such concentrations do not occur normally in well-ventilated air spaces. However performance decrements may occur for shorter exposures to lower concentrations of carbon monoxide (under 100 ppm). We survey the performance literature below. Studies of the toxic effects of carbon monoxide are reviewed elsewhere.[35]

Task Performance During Carbon Monoxide Exposure.   A variety of laboratory experiments have been made in which subjects are required to perform calculations, monitor light panels, or respond to signals while they are being exposed unknowingly to carbon monoxide. Schulte exposed firemen to carbon monoxide at 100 ppm. During each of four experimental cycles the subjects breathed either air or the carbon monoxide–air mixture through a gas mask while working on a battery of tests. Four cycles of testing were completed consecutively by each subject, carbon monoxide exposure being varied systematically from cycle to cycle. Blood samples were taken during each of the four cycles, and test results were then related to carboxyhemoglobin levels. Significant correlations were found on several tests, indicating that as carboxyhemoglobin levels increased, more errors were made on tests of arithmetic, t-crossing, and color and letter responses, and more time was required to complete letter and color responses, noun underlining, arithmetic, and t-crossing tests. No physiological changes other than increased carboxyhemoglobin were detected, and no subjective symptoms attributable to carbon monoxide were reported except by one subject who said he had a headache.

Schulte concludes that many people who must make rapid and correct decisions and responses in their work situation (e.g., astronauts, pilots, and train engineers), could be adversely affected even by the relatively low levels of carbon monoxide typically found in such settings.[36]

Beard and Wertheim used a specially constructed environmental chamber to expose subjects to carbon monoxide without using a gas mask. Sound stimuli at 1000 Hz were presented to subjects in pairs. The first sound always lasted one second; the other could last from 0.675 to 1.325 seconds. Subjects judged whether they thought the second sound was longer, shorter, or of the same duration as the first, but they received no indication of the correctness of their responses. During a 4-hour session, 600 sound pairs were presented. Each of 18 subjects participated in a minimum of 15 testing sessions during which the carbon monoxide level might have been at 0, 50, 100, 175, or 250 ppm. Response accuracy fell even for small doses of carbon monoxide and deteriorated by 50% at 250 ppm relative to 0 ppm. Performance deteriorated drastically within the first 90 minutes of exposure at 50 ppm, and within 20 minutes at 250 ppm.[37]

Beard and Grandstaff found an additional effect of 250 ppm carbon monoxide on an experimental task using a visual light display. Subjects were supposed to learn the correct sequence of 15 different symbols displayed on a screen. A subject touched a symbol with a light pen, whereupon the computer-controlled machine indicated whether the choice was correct. After the subject had learned the complete sequence of 15 symbols while breathing either pure air or air with 250 ppm carbon monoxide, he was required to repeat the sequence twice without any feedback from the computer. The number of errors on the last two repetitions of the sequence was nearly doubled, and subjects took more time to learn the correct sequence of symbols, when breathing carbon monoxide at 250 ppm.[38]

Another study indicated that vigilance may be impaired at the relatively low levels of carbon monoxide commonly found in urban freeway driving. Subjects seated in an air-conditioned chamber breathed air with carbon monoxide at 0, 26, or 111 ppm. The higher levels of carbon monoxide were chosen to represent the average and peak levels found on Los Angeles freeways. The subjects monitored a light that went on for a second every 3 seconds. The intensity of the light varied between a constant nonsignal level and a brighter signal level. Subjects indicated detection of a signal by pressing a button. When the subjects breathed 111 ppm carbon monoxide, fewer signals were detected.[39] Other investigators have found that carbon monoxide raises the visual threshold, the intensity of the dimmest light signal that a subject can detect.[40]

Hackney and his colleagues exposed adult male volunteers to purified air or to ozone, alone or in combination with nitrogen dioxide and carbon monoxide in a simulation of the conditions of a smoggy southern California summer.[41] The ozone exposures produced symptoms sufficient to restrict normal activity. Subjects with histories of cough, chest discomfort, or wheezing were more reactive than subjects without such backgrounds. The addition of carbon monoxide produced small variable decrements in psychomotor performance. The authors concluded that exposures to photochemical oxidants at concentrations sometimes achieved in California urban areas may render sensitive subjects unable to carry on normal activities.

Poorer performance on mental tests, learning tasks, time judgments, and signal detection tests have been associated with increasing concentrations of carbon monoxide. It is particularly significant that connections have been found between concentrations typical of freeway driving and impaired signal detection and time judgment. Both abilities are obviously crucial to driving, and if the laboratory findings generalize to actual driving experiences, one would expect driving performance to be adversely affected.

Automobile Driving.   Several analyses of driving performance at various carbon monoxide levels have been completed. This work was motivated by studies that sampled the carbon monoxide levels of air on various streets in Paris and Los Angeles and related the carbon monoxide levels to the resultant carboxyhemoglobin levels in the blood of pedestrians, drivers, traffic policemen, garage attendants, and other persons often exposed to automobile exhaust. Carboxyhemoglobin levels were not high enough to endanger the health of the populations examined, but the levels found did indicate that drivers' reaction times could have been increased, thereby contributing to accidents. Chovin reported that drivers involved in accidents in Paris had somewhat higher carboxyhemoglobin levels than workers with occupational exposures or urban residents tested at their homes.[42]

Clayton et al. investigated the occupations of persons involved in traffic accidents in Detroit during three months of 1957. They found no relationship between occupational exposure to carbon monoxide and involvement in auto accidents. Blood samples were also obtained from accident victims admitted to hospitals. Carboxyhemoglobin levels were almost all below 10%, which would probably not impair the driving ability of healthy drivers.[43]

Ramsey recruited 30 male university students with automobiles and 30 older hypoxic males as experimental subjects for a study of reaction times following a 90-minute exposure to driving in commuting traffic. Thirty nondriving male university students and 30 older but healthy males were recruited to serve as control subjects. Medical diagnoses indicated that hypoxia, or insufficient oxygenation of the blood, was probably a chronic condition for the hypoxic older males. These men had a slightly lower volume percentage of oxygen in their blood than did the other subjects, including the older, nonhypoxic controls.

Blood samples were taken from the younger controls and from all the experimental subjects, and reaction times were measured on a visual stimulus test. The experimental subjects then went for a 90-minute drive during afternoon rush hour traffic, using a prescribed route, while the control subjects remained behind on campus. When the experimental subjects had returned to the campus, additional blood samples were collected from all subjects and reaction times were again measured. Carbon monoxide levels during the driving averaged 38 ppm. Twenty-seven of the 30 older hypoxic drivers had slower reaction times after the drive, as did 27 of the 30 normal drivers. But the increase in reaction time was greater for the hypoxic than the normal drivers. The nondriving student control group slightly reduced their reaction time during the 90 minutes they spent on campus.[44] Thus 90 minutes of driving in congested traffic while breathing polluted air may not importantly affect young healthy drivers, but the possibility exists that older drivers with hypoxia may be affected by carbon monoxide, by driving in congested traffic, or by the combination of both noxious experiences. If the control drivers had been exposed to the stresses of driving without breathing any carbon monoxide, perhaps by using driving simulators or oxygen tanks in the cars, one could be more confident that the increased reaction times were due to carbon monoxide exposure.

Ury developed a method of comparing automobile accidents and air pollution levels when factors vary simultaneously because of a third variable. Most people work Monday through Friday, from 8 a.m. to 5 p.m., and pollution from transportation and industrial sources thus will have daily and weekly patterns resulting from this institutional arrangement. More accidents may occur during peak traffic periods as people go to and from work. Thus pollution and accident data coded by day of occurrence should show a high correlation, not because they are causally related but because both are partially due to traffic flow rates. Ury's method tests for an association between pollution levels and accident rates that might exist independently of the time pattern both follow by day and week and thus might be attributable to pollution.

Accident and pollution data were recorded to the hour for four years of data. Each datum was compared to the datum for the same hour one week earlier. If both the accident datum and the pollution datum had changed in the same direction relative to one week earlier, a score of + was given. If the two data had changed in opposite directions (e.g., pollution increased but accidents decreased), a score of − was given. If neither had changed, a score of 0 was given. The +'s, −'s and 0's were then summed for all successive pairs of weeks and compared to what would be expected, given random probability estimates. The results indicated that oxidants were related to accidents; that is, when oxidant levels increased from one week to the next, accidents also increased, and when oxidants decreased, accidents also decreased. However carbon monoxide level was not consistently related to accidents.[45]

One cannot state with confidence that air pollution is related to highway accidents. The possibility certainly exists that signal detection (e.g., seeing tail lights and stop lights), may be impaired after exposure to carbon monoxide and that reaction times may be increased. Both these changes should result in more automobile accidents. The extent to which these effects are associated with carbon monoxide, rather than with the stresses of driving in congested traffic, remains to be tested. In addition, no one has compared nonaccident drivers to drivers involved in accidents, nor drivers just involved in an accident to another period when they drove without accidents. Individual differences in susceptibility to the deleterious performance and reaction time effects of carbon monoxide need to be investigated.

Air Pollution and Health.   The health effects of air pollution have been dramatically emphasized by acute pollution episodes in the twentieth century. The first of these was in the Meuse Valley of Belgium in 1930. During December of that year an inversion trapped pollutants from coke ovens, blast furnaces, steel mills, glass factories, zinc smelters, and sulfuric acid plants in the valley for an entire week. Many people became ill with chest pain, cough, shortness of breath, and eye and nasal irritation. Sixty persons had died by the end of the week; older persons with preexisting heart and lung diseases had the highest mortality rates. Sulfuric acid mist was the most probable killer, although no pollutant measurements were made.

Subsequent pollution disasters have occurred in Donora, Pennsylvania (October 1948, 20 deaths, sulfur dioxide emitted from a variety of industrial plants), Poza Rica, Mexico (November 1950, hydrogen sulfide leak from a natural gas plant, 22 killed), London (December 1952, 3500 excess deaths due to sulfur dioxide), and Osaka, Japan (December 1962, 60 excess deaths from a variety of pollutants). These episodes were precipitated by a temperature inversion that trapped industrial emissions near the ground and caused pollutant concentrations in the air to rise to lethal levels. Sulfuric acid mist appears to be the most common of these lethal pollutants. Inversions are particularly likely to occur in the winter months in the Northern hemisphere. A broad section of the population shows some signs of respiratory tract illnesses, and the old and/or already ill are in danger of dying during the pollution episode.[46]

At such extreme concentrations air pollutants such as sulfur oxide, hydrogen sulfide, and carbon monoxide clearly have deleterious health effects. In many urban areas people are chronically exposed to lower levels of air pollutants. For example, studies on the effects of carbon monoxide in cigarette smoke indicate that heart rate, blood pressure, and reaction times may be negatively affected in both smokers and nonsmokers.[47]

Physicians and psychiatrists have been confronted with patients suffering from a variety of gastrointestinal and respiratory complaints accompanied by headaches and back pains. Some doctors have called these symptoms air pollution syndrome (APS). LaVerne performed an experiment with 100 patients who complained of headache, fatigue, irritability, lassitude, insomnia, burning of the eyes, depression, impaired judgment, and difficulty in concentration. Half the patients breathed compressed pure air during their sleeping hours, the other half breathed compressed polluted air. Of those breathing pure air, 72% showed some improvement during the next 12–24 hours but the patients breathing polluted air showed no improvement. Thus LaVerne concludes that the second group of patients were suffering from a symptom complex he labels nonspecific air pollution syndrome.[48]

Hart distinguishes two distinct symptom complexes found in geographically separated areas: APS-α was found in patients seen in New York and consists of backache, chest pains when breathing, neck pain, and gastrointestinal upsets; APS-β was found in Charleston, North Carolina, and is characterized by a greater degree of abdominal discomfort, whereas chest and neck pains are less evident. Hart feels that differences in these syndromes may be due to the particular combinations of air pollutants found in each area.[49]

The strength of the association of these syndromes with air pollution is debatable; other features of urban life may well be involved. LaVerne's patients breathing pure or polluted compressed air provide the only evidence that air pollution is specifically involved in the variety of complaints described, and strictly speaking, his results show only that breathing pure air cures the problem, not that pollution causes it.

Several epidemiological studies have attempted to discover a connection between air pollution and respiratory complaints. Sterling et al.

related the frequency of hospital admission and length of stay in the hospital to air pollution conditions for a sample of Blue Cross insured patients admitted to large hospitals in the Los Angeles Basin. They calculated the difference between the expected and actual number of admissions on each day of the week and compared this number to a similar index of air pollution. Diseases were grouped into categories of diseases likely to be affected by pollution (allergies, eye and upper respiratory infections, and cardiovascular diseases) and diseases not likely to be affected. The most-likely-to-be-affected disease categories were rather highly related to all pollutant measures (i.e., there were more admissions than expected in these disease categories on days of worse-than-expected pollution). There were fewer admissions than expected on higher-than-expected pollution days for the categories not likely to be affected by pollution. If a number of pollution-related cases come in on a polluted day, the admission of other types of patients presumably had to be delayed.[50]

Japan is a very densely populated country, and its inhabitants suffer from a great deal of air pollution emitted by industries and automobiles. Toyama found that dustfall during 1956–1959 in Tokyo was correlated with bronchitis deaths but not with deaths from pneumonia or cardiovascular diseases. Morbidity surveys in Japan showed higher rates of respiratory disease for polluted urban areas than for rural areas with cleaner air. Physiological examinations were conducted at a school having urban, polluted air and at a rural school with much cleaner air, both near Kawasaki. The children attending the "polluted" school had less lung capacity on the average and more often complained of cough and mucous membrane irritation and secretion. The variety of effects detected all support the hypothesis that air pollution in Japan has deleterious effects on the respiratory functioning of Japanese citizens.[51] Using the records of a national health insurance system for self-employed persons and employees of small businesses, Yoshida et al. showed that common cold, bronchial asthma, and upper respiratory inflammations had a higher incidence in districts more highly polluted by dust and sulfur dioxide. Persons over 40 years of age were especially afflicted.[52]

Acute pollution crises can kill, and periodic pollution episodes have been associated with increased morbidity and mortality. The more serious health effects are found usually among the old and/or already ill. Long-term occupational exposure to dusts or gases may have permanent deleterious effects. There remains the possibility that ordinary, healthy people may be affected by "normal" air pollution. People who are exposed to the normal range and incidence of air pollution found in modern cities and who are not chronically or unusually sick have been analyzed in two detailed series of studies.

Nashville Air Pollution Study. The Nashville Air Pollution Study was conducted in the Nashville, Tennessee, area, which has a chronic but rather moderate air pollution problem distinctly different from that of Los Angeles. Automobile pollution is of minor importance in Nashville compared to the by-products of coal combustion. Coal is extensively used in the area for home and industrial heating. Various compounds of sulfur and dust are the most irritating pollutants resulting from the widespread use of coal.

Zeidberg and his colleagues found that patients with chronic bronchial asthma suffered more attacks when sulfur dioxide levels were high. They collected morbidity data by interview from a sample of 3000 Nashville residents over a 3-month period in 1959. Pollution data were obtained from pollution monitoring stations set up in the same neighborhoods. Total morbidity of middle-income persons over 55 years of age went up significantly as dust and sulfur dioxide pollution rose. White housewives and both housekeeping and employed nonwhite females had higher morbidity rates during high pollution periods.[53] Other studies in this series related infant mortality and total mortality from respiratory disease, cardiovascular disease, and cancer to air pollution.[54]

Whereas most air pollution studies have concentrated on pollution from automobiles and combustion of relatively "clean" heating fuels such as natural gas and oil, the Nashville study indicates that a wide variety of health effects are related to sulfur and dust pollution. As this country depletes its oil reserves, it is likely to use its abundant supplies of sulfur-rich coal to a much greater extent. Work on the health effects of coal combustion is therefore of great importance. The Nashville study currently furnishes the best available evidence on the health effects of extensive combustion of coal.

Cornell Family Illness Study. The Cornell Family Illness Study (CFIS) monitored the weather and air pollution of a New York City neighborhood and simultaneously monitored the health of a sample of the area's population, on a daily basis for several years. The area selected, on the Lower East Side of Manhattan near the East River, included an old, somewhat rundown tenement slum area, a low-income, modern public housing project, and a middle-income, privately owned housing project. The housing projects were comparable in terms of age, condition and appearance of the buildings, and size of the individual apartments. White, black, and Puerto Rican families were included in the sample, which totaled nearly 1800 persons. Participation entailed devoting up to one hour per week per family to answering an interviewer's questions about the health of the family during the previous 7 days; blood samples and throat cultures were collected from each family member twice a year.[55]

An attempt was made to follow each family for a minimum of 1 year and for up to 3 years if the family agreed to participate. The average length of participation was 45 weeks.[56]

Cassell and his colleagues reported no remarkable health symptom changes in the entire CFIS sample during two acute pollution episodes. They speculated that only a small group of sensitive individuals may react to pollution and that the effects on these individuals could not be detected by graphs of total symptom incidence.[57] In another study the incidence of common cold in the sample was related to weather and pollution. There was some relationship between colds and low temperature and humidity (low humidity in winter and high humidity in summer) but none with air pollution variables.[58] In a third study no relationship was found between pollution levels and headache and eye irritation, with one exception. Heavy cigarette smokers reported headaches more often on days of high atmospheric carbon monoxide. Cold and cough were more prevalent symptoms during the winter, when particulate matter and carbon monoxide concentrations were higher.[59]

The CFIS team identified five patterns of association or interaction of environmental and illness variables over time. The first consisted of high air pollution associated with common cold symptoms. The second represented the period when air pollution is just beginning to build up; few health symptoms were reported. The third associated inclement winter weather with colds, sore throat, and cough. The fourth associated automobile pollutants and little wind with headaches and eye and throat irritation. The fifth pattern was typified by warm, sunny, nonpolluted days and general good health.[60]

Thus different commonly occurring combinations of weather and pollution variables affect health differentially. Two distinct environmental conditions are associated with cold and sore throat. Eye and throat irritations plus headaches are associated with a third weather-pollution configuration. Good health is found on days when the air is clear and the weather pleasant and on days when pollution levels are just beginning to build up. Not all people react to these weather-pollution patterns in the same way, but on the average enough people react in the noted ways to justify associating the health variables and the environmental patterns. The study also makes an important contribution by putting pollution into a meteorological context. Pollution can not build up without certain weather conditions (i.e., little wind, temperature inversion, or cold spell leading to pollution from heating sources).

The Cornell Family Illness Study is a unique research effort that monitored the health symptoms of a group of typical New York City residents for a period of several years. Among the many findings, some are especially interesting. A few residents in the sample were chronically ill; these persons reported various illness symptoms nearly every time they were interviewed. Most people were healthy most of the time. A small subsample of the normally healthy individuals seemed to be slightly more sensitive to air pollution than the rest of the sample. These sensitive individuals became acutely ill after or during severe air pollution with somewhat greater regularity than the rest of the sample, and they remained ill a little longer.[61] The other normally healthy individuals sometimes became ill during or after significant air pollution and sometimes remained healthy. Air pollution thus may be a contributing factor in colds, coughs, headaches, eye and throat irritation, and other minor ailments, but other factors are obviously involved. Colds and coughs are associated with inclement weather in the winter, with particulate pollution, and with an environmental pattern of temperature inversion and general air pollution buildup. Eye and throat irritation with headaches occurred in periods of little wind and extensive hydrocarbon pollution. Very good weather with no pollution and deteriorating, pollution-building periods were associated with few health complaints.

An important finding in all these studies is that different people react to pollution differently, and a given person's reaction may vary over time. Thus a simple comparison of illness rates with pollutant concentrations in the air is unlikely to yield interesting results unless the pollution is very severe, even critical. More sensitive analytic methods such as multiple correlation and factor analysis may help to clarify the associations that exist between air pollution and health. The nature and role of stressful life events, waves of infection, institutional arrangements, seasonal variation in susceptibility, and activity patterns need to be analyzed to gain an understanding of the "some of the people some of the time" characteristic of air pollution-health associations.

Cardiovascular Diseases.   The epidemiological studies have generally concentrated on maladies such as asthma, common cold, and other upper respiratory diseases. A smaller body of work has considered the effects of pollutants on cardiovascular diseases. The presence of significant amounts of carbon monoxide in the air raises the carboxyhemoglobin content of a person's blood, thus reducing the oxyhemoglobin available at the tissues. The significance of these blood content alterations for patients with heart diseases has been explored in both experimental and epidemiological studies.

Carbon monoxide in the air may reduce the chances of survival for a person who has just suffered a myocardial infarction. Cohen et al. compared carbon monoxide levels measured by Los Angeles County to the case fatality rates among 3080 admissions for cardiac problems. Cases from hospitals with relatively high carbon monoxide concentrations in the surrounding air were compared against cases in hospitals in lower carbon monoxide areas. During a one-week period, the fatality rate for patients admitted to hospitals in high carbon monoxide areas was 27.3 deaths per 100 admissions, whereas for patients admitted to low carbon monoxide area hospitals the rate was 19.1 deaths per 100 admissions. Within the high carbon monoxide area, more patients died during higher carbon monoxide periods.[62] Other pollutants, hospital procedures, or patient characteristics may have varied within the high and low carbon monoxide areas, but carbon monoxide cannot be ruled out as an important explanatory factor. Alternative explanations of the findings are also possible. For example, the high carbon monoxide areas may have had more traffic. An ambulance would then take longer to reach the hospital, thereby reducing the cardiac patient's chances of survival.

Angina pectoris is a heart condition characterized by spasms of chest pain and feelings of suffocation, usually due to anemia of the heart muscle. Hence angina pectoris is particularly likely to be influenced by carbon monoxide concentrations, since elevated carboxyhemoglobin can produce a condition resembling anemia. Ambient carbon monoxide levels in urban areas normally are not high enough to seriously affect angina pectoris symptoms, but persons riding in automobiles on urban freeways may experience dangerously high levels. Aronow and his colleagues took 10 patients with angina pectoris for 90 minute rides in heavy morning traffic on the infamous freeways of Los Angeles. On a subsequent morning the patients took the freeway excursion again but breathed pure compressed air during the ride. Carbon monoxide in expired air and carboxyhemoglobin in the blood of these patients were higher after the freeway trip during which they breathed freeway air. Patients exercising on a bicycle exercise machine were able to exercise for less time before angina was noted after breathing the freeway air. This change in exercise ability was not found when the patients breathed compressed pure air during the freeway trip.[63]

These findings were reinforced by another study of patients with angina pectoris. Pure air or air with 50 or 100 ppm carbon monoxide was administered by face mask to 10 adult male patients for 4 hours on five successive days. Pure air was given on 2 days and air with carbon monoxide in one of the two concentrations on 3 days. Neither the patients nor the technician administering the gas knew which substance was being used. Treadmill exercise tests followed, with the time until onset of angina and the duration of the pain after onset and cessation of exercise recorded. As in the case of single exposure to freeway air, exposure to carbon monoxide shortened the length of time during which exercise could proceed painlessly. After onset of pain and cessation of exercise, the duration of the pain was longer after exposure to one of the carbon monoxide concentrations.[64] The carbon monoxide levels used in this study were comparable to those experienced in expressway and freeway driving in urban areas.

Overview of Pollution Studies.   Annoyance or irritation responses to air pollution have not been widely studied. Carbon monoxide, administered by gas masks or in specially constructed chambers, has been associated with impaired signal detection and increased reaction time. These changes may affect one's ability to safely and efficiently operate an automobile. However the studies on automobile driving and carbon monoxide are far from definitive. In experimental studies of human performance, it is difficult to be sure that only the effect one has set out to measure is in fact being measured. Vigilance (the ability to detect signal changes over a long period of time) may become confused with visual threshold (the dimmest increase of light intensity that can be detected) because a very bright light cannot be used in a vigilance study. The complexities of studying human performance may be one reason for investigators' failure to find more than a few performance effects of pollution.

The health effects of air pollution appear to be quite broad. Very severe air pollution crises can kill, as we know from the Donora episode. Sulfur dioxide and sulfuric acid mists have been involved in several of these lethal air pollution incidents. Moderately high air pollution is associated with higher morbidity in respiratory disease categories and with higher than expected hospital admissions for patients with respiratory and cardiovascular problems. Bronchitis and asthma have been associated with sulfur dioxide and particulate pollution both in this country and in Japan. Respiratory, cardiovascular, cancer, and total infant mortality was higher in Nashville during periods of high pollution by coal combustion by-products. In New York colds and coughs have been associated with two distinct weather-pollution patterns, and headaches and eye and throat irritation have been associated with a third weather-pollution pattern. Finally, a variety of psychosomatic symptoms have been associated with air pollution in two urban areas.

The identity of the pollutant or combination of pollutants implicated in health and performance studies is often unclear. Pollutants occur in complex combinations in the air we breathe. The one pollutant measure that correlates most highly with the effect being studied may not necessarily be causally linked. Pollutants may have synergistic effects; the effect of a combination of pollutants is not necessarily the same as the sum of the effects of each pollutant by itself.

It is important to note that pollution can build to significant levels only in certain kinds of weather. A temperature inversion or lack of wind is usually necessary, and high daytime temperatures often accompany both conditions. Some of the explanation of performance and psychosomatic and other health effects of pollution may be in the weather prevailing at the time. High temperature has been linked to excess mortality, for example (see Chapter 3), and if high temperature and pollution occur simultaneously, either one, or both together, may be responsible for the observed health effects. The use of weather-pollution patterns as dependent variables in the epidemiological literature makes the point that the two are linked but does not separate out the effects of each by itself, if indeed each has effects by itself. To make matters more complex, some pollutants may play a role in producing modifications in the weather.[65]

A recent study of 29,000 blood donors living in various communities across the United States indicated that exposure to carbon monoxide in excess of that permitted by the Clean Air Quality Standards was regular and widespread.[66] Compliance with the standards presumably prevents blood carboxyhemoglobin (COHb) of more than 1.5% saturation in active nonsmokers. However a shocking 75% of the nonsmokers in Denver and Los Angeles had COHb saturation greater than 1.5%. The COHb saturations of taxicab drivers and of people working in airport terminals were especially high, presumably because of jet engine production of carbon monoxide and heavy automobile exhaust.

Tobacco smoking was consistently associated with the highest COHb saturations (up to 9 and 10%). However significant amounts of carbon monoxide are also absorbed by nonsmokers who are exposed to smoke-filled rooms. In one study the amount of carbon monoxide absorbed by nonsmokers was about the same as if they had smoked one cigarette and inhaled. It was similar to the amount a London taxi driver absorbs during one whole day of driving in heavy traffic. Nonsmoking elementary school age children's heart rate and blood pressure may be adversely affected when they "passively smoke" in a poorly ventilated room.[67]

Thus excessive exposure to carbon monoxide is widespread and occurs regularly, even in rural areas. In addition, there may be synergistic effects, as for example in the smoker who breathes polluted urban air. Many other factors may be operating, but the incidence of lung cancer among smokers is higher in urban than in rural areas. These findings indicate that the behavioral and health effects of air pollution may be considerably greater than has thus far been recognized, particularly in susceptible individuals.

REFERENCES

1. Baron, R. A. *The tyranny of noise.* St. Martin's Press, New York, 1970 (quotation from pp. 3–4).
2. *Ibid.,* p. 5.
3. Berland, T. *The fight for quiet.* Prentice-Hall, Englewood Cliffs, N. J., 1970, pp. 3–5.
4. Baron, *op. cit.,* pp. 39–42.
5. Schultz, T. J. *Community noise ratings.* Applied Science Publishers, London, 1972, pp. 30–31.

   Kryter, K. D. *The effects of noise on man.* Academic Press, New York, 1970, p. 279.
6. *Effects of noise on people.* Environmental Protection Agency, Government Printing Office, Washington, D.C., 1971, pp. 6–42.
7. Leggett, R. F. and Northwood, T. D. Noise surveys of cocktail parties. *Journal of the Acoustical Society of America,* **32:**16–18, 1960.
8. Beranek, L. L. Criteria for office quieting based on the questionnaire rating studies. *Journal of the Acoustical Society of America,* **28:**833–852, 1956.
9. Appleyard, D. and Lintell, M. The environmental quality of city streets: The residents' viewpoint. In W. J. Mitchell (Ed.), *Environmental design: Research and practice.* Proceedings of the third Environmental Design Research Association Conference, University of California, Los Angeles, January 1972.
10. McKennell, A. C. and Hunt, E. A. *Noise annoyance in central London.* Building Research Station, London, 1966.
11. *Public health and welfare: Criteria for noise.* Environmental Protection Agency, Government Printing Office, Washington, D.C., 1973, p. 3-1.
12. McKennell and Hunt, *op. cit.*
13. Burrows, A. A. and Zamarin, D. M. Aircraft noise and the community: Some recent survey findings. *Aerospace Medicine,* **43:**27–33, 1972.
14. Bragdon, C. R. *Noise pollution: The unquiet crisis.* University of Pennsylvania Press, Philadelphia, 1970.
15. Gattoni, F. and Tarnopolsky, A. Aircraft noise and psychiatric morbidity. *Psychological Medicine,* **3:**516–520, 1973.

    Aba'ey-Wickrama, I., a'Brook, M., Gattoni, F. and Herridge, C. F. Mental-hospital admissions and aircraft noise. *Lancet,* **2**(7633):1275–1278, 1969.
16. Graeven, D. The effects of airplane noise on health: An examination of three hypotheses. *Journal of Health and Social Behavior,* **15:**336–343, 1974.
17. McKennell and Hunt, *op. cit.,* Ch. VI.

18. Ward, L. M. and Suedfeld, P. Human responses to highway noise. *Environmental Research,* **6:**306–326, 1973.

19. Kryter, K. D. The effects of noise on man. *Journal of Speech and Hearing Disorders Monograph Supplement,* **1:**7–26, 1950, see pp. 8–9.

20. *Ibid.,* p. 10.

21. Broadbent, D. E. Effects of noise on behavior. In C. M. Harris (Ed.), *Handbook of noise control.* McGraw-Hill, New York, 1957.

22. *Ibid.,* pp. 10–24.

23. Woodhead, M. M. The effect of bursts of noise on an arithmetic task. *American Journal of Psychology,* **77:**627–633, 1964.

24. Azrin, N. H. Some effects of noise on human behavior. *Journal of the Experimental Analysis of Behavior,* **1:**183–200, 1958.

25. Glass, D. C. and Singer, J. E. *Urban stress: Experiments on noise and social stressors.* Academic Press, New York, 1972.

26. Frankenhaeuser, M. and Lundberg, V. Immediate and delayed effects of noise on performance and arousal. *Biological Psychiatry,* **2:**127–133, 1974.

27. Ozerengin, M. and Cowen, M. Environmental noise levels as a factor in the treatment of hospitalized schizophrenics. *Diseases of the Nervous System,* **35:**241–243, 1974.

28. Chambers, L. A. Classification and extent of air pollution problems. In A. C. Stern (Ed.), *Air pollution,* 2nd ed. Academic Press, New York, 1968, pp. 1–21.

29. McCormick, R. A. Air pollution climatology. In A. C. Stern (Ed.), *Air pollution,* 2nd ed. Academic Press, New York, 1968, pp. 275–320.

30. Rose, E. F. and Rose, M. Carbon monoxide: A challenge to the physician. *Clinical Medicine,* **78**(8):12–19, 1971.

31. Haagen-Smit, A. J. Carbon monoxide levels in city driving. *Archives of Environmental Health,* **12:**548–551, 1966.

32. Chovin, P. Carbon monoxide: Analysis of exhaust gas investigations in Paris. *Environmental Research,* **1:**198–216, 1967.

33. Clayton, G., Cook, W. A., and Fredrick, W. G. A study of the relationship of street level carbon monoxide concentrations to traffic accidents. *American Industrial Hygiene Association Journal,* **21:**26–54, 1960.

34. Rose and Rose, *op. cit.*

35. Beard, R. R. Toxicological appraisal of carbon monoxide. *Journal of the Air Pollution Control Association,* **19:**722–729, 1969.

36. Schulte, J. H. Effects of mild carbon monoxide intoxication. *Archives of Environmental Health,* **7:**524–530, 1963.

37. Beard, R. R. and Wertheim, G. A. Behavioral impairment associated with small doses of carbon monoxide. *American Journal of Public Health,* **57:**2012–2022, 1967.

38. Beard, R. R. and Grandstaff, N. Behavioral responses to small doses of carbon monoxide. Wright-Patterson Air Force Base, AMRL-TR-102(7):92–105, 1970.

39. Horvath, S. M., Dahms, T. E., and O'Hanlon, J. F. Carbon monoxide and human vigilance: A deleterious effect of present urban concentrations. *Archives of Environmental Health*, **23:**343–347, 1971.

40. Halperin, M. H., McFarland, R. A., Niven, J. I., and Roughton, F. J. W. The time course of the effects of carbon monoxide on visual thresholds. *Journal of Physiology*, **146:**583–593, 1959.

    McFarland, R. A., Roughton, F. J., Halperin, M. H., and Niven, J. I. The effects of monoxide and altitude on visual thresholds. *Journal of Aviation Medicine*, **15:**381–394, 1944.

41. Hackney, J. D. Physiological effects of air pollutants in humans subjected to secondary stress. Final Report, State of California Air Resources Board, Sacramento, 1974.

42. Moureu, H. Carbon monoxide as a test for air pollution in Paris due to motor-vehicle traffic. *Proceedings of the Royal Society of Medicine*, **57:**1015–1020, 1964.

    Chovin, *op. cit.*

43. Clayton et al., *op. cit.*

44. Ramsey, J. M. Oxygen reduction and reaction time in hypoxic and normal drivers. *Archives of Environmental Health*, **20:**579–601, 1970.

45. Ury, H. K. Photochemical air pollution and automobile accidents in Los Angeles: An investigation of oxidant and accidents, 1963 and 1965. *Archives of Environmental Health*, **17:**334–342, 1968.

46. Goldsmith, J. R. Effects of air pollution on human health. In A. C. Stern (Ed.), *Air pollution*, 2nd ed. Academic Press, New York, 1968, pp. 547–615.

47. Ashton, H., Savage, R. D., Telford, R., Thompson, J. W., and Watson, D. W. The effects of cigarette smoking on the response to stress in a driving simulator. *British Journal of Pharmacology*, **45:**546–556, 1972.

    Cameron, P. The presence of pets and smoking as correlates of perceived disease. *Journal of Allergy*, **40:**12–15, 1967.

    Luquette, A. J., Landiss, C. W., and Merki, D. J. Some immediate effects of a smoking environment on children of elementary school age. *Journal of School Health*, **40:**533–536, 1970.

    Russell, M., Cole, P., and Brown, E. Absorption by non-smokers of carbon monoxide from room air polluted by tobacco smoke. *Lancet*, **1**(7803):576–579, 1973.

48. LaVerne, A. A. Nonspecific Air Pollution Syndrome (NAPS): Preliminary report. *Behavioral Neuropsychiatry*, **2**(7–8):19–21, 1970.

49. Hart, R. H. The concept of APS: Air Pollution Syndrome(s). *Journal of the South Carolina Medical Association*, **66**(3):71–73, 1970.

50. Sterling, T. D., Phair, J. J., Pollack, S. V., Schumsky, D. A., and DeGroot, I. Urban morbidity and air pollution. *Archives of Environmental Health*, **13:**158–170, 1966.

51. Toyama, T. Air pollution and its health effects in Japan. *Archives of Environmental Health*, **8:**153–173, 1964.

52. Yoshida, K., Oshima, H., and Imai, M. Air pollution and asthma in Yok-kaichi. *Archives of Environmental Health*, **13:**763–768, 1966.

53. Zeidberg, L. D., Prindle, R. A., and Landau, E. The Nashville Air Pollution Study: I. Sulfur dioxide and bronchial asthma. A preliminary report. *American Review of Respiratory Diseases*, **84:**489–503, 1961.

   Zeidberg, L. D., Prindle, R. A., and Landau, E. The Nashville Air Pollution Study: III. Morbidity in relation to air pollution. *American Journal of Public Health*, **54:**85–97, 1964.

54. Hagstrom, R. M., Sprague, H. A., and Landau, E. The Nashville Air Pollution Study: VII. Mortality from cancer in relation to air pollution. *Archives of Environmental Health*, **15:**237–248, 1967.

   Sprague, H. A. and Hagstrom, R. The Nashville Air Pollution Study: Mortality multiple regression. *Archives of Environmental Health*, **18:**503–597, 1969.

   Zeidberg, L. D., Horton, R. J. M., and Landau, E. The Nashville Air Pollution Study: V. *Archives of Environmental Health*, **15:**214–224, 1967.

   Zeidberg, L. D., Horton, R. J. M., and Landau, E. The Nashville Air Pollution Study: VI. Cardiovascular disease mortality in relation to air pollution. *Archives of Environmental Health*, **15:**225–236, 1967.

55. McCarroll, J. R., Cassell, E. J., Ingram, W., and Wolter, D. Health and the urban environment. Air pollution and family illness: I. Design for study. *Archives of Environmental Health*, **10:**357–363, 1965.

56. Cassell, E. J., Lebowitz, M. D., Mountain, I. M., Lee, H. T., Thompson, D. J., Wolter, D. W., and McCarroll, J. R. Air pollution, weather, and illness in a New York population. *Archives of Environmental Health*, **18:**523–530, 1969.

57. Cassell, E. J., McCarroll, J. R., Ingram, W., and Wolter, D. Health and the urban environment: Air pollution and family illness: III. Two acute air pollution episodes in New York City: Health effects. *Archives of Environmental Health*, **10:**367–369, 1965.

58. Thompson, D. J., Lebowitz, M., Cassell, E. J., Wolter, D., and McCarroll, J. R. Health and the urban environment. VIII: Air pollution, weather, and the common cold. *American Journal of Public Health*, **60:**731–739, 1970.

59. Mountain, I. M., Cassell, E. J., Wolter, D. W., Mountain, J. D., Diamond, J. R., and McCarroll, J. R. Health and the urban environment: VII. Air pollution and disease symptoms in a "normal" population. *Archives of Environmental Health*, **17:**343–352, 1968.

60. Cassell, E. J., Lebowitz, M. D., Mountain, I. M., Lee, H. T., Thompson, D. J., Wolter, D. W., and McCarroll, J. R. Air pollution, weather, and illness in a New York population. *Archives of Environmental Health*, **18:**523–530, 1969.

61. Lebowitz, M. D., Cassell, E. J., and McCarroll, J. R. Health and the urban environment: XV. Acute respiratory episodes as reactions by sensitive individuals to air pollution and weather. *Environmental Research*, **5:**135–141, 1972.

62. Cohen, S. I., Deane, M., and Goldsmith, J. R. Carbon monoxide and survival from myocardial infarction. *Archives of Environmental Health*, **19:**510–517, 1969.

63. Aronow, W. S., Harris, C. N., Isbell, M. W., Rokaw, S. N., and Imparato, B. Effect of freeway travel on angina pectoris. *Annals of Internal Medicine,* **77:**669–676, 1972.

64. Anderson, E. W., Andelman, R. J., Strauch, J. M., Fortuin, N. J., and Knelson, J. H. Effect of low-level carbon monoxide exposure on onset and duration of angina pectoris. *Annals of Internal Medicine,* **79:**46–50, 1973.

65. Hobbs, P. V., Harrison, H., and Robinson, E. Atmospheric effects of pollutants. *Science,* **183:**909–915, 1974.

66. Stewart, R., Baretta, E., Platte, L., Stewart, M. T., Kalbfleisch, J., Van Yserloo, B., and Rimm, A. Carboxyhemoglobin levels in American blood donors. *Journal of the American Medical Association,* **229:**1187–1195, 1974.

67. Luquette, A., Landiss, C., and Merki, D. J. Some immediate effects of a smoking environment on children of elementary school age, *op. cit.*

    Russell, M., Cole, P., and Brown, E., Absorption by non-smokers of carbon monoxide from room air polluted by tobacco smoke, *op. cit.*

PART THREE

Social Environments

CHAPTER SEVEN

Behavior Setting Theory and Research[a]

For more than 20 years Roger Barker and his colleagues at the Midwest Psychological Field Station and the University of Kansas have been studying the ecological psychology of naturally occurring environments. Barker's work represents a major pioneering effort in this field. He and his coworkers have a long history of dealing with theoretical and empirical questions that have only recently captured the interest and imagination of other workers in the behavioral sciences.

The intellectual yield of the Midwest Psychological Field Station has been impressive. Barker's work has had a major impact on the fields of psychology, child development, naturalistic research methods, education, and environmental studies. This chapter reviews theory and research in ecological psychology and attempts to capture the unique perspective on man-environment relations that has guided Barker, his colleagues, and his students.

The *behavior setting* is a central concept in Barker's theory of ecological psychology. We examine the attributes of behavior settings and ask how behavior settings come to exert their influence over the behavior of people who occupy them. Next the question of how to classify behavior settings is discussed. Several advantages of developing a taxonomy of behavior settings are considered, and an empirical classification of set-

---

[a] This chapter is authored by Richard Price.

tings is presented. Barker's theory of undermanning is also set forth, and recent reformulations of that theory are considered.

In reviewing applications of Barker's concepts, methods, and theories in widely different settings, we discover that the theory and method of ecological psychology are appropriate to a broad range of milieus, including the behavior of young children in their homes, the structure and dynamics of a rehabilitation hospital, and the relationship between the personality of college students and the types of settings they choose to enter in the conduct of their everyday lives.

Finally, an important aspect of Barker's contribution to the behavioral sciences is methodological. Barker has been a champion of naturalistic methods of observation in a time when psychology and related disciplines have primarily focused on manipulative experimental paradigms as the primary source of empirical data.

The Behavior Setting.

Attributes of Behavior Settings.   Barker and his colleagues have developed the behavior setting as a basic environmental unit. In a sense, this unit is the "building block" of ecological psychology. Behavior settings are extraindividual. That is, behavior settings refer not to the behavior of particular individuals but to groups of individuals behaving together. When you attend a lecture, go to a baseball game, shop in a grocery store, or go to the dentist, you are participating in a behavior setting.

Let us consider a concrete example in detail. Imagine yourself listening to Roger Barker deliver the Kurt Lewin Memorial Award address in 1963 in Philadelphia.

> It is not often that a lecturer can present to his audience an example of his phenomena, whole and functioning *in situ*—not merely with a demonstration, a description, a preserved specimen, a picture, or a diagram of it. I am in the fortunate position of being able to give you, so to speak, a real behavior setting.
>
> If you will change your attention from me to the next most inclusive, bounded unit, to the assembly of people, behavior episodes, and objects before you, you will see a behavior setting. It has the following structural attributes which you can observe directly:
>
> 1.   It has a space-time locus: 3:00–3:50 p.m., September 2, 1963, Clover Room, Bellevue-Stratford Hotel, Philadelphia, Pennsylvania.
> 2.   It is composed of a variety of interior entities and events: of people, objects (chairs, walls, a microphone, paper), behavior (lecturing, listening, sitting), and other processes (air circulation, sound amplification).

3. Its widely different components form a bounded pattern that is easily discriminated from the pattern on the outside of the boundary.

4. Its component parts are obviously not a random arrangement of independent classes of entities; if they were, how surprising, that all the chairs are in the same position with respect to the podium, that all members of the audience happen to come to rest upon chairs, and that the lights are not helter-skelter from floor to ceiling, for example.

5. The entity before you is a part of a nesting structure; its components (e.g., the chairs and people) have parts; and the setting, itself, is contained within a more comprehensive unit, the Bellevue-Stratford Hotel.

6. This unit is objective in the sense that it exists independently of anyone's perception of it, *qua* unit.[1]

Barker's example makes something clear that is difficult to comprehend by considering only the abstract properties of behavior settings. The behavior setting is a naturally occurring unit, having physical, behavioral, and temporal properties, and it reveals a variety of complex interrelationships among its parts.

Barker has described several essential attributes of behavioral settings. These attributes will help us understand some particular characteristics of behavior settings.

First, behavior settings have one or more *standing patterns of behavior*. These patterns of behavior are not the behavior of individuals, but of people *en masse*. They are the overall behavior patterns that you would observe if you went to a worship service, a band concert, or a baseball game. In the example just offered by Barker during his Lewin Memorial Address, the standing patterns of behavior would include sitting, listening, lecturing, and perhaps note taking. Another important aspect of standing patterns of behavior is that they are not dependent on the particular people in a behavior setting at a particular point in time. That is, if we replaced all the individuals at the baseball game with other individuals to serve as players, spectators, and umpires, the new people would engage in the same behaviors.

A second characteristic of behavior settings is that they involve not just behavior but also a *milieu* that is physical and may include man-made objects such as buildings, streets, or chairs. It may also entail natural features of the environment, such as hills or streams. The milieu exists independently of the standing pattern of behavior in the setting, and it exists independently of anybody's perception of the setting. Thus, for example, the meeting room in Barker's example may still contain chairs and perhaps a podium and tables even when the behavior setting itself is not occurring.

A third characteristic of behavior settings is that *the physical milieu surrounds or encloses the behavior.* The milieu, both in terms of its temporal and physical aspects, surrounds whatever standing patterns of behavior exist in the setting. Thus when Barker refers to the "circumjacent" milieu, he means the walls, ceiling, and other physical aspects of the setting.

A fourth aspect of behavior settings is that the standing patterns of behavior in the setting are *similar in structure* to the milieu. That is, the physical and temporal aspects of the setting and the standing patterns of behavior in the setting are interdependent. We see an example of this similarity when we observe that in Barker's description, chairs face a speaker for listening. Given this characteristic of behavior settings, Barker says that the milieu is "synomorphic" to the behavior.

Some Advantages of the Behavior Setting as an Environmental Unit.   The concept of behavior setting is certainly not the only basic unit that has been offered to characterize human environments. Wicker points out that one way of conceiving of the environment is to exclude all but inanimate physical features, such as the spatial arrangement of objects, furniture, and walls.[2] This approach has a distinct advantage, since these features can be readily specified in terms of physical characteristics. The problem with this approach, however, is that it entirely ignores the social inputs to which people are exposed.[3]

Alternatively, we can think of the environment as a complex of expectations, rules, norms, and social roles controlling behavior. This approach has both advantages and disadvantages. For example, it allows us to simultaneously represent a number of different sources of social influence on the behavior of an individual. Unfortunately, however, the physical aspects of the environment are given secondary status or are entirely forgotten. The behavior setting unit has the distinct advantage of including temporal and physical aspects of the environment, the standing patterns of behavior in the environment, and the relationship between the two.

Another important advantage of the behavior setting unit is its intermediate size. It is not as small as the behavior of a single individual, nor is it as large as that of a school or hospital. Since the behavior setting unit is of intermediate size, it provides a context for what Barker describes as "behavior episodes." Actual human behavior may be best understood in the context of an environmental unit the size of a behavior setting.

Behavior settings can also serve as an important link between the behavior of a particular individual and that of larger contexts, such as organizations or schools. Gump prefers the concept of behavior setting to that of "group" as an intermediate-sized environmental unit. He argues that unlike the concept of group, "the behavior setting conception is the result of a research orientation which assumes that behaviors and environments form a patterned reality. This reality exists independently of those organizations imposed by scientific investigations; its nature is more adequately comprehended if one 'listens' to the phenomenon before applying traditional conceptualization."[4]

Another important advantage of the behavior setting is its multidimensionality. Neither physical objects alone nor behaviors alone are the defining criteria of behavior settings. Instead, behavior settings involve specific places, objects, standing patterns of behavior, and occurrences in time. Recent work by Barker has designated the inhabitants of behavior settings in terms of different roles they may enact as they function in each respective setting.[5] Setting occupants may take on peripheral roles as outside observers or members, or more central roles as performers. Thus the role-related behavior of performers and members within a behavior setting can be specified, as well as certain demographic characteristics such as age and sex of setting occupants.

The Problem of Behavior Setting Taxonomies. The development of classification systems, or taxonomies, is fundamental to scientific investigation. In botany, for example, plants of various types are classified into groups. In medicine, diseases of various types are classified according to symptom patterns, causes, or both. In astronomy, stars may be classified into types according to their size, age, brightness, and chemical composition.

Are there distinct types of settings? If so, how can we discover and describe them? One important approach to this problem is the development of taxonomies of settings. There is currently a good deal of interest in this problem.[6] In a recent review of work on environmental psychology, Craik states that "a taxonomic interest in the descriptive properties of places is a prerequisite to substantive research on man-environment relations."[7] Cowen expresses a similar concern in his review of social and community interventions: "to understand the effects of settings on growth requires that we first develop systematic frameworks for describing settings—something we currently lack."[8]

A taxonomy of behavior settings would be useful to scientists studying the environment for at least four reasons.[9] First, we do not have a *common language* for describing various types of situations or settings. A standard taxonomy or list of setting types would greatly aid communication among scientists studying social settings. Second, a taxonomy of settings would allow scientists to begin to *describe* important similarities and differences among various types of settings. Third, a taxonomy would aid us in *predicting* the behavior of individuals in various types of settings, since the type of setting one is in may substantially influence the type of behavior in which he engages. Finally, a taxonomy can aid us in *theory construction*. Hempel has argued that the process of classification can be thought of as a kind of scientific concept formation.[10] Thus we can treat the setting types enumerated in a setting taxonomy as initial organizing concepts in the field.

When scientists begin to work out a taxonomy in any given field, they may use one of two strategies. The first strategy is to simply speculate on what types of settings should exist, based on a particular theory or simply on intuition. The intuitions could then be checked against a sample of real settings to see how well the speculations compare with the empirical world.

A second, perhaps preferable strategy is empirical. In this case, a sample of settings is obtained first. The investigator then asks how the sample could be divided into smaller groups or types so that each group contains settings that are very similar to one another yet keeping various types as distinct as possible. If the scientist chooses the second strategy, at least three major questions must be confronted.

"What is it precisely that we propose to classify?" The extensive work on the description and identification of behavior settings mentioned earlier in this chapter suggests that the behavior setting provides a clear-cut, theoretically based entity ideal for the purposes of classification.

But if the first question can be answered, we still must ask, "What variables should be selected to describe settings and how should these variables be summarized?" Barker and his associates have developed a large number of variables designed to measure salient characteristics of behavior settings.[11] The variables reflect such characteristics as (1) the authority system to which the setting belongs; (2) the action patterns that predominate in the setting; (3) the age and sex characteristics of setting inhabitants according to their role status as performers, members, or targets; (4) the population size of the setting; (5) the duration of the setting; and (6) its frequency of occurrence. These variables provide an extremely broad multidimensional basis for the isolation of important behavior setting attributes.

The final question to be answered is, "How will settings be sampled and classified once they have been defined and described according to a set of variables or dimensions?" The answer involves sampling settings from some larger population and classifying them into a number of relatively homogeneous and distinct groups or classes. To accomplish this we must have (1) some definition of the population of settings, (2) a procedure for sampling the population, and (3) a basis for classification.

The behavior setting surveys of Barker and his colleagues lend themselves quite well to the first two requirements. They define an entire town as a naturally occurring, ecologically relevant population of behavior settings. Such a definition provides a large number and variety of settings for classification. Furthermore, once the population of settings has been defined in this way, either it may be sampled randomly with some assurance that the sample is representative of the population, or the entire population of settings may be classified.

A recent study reported by Price and Blashfield examined the entire population of behavior settings in a small midwestern town surveyed by Barker and his colleagues.[12] The goal of the study was to develop an empirical classification of behavior settings based on the measured similarities and differences among them. Price and Blashfield examined all 455 settings in the town in terms of 43 descriptive variables used to describe each setting. A statistical cluster analysis method was used to obtain behavior setting types. This method grouped the 455 settings into smaller groups or types, which ensured that the settings within each type were as similar as possible to one another in terms of the descriptive variables.

The results of the study are summarized in Table 7.1. Twelve distinct types of behavior setting were obtained. Also listed in Table 7.1 are the variables of characteristics that most strikingly distinguished each behavior setting type and examples of the kinds of behavior settings that each type contained.

This classification of social settings may provide hypotheses concerning the socialization, economic, political, and behavior control functions of social settings in the context of an entire community. For example, there exist some interesting correspondences between the results of the present analyses and other attempts to offer broad classifications of organizations or settings. When Parsons classified organizations according to the social needs to which the organizations are directed, he divided organizations into (1) those oriented toward economic production, (2) those oriented toward political goals, (3) those primarily concerned with social integration, and (4) those concerned with pattern maintenance.[13]

It could be tentatively suggested that Parsons' economic production category is similar to the present "local business settings" cluster. Parsons' category describing political organizations corresponds to our "government settings" cluster. In addition, a number of setting clusters appear to be concerned with social integration, in particular, youth performance settings, elementary school settings, and high school settings, whereas the religious settings cluster might be thought of as involving pattern maintenance in the context of Parsons' system.

Table 7.1 Taxonomy of Behavior Settings

Behavior Setting Type	Distinctive Characteristics	Typical Examples
Elementary school settings	1. Settings intended for children 6–11 years old 2. Settings under school sponsorship	1. Elementary school parties 2. Field trips 3. Elementary school classes
High school settings	1. Settings intended for adolescents	1. High school classes 2. Club meetings 3. Class trips 4. Dances
Youth performance settings	1. Contains large numbers of young performers	1. Christmas programs 2. Scout banquets 3. Amateur talent shows
High school performance settings	1. High-school sponsored 2. Large proportion of performers in adolescent age range	1. School assemblies 2. Class plays 3. Athletic events 4. Homecoming parades, rallies
Adult settings	1. Intended for adults 2. Excludes adolescents and children	1. PTA conferences 2. Nursing home activities 3. School county administration meetings 4. Electrical cooperative meetings
Women's organizational settings	1. Almost exclusively female members and performers	1. Sewing clubs 2. Garden clubs 3. Women's auxiliaries
Men's organizational settings	1. Almost exclusively male members and performers	1. Church deacons' meetings 2. Kiwanis Club meetings 3. Athletic banquets

Table 7.1 (Continued)

Religious settings	1. Religious behavior patterns 2. Settings under church sponsorship	1. Religion classes 2. Worship services 3. Fellowship meetings
Government settings	1. Sponsored by local or other governments 2. Political or governmental behavior patterns	1. Township board meetings 2. City council meetings 3. Election polling places
Local business settings	1. Oriented to private enterprise 2. Large number of occurrences per year	1. Service stations 2. Banks 3. Barber shops 4. Grocery stores 5. Lumber yards
Family-oriented settings	1. Includes members from entire age range 2. Sponsored by voluntary organizations	1. Picnics 2. Dinners for the public 3. Family nights
Large membership settings	1. Large numbers of members 2. Typically voluntary organizations 3. Long duration per occurrence	1. Street fairs 2. Parades 3. Auto displays 4. Refreshment stands

Because this study is based on the entire population of behavior settings in the community under investigation the results may be of considerable use to researchers interested in the impact of situational variables on individuals. For example, the setting clusters obtained in this study may provide an empirical basis for selecting a stratified sample of settings in new communities with some assurance that the settings selected represent distinctive and important setting types.

How Behavior Settings Promote Behavior—Environment Congruence. We have discussed the concept of behavior setting and its various characteristics and advantages as if settings were static units. But the behavior setting is dynamic. Behavior settings exert a substantial degree of influence over the behavior of their occupants. Wicker has referred to this phenomenon as behavior-environment congruence.[14] It is not just that settings act on people to affect their behavior. Nor is it only that people act on settings. Instead, a continual interaction between the people in a setting and other aspects of the setting itself produces a stable, patterned, state of affairs.

To understand Barker's view of the stability of settings and how behavior-environment congruence occurs, we must consider two questions. First, "How are behavior settings and people related to one another?" That is, what are the channels or circuits that connect the people in a behavior setting to the setting itself? Once we have an idea of what these circuits are, we must ask a second question, "How do they work?"

Let us begin by trying to determine how behavior settings and the people in them are joined together. Barker suggested that the following "circuits" exist between settings and their occupants: (1) goal circuits, (2) program circuits, (3) deviation-countering circuits, and (4) vetoing circuits.

Barker assumes that people actively attempt to maintain the settings they occupy because they obtain satisfactions from these settings. If the inhabitants of a behavior setting are not at least minimally satisfied, they will leave the setting or will not return to it on another occasion. In this case, of course, the setting will cease to be maintained and will cease to exist.

Thus one of the important relationships between behavior setting inhabitants and the setting itself is the *goal circuit,* which involves people's perception of goals within the setting, ways to obtain and achieve those goals, and the satisfaction derived from their achievement. Thinking in these terms, we see that people and settings are linked by paths or routes to goal satisfaction. For example, if a store fails to carry products that satisfy customers, the customers will not return to that setting. If a professor's lectures are boring or have little to do with students' final grades, it would not be surprising to see him soon lecturing to an empty hall.

Barker uses the term *program circuits* to designate a second way in which people and settings are linked. The essential features of program circuits are knowledge by the people in a behavior setting of the program of that setting and knowledge of how to control and organize that program.

Programs are much like agendas in a meeting. They specify the behaviors to be enacted in a setting, and they are usually carried by people who act as performers in the setting. For example, the program circuit for a course in Environmental Psychology may involve a list of class meeting times, a syllabus of required readings, an outline of lecture material to be presented by the principal performer in the setting, and a description of course requirements. Program circuits, then, specify in a fairly precise way the behaviors to be enacted by members and performers in the setting and the nature of the transactions between performers, members, and other components of the setting.

Two other circuits link people and settings to maintain the stability of the settings and of the people's behavior. The first is called the *deviation-countering circuit*. For a setting to be maintained intact, deviations in the setting must be dealt with. Deviations are inadequacies or modifications that prevent the inhabitants from achieving the satisfactions that they seek. If, for example, a proprietor corrects a clerk's errors in pricing articles, he is using a deviation-countering circuit to maintain the setting, grocery store, intact.

Deviation-countering circuits need not deal only with the behavior of setting inhabitants. Physical aspects of the setting may require maintenance as well. In the same setting, the grocery store, if the refrigerator cooling frozen goods breaks down, a deviation-countering circuit is used when the refrigerator is repaired. The setting will thus be maintained. As Barker notes, deviation-countering circuits are characterized by people's ability to sense the presence in the setting of conditions that prevent the program of the setting from being carried out. They are also characterized by action designed to counteract the interfering conditions and maintain stability in the setting.

The final type of circuit or channel that specifies a mode of relationship between the setting itself and its inhabitants, is what Barker calls the *vetoing circuit*. Vetoing circuits are much like deviation-countering circuits except that the deviant component of the setting is eliminated rather than repaired or altered. To consider our example of the grocery store once more, a clerk who consistently misprices items may not be corrected after numerous mistakes; he may be fired. Or consider this example offered by Barker. "Oran was acting silly. Miss Rutherford said, 'Evidently you do not wish to play in our band, Oran.' She took his cymbal away from him and gave it to Selma Bradley. . . . Miss Rutherford put Oran on the far side of the piano away from the class."[15] Most of us have known a Miss Rutherford at some time during our school years, but it is doubtful that we thought of her as part of a vetoing circuit. Nevertheless, Miss Rutherford's removal of Oran from the music class is an excellent example of the use of vetoing circuits to maintain the music class behavior setting.

Now we have an idea of the channels or circuits that connect people with settings. To summarize briefly, people are connected to the settings they occupy by (1) goals they wish to and do achieve in the settings, (2) a program that specifies how the setting "works," and (3) deviation-countering circuits and (4) vetoing circuits that maintain the setting either by altering or removing components of the setting that threaten its maintenance and stability.

Now that we have considered the abstract structural attributes of behavior settings and have gained some insight into their dynamics, we are still left with a question. Behavior settings are made up of two very different sets of phenomena: (1) people and their behavior, and (2) physical objects. These two sets of phenomena probably function according to very different sets of laws, at least as we currently think about them. They are, as Barker notes, "incommensurable." What then is the essence of the behavior setting? Is not the behavior setting a kind of artificial composite of people and places?

Barker's answer to this question is intriguing and very much in the ecological tradition. He says, "The reality and nature of behavior settings of eco-behavioral entities do not reside in psychological processes of the inhabitants, but in the circuitry that interconnects behavior settings, inhabitants and other behavior setting components."[16] Thus the "essence" of behavior settings is not just people, nor is it just places. It is instead a complex network of *relationships* between individual psychological processes and setting components.

Theory and Research on Undermanned Environments.   Barker has outlined a theory discussing the effects of behavior setting size stimulated in part by a comparison of two small towns, one in Kansas ("Midwest") and one in Yorkshire, England ("Yoredale"). A number of striking differences emerged from this cross-cultural study, but among the most interesting was the fact that although Midwest has a considerably smaller population than Yoredale, it had approximately 1.2 times as many behavior settings. In addition, residents of Midwest performed at least three times as often in their behavior settings as residents of Yoredale did in theirs. Barker reasoned that to maintain the more numerous settings in Midwest, the residents were required to accept more positions of responsibility and to include in the settings larger proportions of people who were only marginally qualified to function in those settings. Thus Barker argued that the behavior settings of Midwest were "undermanned," at least when compared with those of Yoredale.[17]

Since there were relatively fewer people available to maintain the settings, Barker concluded that Midwest residents needed to participate in a wider variety of settings if the settings were to be maintained. In fact, according to the theory, a larger number of behavioral consequences should occur for individuals participating in undermanned settings. Barker hypothesized that undermanned settings made a greater "claim" on people both by requiring greater effort and because relatively more difficult and more important tasks would be assigned to their occupants.

In addition, the range and direction of forces acting on individual occupants was hypothesized to be greater. For example, a wider variety of activities would be required of each occupant, and because every individual in the setting was crucial for the maintenance of the setting, there would be less sensitivity to, and evaluation of, differences among people. Furthermore, since performers in the setting would be required to carry out a variety of different tasks, it was expected that there would be a lower level of maximum performance for occupants of the setting. Since many setting occupants would have to carry out a number of tasks, it seemed unlikely that any single occupant would achieve great proficiency at any one task.

Barker believed that the joint influence of greater strength of forces on occupants of undermanned settings as well as a greater range of forces would result in each individual having greater functional importance within a setting, more responsibility, and a greater feeling of functional self-identity. There would be lower standards and fewer tests for admission to the setting. However there would also be greater feelings of insecurity, since each person would be in more jeopardy of failing to carry through the tasks assigned him. Finally, Barker predicted that undermanned settings should produce more frequent occurrences of success and failure.

Thus if a behavior setting is to be maintained, and few people are available to perform in that setting, very real forces will operate on the occupants of the setting. These forces will push the individual into roles of greater responsibility and participation, but at the same time, undermanned settings will create greater insecurity and more opportunities for failure. As Barker put it, "The underpopulated setting is one where self-esteem and social status can both flourish, and also wither."[18]

Let us summarize the *impacts* of undermanned settings on setting occupants, as hypothesized by Wicker.

The greater *claim* of undermanned behavior settings is said to produce the following consequences for setting occupants:

1.   Greater effort to support the setting and its functions, either by "harder" work or by spending longer hours.
2.   Participation in a greater diversity of tasks and roles.
3.   Involvement in more difficult and more important tasks.
4.   More responsibility in the sense that the setting and what others gain from it depend on each individual occupant.
5.   Viewing oneself and others in terms of task-related characteristics, rather than in terms of social-emotional characteristics.
6.   Greater functional importance of individuals within the setting.
7.   Less sensitivity to and less evaluation of differences between people.
8.   Setting of lower standards and fewer tests for admission into the setting.
9.   A lower level of maximal or best performance.
10.   Greater insecurity about the eventual maintenance of the setting.
11.   More frequent occurrences of success and failure, depending on the outcome of the setting's functions.[19]

It was not until the publication of *Big School, Small School* that detailed and careful studies were done within the behavior setting framework to support the undermanning hypothesis. What are some of the striking differences between big and small schools? Barker and Gump suggest that they may not be the ones we would initially expect:

> The large school has authority: its grand exterior dimensions, its long halls and myriad rooms, and its tides of students all carry an implication of power and rightness. The small school lacks such certainty: its modest building, its short halls and few rooms, and its students, who move more in trickles than in tides, give an impression of a casual or not quite decisive educational environment.
>
> There are outside views. They are illusions. Inside views reveal forces at work stimulating and compelling students to more active and responsible contributions to the enterprises of small than of large schools.[20]

Thus Barker and Gump argue that bigger is not necessarily better, and smaller schools might have some distinct advantages over larger ones. The major findings reported in Barker and Gump's work in the comparison of big and small schools can be summarized as follows. First, larger schools tend to offer a wider variety of instruction. However, the increase in curriculum variety as school size increased was relatively small. As a rule, a 100% increase in the size of the school was required to yield 17% increase in variety in instruction. In addition, there was no clear evidence that the greater variety that typified big schools meant that the average students in the larger school really experienced a broader range of academic classes.

A second major finding was that students in larger schools participated in slightly more out-of-class activities than students in small schools. But students in smaller schools participated in a much wider range of different settings. Perhaps of even more interest was the finding that the student coming from a small school tended to be a *performer* in more than twice as many instances as the student in a large school. As Gump notes, "The chance to be essential, to gain the active or demanding role in activity comes much more often to the average small school student."[21]

Another important difference between large and small schools had to do with the kinds of satisfactions reported by students from each type of school. Students from large schools tended to experience satisfactions that were mainly vicarious and were associated with the feeling of being part of a large and imposing institution. Students from small schools, on the other hand, reported satisfactions having to do with the development of competence, close cooperation with fellow students, and the meeting of challenges.

As intriguing as these findings are, one can raise questions about their generality. As Baird points out, most of the research reported in *Big School, Small School* was based on only five high schools in Kansas.[22] Furthermore, the definition of participation used by Barker and Gump classified many different types of activities under one heading. Finally, the question of the different levels of participation in large and small schools, although real, may or may not be educationally relevant.

Baird set out to test Barker and Gump's major hypothesis and at the same time to deal with the limitations just mentioned. Baird's study used very large samples and measures of nonacademic accomplishment in six different areas previously shown to have great educational relevance. A 3% sample of college applicants who took the assessment administered by the American College Testing Program (ACT) was obtained, producing a research sample of 21,371 students. Baird broke the sample up according to the size of the graduating class and the degree of urbanization of the community setting, examining extracurricular accomplishment in the following areas: leadership, music, drama and speech, art, writing, and science. Thus it was possible to study the effects of the size of the school and also the degree of urbanization. Baird found that students from small schools tended to participate to a greater extent in a variety of areas than did students from large schools. The differences found were especially pronounced in the areas of leadership, speech, and drama. Thus Baird's evidence appears to support the theory of undermanning.

If students from smaller schools participate in a wider range of activities than those of larger schools, do these differences carry over to college experiences? Baird found that the differences did not generalize to the college experience, since the college achievements of students from large and small high schools did not differ. However the size of the college itself was related to college achievements. Smaller colleges produced higher degrees of participation, even when controls were introduced to check for differential ability of students in large and small colleges. These results suggest that students' participation and achievement are strongly influenced by their immediate situation. But the effect of school size does not carry over when a student moves out of a small school to a larger one. In general, however, Baird's findings support the undermanning hypothesis.

Another question we might ask is whether the effects of small schools or other undermanned settings affect all students in the same way. In particular, do differences in the size of school settings have the same effects on marginal students and on average students? This question is of considerable social importance, particularly in the light of recent concern about school dropouts.

Willems has addressed this question in a study of school size as it affects the sense of obligation to high school activities felt by marginal and regular students. In two field studies Willems demonstrated that small schools produced a much higher average sense of student obligation; indeed the difference between marginal and regular students in small schools with respect to their sense of obligation was virtually nonexistent. In large schools, on the other hand, marginal students felt a much lower sense of obligation when compared with regular students. As Willems puts it, "It would appear that the small school marginal students were not experientially and behaviorally marginal, while their large school counterparts were a group of relative outsiders."[23] Willems has replicated these original findings in a much larger sample of 80 schools.[24]

In yet another replication of the small school phenomenon, Wicker demonstrated that small school students entered a much wider range of school settings and engaged in more performances as measured by the number of positions of responsibility in the settings.[25] Small school students also had higher levels of cognitive complexity. That is, the relative number of distinct concepts or dimensions used by small school students in evaluating behavior settings was greater. Thus Wicker demonstrated that students in small schools had a more complex and differentiated set of perceptions of their social environment than did students in large schools.

A series of studies by Wicker and his colleagues has shown that these findings are not specific to school settings. They are observed in large and small churches.[26] For example, Wicker obtained complete lists of all organized group activities in five Methodist churches for a one-year period. He showed that the ratio of members to activities consistently increased with church size. A more detailed comparison of a large church and small church indicated that members of small churches participated in more different activities, had more positions of leadership, spent more time in the activities, attended church more often, and contributed more money. Still another measure used by Wicker involved the examination of archival data on a much larger sample of 104 churches. These data also indicated that support of church activities was much greater in small churches.

Thus the general outlines of Barker's theory of undermanning have received widespread empirical support. In the next section we examine a more precise statement that both sharpens the theory and allows us to extend it to the problems of crowding and population density.

Reformulation and Extension of the Theory of Undermanning. In most of the research on the manning issue, size has been the principal indicator of whether a setting is undermanned or overmanned. Thus settings in small organizations are assumed to be relatively undermanned and those in large organizations are assumed to be relatively overmanned.

Wicker and his colleagues, unsure that the original theory had been adequately tested, recently presented a reformulation of the theory of manning. They note that Barker originally formulated his theory to refer to the effects on occupants of undermanned behavior settings, rather than to the consequences of belonging to organizations of different sizes: "The key issue here is whether the worship service and church school behavior settings in the small churches of the present sample were indeed, undermanned, while those in the larger churches were overmanned."[27]

Thus they offer a reformulation of the theory of manning that is directly derived from Barker's formulation. It has the dual advantages of (1) allowing more adequate tests of the undermanning hypothesis, and (2) extending the theory to the conditions of crowding and population density.

The restatement contains three basic definitions. The first is the *maintenance minimum,* which is the minimum number of persons required for the setting to be maintained. The second definition is that of *capacity,* which is the maximum number of persons the setting can accommodate. Finally, they define the concept of *applicants*. The total number of persons who seek to participate and who meet the eligibility requirements of the setting is the number of applicants to the setting.

In addition, a distinction is made between two kinds of setting occupants: *performers* and *nonperformers*. This distinction between the roles potentially existing in any behavior setting is derived from Barker's earlier formulation. By differentiating between two roles that occupants may take and adding the concept of "capacity," we can describe behavior settings as either undermanned or overmanned in terms of either performer or nonperformer roles. Let us now summarize this reformulation by defining maintenance minimum, capacity, and applicant concepts in terms of performer and nonperformer roles.

The maintenance minimum for performers is the smallest number of functionaries required by the setting for the setting to continue, with performers carrying out the necessary tasks in proper sequence. Maintenance minimum for nonperformers is the smallest number of people who must be present as consumers in the setting for the setting to continue.

Capacity for performers could be constrained by either physical or social structural factors. Thus both the physical size of the setting and the number of roles available may affect this variable. For nonperformers, capacity is usually constrained by merely physical factors, such as the available space or number of seats in the setting. Capacity for performers depends on the role requirements of the setting.

Finally, applicants for performer roles are people who are eligible to participate and wish to do so at the performer level. Applicants for the nonperformer role are people who meet the admission requirements and also wish to enter the setting.

Consider the following example, provided by Wicker, which applies all these concepts to the behavior setting of a high school play.

> For example, in a high school play, the maintenance minimum for performers would include the director, members of the cast, persons to handle lighting, props, and costumes, a ticket seller, and possibly a few others. The maintenance minimum for nonperformers would be the smallest audience size which would be tolerated before the setting would be altered or eliminated. Capacity of performers would be the total number of persons who could be accommodated in all functionary roles, including in addition to those listed above, ushers, a house manager, an assistant director, understudies, concession sellers, and others. Capacity of nonperformers would be the number of persons who could be seated in the auditorium. Applicants at the performer level would be the number of people who sought to or at least were willing to serve as a functionary in the setting, i.e., to direct, act, usher,

serve on the stage crew, and so on. Applicants at the nonperformer level would be the number of persons who have the admission fee and seek to enter the play performance.[28]

This rather elaborate and careful reformulation of the factors affecting manning allows us to specify quite precisely the three major conditions of manning (undermanned, adequately manned, or overmanned). In the context of this new formulation, whether a setting is undermanned, adequately manned, or overmanned depends on the relationship between the number of applicants (either performers or nonperformers) relative to the maintenance minimum and the capacity of the setting for either performers or nonperformers. Thus if the number of applicants falls below the maintenance minimum, the setting is defined as undermanned. If, on the other hand, the number of applicants falls somewhere between the maintenance minimum and the capacity, the setting is adequately manned. Overmanning occurs when there are more applicants than can be accepted, given the capacity of the setting.

This reformulation is a substantial contribution because of the more precise specification of manning and its extension to both performer and nonperformer roles. Moreover, as Wicker points out, the conception now encompasses the serious contemporary problem of excess populations (see Chapter 5).

> The theory of undermanning, and the revised formulation for defining degrees of manning, point to some additional factors which need to be considered in dealing with consequences of excess populations. They stress the need to consider not merely the number of persons present in a setting, but rather how that number relates to the personnel requirements of the setting, and to the number of persons the setting can accommodate. It follows from this view that population density, in terms of number of people per acre, household, or square yard of floor space, at least within the range of which they naturally occur, may not be crucial in determining human experiences and behavior. What one needs to know is what are the maintenance minima and capacities of the settings which are located within the physical spaces.[29]

Wicker makes it clear that the reformulation of the problem of manning can be applied to the problem of crowding or population density. The reformulation focuses not on physical variables alone, which have been the principal measures used in studying population density. Instead it considers the behavioral requirements of the setting as the critical factors in the problem of excess population.

This reformulation is not merely of academic interest, however. Both Zlutnick and Altman[30] and Wicker remind us that *how excess population is defined* is very likely to affect one's perception of how the behavioral problems that may be associated with crowding or excess population will be dealt with. As Wicker remarks, conceptualizations based on sheer numbers of persons per unit of space are likely to imply solutions dealing either with increasing the amount of available physical space or somehow reducing the number of people in that area. The present reformulation suggests a much broader range of change strategies.

For example, Wicker has focused his work on service behavior settings. In particular, the concern of this work has been to study the *adaptive mechanisms* that develop spontaneously in settings to deal with the problem of having more clients in the setting than can be readily served. Wicker believes that the adaptive mechanisms work to deal with the problem of overpopulation in at least three ways: (1) by regulating the capacity of the setting, (2) by regulating the entrance of clients into the setting, and (3) by regulating the length of time clients spend in the setting. Let us examine some examples of how each of these adaptive mechanisms might work in specific instances described by Wicker.[31]

A. Regulation of the entrance of clients into the setting
    1. Adjusting standards of admission
    Example: A national park whose wilderness areas are heavily visited might begin to require all backpackers to demonstrate knowledge of how to minimize the environmental impact of their visit before issuing them wilderness permits.
    2. Channeling clients into holding areas
    Example: Patrons of a busy restaurant might be directed to the cocktail lounge to wait until a table is free.
B. Regulation of the capacity of the setting
    1. Altering physical facilities and spaces
    Example: Ushers at an Easter worship service might place folding chairs at the back of a church sanctuary to accommodate a large crowd.
    2. Adjusting size of staff
    Example: A bank manager might assign an additional employee to teller duty on Fridays.
    3. Varying assignments of nonservice tasks to staff
    Example: Lifeguards at a beach might be asked to suspend all equipment maintenance tasks during heavy visitation periods.
C. Regulation of the amount of time clients spend in the setting
    1. Varying rate of processing clients

Example: A barber with a number of customers waiting might spend less time on each haircut.

2.   Establishing priorities among clients in the setting on such bases as time of arrival, waiting costs, and service time required

Example: A computer consultant might serve clients having brief questions before helping those with more involved problems.

3.   Altering the standing patterns of behavior by means of procedures, rules, and/or physical facilities affecting the rate of flow of clients into and out of the setting

Examples: A busy bus system might begin to accept only the exact fare. A restroom in a large sports arena might be redesigned with separate entrance and exit doors. A savings and loan bank might post signs asking customers to complete their deposit slips before approaching a teller.

These examples suggest that settings adapt to increased population pressure in a variety of ways. These changes will surely affect the quality of life of individuals for better or for worse. There can be no doubt, however, that not just individual behavior but also settings must be modified to cope with the increasing demands of excess populations.

The view of under- and overmanned settings presented here has implications for the potential impact on persons with average or better than average abilities and also for those less well endowed. The work of Willems, it will be recalled, suggests that under- and overmanned settings may have their principal impact on those marginal persons who are most in need of environmental supports and are most at risk as school drop-outs. It is these people who could most benefit by the adaptive skills potentially provided by optimally manned settings. They might also benefit most by the motivational forces generated by undermanned settings. Thus the theory of undermanning developed by Barker and extended by Wicker and his colleagues may prove to have great practical as well as theoretical significance.

Some Applications of Behavior Setting Theory and Methods.   The three types of research project reviewed in this section indicate the range of application of behavior setting theory. Although very different from one another, all display a distinctive ecological quality and all are derived from the basic conceptions of behavior setting theory outlined earlier. Other relevant examples involve the comparison of open and traditional classrooms and the cross-cultural study of qualities of community life.[32]

Children in Their Homes.   Maxine Schoggen and her associates have collected large amounts of data on the behavior and home milieu of 3-year-old children. The data take the form of *specimen records*—running, narrative descriptions of a child's behavior and of the behavior of other people toward the child, plus information about the environment of the child. One of the units developed by Schoggen and her associates and measured in the context of specimen records is the Environmental Force Unit (EFU), an action of an environmental agent (associate) of a child that is directed toward a particular goal or end state with respect to that child.[33]

Schoggen and her associates studied 24 children 3 years of age, varying in sex, socioeconomic background, race, and rural or urban residence. When they compared middle-income with lower-income homes, the investigators discovered that the EFUs in the middle-income homes more frequently involved (1) the giving or asking of information, (2) extended interactions, (3) an obligation to perform some specific action, (4) goals in harmony with those of the agent, and (5) largely verbal interactions. Children in low-income homes received less verbal input, more negative or inhibiting behavior, and less input directed toward their specific behavior. The vast majority of EFUs given to these children involved neutral rather than positive or negative affect. This finding is quite surprising when one realizes that the child and the agent delivering the EFU were in conflict approximately 40% of the time.

Wicker and Farrell selected 1290 EFUs (from approximately 9000 EFUs identified by Schoggen and her colleagues) in which the mother's goal—to have the child perform an overt act—was either neutral or in conflict with the child's goal. Examples were attempts to get the child to wash his hands, close the door, wipe his nose, or clean up spilled milk. These EFUs were rated on a number of dimensions, including location of occurrence, whether the mother provided any reason for her behavior influence attempt, whether the child complied with the attempt, and so on.

There were several important findings. For example, in 80% of the cases, the child's only source of information about what was expected of him was the spoken words of the mother. Mothers modeled the desired behavior for their children in less than 1% of the cases. In light of recent research and theoretical work on modeling, this is a striking result. It illustrates how different behavior in the natural environment can be from that observed in laboratory settings. Perhaps the most interesting finding was that the mother rarely rewarded or punished the child for compliance or noncompliance with her wishes.

When Wicker and Farrell examined subgroups by race, socioeconomic status, and rural-urban location, they found an overall difference between black and white homes. There were many more instances in which white mothers provided a goal, plus a reason or rule in their behavior influence attempts. In addition, a number of similarities were discovered between the situations of lower-class black and middle-class white children. In both groups there was a high percentage of behavior influence attempts in which the mother was physically distant from the child, and the influence attempts lacked extended explanations, helping cues, or lengthy communicative interchanges. Lower-class black and middle-class white children received fewer behavior influence attempts per minute than did middle-class black or lower-class white children.[34]

Research of this kind allows fine-grained analyses of one of the most important socialization milieus of young children, their own home. By focusing on inputs to the child, such as Environmental Force Units, it is possible to begin to understand processes by which class and race differences may develop.

Patients and Staff in a Rehabilitation Hospital.   Willems and LeCompte have engaged in an intensive behavior setting survey of a rehabilitation hospital for spinal cord injury patients. LeCompte has reported a survey of all the behavior settings (122) existing in the rehabilitation hospital during 1968 and 1969.[35] He reports relatively high reliabilities in the identification of behavior settings.

One basic distinction made by LeCompte had to do with whether patients were present or absent in each behavior setting. A number of settings were never entered by patients (offices of heads of departments, departmental staff meetings, nursing stations, etc.). Having made this distinction it was possible to examine the degree to which treatment personnel spent time in patient and nonpatient settings. LeCompte found, for example, that the physicians and administrative personnel inhabit nonpatient settings for approximately 4 hours for every hour that they spend in the patient treatment environment. Other professional staff, such as physical therapists, social workers, and vocational counselors, spent about equal time in the two types of settings.

Assuming this basic distinction between patient and nonpatient settings, LeCompte went on to ask what behaviors occurred in each of the 122 settings. By examining the behavior of the dominant performer in each setting, it was possible to rate characteristic behavior patterns and examine these settings according to the professional discipline of the treatment personnel. For example, physicians engaged in specialized evaluation and treatment activities, but participated in little if any social interaction. Social service personnel, on the other hand, exhibited a great

deal of social interaction in their specialized settings but very little evaluative behavior. Thus groups of behavior settings selected in terms of the
dominant performer in the setting show very different behavior patterns
and contain quite different professional groups.

LeCompte also derived some other measures from his behavior setting
survey which speak directly to the question of the relative importance of
staff members in maintaining the function of the treatment settings. One
index he derived, the "Pied Piper Index," was a measure of the hospital's
loss "if the group in question were to be piped away." This was a measure,
then, of the number of performances someone else would have to enact if
the hospital were to maintain its level of functioning, having lost a particular professional group. If we arrange treatment personnel in terms of the
Pied Piper Index, we gain some information about the ecological impact
of various professional groups. Not surprisingly, aides and orderlies
scored highest on the Pied Piper Index, whereas physicians and nurses
occupied intermediate levels of importance.

In a second study Willems observed patients for a full 18-hour day
during which observations of behavior were continuously recorded, as
were the settings in which the behavior occurred. Willems coded behavior
into large units called "chunks" (e.g., "eating a scheduled meal," "watching television," "conversing with a physician"). Behavior was also coded
into smaller units called "bits," which were fleeting social encounters or
brief intrusions by other people into the patient's stream of behavior. For
example, an isolated "How are you?" by a passerby might qualify as a "bit."

With the basic data in hand it was possible to examine the distribution
of patient behavior throughout the hospital's 122 behavior settings. Willems found that the behavior was very unevenly distributed throughout
the settings: almost 90% of the behavior occurred in the two treatment
wards, the physical therapy area, the hallways, and the occupational
therapy area—only five settings.

In another analysis Willems examined two different types of behavior
obtained from factor analyses of the behavior settings and of the behaviors in which the patients engaged. One type of behavior was called
"independent behavior" because it was patient-instigated and was carried
out alone. A second type was called "complexity" because it involved the
proportion of time during which patients did more than one thing at
once. Both these behavioral factors are of considerable importance in a
physical rehabilitation setting; therefore it is of some interest to discover
where these behaviors occurred and under what circumstances. One of
the most interesting findings was that Behavioral Complexity was relatively low in patients early in the rehabilitation program and quite high in
patients about to leave the program. This suggests that complexity is a

relatively good measure of patient progress and a good indication that the hospital is accomplishing an important part of its mission. Behavioral Independence, on the other hand, was more surprising when examined in terms of the behavior settings in which it occurred. As Willems notes,

> Among the settings displayed, the two that are most public and most tangential to comprehensive rehabilitation—cafeteria and hallways— —produce the most Behavioral Independence on the part of the patients, while PT (physical therapy), OT (occupational therapy), and RT (recreational therapy)—three settings at the heart of comprehensive rehabilitation—produced the least.[36]

The work of LeCompte and Willems illustrates nicely how a behavior setting survey can be carried out in a hospital milieu. It points to important aspects of the behavior of treatment personnel and patients as well as to the settings in which they typically occur. Such information is, of course, critical in changing or improving the effectiveness of rehabilitative settings of all kinds.

Selection of Behavior Settings by Emotionally Disturbed College Students.
A recent study by Eddy and Sinnett illustrates another application of the behavior setting approach to understanding the behavior of people in their natural context.[37] This study is particularly notable because it took into account personality differences among individuals as well as the settings in which they tended to spend their time. In fact, Eddy and Sinnett suggest that their primary purpose was to understand the relationship of personality to the utilization of space. They believe that an individual's behavior in a particular environment, or his choice of environments, may reveal a great deal about his personality.

These investigators selected 46 client members of a rehabilitation living unit at a large university. Each student was evaluated using three different measures: activity records, which provided a chronological account of the behavior of each person and the setting in which it occurred; clinical judgments from treatment personnel concerning the degree to which each person was thought to be action-oriented as opposed to inhibited; and a personality test administered to each subject.

With this information it was possible to ask whether there were relationships between personality factors, clinical judgments of activity orientation, and where and how students spent their time. Eddy and Sinnett hypothesized that subjects who were inhibited would spend more time in their rooms and less time in socialization areas than subjects judged to be highly action-oriented. A factor analysis of the data obtained from the activity records, the personality test, and the clinical judgments yielded four general sets of relationships.

Strong relationships were found between clinical judgments of action orientation, personality variables indicative of extroversion, and social settings. Examples of social settings were the lobby on weekends, the park during the weekend, and bars. Thus extroverted, action-oriented people appear to spend more time in settings that provide opportunities for social interaction.

Strong relationships were also found between ego strength on the one hand, and behavior activities such as work on the weekend, basement recreation on the weekend, and behavior in the lobby on the weekend. Still another set of relationships was found between settings located outside the students' living area and unconventional action or behavior. This set of relationships also represented an action orientation, but one related to an unconventional life style and suspicious or brooding personality characteristics.

Finally, relationships were found between being male or female and the settings occupied. Being female was associated with activities such as spending time in the bathroom and spending time shopping or visiting in another student's room.

Thus the Eddy and Sinnett study suggests that there are clear relationships between activity orientation, personality, and where and how people spend their time in the relatively unconstrained college milieu. This research also indicates that one of the most important relationships between individual characteristics and setting characteristics lies in the way people select settings and settings select people.

Naturalistic Methods in Ecological Psychology.   One of the distinguishing characteristics of ecological research is its heavy reliance on a class of methods variously called "naturalistic approaches," "field methods," and "observational techniques." Although these methods have been commonly used in the field of ethology, their growing use by environmental psychologists is particularly interesting because much of psychology was until recently largely oriented toward experimental laboratory research.

Barker has remarked that the phenomena of science "occur without the benefit of scientists, but the data of a science are the joint product of scientists and the phenomena coupled within specially contrived data-generating systems."[38] He goes on to distinguish between two different types of data-generating system in behavioral science. The first involves the scientist as *transducer;* the second involves the scientist functioning as an *operator.*

In the case of transducer data-generating systems, the behavioral scientist merely receives, codes, and transmits information. He is attempting to answer the question "What goes on here?" The scientist is essentially a translating machine when he uses transducer data-generating systems.

Behavioral scientists as operators, on the other hand, are functioning in the context of a data-generating system in which they not only act as transducers, recording and transmitting information, but also as operators. That is, they quite consciously manipulate, influence, or regulate the phenomena in question to gain control and to focus on particular aspects of interest. The scientist as operator, then, is engaging in what we commonly call "experimental manipulations."

As we shall see, experimental and naturalistic research methods can and should function in complementary ways in the investigation and understanding of behavioral phenomena. Each method has strengths and weaknesses of its own, and in many cases the strength of one method is the weakness of the other. It follows from this rather straightforward premise that behavioral scientists interested in transducer methods and those interested in experimental methods should work together. At the very least, scientists with one preference in methodology should be aware of and interested in the approach of the other.

Unfortunately, this kind of complementary relationship is seldom seen in practice. Instead, many people have argued for the alleged superiority of one method over the other. Advocates of the experimental mode of research speak glowingly about the "control" provided by the experimental method.[39] They disparage naturalistic methods as being "only for avocational purposes."[40] On the other hand, partisan advocates of naturalistic research believe that the naturalistic method allows the researcher to have access to "the proper subject matter of psychology."[41] They speak in a mildly condescending way about the "artificiality" of laboratory experimentation.[42] Thus the positions taken by advocates of experimental or naturalistic methods have hardly been the models of the scientific detachment that one would expect from problem-oriented behavioral scientists.[43]

Dichotomizing naturalistic and experimental methods is not merely a waste of time, in fact, it may significantly distort the issues to which behavioral scientists should be addressing themselves. Willems has taken an important step beyond polemics in his analysis of the issues involved in the experimental versus naturalistic methodology controversy. Instead of putting all research into either "naturalistic" or "experimental" categories, he has suggested the arrangement of research activities along two independent dimensions. The first describes "the degree of the investigator's influence upon, or manipulation of, the antecedent conditions of the behavior studied." This dimension is the one most commonly used to characterize the distinction between naturalistic and experimental laboratory research.

Willems proposes a second dimension that describes "the degree to which units are imposed by the investigator upon the behavior studied." He suggests that it is possible to locate most research studies in a two-dimensional space (Figure 7.1) formed by combining these dimensions.[44] Thus the degree of manipulation of antecedent conditions can be judged to be low, medium, or high, and the degree of imposition of units on the behavior studied can also be characterized as low, medium, or high.

The bulk of behavioral studies probably fall along the main diagonal of the two-dimensional space illustrated. That is, if the degree of imposition of units on the behavior under study is low, so also is the degree of manipulation of antecedent conditions. And if the degree of imposition of units on the behavior is high, the degree of manipulation of antecedent conditions is also likely to be high. The apparent correlation may reveal one of the underlying aspects of the naturalistic versus experimental controversy. Often experimentally oriented researchers are fond of de-

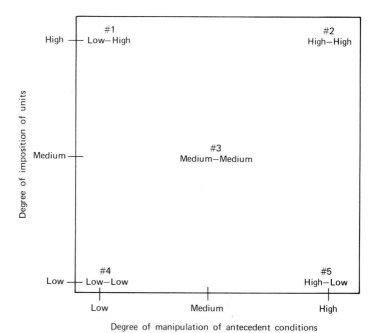

Figure 7.1 Two-dimensional space characterizing psychological research (adapted from Willems, 1969).

scribing their own research as "rigorous" (high on both dimensions), whereas field-oriented scientists, whose research is frequently low on both dimensions, like to say that this work involves "behavior in the real world."

In any case, the question is not which method—the naturalistic or the experimental—is "better," but whether there are problems for which each of these methods is uniquely suited. Willems has listed some of the purposes for which naturalistic research appears to be uniquely suited, and we consider these next.

Naturalistic studies are particularly important if one is concerned about the distribution of phenomena in nature. It is ironic that even with the present geometric increase in published research reports and professional journals dedicated to the reporting of behavioral science data, we know very little about how the relevant phenomena are distributed in nature. Barker makes this point particularly well when he says

> This state of affairs is most surprising in view of the situation in the old, prestigeful sciences that psychology so admires and emulates in other respects. In these sciences, the quest for the phenomena of science as they occur unaltered by the techniques of search and discovery is a central, continuing task; and the development of techniques for identifying entities and signalling processes without altering them (within organisms, within cells, within physical systems, and within machines) is among the sciences' most valued achievements. Handbooks and encyclopedias attest to the success of these efforts. We read, for example, that potassium (K) ranks seventh in order of abundance of the elements, and constitutes about 2.59% of the igneous rocks of the earth's crust; that its compounds are widely distributed in the primary rocks, the oceans, the soil, plants, and animals; and that soluble potassium salts are present in all fertile soils. The fact that there is no equivalent information in the literature of scientific psychology (about playing, about laughing, about talking, about being valued and devalued, about conflict, about failure) confronts psychologists with a monumental incompleted task.[45]

Naturalistic observation offers the promise of remedying this deficiency. For example, Barker and his colleagues have provided *specimen records* of day-long observations of children in their natural surrounding.[46] The records include descriptions of the subjects' behavior, conversations, interactions, and locations. Such data provide an opportunity to discover the distributions of children's behavior in their natural settings.

A second purpose to which naturalistic studies are uniquely suited is the study of the behavioral achievements that persons make in their everyday environments. That is, if one wishes to know how well individuals make use of their abilities in their everyday world and how they go about it, naturalistic observation appears to be the method of choice.

Another research problem to which naturalistic studies are particularly well adapted is that of describing the behavioral repertoire of individuals or of lower animals. In many cases it will be informative to discover how a particular species functions in its natural habitat and what kind of behaviors commonly occur in that natural context. Ethologists have made important strides in collecting such observations, and there are a variety of questions that can probably be answered in no other way.

A fourth class of cases in which naturalistic methods have a clear advantage are those in which it is unethical, dangerous, or not feasible to apply experimental methods. Willems suggests that natural disasters, physical disabilities, child-rearing regimens, deaths, and accidents are all examples of phenomena that are perhaps best studied using naturalistic methodology.[47]

There is a final advantage of data derived using what Barker describes as transducer methods. Barker has called for the accumulation of archives of data collected by naturalistic methods.[48] One prime example is the data available from the Midwest Psychological Field Station. These records, especially those of children's behavior, have been used for innumerable studies for which they were not originally intended. The specimen records of children's behavior have been used to test diverse hypotheses concerning, for example, children's attitudes toward food and Freudian theories of mother-son and father-daughter relations. Barker notes that these problems were far from the minds of the data collectors, yet data drawn selectively from the archives have provided valuable experimental leads in a wide variety of instances. Experimental methodology, on the other hand, furnishes data that are explicitly aimed at answering a particular question and are usually of little value outside the specific experimental context and questions originally posed. The taxonomic work on behavior settings discussed earlier in this chapter would have been impossible without the extensive data archives provided by Professor Barker and the Midwest Psychological Field Station.

Of course in some cases naturalistic methods are at a distinct disadvantage and experimental methodology is the research method of choice. One of the clearest instances of this kind is the case of the frequency of the phenomenon being so low that the data yield using naturalistic methods would be extremely small and very costly. Gump and Kounin, who studied the behavior of children in summer camp, discovered that the behavior in which they were interested occurred at the rate of about only one incident per 18 pages of specimen record material. Their reaction to this dilemma is nicely understated when they say, "This low yield was a sobering experience."[49]

Another major issue that must be considered in comparing experimental and naturalistic methodologies has to do with the thorny question of *generalization*. Perhaps the most obvious and most frequently cited reason for doing observational or naturalistic research is that the findings, whatever they may be, will be generalizable to the "real world." This seems to be a simple and straightforward proposition and a compelling motive for doing naturalistic observation. However Willems and Raush discuss this proposition in detail and suggest that it is not nearly as simple as has sometimes been thought. The issue of generalizability, or as Campbell and Stanley[50] describe it, "external validity," has often been discussed as if the use of naturalistic observation or unobtrusive measures were the only solution to the generalization problem.[51]

Willems and Raush have listed a number of limits to generalization associated with the use of experimental methods including (1) the use of arbitrarily demarcated spans of experimental time that may limit generalizability to sequences of behavior that emerge over extended periods of time outside the laboratory, (2) experimental involvement in a task that is perceived as being very brief by the subject and therefore free of long-range consequences for him, (3) the problem of subject selection, either for homogeneity or through volunteering, and (4) the arbitrary demarcation of "correct" responses.[52]

As Willems and Raush point out, the same features of experimental techniques that potentially jeopardize generalizability are also the experimental method's greatest strength. On the one hand, experimental methods provide us with precision and the opportunity to rule out competing explanations for an observation. On the other hand, the stringent application of experimental control and manipulation may produce findings that are quite relevant to the experimental question under consideration in the laboratory, yet tell us little about the world as we describe and experience it in the conduct of everyday life.

Conclusion. The research and theory reviewed in this chapter suggest that the behavior setting conception is an extremely fertile one. We have examined the characteristics and inner dynamics of behavior settings themselves and have noted that whether a setting is over- or undermanned can have a profound impact on the inhabitants of the setting. Behavior settings can serve as a basic environmental unit whose attributes can be measured, thus providing the basis of an empirical taxonomy of settings. The behavior setting is also a naturally occurring unit. It is not surprising, then, that much of the recent work in naturalistic observation has developed in the context of behavior setting theory and research. Finally, the behavior setting unit is a useful unit in a wide range of environments.

It is a reasonable guess that little of the work reviewed in this chapter would have been accomplished without Barker's unique vision. Like Darwin, Barker looked at phenomena that other men took to be commonplace, seeing in them structures and dynamics that promise to contribute substantially to our understanding of man-environment relationships.

REFERENCES

1. Barker, R. G. On the nature of the environment. *Journal of Social Issues,* **19:**26–27, 1963.

2. Wicker, A. W. Processes which mediate behavior-environment congruence. *Behavioral Science,* **17:**265–277, 1972.

3. Gump, P. V. Environmental guidance of the classroom behavioral system. In B. J. Biddle and W. J. Ellena (Eds.), *Contemporary research on teacher effectiveness.* Holt, Rinehart & Winston, New York, 1964, pp. 165–195.

4. Gump, P. V. Persons, settings and larger contexts. In B. P. Indik and F. K. Berrien (Eds.), *People, groups and organizations: An effective integration.* Columbia University Press, New York, 1968, pp. 247–248.

5. Barker, R. G. *Ecological psychology: Concepts and methods for studying the environment of human behavior.* Stanford University Press, Stanford, Calif., 1968.

6. Frederiksen, N. Toward a taxonomy of situations. *American Psychologist,* **27:**114–123, 1972.
   Moos, R. H. Conceptualizations of human environments. *American Psychologist,* **28:**652–665, 1973.
   Price, R. H. The taxonomic classification of behaviors and situations and the problem of behavior-environment congruence. *Human Relations,* **27:**567–585, 1974.
   Price, R. H. and Moos, R. H. Towards a taxonomy of inpatient treatment environments. *Journal of Abnormal Psychology,* **84:**181–188, 1975.
   Sells, S. B. General theoretical problems related to organizational taxonomy: A model solution. In B. P. Indik and F. K. Berrien (Eds.), *People, groups and organizations.* Columbia University Press, New York, 1968.

7. Craik, K. H. Environmental psychology. *Annual Review of Psychology.* Annual Reviews, Palo Alto, Calif., 1973, p. 404.

8. Cowen, E. Social and community interventions. *Annual Review of Psychology,* Annual Reviews, Palo Alto, Calif., 1973, p. 434.

9. Blashfield, R. K. *An evaluation of the DSM-11 classification of schizophrenia.* Doctoral dissertation, Indiana University, Bloomington, 1972.

10. Hempel, C. G. *Aspects of scientific explanation.* Free Press, New York, 1965.

11. Barker, *Ecological Psychology, op. cit.*

12. Price, R. H. and Blashfield, R. K. Explorations in the taxonomy of behavior settings: Analysis of dimensions and classification of settings. *American Journal of Community Psychology,* 1975 (in press).

13. Parsons, T. Suggestions for a sociological approach to the theory of organizations. *Administrative Science Quarterly,* **1:**63–85, 1956.

14. Wicker, Processes which mediate behavior-environment congruence, *op. cit.*

15. Barker, *Ecological Psychology, op. cit.,* p. 171.

16. *Ibid.,* p. 174.

17. Barker, R. G. Ecology and motivation. In M. R. Jones (Ed.), *Nebraska symposium on motivation.* University of Nebraska Press, Lincoln, 1960, pp. 1–49.

18. *Ibid.,* p. 33.

19. Wicker, A. W. and Kirmeyer, S. From church to laboratory to national park: A program of research on excess and insufficient populations in behavior settings. In S. Wapner, B. Kaplan, and S. Cohen (Eds.), *Experiencing the environment.* Plenum, New York, 1976.

20. Barker, R. G. and Gump, P. V. *Big school, small school.* Stanford University Press, Stanford, Calif., 1964, p. 20.

21. Gump, Environmental guidance of the classroom behavioral system, *op. cit.*

22. Baird, L. L. Big school, small school: A critical examination of the hypothesis. *Journal of Educational Psychology,* **60:**253–260, 1969.

23. Willems, E. P. Sense of obligation to high school activities as related to school size and marginality of student. *Child Development,* **38:**1257–1258, December 1967.

24. Willems, E. P. Planning a rationale for naturalistic research. In E. P. Willems and H. L. Raush (Eds.), *Naturalistic viewpoints in psychological research.* Holt, Rinehart & Winston, New York, 1969.

25. Wicker, A. W. Cognitive complexity, school size, and participation in school behavior settings: A test of the frequency of interaction hypothesis. *Journal of Educational Psychology,* **60:**200–203, 1969.

26. Wicker, A. W. Undermanning, performances, and students' subjective experiences in behavior settings of large and small high schools. *Journal of Personal and Social Psychology,* **10:**255–261, 1968.

Wicker, A. W. Size of church membership and members' support of church behavior settings. *Journal of Personal and Social Psychology,* **13**(3):278–288, 1969.

Wicker, A. W. and Mehler, A. Assimilation of new members in a large and a small church. *Journal of Applied Psychology,* **55:**151–156, 1971.

27. Wicker, A. W., McGrath, J. E., and Armstrong, G. E. Organization size and behavior setting capacity as determinants of member participation. *Behavioral Science*, **17**:510, 1972.

28. Wicker, A. W. Undermanning theory and research: Implications for the study of psychological and behavioral effects of excess populations. *Representative Research in Social Psychology*, **4**:190–191, 1973.

29. *Ibid.*, p. 193.

30. Zlutnick, S. and Altman, I. Crowding and human behavior. In J. F. Wohlwill and D. H. Carson (Eds.), *Environment and the social sciences: Perspectives and applications*. American Psychological Association, Washington, D.C., 1971.

31. Wicker and Kirmeyer, From church to laboratory to national park, *op. cit.*

32. Gump, P. Operating environments in schools of open and traditional design. *School Review*, **82**:575–593, 1974.

    Barker, R. and Schoggen, P. *Qualities of community life*. Jossey-Bass, San Francisco, 1973.

33. Schoggen, M. and Schoggen, P. Environmental forces in the home lives of three-year old children in three population subgroups. DARCEE papers and reports, **5** (2), John F. Kennedy Center for Research on Education and Human Development, George Peabody College for Teachers, Nashville, Tenn., 1971.

34. Wicker, A. and Farrell, B. How do children behave appropriately to their every day environments? An ecological study of some processes suggested by learning theories. Unpublished manuscript, Psychology Department, Claremont Graduate School, Claremont, Calif., 1973.

35. LeCompte, W. F. Behavior settings: The structure of the treatment environment. Proceedings of the Environmental Design and Research Association Conference, Vol. 1, University of California, 1972, p. 4.2.

36. Willems, E. P. Place and motivation: Independence and complexity in patient behavior. Proceedings of the Environmental Design and Research Association Conference, Vol. 1, University of California, 1972, p. 4.3.6.

    See also Willems, E. The interface of the hospital environment and patient behavior. *Archives of Physical Medicine and Rehabilitation*, **53**:115–122, 1972.

37. Eddy, G. L. and Sinnett, R. Behavior setting utilization by emotionally disturbed college students. *Journal of Consulting and Clinical Psychology*, **40**:210–216, 1973.

38. Barker, *Ecological psychology, op. cit.*, p. 139.

39. Rosenthal, R. Covert communication in the psychological experiment. *Psychological Bulletin*, **67**:356–367, 1967.

40. Harlow, H. F. Behavioral contributions to interdisciplinary research. In H. F. Harlow and C. N. Woolsey (Eds.), *Biological and biochemical bases of behavior*. University of Wisconsin Press, Madison, 1958, p. 4.

41. Cartwright, D. Lewinian theory as a contemporary systematic framework. In S. Koch (Ed.), *Psychology: A study of a science*, Vol. 11, No. 11. McGraw-Hill, New York, 1959.

42. Epstein, S. Comments on Dr. Bandura's paper. In M. R. Jones (Ed.), *Nebraska symposium on motivation*. University of Nebraska Press, Lincoln, 1962, pp. 269–270.

43. Willems, E. P. and Raush, H. L. *Naturalistic viewpoints in psychological research*. Holt, Rinehart & Winston, New York, 1969.

44. Willems, Planning a rationale for naturalistic research, *op. cit.*

45. Barker, *Ecological psychology, op. cit.*, p. 145.

46. Barker, R. G. and Wright, H. F. *One boy's day*. Harper & Row, New York, 1951.

    Barker, R. G. and Wright, H. F. *Midwest and its children*. Harper & Row, New York, 1955.

    Barker, R. G. (Ed.). *The stream of behavior*. Appleton-Century-Crofts, New York, 1963.

47. Willems, Planning a rationale for naturalistic research, *op. cit.*

48. Barker, R. G. Wanted: An eco-behavioral science. In E. P. Willems and H. L. Raush (Eds.), *Naturalistic viewpoints in psychological research*. Holt, Rinehart & Winston, New York, 1969.

49. Gump, P. V. and Kounin, J. S. Issues raised by ecological and "classical" research efforts. *Merrill-Palmer Quarterly*, **6:**145–152, 1959–1960.

50. Campbell, D. T. and Stanley, J. C. *Experimental and quasi-experimental designs for research*. Rand McNally, Skokie, Ill., 1963.

51. Webb, E. J., Campbell, D. T., Schwartz, R. D., and Sechrest, L. *Unobstrusive measures*. Rand McNally, Skokie, Ill., 1966.

52. Willems and Raush, *op. cit.*

CHAPTER EIGHT

The Impact of Organizational[a] Structure and Change

Historians give labels to periods in history to capture their unique characteristics. For example, the Renaissance denotes the rebirth of Greco-Roman civilization beginning in the 1400s; the Age of Enlightenment symbolizes the rational and scientific spirit of the eighteenth century; and the Industrial Revolution epitomizes the accelerated process of shifting from hand tools to power machinery in the nineteenth century.[1] How might our century be labeled? One dominant characteristic is the rapid expansion and increased scope of large organizations. Although formal organizations (e.g., the Catholic Church) have existed throughout modern history, the twentieth century might well be called the Organization Age because of the pervasiveness of large organizations. Consider the range of activities we pursue in organizational settings.

> We are born in organizations, educated by organizations, and many of us spend much of our lives working for organizations. We spend much of our leisure time paying, playing, and praying in organizations. Most of us will die in an organization, and when the time comes for burial, the largest organization of all—the state—must grant official permission.[2]

Since organizations are an integral part of modern society, their impact has generated a great deal of discussion and research.

---

[a] This chapter is co-authored by Evelyn Bromet and Rudolf Moos.

An organization is in part a formal structure "established for the pursuit of relatively specific objectives."[3] As a formal structure it has both size (number of employees) and shape (number of levels of authority). An organization is also an environment with explicit rules, roles, and responsibilities. Like most environments, an organization influences the behaviors and attitudes of the people who participate in it. This influence can often be traced to the very structure of an organization (i.e., its size and shape). Organizations, like other environments, are dynamic settings whose structures grow and change over time, and the changes or innovations have an impact on the behaviors and attitudes of the persons involved. This chapter examines the effects of both structure and change on people in work organizations, such as industries and business concerns, and service organizations, such as hospitals and correctional facilities.

The expansion of organizations has been accompanied by a lively debate about the nature of organizational functioning. The different theories provide a frame of reference for viewing the impact of structure and change and the mechanisms that mediate their influence. Thus we begin by considering some major perspectives in organization theory and offering a conceptual model for understanding research on structure and change. We then critically review some effects of structure and change in work and service organizations.

Theoretical Perspectives on Organizations.   Organization theory was first applied to the pragmatic concern of maximizing efficiency, productivity, and profits in industry. As the debate about these issues developed, three factors attracted considerable attention: the formal structure of an organization, the behavioral determinants of individual functioning, and the role of informal groups. Many social theorists have elaborated on the elements and interrelations of these factors. Since the turn of the century, four distinct schools of thought have emerged: (1) scientific management, which took a thoroughly economic stance, (2) human relations, which reacted by emphasizing the social inputs, and (3) structuralism and (4) open systems, which tried to bridge the first two perspectives.

Scientific Management.   Scientific management grew out of the classical theory of organizations, which emphasized the sharp division of labor and the vertical chain of command depicted on an organizational chart.[4] The division of labor entails breaking each job into its simplest components, thus enabling individual workers as well as production systems to operate at maximum efficiency. Workers are assumed to be motivated primarily by material rewards. To ensure maximum productivity, incentives (pay) are manipulated to correspond closely to workers' output. Communication takes place vertically through a pyramidlike hierarchy where each supervisor is responsible for his or her subordinates (the number of subordinates, or span of control, decreases with higher organizational levels, thus creating the pyramid-shaped hierarchy). At the apex of the structure sits the president or board of directors who controls, directs, and coordinates all activities toward the organization's goals.

Frederick Taylor closely adhered to the tenets of classical organization theory in his attempt to optimize worker productivity. Underlying the principles of scientific management was the conviction that workers were motivated only by pay; in a system where pay is tied to productivity, money would induce people to work as fast as physically possible. Going beyond mere task specialization in the division of labor, Taylor focused on the physical requirements of a job, determining the best pace, body movements, illumination, and the like. Besides the physical conditions that produced maximum efficiency and productivity, Taylor also formulated an ideal span of control (number of subordinates per supervisor) for each job.

The nature of scientific management was cogently illustrated by Taylor's description of Schmidt the pig-iron handler, (whose job consisted in moving a 92-pound pig of iron from one pile to another).[5] Prior to a careful analysis of the job, Schmidt had been handling 12.5 tons of pig iron per day. By "scientifically" dissecting every aspect of the job, Taylor determined the procedure that would achieve the maximum output. The new design required Schmidt's supervisor to watch him all day, telling him when to lift a pig, when to walk, and when to rest. As a result, Schmidt's output rose to 47 tons of pig iron per day. Obviously Schmidt was subjected to enormous pressure under the new system. To induce him to cooperate, Taylor played up the material rewards of handling more pigs "fixing his attention on the high wages which he wants and away from what, if it were called to his attention, he probably would consider impossibly hard work."[6]

Middle-class managers in the early 1900s, were favorably impressed with this account of the advantages of scientific management. Productivity and profits were both enhanced. Far from being unusual, Taylor's total concern with physical capacity and neglect of human emotions corresponded with prevailing attitudes toward unskilled immigrant laborers such as Schmidt. However by the 1920s the moral climate had shifted, and managers were cautioned to "treat workers as human beings."[7] Moreover, the classical organization model and its derivative, scientific management, had been challenged by the discovery of informal social networks in industry. These social groupings were found to play a central role in controlling productivity and communication. In reality, the formal chain of command depicted on an organizational chart was often bypassed and even avoided. The discovery of informal social networks added a human dimension to organization theory and led to a new approach called human relations.

Human Relations. How was the "social environment" of organizations discovered? Following Taylor's lead, many studies were conducted to determine which working conditions and pay incentives increased worker efficiency and output the most. At the Western Electric Company's Hawthorne Works in Chicago, researchers manipulated lighting levels and the length and frequency of rest periods among small groups of workers.[8] They were unable to demonstrate the best possible working conditions. Instead they were surprised to find that productivity increased in every one of the test conditions! Even in the most extreme circumstances, when illumination was reduced to the level of "bright moonlight" and rest periods were eliminated, the workers produced more than their counterparts in the rest of the plant. These findings could not be explained by the assumptions of scientific management. After extensive interviews with workers in the plant, the investigators were forced to conclude that there were social influences—both the special attention from the experimenters and the interactions between the workers—that accounted for the increased production.

To test this hypothesis the researchers carried out the famous Bank Wiring Room experiment in which 14 telephone switchboard assemblers were isolated in a special room and observed over a 7-month period.[9] Workers were paid individually according to their average weekly output, and, in addition, received a bonus depending on the average group output. Despite the individual work incentives, group pressure was the primary influence of productivity. With daily output established informally, both "rate busters" and "chiselers" were subject to ostracism, sabotage, and even physical reprisals. Records were falsified, unpopular supervisors were duped, and certain workers were protected. These actions were not taken out of malice against the company but out of fear that greater output would result in layoffs and pay cuts (the study was conducted during the Great Depression).

The important conclusions from this study formed the crux of human relations theory, which contradicted the principles of scientific management. (1) *Social* norms rather than physical capacity determine the level of productivity. (2) Social sanctions (i.e., coworker respect) rather than economic incentives determine productivity. (3) Individual behavior is determined by the group rather than by an individual or his or her supervisor. In short, informal communication and the informal social environment are more directly related to worker productivity than are formal communication networks, physical conditions of workers, or exact monetary incentives.

If the source of inefficiency lies with the group, the solution must also be found in the group. Once this was realized, problems were taken directly to the workers, and management let them share in planning a suitable solution. Coch and French demonstrated the desirability of this approach (known as "participative management").[10] They showed that technological changes in a pajama factory were facilitated among groups of employees given orientational lectures about the reasons for the changes, and among groups given an opportunity to help design retraining programs. Workers who did not receive an explanation for the changes, and workers not participating in designing retraining programs, tended to resist the changes.

The human relations movement has had a substantial impact on managerial practice. Influential writers such as Rensis Likert have advocated group decision making as a means of changing employee attitudes to conform more closely to an organization's goals.[11] The aim was to successfully balance workers' needs with the organization's goals to create a stable, happy environment.

Thus the human relations movement constituted a strong attack on the principles of motivation and efficiency espoused by scientific management and the classical model of organizations. Ironically, it too offered a one-dimensional view of human motivation and organizational efficiency by focusing primarily on social concerns and informal group membership. To think of worker motivation as purely social is as narrow as a simple economic stance; to change employee attitudes using group pressure is as limited as manipulating pay incentives. In reaction to the one-sidedness of human relations theory, and drawing on the newly translated writings of Max Weber, a new perspective emerged.

Structuralism. The structuralist approach is a synthesis of such diverse conceptions as classical organization theory, human relations, the writings of Max Weber, and to some extent the work of Karl Marx.[12] In combining these traditions, the structuralists offered a totally encompassing analysis of organizations, one that included both formal and informal elements and material and social rewards. It also added nonwork settings to the realm of organization theory and viewed the organization as a *dynamic* structure.

The conceptual foundations of the structuralist school are contained in the writings of Max Weber.[13] Briefly, Weber enumerated three features that formed the basis of the ideally efficient (i.e., bureaucratic) organization: (1) a division of labor comprised of technical specialists or experts who regard their employment as a life-long career, (2) a pyramid-shaped authority structure in which each official is responsible for those beneath him and reports to those immediately above him, and (3) formal rules and regulations governing decisions and behavior. In addition, Weber outlined other characteristics of a bureaucratic (efficient) organization. Management and workers were to be recruited, ensuring that they shared a common view of the organization and its goals, thus legitimizing the manager's authority over the workers (although some degree of conflict was considered inevitable). This model has the formal structure of the classical model, but it spells out the role characteristics of an organization's members and the mechanics of hierarchical control.

The structuralists were also sensitive to another critical issue, and here they borrowed from Marx as well as Weber. By concentrating on managerial goals both scientific management and human relations thinkers assumed that a conflict of interest was inherently negative. The structuralists accepted the existence of conflicting interest groups (e.g., employees and managers) and saw them as potentially useful for improving an organization.

Weber's description has important implications for a manager trying to deal with inefficiency. It suggests that the causes of inefficiency probably include factors other than *workers'* attitudes or *workers'* physical routines—for example, deficiencies in managerial control and technical knowledge, or imperfections in existing regulations. It could also include structural defects in the pyramid—there might be too many workers at certain levels and too few at others. Thus by detailing the ideally efficient organization, Weber provided clues for identifying diverse sources of inefficiency.

Although the structuralist model of organizations has enlarged the list of possible causes of inefficiency, there is one other contributing factor to be considered, and the open systems approach is particularly emphatic about the environment in which the organization operates.

Open Systems. The open systems approach sees an organization as a dynamic enterprise composed of many subsystems, all interrelated within an organization and interacting with the external environment.[14] Since the external environment is never stable, to survive, an organization must be flexible and adaptive. For example, following the launch of the first Sputnik in 1957 (external event), high schools and universities (organizations) began to emphasize physical sciences in their curricula (adaptation). Thus knowledge of the external environment is necessary to explain an intraorganizational change. It is also the case that organizations often shape the external environment to suit their own needs. Adaptation can occur on both sides of an organization's doors.

A Conceptual Model.   Figure 8.1 presents a conceptual model designed to illustrate the major factors mediating the effects of organizational structure and change on people in organizations. It also shows the interrelationships among these factors and the influence of external conditions on all aspects of organizational functioning. The model itself is a synthesis of the major theoretical perspectives on organizational functioning. Before explaining how the components fit together, we describe them individually.

Organizational Factors.   Organizations have many structural properties and experience even more innovations and changes. In work organizations the two structural dimensions most thoroughly studied are size (of work group and of plant) and shape, expressed as the number of supervisory levels relative to the total number of employees. Based on the span of control, the aspect of shape constitutes the "tallness" or "flatness" of an organization. Another facet of shape, degree of centralization, has also received some attention relevant to our discussion. With regard to organizational change in work settings, automation provides a historically significant example of a major structural innovation.

In service organizations the structural properties examined are size (of program and of institution) and resident-staff ratio, or the number of patients or residents per staff member. The interdisciplinary health care team provides a current example of a major structural innovation in health care settings.

Mediating Factors: Roles, Average Background Characteristics, Social Climate.   The influence of organizational characteristics on people's behaviors and attitudes depends on three interrelated factors: roles, average background characteristics, and social climate. In work settings *roles* refer to positions in the organizational hierarchy, and the responsibilities, expectations, and rewards associated with those positions (role concomitants). In service settings roles refer not only to the positions in the staff hierarchy but to the functions of residents or patients. *Average background and personalities* often differ across organizations; this may reflect their location in urban or rural areas, particular ethnic groups attracted to or accepted by certain organizations, and so on. Average background and personality factors also vary among different roles; for example, educa-

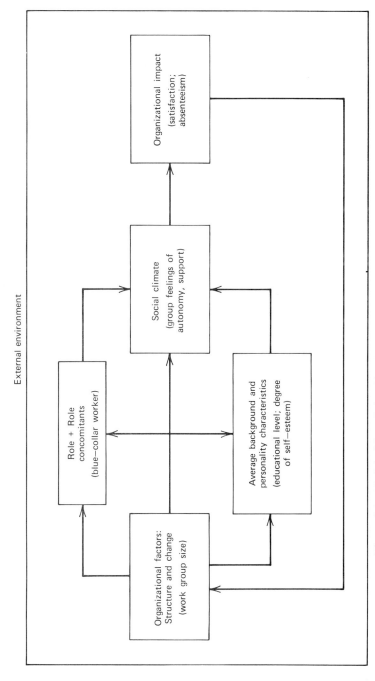

External environment

Figure 8.1 Model of the relationship of organizational factors to organizational impact.

tional levels tend to be lower among blue-collar workers than among managerial personnel. Finally the *social climate* created at different organizational levels can either accentuate or mitigate the structural influences (see Chapter 10).

These three factors condition the effects generated by organizational structure and change, raising two important implications. First, identification of the intermediate factors increases the accuracy in predictions about actual effects. For example, the effects of organization size are not the same across all levels of an organization. Large universities elicit feelings of alienation and insignificance in students; yet the same settings encourage faculty to feel part of the "mainstream" of academia. Second, the presence of mediators implies that negative effects can be changed even if the structural properties that generated them are permanent —that is, the mediators can function as the change agents. Thus in the case of large universities, the social climate of dormitories and classrooms could be modified to increase interpersonal involvement and affiliation.

Organizational Impact.   As we have already indicated, the effects of organizational structure and change are manifested in the behaviors and attitudes of the people in each setting. In work environments, differences in attitudes, such as satisfaction and morale, and in behaviors, such as absenteeism and turnover, have been linked to structural properties. In service environments, attitudes and behaviors, such as satisfaction with the treatment program and release rates, have been assessed.

It is important to maintain a balanced perspective when considering the relationship of organizational properties to people's attitudes and behaviors. Impacts can be positive or negative. Moreover, positive and negative consequences often exist side by side. For example, although students in large universities often feel isolated, they may also report more satisfaction with the range of academic and extracurricular opportunities than students in small colleges.

External Environment.   No organization is "an island," and the world around it influences and is influenced by all aspects of its functioning. If workers respond to inflation by demanding higher wages, for example, to maintain existing profit margins, organizations must increase the costs of their products. The demand for health care might result in the opening of a new outpatient facility; in turn, a new health facility might decrease unemployment if previously unemployed community residents were hired and trained to work there.

The Model as a Whole.   The model suggests that organizational factors determine the role positions and background characteristics of the people who enter an organization. For example, a company adopting a computer (organizational change) may upgrade the job descriptions of clerical employees (role) and hire college-educated people to fill these jobs (average background characteristic). The model also indicates that role positions, members' background characteristics, and organizational factors all contribute to creating a social climate or atmosphere in which daily activities are carried out (see Chapter 10). The climate may be supportive of or antithetical to satisfaction and productivity (indicators of organizational impact). Finally, the impact itself may influence organizational factors. Productivity might generate growth, create new positions, and so on. Lack of productivity might have a negative influence on an organization's structure. The organization, the people who comprise it, and the climate in which the personnel function are also affected by such external circumstances as economic, social, and political conditions.

Structural Factors in Work Organizations.

Organization and Work Group Size.   Most people intuitively believe that small size in organizations is more desirable than large size. In fact throughout history there has been a consensus about the negative effects of large size. During the Exodus from Egypt, Jethro warned his son-in-law Moses that it was inefficient for him to deal single-handedly with large numbers of Israelites demanding his advice. "You and the people with you will wear yourselves out, for the thing is too heavy for you; you are not able to perform it alone."[15] Aristotle felt that democracy could not work effectively in large-sized states where citizens did not know "one another's characters."[16] These concerns were echoed centuries later in the writings of Karl Marx, who reasoned that the lack of interaction between employers and employees in large bureaucracies led to conflict between capital and labor and misunderstanding between management and workers.[17] Emile Durkheim put this very succinctly: " . . . small scale industry . . . displays a relative harmony between worker and employer. It is only in large scale industry that these relations are in a sickly state."[18]

Critics of large size have cited many instances of undesirable effects of this property. Some of the most striking and diverse examples were provided by R. W. Revans,[19] who noted the following:

1.   In 1869 the risk of dying from an amputation was three times greater in the largest hospitals in England than in the smallest ones.
2.   During 1950 absenteeism in the smaller plants of a large British company were one-quarter the rates of the very largest plants.
3.   Between 1948 and 1953 coal mine output fell with increasing size of mine, according to British production data.

    4.   In 1956 industrial accidents in Great Britain rose steadily with increasing factory size.

Revans concluded from this evidence that "some ostensible aims of human beings are difficult to achieve in large organizations; these statistics suggest that size may have a disabling effect on human cooperation."[20]

An impressive testimonial about the advantages of small-sized settings was furnished by Mayo and Lombard (two noted human relations advocates) after visiting an aircraft factory in England during the summer of 1939.[21] Located in a valley along the Thames River, the factory was particularly vulnerable to attack by German bombers. The decision was made to decentralize the factory, and small units were set up in towns far away from the main plant. Many of the shops could not be moved, however, and remained in operation in the original building. Mayo and Lombard reported that absenteeism and turnover dropped considerably in the smaller units, but remained at the original rate in the large factory. Quantity and quality of work were higher in the smaller units, even in the absence of qualified supervisors to oversee the work.

Thus there are many anecdotal reports of the negative impact of large size. Do our speculations and preliminary findings hold up under more careful scrutiny? Research on the relationship of organization size and employees' attitudes and behaviors has focused on two somewhat different aspects of size—work group size and plant size. Although it is important to distinguish between these two aspects of size, the relevant findings are remarkably similar.

Job-Related Attitudes.   Some of the most interesting research on the impact of size deals with job satisfaction and employee morale. For example, Talacchi[22] examined the effect of plant size on three indices of satisfaction: (1) satisfaction with interpersonal relationships (i.e., employee-employee relationships, employee-supervisor relationships, and employee-management relationships), (2) satisfaction with nonmaterial rewards (i.e., the psychological satisfaction of the job itself), and (3) satisfaction with material rewards. Talacchi reasoned that increased size might reduce nonmaterial rewards but might not be related to such material rewards as salary and fringe benefits. He studied employees of 66 manufacturing (metal, food produce, chemical) plants and of 27 nonmanufacturing (financial, wholesale, and retail—i.e., white collar) firms. The range of plant or firm sizes was extremely large, varying from 10 to 1800 employees. Talacchi found that satisfaction with interpersonal relationships and satisfaction with nonmaterial rewards were considerably lower in the larger plants. Satisfaction with material rewards, however, was not affected by size of plant. The overall level of satisfaction decreased with size in both manufacturing plants (i.e., mostly blue-collar workers) and in nonmanufacturing firms (i.e., mostly white-collar workers).

Many other studies encompassing a variety of settings basically support these findings about satisfaction.[23] A survey of employees working in various departments of a metals fabrication factory revealed that satisfaction was lower in the larger departments. Other investigators learned that workers in large pharmaceutical warehouses were less satisfied than workers in small warehouses. In yet another study it was discovered that in two factories with different pay incentive schemes, workers in the larger groups were less well informed about their earnings. Satisfaction among workers "without knowledge" decreased as size of groups increased. Finally, a study of 32 package delivery departments, varying in size from 15 to 61 workers, disclosed that less satisfaction was expressed among workers in large departments compared with those in smaller departments.[24]

Studies of other job-related attitudes also indicate that increasing size may have negative consequences. In England the Acton Society Trust conducted a widely cited study in which various negative factors were associated with increased size.[25] As size increased, for example, interest in the affairs of the organization, voting on work unit issues, and knowledge of administrators' names all decreased, while acceptance of rumors grew. Another study indicated that increasing size led to less agreement among workers and supervisors on role functions, and less commitment to the ethics and ideals of the work.[26]

Our conceptual model indicated that role position mediates the effects of organizational factors, such as size. The results just described pertain mainly to blue-collar and lower-level white-collar workers. Do these findings generalize to managers? Or do managers feel more satisfied and more important when they supervise large work groups?

In a 5-year follow-up study of graduates of the Stanford Business School, Thomas Harrell compared job satisfaction of men employed in large (1000 or more employees) and small (fewer than 1000 employees) firms.[27] Men in the smaller firms were more satisfied with their work than were men in the larger firms. Importantly, men in the smaller firms also had higher compensation and were able to participate more broadly in management than men in the larger firms. However, Stanford Business School graduates have considerable choice in selecting an employer. Thus there were selective differences between the men who chose (and were chosen by) large firms and smaller firms. It is therefore uncertain whether Harrell's results reflect an impact of organization size or personality traits of people who choose large versus small organizations. Perhaps the people who chose small companies would have been more satisfied with their work regardless of company size. On the other hand, the greater satisfaction of men in small firms may have resulted from size-related differences between the firms.

Porter studied the relationship between size and job attitudes among a nationwide sample of 1900 managers.[28] Three categories of organization size were used: small (fewer than 500 employees); medium (500–5000 employees); and large (more than 5000 employees). People were placed into one of five managerial levels from vice president to low-level administrator. The results showed that at lower and lower-middle levels of management, small company managers were more satisfied than their counterparts in large companies. At upper-middle and vice-presidential levels, however, large company managers reported greater satisfaction.

The same managers also described their jobs in quite different terms, depending on whether they worked in large or small organizations.[29] Managers in large companies were more positive, using adjectives such as "good," "interesting," "challenging," and "imaginative." Small company managers were more likely to see traits such as "caution" and "tact" as important to their positions. These descriptions failed to support the popular assumption that large organizations turn creative, inner-directed individuals into compliant, other-directed "organization men." In fact managerial positions in large organizations were characterized more favorably.

Thus with regard to attitudes, size is an important antecedent for both blue- and white-collar workers. Do these attitudes carry over into actual behavior, such as absenteeism and productivity?

Absenteeism. There is consistent evidence that absenteeism rises with increased size among blue-collar work groups. Two of the earliest studies found this association among both male and female employees. One investigation of construction and maintenance work groups in an electric power company showed that absence rates of larger groups (more than seven men) were greater than those of the smaller work groups (fewer than seven men).[30] In the second study, conducted in a textile factory in England, the number of workers (mostly female) per room was the measure of size.[31] The results showed that absenteeism in the smaller rooms was less than half that of the average for the factory as a whole.

Absenteeism is also higher in larger factories. Revans showed that absenteeism in the largest plants of a British company (composed of 91 factories) was four times as great as the rate for the very smallest units.[32] He also demonstrated that absence rates were relatively higher in larger gas works in the London area, telephone exchange units, coal mines, chemical factories, and factories manufacturing electrolytic products. The Acton Society Trust survey reported the same relationship between size and absenteeism in British factories.[33]

The consistency of this finding in different types of settings is impressive.[34] Baumgartel and Sobol discovered that yearly mean absences among employees of 11 plants of a major American airline ranged from 5.9 in the smallest plant to 9.4 in the largest. Absenteeism in various departments of a metals fabrication company was higher in the larger departments. A study of package delivery firms revealed higher absentee rates in the larger firms.[35] Finally, Ingham showed the same size effect in eight randomly selected light engineering industries.[36]

Clearly for blue-collar workers, factory and work group size are important determinants of absenteeism. Unfortunately, white-collar workers and managers have not been included in these studies (with one minor exception); thus there is no evidence about how size relates to their absence rates.

Turnover. Job turnover can be a costly proposition for an organization, since almost every job requires some training or investment by an employer. Leaving a job can also be expensive for an employee because it may mean losing both wages and seniority. Thus, as might be expected, increased size is associated with greater turnover, but not as highly or consistently as in the case of absenteeism.

Several studies have found higher turnover rates in larger settings.[37] The metals fabrication factory survey (described earlier) reported that turnover rose progressively with size of department. Katzell, Barrett, and Parker, studying employees of 72 pharmaceutical warehouses, found higher employee turnover rates in the larger warehouses. Another study showed the same size effect in large offices compared with smaller ones. Finally, Indik and Seashore examined turnover in 36 automobile sales dealerships and found higher termination rates in the larger dealerships.

On the other hand, two studies were unable to demonstrate any size effects.[38] Although the relationship has been generally confirmed (four out of six studies), it is not quite as strong as it was for the case of absenteeism. It has been demonstrated that satisfaction, absenteeism, and turnover are related to each other, as well as to organization and work group size.[39] That is, satisfied workers exhibit lower average absenteeism and turnover rates than unhappy workers. Thus on the whole it is fair to conclude that size is moderately related to employee turnover.

There have been attempts to link size with other organizational outcomes, such as productivity, accident rates, and labor disputes, but no consistent patterns have been documented. Possibly the type and level of technology are the crucial organizational determinants here.

Organization Shape: Supervisor-Employee Ratios.   After warning Moses about the dangers of dealing personally with a large number of people, Jethro made the following suggestions: "Place [able and trustworthy] men over the people as rulers of thousands, of hundreds, of fifties, and of tens."[40] In other words, Jethro proposed a pyramidal hierarchy where groups of 1000 had a supervisor, every 100 supervisors had a supervisor, and so on. The Incas in South America used this principle in the organization of their society. Every 10 persons reported to a supervisor, and 10 of these reported to a higher-level supervisor. Ten of the next level supervisors reported to the next higher level leader, and so forth, until the 10 highest-level leaders reported to the Inca god. These supervisory ratios are referred to as the "span of control" in modern organization theory. The total number of supervisory levels in an organization is based in part on the span of control. Moses could have set up more or fewer levels between himself and the Israelites by decreasing or increasing, respectively, the supervisory ratios or span of control.

An organization that has many levels of supervision relative to its total size is considered "tall"; conversely, a structure with few levels relative to its total size is considered "flat." Large organizations are generally taller than small ones; therefore, research on the tall-flat dimension must take organization size into account as well.

Many people think that a flat structure provides a milieu conducive to job satisfaction. Specifically, in an organization with few levels of supervision relative to its total size, each supervisor has responsibility for a large number of subordinates (i.e., a large span of control). In this situation, an individual worker *presumably* has a fair degree of autonomy in decision making. Such active participation in the work is thought to facilitate job identification and satisfaction.[41] Conversely, in an organization characterized by a tall structure, there are many levels of supervision, a smaller span of control (i.e., a high ratio of supervisors to subordinates), supposedly less autonomy and responsibility for the average employee, and hence less job satisfaction.

One of the most widely cited advocates of the flat organization structure was J. C. Worthy.[42] Worthy's contentions were based on a survey of Sears, Roebuck and Company, an unusually flat organization which, despite its enormous size, has only four levels of supervision between the president and the salespeople. Worthy's survey showed that 72% of the employees regarded Sears as a better than average work setting. He attributed these favorable attitudes in large part to the flat structure of the

Sears organization. Since that time, several empirical studies have been conducted to evaluate his conclusion.

Porter and Lawler tested Worthy's theories and found that the relationship between the tall-flat dimension and employee attitudes is more complex than the original formulation.[43] They obtained responses to attitude questionnaires from 1900 managers of companies throughout the United States. Organizations were classified as *tall, intermediate,* or *flat* based on the ratio of the number of levels of authority relative to total company size. Managers in flat organizations were no more satisfied than their counterparts in tall organizations. In attempting to determine the effect of size on the relationship between type of structure and satisfaction, they found that in small organizations, managers in flat structures reported greater satisfaction than managers in tall structures. In large organizations, managers in tall companies were more satisfied than managers in flat structures.

Porter and Siegel repeated this study using a sample of 3000 managers from organizations in 13 foreign countries.[44] Once again, the results showed that in smaller organizations, a flat structure was associated with greater satisfaction, and the reverse was found for companies with 5000 or more employees. Thus the work of Porter and his associates suggests that size mediates the impact of organizational shape.

El Salmi and Cummings, who investigated this issue with a sample of managers participating in the Indiana University Executive Development Program,[45] found a U-shaped relationship between shape and satisfaction. Managers from intermediate structures reported the most satisfaction. At the same time, there was a trend for tall structures to be more satisfying than flat structures. Our conceptual model suggested that role position is often an important mediator of structural effects. This study revealed that tall structures were superior only for top management positions; at the lower levels, flat structures offered greater job satisfaction. Thus the impact of organizational shape is a more complex issue than Worthy had assumed.

Another study examined a variety of attitudes, including values, social orientation, and intellectual functioning, among a nationwide sample of male employees.[46] In this case the number of supervisory levels relative to size was called "degree of bureaucratization" in keeping with Weber's terminology. Men in the more bureaucratized (tall) organizations tended to be more intellectually flexible, more open to new experience, and more self-directed in their values than men working in nonbureaucratic (flat) organizations. This suggests that some areas of creative functioning are enhanced in tall organizations.

Thus the relationship between the tall-flat dimension and attitudes is complex. At least two variables are important in mediating its effect: organization size and occupational level (or role). Worthy's unqualified assertions are not supported under critical examination. One interpretation of their failure might be that size and shape must be appropriately matched. For example, in a small organization, a tall structure would be deleterious in that it could create problems in coordination and communication that might not necessarily have existed. Also, Worthy based his conclusions on his observations of Sears Roebuck, which is not only flat but *decentralized*. Since comparable information about decentralization was not supplied in the other studies, it may be that Worthy's comments apply only to smaller-scale and/or decentralized organizations.

Structural Change: Automation. Just as the structural properties of organizations can influence the behaviors and attitudes of workers, structural changes can have a powerful impact. The effects of automation in work settings have been the subject of a long and heated debate. The advocates of automation applaud the material benefits associated with technological progress, whereas social critics blame automation for the discontent of industrial and white-collar workers. In fact, there are both advantages and costs, depending on the level of automation and the type of industry involved.

Automation is an outgrowth of mechanization, a major catalyst of the Industrial Revolution. Mechanization itself had some unfortunate consequences for industrial workers. One of the earliest descriptions was written by Adam Smith. Although he was impressed that 240 times as many pins could be produced by dividing pin-making into 18 separate operations, Smith was nevertheless aware of the human costs.

> The man whose whole life is spent in performing a few simple operations . . . has no occasion to exert his understanding, or to exercise his invention in finding out expedients for removing difficulties which never occur. He naturally loses, therefore, the habit of such exertion, and generally becomes as stupid and ignorant as it is possible for a human creature to become.[47]

Mechanization gradually grew in sophistication and complexity. Its current form, automation, is distinguished by the use of electronic equipment to *direct*, *control*, and *correct* an operation automatically. One important component of the system is the computer. Consider the following description of the baking process at Sara Lee.

> In the kitchens of the Sara Lee Company in Deerfield, Illinois, the computer system not only mixes and bakes twelve different kinds of cakes, but also

packages them, freezes them, stores them, starts them on their way to the store, and even handles some of the bookwork. Their computers direct operations at about 15,000 points in the plant, issue 180,000 instructions every three seconds, monitor some 300 variables in the cake-baking process, and scan 200 incoming messages per second.[48]

There are numerous studies of worker satisfaction showing that the more automated the task, the more dissatisfied workers feel.[49] The man on the assembly line epitomizes the lack of control and meaninglessness associated with automation. We are interested here in the special case in which automation represents a structural *change* in an organization. Specifically, what happens to people, in the short run and in the long run, when automation is experienced as a major innovation in their work setting?

One of the main effects reported in studies of industrial and clerical workers is increased social isolation. When computers were installed in several insurance companies, the following observation was made: "Less face-to-face communication is the consequence, and working inter-dependencies are achieved by communication from one person to another *through* the computer system. The net effect is to increase the amount of time that the individual is at work alone in the performance of his normal duties."[50]

Lipstreu and Reed studied employees of a large baking firm prior to, during, and after a shift to automation. They too found that the amount of communication between workers was drastically reduced.[51] Most employees had neither the time nor the opportunity for verbal interaction because of new work assignments, the need for added speed and more mental concentration, and more automatic work procedures. A later follow-up indicated that some workers were interacting a bit more, but the change was only slight. Thus it appears that the introduction of automated processes can have long-term isolating effects on workers.

Another effect that has been observed is decline in morale. Lipstreu and Reed noted that job satisfaction was affected in several ways.[52] Workers in the baking firm expressed dissatisfaction with their superiors and with their new work. They felt that their new work was less important, and they expressed less confidence in their ability to cope with the new machinery. However this reaction tended to abate over time. Unlike social isolation, decreased morale was a much more temporary phenomenon.

For workers in some settings, automation has meant new responsibility, greater variety and change, and opportunities to learn new skills. Once workers feel competent with the transition, they often report long-term *gains* in satisfaction or morale.[53] On the other hand, automation has created for the majority a more routinized job environment in which people are unable to control either the pace or the style of work. One widely reported effect is mental and emotional fatigue. The physical environment in automated plants is often cleaner, better ventilated, and more spacious, and the work is less demanding physically. However the tasks are more repetitive, while at the same time requiring full concentration. The implications of routinization were cogently described in *Work in America:*

> Intrinsic factors such as challenge appear to affect satisfaction and dissatisfaction most substantially. The aspects of job content that appear most consistent in their negative effects are fractionation, repetition and lack of control, or, in positive terms, variety and autonomy.[54]

The results of studies indicating that automation is experienced as a structural change are consistent with reports of the morale of workers in other automated settings. Dissatisfaction is widespread. Blauner has argued that as industry moves from (1) a traditional craft structure to (2) mechanization to (3) automation, the extent of worker dissatisfaction (alienation) follows "a course that could be charted on a graph by means of an inverted U-curve, with alienation at its peak in the mechanization stage."[55] Other observers are less optimistic and point to the spread of automation and worker dissatisfaction in white-collar work environments.[56] Thus automation has its benefits, but the costs have pressured managerial personnel into devising coping strategies.

Counteracting Negative Effects.   Large size, automation, and in certain circumstances tall or flat shape each can have negative effects on employees, particularly on morale, absenteeism, and turnover. These structural properties are not static; on the contrary, most organizations are expanding and making greater use of automated machinery. To overcome the negative effects, it is necessary to specify the mechanisms mediating the influence of structural factors. In this way interventions can be applied to the intermediary factors. Few studies have systematically investigated the influence of the three variables identified in our conceptual model: roles, average background characteristics, and social climate. But the theoretical perspectives offer different explanations and solutions for the impacts we observed based on these mediating factors.

How would scientific management and the classical theorists explain the effects of size, shape, and automation? Once the best procedure for each job had been scientifically determined, at least two requirements had to be met for scientific management to be effective. First, a certain type of person had to be selected for each job (average background and personality factors); the major qualification Taylor advocated was ignorance ("mental sluggishness"). Second, a particular social climate had to be established, one that was totally authoritarian. "It is only through *enforced* standardization of methods, *enforced* adoption of the best implements and working conditions, and *enforced* cooperation that this faster work can be assured. And the duty of enforcing . . . rests with management alone."[57] Schmidt the pig-iron handler was successful because he was "stupid and phlegmatic" and followed orders from morning till night.

Any systematic effects of size, shape, and automation, in this light, could represent systematic defects in the screening process (average background characteristics) and authoritarian character (social climate) of particular settings. For example, large organizations with relatively high rates of worker dissatisfaction, absenteeism, and turnover might be failing to screen out all "mentally alert" workers or to completely control every minute of their employees' day. To deal with negative effects, scientific management theorists might suggest more careful screening of "alert" applicants and tighter control over workers, that is, a more authoritarian work environment.

Human relations theorists also focused on social climate as the primary mediator of structural factors. In contrast to classical theorists, they advocated a social climate having a high degree of worker participation, responsibility, and identification with the organization. These conditions were thought to promote satisfaction and to discourage absenteeism and turnover. Thus the systematic effects of structural factors could indicate systematic differences in the social climate of certain settings. For example, if low-level managers in tall organizations express less satisfaction than their counterparts in flat organizations, the social climate in which the former work probably inhibits participation, decision making, and identification with the company. To counteract poor morale among such managers, human relations consultants would initiate group meetings to set up a more democratic environment. Thus by altering a mediating variable (social climate), the negative effects of an organization's structure could be overcome.

The structural school was more eclectic than its predecessors. Within this perspective, all three of the mediators could be seen as important in understanding how organizational factors influence behavior. Perhaps most essential to an ideally efficient bureaucracy was a rigid role or communication hierarchy. Thus a student of Weber might interpret the effects we described as indicating systematic shortcomings in the hierarchical network. One study directly tested this hypothesis using data from automobile sales dealerships, package delivery firms, and voluntary educational-political organizations.[58] The organizational factor involved was unit size, and the impacts examined were absenteeism and turnover. It was learned that as size increased, the complexity of communications also increased, resulting in inadequate communication among employees and between employees and supervisors. The overall effect of this pattern was increased absenteeism and turnover. To cope with undesirable effects from organizational factors, structuralists might suggest analyzing and modifying the communications network embodied in the role hierarchy.

The open systems model could similarly explain the negative effects of large size, shape, and automation using all three mediating variables. In fact, some organizations have responded to expressions of poor morale caused by automation and large size by using the open systems approach. General Foods tried to integrate the technological and social systems, reduce status differences among employees, and create a social climate that enhanced self-esteem, feelings of responsibility, and identification with the organization's goals. Their far-reaching philosophy has been labeled an "open systems" approach.[59]

The General Foods pet food factory in Illinois, a large, automated plant, had been plagued by high absenteeism, low morale, and frequent shutdowns and acts of sabotage. When management analyzed the situation, they realized that workers had little autonomy, made no major decisions about their work, had no sense of accomplishment, and had no opportunities to learn new skills. In terms of the mediators we identified, the division of labor was rigid and narrow (roles), employees' personal needs went unfulfilled (average personality characteristic), and the atmosphere was controlling (social climate). The open systems solution was designed not only to remodel the entire organization but to take into account "present business, educational and social trends" (i.e., the external environment).

In implementing the solution, a new fully automated plant was created in Topeka, Kansas. Employees were divided into relatively autonomous work groups or teams and were given responsibility for planning and scheduling the work, checking for quality, changing the design of jobs, and hiring and firing replacements. Workers were trained to do almost all the jobs in the plant, from menial tasks to handling the complicated controls of machines that cook and mix the pet food. Jobs were rotated, and the pay scale was based on the number of jobs a person learned. In addition to the formal aspects of the job, the plant was designed to minimize status differences by having, for example, equal access to parking spaces, a single entrance, and similar decor in the office, cafeteria, and locker room facilities for managers and workers alike.

After a year and a half of operation, the outcome of the reorganization has been described as overwhelmingly positive. In comparison with the older plant in Illinois, absenteeism dropped from 5 to 1%, morale improved markedly, and even productivity was 20 to 30% higher at the Kansas plant. According to *Work in America,* the economic benefits were largely a result of the work attitudes of the operators. Workers have stated that they feel a strong attachment to the company. In short, the reorganization was felt to have benefited both the employees and the company as a whole.

Research from work organizations suggests that structural factors such as size, shape, and automation have an impact on employees, and some of the effects are negative. By understanding the mediators involved—role position, average background and personality characteristics, and social climate—it is possible to devise strategies to overcome the negative effects.

Structural Factors in Service Organizations.   Service organizations have the goal of providing clients with professional services.[60] The effects of size and staff-patient ratios in service organizations were investigated independently from research in work settings. These parallel studies focused primarily on mental hospitals and correctional facilities. After reviewing research performed in these settings, we draw on the four theoretical perspectives, as well as on our conceptual model, to show how some of the negative effects can be diverted. In medical settings of other types, a major structural change has been introduced—the interdisciplinary health care team. Like the work teams at General Foods, health care teams embrace the three mediating factors and have had a positive impact on the clients being served.

Mental Hospitals.   How is organizational impact assessed in studies of mental institutions? One of the major goals of psychiatric hospitalization is to restore a patient's ability to function responsibly in the community. A long hospital stay frequently has a severely detrimental effect on the physical and psychological conditions of patients.[61] By adapting to an unhealthy hospital environment, long-term patients often become withdrawn, passive, and spiritless—in short, "institutionalized." Moreover, the longer patients remain in the hospital, the more dependent they become on the institution and the poorer are their chances for release. Hence two measures are often used in studies of mental hospital effectiveness. (1) "Release rates" refer to the proportion of *newly admitted* patients released from the hospital during a designated period of time, such as 90 days or one year. (2) "Turnover rates" are based on the proportion of *all* patients discharged during a specific period, regardless of time of admission. Most studies considering the effects of structural factors in psychiatric hospitals focus on one or both measures.

Leonard Ullmann completed one of the first large studies of the effects of size and staff-patient ratio at 30 Veterans Administration psychiatric hospitals across the country.[62] Both release and turnover rates were used to assess organizational impact. Release rate was defined as the number of patients leaving the hospital within 9 months of admission and remaining in the community for at least 90 consecutive days. Several measures of patient turnover were used, including the number of patients discharged divided by the total patient population, and the proportion of patients who had lived in the hospital 2 years or more.

Ullmann found that patients in small hospitals were much more likely to be released early, and the occurrence of this effect was independent of how well the hospital was staffed. He also discovered that patient turnover was much more rapid in the better staffed hospitals, independent of hospital size. Ullmann concluded that both small size and high staffing had independent positive impacts and were important structural determinants of hospital effectiveness.

Some investigators have argued that the crucial determinants of hospital effectiveness are the kinds of patients admitted (average background and personality characteristics), the facilities available to patients, and hospital policy regarding discharge. Lawrence Linn examined these variables, as well as size and staff-patient ratios, using 12 state mental hospitals varying in size from 700 to more than 12,000 patients.[63] His findings were quite striking. Hospital rates of patient discharge (turnover) were not related to the average background and personality characteristics of the patient population (e.g., patient's age, level of physical disability or mental condition). Hospital discharge rates were also unrelated to the quality of the hospital living conditions (e.g., physical conditions of the ward, facilities available for patients). Moreover, discharge rates were unrelated to hospital rules and policies regarding patients' freedom of movement or work activities. These are somewhat surprising results.

Two structural characteristics of hospitals were related to the rate of patient discharge. Smaller hospitals and those with higher attendant-patient ratios were much more likely to have higher rates of patient discharge. Patients were also discharged more rapidly from hospitals with higher nurse-patient ratios. Some of the other variables that were related to patient discharge appear to be a function of small size and high staffing. For example, patients were discharged more rapidly from hospitals in which doctors spent more time on wards and a higher frequency of staff-patient interaction was observed. (It should be noted that Linn did not ascertain whether average background characteristics *mediated* the relationship between the structural factors and hospital effectiveness. According to our model, this may in fact have occurred.)

Two studies focused exclusively on staff-patient ratios, which are important for treatment outcome because they indicate the potential amount of staff-patient interaction. Higher ratios, allowing greater interaction between staff and patients, are presumably more beneficial. One study gathered data on the mean release rates and staff-patient ratios of state mental institutions from all 50 states and the District of Columbia.[64] Rich staffing was associated with higher release rates in each of four different years. The second study refined the staff-patient ratio to assess more precisely the amount of staff-patient interaction.[65] To do this the author developed a staff-patient attention ratio—the total number of minutes per week each staff member spent in formal meetings, divided by the number of patients in the program. The results indicated that the higher the staff-patient attention ratio, the shorter the hospitalization.

Thus there is considerable evidence that small size and rich staffing relate to various indices of mental hospital effectiveness. In our conceptual model we identified social climate as the mediator most closely linked to organizational impacts. Inherent in this suggestion are the assumptions that different levels of size and staffing produce differential social climates and that certain types of social atmospheres, which develop partly as a function of size and staffing ratios, benefit patients more than other types. Both these issues have been addressed in the literature on mental hospital effectiveness.

How are size and staff-patient ratios related to the social climate or treatment environment of a psychiatric ward? This question was the focal point of a large study encompassing 143 American and 36 British psychiatric wards.[66] The social environments were measured by the Ward Atmosphere Scale (WAS), which assesses 10 dimensions of the social environment of psychiatric treatment programs (e.g., manner and quality of patient-staff relationships, type and direction of the treatment program, and program clarity and structure). (See Chapter 10). The results showed that with greater numbers of patients in a program and lower staff-patient ratios, there was less supportiveness from the staff and among the patients themselves. Moreover, patients were less strongly encouraged to act openly and to express their feelings freely. Larger size and poor staffing also meant greater staff control.

Some of the specific items to which patients and staff on larger programs answered "true" much more often than patients and staff on smaller programs included: "Doctors have very little time to encourage patients," "Patients rarely help each other," "Nurses have very little time to encourage patients," and "The staff discourage criticism." Patients and staff on smaller programs were more likely to answer "true" to the following items: "Patients are encouraged to show their feelings," "Patients can wear what they want," "Patients can leave the ward without saying where they are going," "Patients here are encouraged to be independent," and "This ward emphasizes training for new kinds of jobs."

Another interesting finding emerged from the WAS study. The degree of agreement between patients and staff about what their program was like was significantly higher in programs with richer staff-patient ratios. There was also considerably less agreement within both patient and staff groups about the characteristics of the treatment milieu in larger programs. Thus size and staffing ratios appear to have important effects on the social climates of psychiatric treatment programs.

Do certain social climates benefit patients more than other types? Cohen and Struening related the social atmospheres of psychiatric hospitals to the length of time patients spent in the community after discharge.[67] They found that hospitals with authoritarian and restrictive social atmospheres were less effective in keeping patients out in the community. On the other hand, hospitals with benevolent, humanistic, or religious atmospheres were more successful. In an interesting exchange of views, Leonard Ullmann argued that these results could be explained by differences in size and staffing among the hospitals studied.[68] That is, the less effective hospitals, characterized by authoritarian atmospheres, were also larger and more poorly staffed. Responding to this critique, Cohen and Struening cogently stated that size and staffing were not psychological variables and could not *directly* affect patients.[69] Rather, the importance of size and staffing derived from their effects on staff attitudes and values, which in turn influence patients directly. In terms of our conceptual model, social climate was viewed as mediating the impact of size and staffing ratios.

Moos also found different social climates on wards with high and low turnover rates and high and low community tenure rates.[70] Programs with higher turnover rates placed a strong emphasis on practical decision making and inhibited open, spontaneous expressions of feelings. Thus they discouraged patients from becoming involved with the ward, while at the same time preparing them for release by focusing on practical ways of getting things done. Wards with more successful community tenure rates also emphasized a practical orientation. Unlike the higher turnover wards, these wards encouraged open, spontaneous expressions of feelings.

Thus there is considerable evidence from psychiatric settings that size and staffing ratios influence treatment outcome (organizational impact) and that this effect is mediated by the programs' social climate.

Correctional Facilities.   Researchers studying juvenile offenders have corroborated the importance of size and staffing in studies of correctional units. Carl Jesness did a carefully designed study of the effects of size and staffing at Fricot, a correctional ranch operated by the California Youth Authority.[71] Fricot residents were housed in 50-bed cottages staffed by a cottage supervisor and a small number of assistants. A 20-bed unit was constructed to house especially disturbed boys. Jesness used the 20-bed unit and one of the 50-bed cottages in his research. Boys were randomly assigned to the 20- and 50-bed units from the pool of delinquents eligible for the 20-bed unit. Every effort was made to keep the therapeutic programs of the two units comparable. Since both units had the same number of staff, however, more staff time was available to boys in the small cottage.

Fifteen months after release from Fricot, 42% of the boys from the small unit had violated parole, compared with 68% of the boys in the large cottage. Moreover, boys classified as "neurotic" (average personality characteristic) had a parole violation rate of only 30% from the small unit, compared with 61% from the large one. Thus size and staffing had a significant impact on outcome, which was mediated by personality characteristics of the delinquents.

Jesness also found that the social climates of the two units were substantially different. The 20-bed unit was less regimented, friendlier, and more informal. Strict group discipline was minimal, and staff used reason and rewards as sources of positive motivation. They were also more supportive, becoming involved with residents' personal problems and interacting with them informally. By contrast, the large unit with a lower staff-resident ratio was described as regimented and less friendly. Staff made frequent use of stringent punishments. To control the boys, who were often immature and hostile, staff established tight limits and regulations. Thus the effects of size and staffing on the social climates were dramatic.

Two other studies concerned with structural factors concluded that smaller living units were indispensable to the success of different treatment strategies. In one study boys in a large custodial reformatory were compared with a similar group assigned to a small residential treatment program.[72] A follow-up of the boys showed that graduates of the smaller program were more successful than their counterparts in the larger one. The author noted that small size was essential to creating an informal, homelike atmosphere (social climate) aimed at reproducing appropriate community roles. According to this logic: "Treatment organizations which permit the duplication of community behavior are more likely to be successful . . . than organizations which foster behavior in response to the special conditions of a total institution."[73]

The second study compared delinquent boys living in groups of 12 with a matched sample of boys housed in groups of 35 at another institution.[74] Here again, greater progress was recorded for boys organized into smaller living units. Adjustment to society (organizational impact), defined as a lack of criminal convictions during a 3 year period after release from the institution, was 71% at the smaller facility and only 53% at the larger one. Greater rapport with the counselors and a more intimate living environment also characterized the smaller institution. These effects were probably enhanced by small group size.

One final study focused on the influence of size and staffing on the social milieus of correctional programs.[75] The units investigated ranged in size from fewer than 20 to more than 500. Staffing patterns varied from a high of one full-time staff member for every two residents to a low of not even one full-time staff member for every 50 residents. The results revealed much more supportive interaction among residents and between residents and staff in smaller, more heavily staffed programs. Also there was more emphasis on residents' autonomy and independence, on staff's understanding the personal problems of the residents, and on the clarity of rules and expectations in these programs. As with psychiatric programs, there was also more agreement about characteristics of the social climate within the resident and the staff groups in smaller, more highly staffed programs. Thus smaller and more highly staffed correctional programs had more coherent and integrated social environments.

Coping with Large Size and Poor Staffing. How would our four theoretical perspectives explain and deal with the negative effects of large size and poor staffing in mental hospitals and correctional facilities? Although classical theory was not applied to service organizations, it is interesting to speculate about how "classicists" might have treated the findings. An effective organization required a highly authoritarian social climate. For service organizations this means a high degree of staff control and clarity of rules and regulations. Classical theorists might suggest that larger units with poorer staffing were less successful because of inadequate staff supervision and lack of clarity in the rules and regulations. That is, as units increased in size and decreased in staffing, there was a systematic decline in supervision, hence in clarity of communication between staff and residents. One way to ensure adequate supervision would be to manipulate the division of labor by creating an intermediate level between staff and patients. Specifically, residents or patients nearing discharge could take on certain staff functions (e.g., explaining rules and regulations to other patients). In this way role position, one of the mediating factors, would be changed. Another component of classical theory is the notion that incentives should correspond with output. If it were discovered that larger and more poorly staffed units did not employ appropriate, positive incentives, encouraging patients to succeed in the community, this aspect of social climate could be improved.

Human relations theory also was not formally applied to service organizations, yet many explanations of size and staffing effects emphasize factors such as identification and participation. In a review of the literature on size and staffing effects, Knight discussed several such mechanisms by which increased size and/or decreased staffing might operate.[76] First, large living units reduce the proportion of intimate or close relationships. Group cohesion tends to decrease as group size increases. Second, large living units limit the time available per event and per group member. These time limitations provide an impetus for greater control and reduce the opportunity for personal intimacy. Third, wider social distance between residents and staff in larger living units facilitates the development of separate resident and staff groups. Fourth, shared misunderstandings may occur among residents as a result of reduced intimacy, decreased group cohesion, and increased distance between residents and staff. People in large groups have less information and are especially susceptible to misinterpreting others' real feelings and intentions. Fifth, increasing regimentation leads to restriction of the personal satisfactions and social rewards of residents.

Moos has pointed out that it is possible to manipulate the social climate even of large, poorly staffed wards to develop a coherent program.[77] In one study he described a Veterans Administration hospital program that was both large (more than 150 patients) and relatively poorly staffed (only one staff member for each 11 patients) but nevertheless had a positively perceived treatment environment. Patients and staff on this program agreed that there was considerable emphasis on involvement in the program, on supportive interactions among patients and between patients and staff, on facilitative autonomy and independence among the patients, and so on. On these grounds, human relations theorists might promote a coping strategy in which staff and residents would meet together to improve the social climate of their program.

The structuralist approach might focus on the systematic lack of clarity in larger units, perhaps attempting to reduce the negative impact by altering the structural pyramid itself. Ullmann has pointed out that the negative effects of large hospitals may be partially alleviated by a unit system in which the hospital is functionally divided into smaller sections.[78] The Veterans Administration has tried to deal with the size problem by decentralizing some large hospitals into separate independent units that admit and discharge their own patients. Of the 41 psychiatric hospitals within the VA system, 39 initiated some form of unit system between 1950 and 1968. These units vary on many dimensions including size, staff-patient ratios, composition of patient populations (mixed-age groups vs. stratified age groups, chronic and acute patients, etc.), and coordination among units within a hospital.

In a large study of Veterans Administration psychiatric hospitals, the investigators examined the relationship of size and staff-patient ratio to the effectiveness of these decentralized units.[79] Effectiveness was defined as a rise in patient turnover and a reduction of a hospital's long-term patient population (those hospitalized 2 years or more). The hospitals with the smallest units and with the most favorable doctor-patient ratios tended to have the highest increase in patient turnover and the greatest reduction in long-term residents. Next the 10 hospitals with the best turnover and long-term reduction rates were compared with the 10 least effective hospitals. Among the many differences that appeared between the two groups of hospitals were differences in size and staff-patient ratio. More specifically, the average number of patients per unit in the more effective settings was about half that found in the less effective settings. Thus the evidence from this study again indicates the advantages of smaller size units and higher staff-patient ratios.

The Interdisciplinary Health Care Team.   The open systems model has recently been used in an attempt to cope with the negative effects of large size in general medical facilities. Within these service organizations, a major ramification of large size (and increased specialization) has been fragmented care. Consider a cardiac patient's account of his stay in the hospital.

> Although my admission was primarily for total rest, I met more than fifty new and different people during the first twenty-four hours. During my two-week stay about thirty-five different people entered my room every twenty-four hours (not counting those who came while I was sleeping). Most of these people performed one or at most two functions, with a different person performing this function each eight-hour shift, swing shift people covering two days out of seven, and no consistent assignments even within regular shifts.[80]

To counteract these effects, a major structural innovation, the interdisciplinary health care team, has been initated.

This reorganization is designed to provide patients with an *integrated* program of comprehensive health services. Health care teams use an open systems approach to the delivery of medical care. Unlike most clinic and hospital settings, which are self-contained or "closed" systems, interdisciplinary teams draw on existing medical and social-welfare resources in the community. The traditional focus on a patient's illness is replaced by a total or open systems approach to the patient. In this view, patients' medical, social, and psychological needs are interrelated, and characteristics of their family and community environments are perceived as influencing the treatment process. By way of illustration, a health care team treating a diabetic child might offer nutritional guidance to the child and his or her family, deal with the family's emotional reactions to the illness, initiate contact with the school nurse about the child's illness, and arrange for a public health nurse to visit the home regularly.

The health care team also provides a new organizational system in which to evaluate, diagnose, and treat health problems. Since health problems are often interdependent and complex, the team can collaboratively perform a variety of tasks. Although the exact composition of interdisciplinary health care teams varies in different settings, an example of an existing team is instructive. The Hill Health Center, in New Haven, Connecticut, offers comprehensive health services through family-centered teams composed of community health workers, nurses, a pediatrician, an internist, a dentist, a dental assistant, a social worker, a psychiatrist, health educator, and a medical records clerk.[81] The teams meet twice weekly to discuss progress and problems of the families under their care and to plan and coordinate future treatment.

How effective are these health care teams? Beloff and his associates studied the utilization pattern of 31 families enrolled for a minimum of 2.5 years in the Family Health Care Program in New Haven.[82] In this program families were cared for by a health team consisting of a physician, a public health nurse, and a health aide. Services included regular preventive care (e.g., periodic examinations, prenatal and postnatal care, and nutritional guidance), treatment of illnesses on a 24-hour basis, and social services.

The evaluation showed that the number of necessary contacts with the Family Health Care Program (per family member per month) declined steadily over a 2-year period (the first 6 months were considered a "breaking-in" period and were not included in the analysis). The majority of the contacts were made for "health supervision." When families were queried by an interviewer independent of the program about their satisfaction with the team approach, 95% said that they " . . . preferred the care of the health team to care by a private physician, if both had been available from a financial point of view."[83] The majority of the families also identified the principal benefits of the program as social counseling and support in health-related areas of functioning. The investigators concluded that using the same number of physicians, the team model has the potential for providing better as well as more health care.

In addition to improved patient care, one study reported greater job satisfaction among nurses working in partnership with physicians.[84] Reasons for the increased satisfaction included easier access to medical records and closer scrutiny of the patients' progress, better and more appropriate use of their skills, and frequent contact with physicians. Thus the impact of health care teams, which represent a major reorganization in the delivery of medical services, may have broad positive results.

Reflections.   We have considered some of the human problems encountered in large organizations. The problem that has received the most attention from the research literature and the mass media has been low morale, or alienation. A great deal has been written about "blue-collar blues" and "white-collar woes" in work organizations, deindividuation and institutionalization in mental hospitals, and anonymity and isolation in large universities. Because so many people participate in one or more large organizations, the issue of alienation is a major societal problem.

The attitudes and behaviors observed in these settings can be traced, in part, to certain structural properties. We found that morale is influenced by size of organization, subunit size, supervisory ratios, automation, and a teamwork approach. The principal factor mediating the effects of these structural properties is the social climate of an environment. That is, the social atmospheres created by different structural properties influence the behaviors and attitudes of people in organizations.

A manager or administrator must identify the factors that contribute to alienation and must find constructive ways of improving the situation. Although very often the structural features of an organization are permanent, by focusing on the factors that mediate the effects of structural properties, an environment can be shaped to meet more humanistic ends. We have suggested here that organizations with structural factors that promote dissatisfaction and alienation can be improved by increasing the level of autonomy and responsibility. We also stressed that the specific goals that are chosen, and, to an extent, how successfully those goals are implemented, reflect one's theoretical orientation and the moral climate and culture in which one lives.

In our Age of Organizations, the organizations themselves are expanding in size and scope. The problems we encounter now will grow during the next 50 years. Knowledge about the influences of organizational structure and climate should help to enhance the congruence between individuals and their work environments, thus contributing to greater employee morale and satisfaction. It is hoped that such knowledge will help reverse the growing trend toward worker alienation and apathy.

REFERENCES

1. Palmer, R. R. and Colton, J. *A history of the modern world.* Knopf, New York, 1965.

2. Etzioni, A. *Modern organizations.* Prentice-Hall, Englewood Cliffs, N.J., 1964.

3. Scott, W. R. Theory of organizations. In E. Faris (Ed.), *The handbook of modern sociology.* Rand McNally, Skokie, Ill., 1964, p. 488.

4. Taylor, F. W. *Scientific management.* Harper & Row, New York, 1911.

5. *Ibid.,* pp. 43–48 (Part 1).

6. *Ibid.,* p. 46 (Part 1).

7. Perrow, C. *Complex organizations: A critical essay.* Scott, Foresman, Glenview, Ill., 1972, p. 69.

8. Roethlisberger, F. J. and Dickson, W. J. *Management and the worker: An account of a research program conducted by the Western Electric Company, Hawthorne Works, Chicago.* Harvard University Press, Cambridge, Mass., 1939.

9. An interesting account of this experiment can be found in G. Homans, *The human group.* Harcourt Brace Jovanovich, New York, 1950, pp. 48–80.

10. Coch, L. and French, J. R., Jr. Overcoming resistance to change. *Human Relations,* **1:**512–532, 1948.

11. Likert, R. *New patterns of management.* McGraw-Hill, New York, 1961.

12. The material on the origins of the structuralist approach follows the discussion by Etzioni, *op. cit.,* pp. 41–67.

13. Weber, M. *The theory of social and economic organization.* A. M. Henderson and Talcott Parsons (Transl.) and Talcott Parsons (Ed.), Free Press and Falcon's Wing Press, Glencoe, Ill., 1947.
    Blau, P. and Scott, W. R. *Formal organizations: A comparative approach.* Chandler, Scranton, Pa., 1962, pp. 27–36.

14. Katz, D. and Kahn, R. L. *The social psychology of organizations.* Wiley, New York, 1966.

15. Exodus, 18:18.

16. Barker, E. (Ed. and Transl.) *The politics of Aristotle.* Oxford University Press, New York, 1962, Book VIII, p. 292.

17. Bottomore, T. B. (Ed. and Transl.) and M. Rubel (Transl.) *Karl Marx: Selected writings in sociology and social philosophy.* Watts, London, 1956.

18. Durkheim, E. *The division of labour in society.* G. Simpson (Transl.), Free Press, New York, 1933, p. 356.

19. Revans, R. W. Human relations, management and size. In E. M. Hugh-Jones (Ed.), *Human relations and modern management.* North Holland, Amsterdam, 1958, pp. 177–181.

20. *Ibid.,* p. 182.

21. Mayo, E. and Lombard, G. *Teamwork and labor turnover in the aircraft industry of southern California.* Harvard Business School, Cambridge, Mass., 1944.

22. Talacchi, S. Organization size, individual attitudes and behavior: An empirical study. *Administrative Science Quarterly,* **5:**398–420, 1960.

23. A review of these studies can be found in L. W. Porter and E. E. Lawler, Properties of organization structure in relation to job attitudes and job behavior. *Psychological Bulletin,* **64:**23–51, 1965, see pp. 36–37.

24. Indik, B. P. Organization size and member participation: Some empirical tests of alternative explanations. *Human Relations,* **18:**339–350, 1965.

25. Acton Society Trust. *Size and morale.* London, 1953.

26. Thomas, E. J. Role conceptions and organizational size. *American Sociological Review,* **24:**30–37, 1959.

27. Harrell, T. W. Differences between men in big and small businesses. *Personnel Psychology,* **24:**649–652, 1971.

28. Porter, L. W. Job attitudes in management: IV. Perceived deficiencies in need fulfillment as a function of size of company. *Journal of Applied Psychology,* **47:**386–397, 1963.

29. Porter, L. W. Where is the organization man? *Harvard Business Review,* **41:**53–61, 1963.

30. Metzner, H. and Mann, F. Employee attitudes and absences. *Personnel Psychology,* **6:**467–485, 1953.

31. Hewitt, D. and Parfitt, J. A note on working morale and size of group. *Occupational Psychology,* **27:**38–42, 1953.

32. Revans, Human relations, management, and size, *op. cit.*

33. Acton Society Trust, *op. cit.*

34. Porter and Lawler, *op. cit.* (Ref. 23), pp. 37–38.

35. Indik, *op. cit.*

36. Ingham, G. K. *Size of industrial organization and worker behavior.* Cambridge University Press, Cambridge, 1970.

37. Porter and Lawler *op. cit.,* p. 38.

38. Argyle, M., Gardner, G., and Cioffi, I. Supervisory methods related to productivity, absenteeism, and labor turnover, *Human Relations,* **11:**23–40, 1958.
   Ingham, *op. cit.*

39. Brayfield, A. H. and Crockett, W. H. Employee attitudes and employee performance. *Psychological Bulletin,* **52:**396–424, 1955.
   Lawler, E. E. Job attitudes and employee motivation: Theory, research and practice. *Personnel Psychology,* **23:**223–237, 1970.
   Porter, L. W. and Steers, R. M. Organizational, work, and personal factors in employee turnover and absenteeism. *Psychological Bulletin,* **80:**151–176, 1973.

40. Exodus 18:22.

41. Vroom, V. H. Some personality determinants of the effects of participation. *Journal of Abnormal and Social Psychology,* **59:**322–327, 1959.

42. Worthy, J. C. Organizational structure and employee morale. *American Sociological Review,* **15:**169–179, 1950.

43. Porter, L. W. and Lawler, E. E. The effects of tall vs. flat organization structures on managerial job satisfaction. *Personnel Psychology,* **17:**135–148, 1964.

44. Porter, L. W. and Siegel, J. Relationships of tall and flat organization structures to satisfactions of foreign managers. *Personnel Psychology,* **18:**379–392, 1965.

45. El Salmi, A. M. and Cummings, L. L. Managers' perceptions of need and need satisfactions as a function of interactions among organizational variables. *Personnel Psychology,* **21:**465–477, 1968.

46. Kohn, M. L. Bureaucratic man: A portrait and an interpretation. *American Sociological Review,* **36:**461–474, 1971.

47. Smith, A. *The wealth of nations.* Random House, New York, 1937, pp. 734–735 (originally published 1776).

48. Bell, G. Introduction. In G. Bell (Ed.), *Organizations and human behavior: A book of readings.* Prentice-Hall, Englewood Cliffs, N.J., 1967.

49. Blauner, R. *Alienation and freedom: The factory worker and his industry.* University of Chicago Press, Chicago, 1964.

    Kornhauser, A. *The mental health of the industrial worker.* Wiley, New York, 1965.

    Work in America. Report of a special task force to the Secretary of Health, Education and Welfare. MIT Press, Cambridge, Mass., 1972.

50. Whisler, T. L. *The impact of computers on organizations.* Praeger, New York, 1970, p. 138.

51. Lipstreu, O. and Reed, K. *Transition to automation: A study of people, production, and change.* University of Colorado Press, Boulder, 1964.

52. *Ibid.*

53. Mann, F. C. and Hoffman, L. R. *Automation and the worker: A study of social change in power plants.* Holt, Rinehart & Winston, New York, 1960.

54. *Work in America, op. cit.,* p. 94.

55. Blauner, *op. cit.,* p. 182.

56. Jenkins, D. *Job power: Blue and white collar democracy.* Doubleday, Garden City, N. Y., 1973.

    Mills, C. W. *White Collar.* Oxford University Press, New York, 1953.

57. Taylor, *Scientific management, op. cit.,* p. 83 (Part 2).

58. Indik, Organization size and member participation, *op. cit.*

59. Jenkins, *op. cit.,* pp. 225–231.

60. Blau and Scott, *Formal organizations, op. cit.,* pp. 51–54.

61. Goffman, E. *Asylums.* Doubleday, Garden City, N.Y., 1961.

    Wing, J. K. Institutionalism in mental hospitals. In T. Scheff (Ed.), *Mental illness and social processes.* Harper & Row, New York, 1967, pp. 219–238.

62. Ullmann, L. P. *Institution and outcome: A comparative study of psychiatric hospitals.* Pergamon Press, Oxford, 1967.

63. Linn, L. State hospital environment and rates of patient discharge. *Archives of General Psychiatry*, **23**:346–351, 1970.

64. Lasky, D. L. and Dowling, M. The release rates of state mental hospitals as related to maintenance costs and patient-staff ratio. *Journal of Clinical Psychology*, **27**:272–277, 1971.

65. Becker, R. E. Staffing level and treatment effectiveness. *British Journal of Psychiatry*, **115**:481–482, 1969.

66. Moos, R. *Evaluating treatment environments: A social ecological approach*. Wiley, New York, 1974, pp. 130–133.

67. Cohen, J. and Struening, E. Opinions about mental illness: Hospital social atmosphere profiles and their relevance to effectiveness. *Journal of Consulting Psychology*, **28**:291–298, 1964.

68. Ullmann, L. A discussion of hospital social atmosphere profiles and their relevance to effectiveness. *Journal of Consulting Psychology*, **29**:277–278, 1965.

69. Cohen, J. and Struening, E. Simple-minded questions and twirling stools. *Journal of Consulting Psychology*, **29**:278–280, 1965.

70. Moos, *op. cit.*, Ch. 8.

71. Jesness, C. F. *The Fricot Ranch study*. California Youth Authority, Research Report No. 47, Sacramento, 1965.

72. Weeks, H. A. *Youthful offenders at Highfields*. University of Michigan Press, Ann Arbor, 1958.

73. Rabow, J. and Elias, A. Organizational boundaries, inmate roles, and rehabilitation. *Journal of Research in Crime and Delinquency*, **6**:8–16, 1969. Quoted in D. Knight, *The impact of living-unit size in youth training schools*. California Youth Authority, Division of Research and Development, Sacramento, 1971, p. 10.

74. McCord, W. and McCord, J. *The psychopath*. Van Nostrand, Princeton, N.J., 1964.

75. Moos, R. *Evaluating correctional environments and community settings*. Wiley, New York, 1975.

76. Knight, *op. cit.*, (Ref. 73), pp. 23–32.

77. Moos, *Evaluating treatment environments, op. cit.*

78. Ullmann. *Institution and outcome, op. cit.*

79. Ellsworth, R. B., Dickman, H. R., and Maroney, R. J. Characteristics of productive and unproductive unit systems in VA psychiatric hospitals. *Hospital and Community Psychiatry*, **23**:261–268, 1972.

80. Straus, R. Hospital organization from the viewpoint of patient-centered goals. In B. Georgopolous (Ed.), *Organization research on health institutions*. University of Michigan Press, Ann Arbor, 1972, p. 217.

81. Novack, A., Bromet, E., Neill, T. K., Abramovitz, R., and Storch, S. Children's mental health services in an inner city neighborhood. 1. A three-year epidemiologic study. *American Journal of Public Health*, **65**:133–138, 1975.

82. Beloff, J. S. and Korper, M. The health team model and medical care utilization: Effect on patient behavior of providing comprehensive family health services. *Journal of the American Medical Association,* **219:**359–366, 1972.

Beloff, J. S. and Willet, M. Yale studies in family health care: III. The health care team. *Journal of the American Medical Association,* **205:**663–669, 1968.

83. Beloff and Korper, *op. cit.,* p. 365.

84. Hockey, L. The family care team: Philosophy, problems, possibilities. In G. Wolstenholme and M. O'Connor (Eds.), *Teamwork for world health.* J. & A. Churchill, London, 1971, pp. 103–110.

CHAPTER NINE

The Human Aggregate[a]

Consider an admissions committee at a private, liberal arts college in the Northeast. Admission to the college has always been very competitive, and requirements include high motivation and self-esteem in addition to academic excellence. Students typically come from high-income, well-educated families. Half the student body attended private high schools; of the remainder, the vast majority attended public high schools with strong college preparatory curricula.

Very often, the choice between two candidates from the same geographical region is a difficult one. Consider the following applicants.

Heather is a bright, extroverted student from _____, Rhode Island, a suburb of Providence. She has excelled in all her classes and is valedictorian. She has been active in various athletic activities and was selected most valuable player of the women's basketball team. During her interview, she was seen as mature and articulate, and she expressed an interest in becoming a clinical psychologist.

Heather's father is an insurance broker; an older brother graduated from Yale and an older sister is a senior at Wellesley. SAT (V+M): 1350

Angela is an honors student from _____, Rhode Island, an industrial community near Providence. She has earned awards for scholastic achievement and ranks first in her class. She has taken an active part in a few extracurricular activities, particularly through the Music Club. During her interview, Angela appeared shy and reticent and was uncertain about major field or career plans.

Angela's father is a tool and die maker; an older sister attended nursing school and an older brother is in the Armed Forces. SAT (V+M): 1320

[a] This chapter is co-authored by Evelyn Bromet and Rudolf Moos.

284

Admissions officers consider personal profiles, but they also note the quality of the applicants' high schools in weighing academic records. The suburban school is similar to most schools in upper-middle-class areas in maintaining a high-quality teaching staff and emphasizing a college-oriented curriculum. The industrial city high school is poorly funded, with its teachers' salaries ranked third lowest in the state; its college preparatory program is very weak.

Clearly the chief differences between Heather and Angela lie in their social backgrounds. Heather's social and personality profile more closely resembles that of the average student at this college. From previous experience, the committee could be confident that Heather will "fit in" easily and do well academically. Angela, on the other hand, is from a social and cultural setting different from that of the typical student at the college. In this respect she might enrich the college environment, but the adjustment required of her would be greater. Thus prediction of her success at this college cannot be as certain.

Important features of an environment are often determined by the average background characteristics of its members. Most people routinely apply this principle in their daily lives. For example, we tend to choose as friends people similar to ourselves on factors such as age, educational level, and ethnicity and attitudes. We often feel more comfortable when we share these characteristics with most people in a group situation, since this information allows us to infer the dominant value orientations, concerns, and ideologies of the group (or at least to reduce the range of possibilities).

How are social background characteristics linked to behavior? In the last chapter we identified *social climate* as the mediator between background factors and behavioral outcomes. Specifically, we suggested that groups with particular configurations of background factors create differential social climates, which in turn contribute to differences in behavioral or attitudinal outcomes. Thus organizations having similar goals but composed of people with dissimilar backgrounds may have distinctly different social climates or atmospheres. For example, the climate of a suburban high school, where students are primarily from upper-middle-class families, has been described as warm and pleasant, with an emphasis on independent study and mutual support between students and teachers. By contrast, an inner-city school is often grim and angry, with regimented class structure and hostility between students and teachers. It has been pointed out that such "differences in climate can have serious effects on student attitudes toward school, student achievement, and the accomplishment of the school's objective."[1] To continue with our illustration, Heather's career plans are in part a product of exposure to an intellectual climate that gave her confidence in her ability to realize her aspirations. By contrast, the climate of Angela's high school probably did not foster high expectations or motivate students toward goals requiring advanced academic training.

The use of average background characteristics in differentiating environments and predicting behavior has a long tradition in the social sciences. This general idea is based on the suggestion by Linton that most of the social and cultural environment is transmitted through other people.[2] Thus the character of an environment is implicitly dependent partly on the typical characteristics of its members.

This chapter describes two areas of research that have examined the effects of average background characteristics on behavior. First we focus on colleges and universities and the relationship between average background characteristics, social climate, and student performance. A second set of studies deals with social epidemiology, particularly ecological studies of mental illness. These investigations identify the average background characteristics of areas of a community, to compare rates of crime or illness among residential neighborhoods with different characteristics.

College and University Environments.

The Environmental Assessment Technique.   The most extensive body of research using average background characteristics to differentiate college environments has been done by John Holland and his colleagues.[3] Holland began his career as a vocational counselor in educational, military, and psychiatric settings, and his intellectual antecedents included interest inventories such as the Strong Vocational Interest Blank (SVIB) and the Kuder Preference Record.[4] The Strong inventory is based on determining the unique patterns of interest that differentiate successful members of various occupational groups (actors, astronomers, librarians, etc.) from people in general. The SVIB profile of interests of college students or prospective employees is used to indicate which occupational groups their interests most closely resemble, therefore which occupations will be most suitable for them. The Kuder Preference Record similarly assesses the patterns of activities of people in various occupational groups (e.g., outdoor, mechanical, musical, and clerical) and matches respondents with vocations in which people hold interests similar to their own. Thus both the SVIB and the Kuder are based on the notion that the average background characteristics of an occupational group—dominant interests in this case—contain predictive information about job success and satisfaction.

Holland developed the Vocational Preference Inventory (VPI), a list of 160 occupations from which respondents choose those they find appealing. He theorized that people's vocational choices were expressions of their personalities and that interest inventories, such as the VPI or the SVIB, were essentially personality inventories. Support for this position came partly from the belief that there are commonly shared attitudes (stereotypes) about the personalities of members of different occupational groups. For example, scientists are considered unsociable, accountants dull, and lawyers aggressive. Holland suggested that these stereotypes were valid because occupational choices are determined to a large extent by personality and personal history. Certain kinds of people are attracted to and remain in certain kinds of jobs.

Holland proposed that occupations could be categorized into six groups (Conventional, Artistic, Realistic, Investigative, Enterprising, and Social) and that each group represented a different personality type. These six groups, the occupations encompassed by them, and the personality characteristics are presented in Table 9.1, columns 1, 2, and 3. Thus, for example, persons who resemble the Artistic type are more likely to seek out artistic occupations—for example, photographer, dancer, or journalist. They would be expected to value aesthetic qualities, such as beauty and harmony, and to see themselves as expressive, original, and introspective. Persons resembling the Realistic type would seek out occupations such as mechanic, electrician, or photoengraver. They would value such tangible characteristics as money, power, and status, and would see themselves as conforming, stable, and practical.

Holland also suggested that college major fields could be classified into these six categories and that students within each category more closely resembled the respective personality type.* Column 4 in Table 9.1 indicates that the Conventional types include accounting, business, and economic majors, Artistic types encompass art, music, journalism, and foreign language majors, and so on.

Of central importance to this chapter is Holland's final theory: "Because people in a vocational group [major field] have similar personalities, they will respond to many situations and problems in similar ways, and *they will create characteristic interpersonal environments*"[5] (emphasis added). Thus Holland proposed six types of environments corresponding to the six personality types. The type of environment is determined by the modal personality type, or the category in which the highest percentage of

---

*For purposes of clarity, we have limited this discussion to the six personality *types*. Each person has in addition a personality *pattern* determined by a rank ordering of her or his interest in the six types. Thus there are 720 possible personality *patterns*.

Table 9.1 Holland's System for the Classification of Personalities and Environments[a]

Orientation	Relevant Occupations	Personality Descriptions	Relevant Major Fields	Environmental Descriptions
Conventional	Bookkeeper, traffic manager, statistician, bank teller, IBM equipment operator, payroll clerk	Prefers structured numerical and verbal activities and subordinate roles; conforming; identifies with power, externals, and status	Accounting, secretarial, business and commercial (general and unclassified), business education, library science, economics	Stimulates conventional activities, rewards people for conventional values, and reinforces conscientiousness, obedience, control, efficiency, orderliness
Artistic	Poet, symphony conductor, musician, author, art dealer, drama coach, composer, cartoonist	Asocial; avoids problems that are highly structured or require gross physical skills; need for individualistic expression	Art education, music education, English and journalism, fine and applied arts (all fields), foreign language and literature (all fields)	Stimulates artistic activities, rewards people for artistic values, and reinforces emotionality, independence, nonconformity, introspection, originality
Realistic	Airplane mechanic, master plumber, surveyor, radio operator, tree surgeon, tool designer, photoengraver, electrician	Masculine, materialistic, unsociable, aggressive, stable, uninsightful, practical, persistent	Agriculture, agricultural education, physical education, recreation, industrial arts, engineering, forestry, trade, and industry	Stimulates realistic activities, rewards people for conventional values, and reinforces conformity, thrift, pragmatism, stability, shyness

Investigative	Biologist, anthropologist, independent research scientist, physicist, zoologist	Task-oriented, introspective, asocial, prefers to think through rather than act out; needs to understand	Architecture, biological sciences, geography, medical technology, pharmacy, mathematics, philosophy, physical sciences, anthropology	Stimulates investigative activities, rewards people for investigative values and reinforces precision, rationality, introspection, pessimism
Enterprising	Speculator, buyer, stock and bond salesperson, master of ceremonies, sports promoter, political campaign manager	Verbal skills for dominating, selling, leading others; verbally aggressive	Hotel and restaurant administration, hospital administration, history, international relations, political science, foreign service, industrial relations, public administration	Stimulates enterprising activities, rewards people for enterprising values, reinforces ambition, self-confidence, acquisitiveness, flirtation, arguments
Social	High school teacher, speech therapist, marriage counselor, clinical psychologist, vocational counselor, foreign missionary	Sociable, responsible, feminine; needs attention; avoids intellectual problem-solving; dependent	Health education, education of exceptional children and mentally retarded, speech correction, education (unclassified), nursing, occupational therapy, scholastic philosophy, social science (general), American civilization, sociology, social work	Stimulates social activities, rewards people for social values and reinforces friendliness, responsibility, tact, femininity, kindness, insight

[a] Adapted in part from A. Astin and J. Holland. The environmental assessment technique: A way to measure college environments. *Journal of Educational Psychology*, **52:**308–316, 1961.

people in a setting have been classified. In this way an average background characteristic of a group (i.e., its dominant vocational preference or major field choice) creates a characteristic environment with unique demands, rewards, and opportunities.

Column 5 of the table reveals that *Conventional* environments act as follows: they encourage people to engage in conventional activities, such as keeping records and organizing material; they reward people for displaying conventional *values,* such as business and economic achievement; and they reinforce personality traits, such as conscientiousness, obedience, and self-control. *Artistic* environments encourage people to choose artistic activities and reinforce personality traits such as emotionality, independence, and nonconformity. *Realistic* environments encourage the selection of realistic activities, such as mechanic, electrician, or plumber; they reward people for displaying realistic values, such as respect for power and material possessions; and they reinforce personality traits such as thrift and conformity. *Investigative* environments encourage people to enter investigative activities such as research or scholarly work; they reward investigative values such as intellectualism and empiricism, and they reinforce such personality traits as introspection, precision, and rationality. *Enterprising* environments encourage activities such as selling or leading others, they reward people for displaying enterprising values such as political and economic attainment; and they reinforce such personality traits as ambition, self-confidence, and acquisitiveness. *Social* environments encourage participation in social activities such as teaching or counseling; they reward social values such as humanistic and ethical activities, and they reinforce such personality traits as friendliness, responsibility, and tact. (The six types can most easily be remembered by their acronym, CARIES.)

To measure college environments, Holland developed the Environmental Assessment Technique (EAT). This scale entails a census of major field choices within a college population. The choices are placed into the six categories, the absolute numbers for each type are converted into percentages for the total student body, and the six categories are rank ordered in terms of their importance. For example, a technological college might have the following distribution among the student body: Investigative, 60%; Realistic, 12%; Enterprising, 10%; Social, 7%; Conventional, 6%; Artistic, 5%. Such an environment would be presumed to stress scholarship, independence, and introspection, and to deemphasize sociability and imaginative thinking.

The validity of these environmental descriptions was examined in several studies. Two projects related the EAT types to the 30 scales of the College Characteristics Inventory (CCI) to ascertain whether the dominant major field orientations of 36 colleges and universities systematically affected their social climates in ways predicted by Holland's environmental model.[6] The CCI contains 300 true-false items describing impressions of the college climate (e.g., "Most students are more 'like numbers in a book!' "). Many of the relationships between the EAT and the CCI supported Holland's descriptions. For example, students at institutions with a Realistic orientation expressed a preference for the practical and concrete rather than the abstract, and they disliked humanistic and reflective experiences. Schools scoring high on the EAT Investigative orientation tended to emphasize introversion at the expense of social and interpersonal skills. Institutions with high scores on Conventional orientation emphasized sports and social activities, while discouraging academic and scholarly pursuits. In another study, Astin also found that students in colleges with a Conventional orientation were generally not motivated to obtain a Ph.D.[7]

Pace has developed the College and University Environment Scale (CUES) to measure five social climate dimensions: *Practicality,* which describes the extent to which the environment emphasizes enterprise, organization, material benefits, and social activities; *Community,* which assesses friendliness, cohesion, and feelings of group spirit; *Awareness,* which encompasses interest in self, society, and aesthetic activities; *Propriety,* which reflects a concern with consideration, politeness, and conventionality; and *Scholarship,* which taps the degree to which the environment emphasizes intellectuality and academic competition.[8]

By correlating the CUES (i.e., social climate) with the EAT scores (i.e., average background characteristics) obtained from 100 colleges and universities, Pace provided additional evidence validating Holland's environmental descriptions. Schools characterized by the EAT Conventional orientation emphasized practicality and showed little concern with propriety, scholarship, or community. Colleges with a high proportion of Artistic majors emphasized awareness, propriety, and community, whereas those with a high proportion of Realistic majors placed much less emphasis on these three factors. Institutions with a high proportion of Investigative majors emphasized scholarship and placed little stress on practicality. Finally, schools with a Social orientation emphasized community and propriety and deemphasized scholarship.

Hearn and Moos have disclosed systematic differences in the social climate of college living units depending on their dominant EAT orientation. In this study,[9] the social climate measure was the University Residence Environment Scale (URES), composed of 10 subscales assessing dimensions of three overall types: *Relationship* dimensions (Involvement and Emotional Support), *Personal Growth* dimensions (Independence, Traditional Social Orientation, Competition, Academic Achievement, and Intellectuality) and *System Maintenance and System Change* dimensions (Order and Organization, Student Influence, and Innovation) (see Chapter 10).

Holland's environmental descriptions were supported by the following relationships. Students in living units with a Conventional major field orientation emphasized Traditional Social Orientation and Organization and deemphasized Involvement, Support, Innovation, and Student Influence. Students in dormitories with a high proportion of Investigative majors emphasized Independence, Innovation, and Student Influence, and de-emphasized Traditional Social Orientation and Organization. Living groups with a high proportion of Enterprising majors were characterized by high Independence and low Support, whereas those with a high proportion of Social majors had high Support and low Independence. Thus Holland's environmental models seem to reflect accurately the social climate of colleges and student living units with different scholastic orientations. Students sharing certain average background characteristics create characteristic social environments.

Impact of Environmental Orientation on Student Behavior.

Congruence.   Holland has suggested that people who are congruent with their environment (i.e., people who share the dominant interests of the group) will be more satisfied and more secure in their major field choices, and will perform at a higher level than those who are dissimilar. Thus, for example, physical science majors living in dormitories with a high proportion of similar majors should be more satisfied with their choice of study, less likely to change their major, and more likely to obtain high grades than physical science majors in art-oriented settings.

One of the first studies of congruence effects tested the hypothesis that students whose major field choice resembled that of the majority had more stable goals and higher achievement than those with incongruent interests.[10] National Merit Scholarship finalists were polled during their senior year of high school to assess their major field plans, and again during their senior year of college to determine their actual choices. The students attending a college dominated by types similar to themselves were less likely to have changed their goals than those in institutions in which the dominant orientation was incongruent with their own. Moreover, students who changed their major fields tended to move in the direction of the majority. A congruent choice was also conducive to higher achievement. For example, art majors in Artistic environments displayed higher levels of achievement than their counterparts in schools dominated by the other EAT orientations.

Holland subsequently surveyed college freshmen and sophomores at 27 institutions to examine the influence of congruence on the stability of vocational choice and satisfaction with college.[11] Students were characterized as one of the six types by their initial choices of vocation, and the EAT was chosen to measure the environment. The results suggested that congruence was associated with stability of vocational choice. Only women, however, were found to be more satisfied with a college if their interests were congruent with the college environment.

Astin reviewed the career choices of 3500 high-aptitude males attending 73 institutions and compared their initial choice (at the time they entered college) with their final choice (at the time of graduation).[12] He found that students' choices tended to conform over time to the modal career type (classified according to Holland's EAT system) of their college environment. For example, attending a college dominated by a Realistic orientation increased the chances that a student would later select a Realistic career. It should be emphasized, however, that other variables also influenced these choices, particularly a student's initial career choice.

A second study involving 36,000 students at 246 institutions also indicated a tendency of students' career choices to conform over time with the more popular choices, particularly in the cases of engineering, teaching, law, and business.[13] Astin and Panos considered this effect to be a *process* that both discouraged students planning relatively popular careers from abandoning their initial choice and encouraged those in less popular careers to switch to more popular ones. Appropriately, they labeled this process *progressive conformity*.

Another cleverly designed study examined the effects of the differential distribution of major fields on male freshmen living in a college residence hall.[14] Forty-four science students were paired with 44 humanities students, and 11 roommate pairs were assigned to each of the four floors of a freshmen residence hall. In addition, 66 other science students were assigned to two of the floors, and 66 other humanities students were assigned to the other two floors. Hence two floors were clearly science-dominated and two floors were clearly humanities-dominated. Significantly more of the *minority group* (science majors on humanities-dominated floors, humanities majors on science-dominated floors) *changed their majors* to fields similar to the majority or became *uncertain* of their initial choice during the school year. The three best friends of minority students tended to live outside the residence hall or floor more frequently than was true for the majority students. It was also observed that minority students expressed *less satisfaction* with residence hall life than the majority group.

Those who use the Strong Vocational Interest Blank to counsel students and employees in selecting vocations believe that congruent interests are the key to occupational success. For example, the SVIB has identified the interest pattern of physicians, and college students with the same interests are advised to consider a career in medicine, whereas students with other interests are cautioned against entering the medical profession. There is evidence that persons who initially displayed scores congruent with their subsequent career choices were more successful and satisfied over time than those who entered occupations for which their interests were incongruent.[15]

Congruence in social class background can also have important consequences for college students. Freedman demonstrated that the impact of the first few weeks of college varied for different women, depending on their social class background.[16] The study was conducted at Vassar during the 1950s, when students were drawn primarily from upper-middle-class families. The women who resembled the majority experienced less anxiety and fewer feelings of incompetence than women who were lower in social status and had attended public rather than private high schools. Davie found that Yale students from lower-class families were less satisfied with their college experiences during all 4 years than their peers from wealthier families.[17] Thus incongruence in social class background may produce dissatisfaction and unhappiness among college students.

Consistency.   Most universities are composed of students in all six types of major fields. By rank ordering the students in terms of the proportion in each category, one can draw a profile indicating the most popular types. Certain environmental types have more in common than do others because they exert similar demands and rewards. When the primary elements in an environment are similar, an environment is regarded as *consistent.* For example, an environment dominated by Realistic and Investigative types is consistent because these orientations call for similar qualities , such as perseverance and independence. On the other hand, an environment high on both Conventional and Artistic orientations is inconsistent because it exerts antithetical pressures, such as conformity and nonconformity, self-control and impulsiveness, and unimaginativeness and originality.

As already mentioned, Holland has examined the effect of consistency of the dominant EAT codes on students' vocational choices.[18] He polled 592 National Merit finalists at the end of their senior year in high school and their senior year in college. Students' initial career choices were more likely to be stable in colleges with consistent codes (i.e., Investigative-Realistic) as opposed to those with inconsistent codes (i.e., Artistic-Conventional).

Other work has concentrated on the effects of consistency on a common problem of college freshmen—conflict between roommates.[19] All entering male freshmen had been administered the Vocational Preference Inventory, and the investigator compared the vocational interests of 39 roommate pairs who were reported in conflict by their house staff with 39 roommate pairs not in conflict (picked at random from a population of 131 nonconflict pairs). Roommates not in conflict tended more often to have consistent or compatible interests. Among the conflict roommates, inconsistent pairs were prevalent, particularly Investigative-Enterprising types.

Homogeneity. Homogeneity refers to the degree of uniformity in the composition of background characteristics. The magnitude of difference between the highest and lowest score on the EAT indicates degree of homogeneity in the environment. The greater the difference, the more homogeneous the environment; smaller differences suggest a more diverse environment in which no one orientation is dominant. For example, the environment of a technological school, which emphasizes scientific studies almost to the exclusion of other fields, would be considered "homogeneous." A university with a more equal distribution of majors among the six categories would be "heterogeneous."

Astin and Panos showed that a homogeneous college environment had a strong impact on the stability of vocational choice during a 4-year period.[20] For example, engineers and physical science students attending technological schools were less likely to change their majors than their counterparts in more heterogeneous university settings. Holland also found that homogeneity affected the stability of major field choice. On the other hand, he has reported that students in homogeneous environments were less likely to be satisfied with their college than students in more heterogeneous environments. According to Holland: ". . . heterogeneous colleges have a diverse student population so that a student's opportunity for finding congenial friends is greater than it would be at a college populated largely by a single kind of personality type."[21] Thus homogeneity can have both social and academic effects.

Colleges and universities are more or less homogeneous with respect to other background factors, such as intelligence, social class, race, and sex. Greater homogeneity on these variables has been shown to affect the college climate and student performance. Newcomb suggested that this influence is due to the corresponding homogeneity of student attitudes: "Homogeneity of age, sex, social class, or religious affiliation contributes to effective peer group influence primarily because of the homogeneity of attitudes that tend to go along with such similarities."[22] Just as Holland's environmental types are created by members' having similar personality characteristics, other average background factors are associated with shared personalities and attitudes.

The decision to attend a single-sex versus a coeducational college has been troublesome for many applicants. Astin contrasted the college environments of 246 single-sex and coeducational schools in a study involving some 30,000 college freshmen.[23] *Women's colleges* were characterized by cooperation, cohesiveness, much musical and artistic activity, high classroom involvement, high school spirit, and low emphasis on athletics. *Men's colleges* were characterized by independence, competition, lack of classroom involvement, and permissiveness. Students at *coeducational* institutions saw their environments as less competitive academically and as showing less concern for the individual student than single-sex schools. They also reported an overemphasis on social activities and more informal dating. Thus homogeneity with regard to sex distinguished schools on a variety of dimensions.

Moos and Gerst have discovered that the sex composition of college living groups is associated with systematic differences in social climate.[24] Women's dorms were typified by emotional support, interpersonal involvement, and traditional, culturally valued behaviors. Men perceived their houses as stressing competitive and nonconformist qualities. Coed houses were regarded as high in intellectuality and innovation and low in competition and order. The homogeneity in sex composition has been related to systematic differences in social climate in several investigations.

In another study DeCoster assigned groups of high-ability students so that they formed 50% concentrations in certain residence halls.[25] Control groups of students were randomly assigned to other residence halls. The high-ability students living in close proximity in the homogeneously assigned residence halls surpassed the scattered high-ability students in academic success and also perceived their living quarters as being more desirable. The concentrated high-ability students reported that their living units were conducive to study, that informal talk sessions had educational value, that they were influenced by fellow residents to do better in their studies, and that their fellow residents were considerate and respectful to others. On the other hand, there was some evidence that this concentration of high-ability students may have had negative effects on the academic achievement of the less-talented students in the same residence.

Comment.   Various aggregate factors related to the characteristics of student bodies have been considered situational variables in that they partly define relevant characteristics of the environment. Our discussion has focused on socio-demographic factors and major field or career choices. Many other aggregate characteristics are differentially distributed in high schools and colleges, such as average ability level, study habits, dominant uses of free time, and percentage of students engaged or married. Differences in each of these (average) personal and behavioral characteristics can potentially influence the social climate and the experiences and behavior of an individual student. Centra demonstrated that several of these aggregate factors (in addition to average demographic characteristics) were differentially related to social climate in a study of more than 100 colleges and universities.[26] For example, colleges in which students spent a great deal of time studying were perceived as having greater faculty-student interaction, curriculum flexibility, and academic challenge and emphasis than schools in which students studied less. A similar assessment of the social climate appeared in colleges in which students owned relatively greater numbers of books and came from families with higher socioeconomic status.

Astin has provided a hypothetical example to illustrate how aggregate factors other than demographic ones might be influential.[27] Suppose that a new student enrolls in an institution with high academic standards and that certain environmental stimuli occur relatively frequently: classroom examinations, discussions among students about grades, studying, intellectual arguments among students, and debates between faculty and students. Exposed to these and related stimuli, the new student might feel anxiety about possible academic failure (a change in immediate subjective experience), he might experience increased fear of or hostility toward fellow students, or he might have increased feelings of competitiveness and/or feelings of inferiority. Presumably the student would be affected differently if he attended a different type of college. In terms of short-term behavioral effects, the student may increase the time he devotes to studying, reduce the time he devotes to social activities, and perhaps increase his intellectual aggression. He may consequently experience greater feelings of loneliness and isolation. Finally, there may be longer lasting alterations in his self-concept and/or relatively permanent changes in behavior that may persist beyond college (e.g., devoting a great deal of time to the job or competing constantly with others). Thus a student's experiences, and their short- and long-term consequences, can be influenced by environmental stimuli, which in turn are partly dependent on the typical characteristics of the student body.

The Framework of Social Epidemiology.   It has long been realized that the distribution of illness in a population differs markedly across social groups. For example, infant mortality is higher and life expectancy is shorter in the lower social classes. Accidents and injuries, as well as many communicable and chronic diseases, also occur more frequently in lower-class populations. It seems apparent that certain characteristics of low-income communities, such as crowding, poor nutrition, and inadequate medical care, as well as the impact of illness itself, contribute to the long-term stability of these differences.

Studying disease and social problems "in relation to the characteristics of the group of persons in whom it occurs" has been the traditional concern of epidemiology.[28] Epidemiology is one aspect of the more general field of social ecology, viewing disease and social problems as selected instances of the interaction between individuals and their environment.[29] Within the epidemiological perspective, an environment is often studied in terms of a cluster of average background characteristics. For example, the Bureau of the Census publishes socioeconomic information about the average income, education, and occupational levels for people living in each census tract of a city, and these data often are used in selecting residential areas for study. Vital statistics and health indices, such as birth and death rates, are also routinely computed by city health departments for each census tract. Thus epidemiologists can compare the health status of residents of different socioeconomic areas of a city. The implication of this approach is that one may meaningfully discriminate among environments, in this case neighborhoods, on the basis of a cluster of average sociodemographic (i.e., background) factors.

Ecological investigations, which use geographical areas as their units of analysis, were originally concerned with the geographical distribution of crime and delinquency, and later with mental disorders. Spatial boundaries were determined in the early studies by a preconceived pattern of natural or functional areas of a city—the business area, the industrial section, and residential areas; in later work politically designed census tracts formed the subpopulation groupings. Both schemes resulted in comparisons of populations with divergent sociocultural (i.e., background) characteristics. Recent studies have grouped census tracts with similar configurations of sociodemographic factors into "social areas," which override geographical boundaries. Although less commonly used by epidemiologists, this technique is noteworthy because it directly illustrates the approach of inferring the dominant features of an environment from the average background characteristics of its residents. As Shevky and Bell explain:

> . . . The social area generally contains persons having the same level of living, the same way of life, and the same ethnic background; and we

hypothesize that persons living in a particular type of social area would systematically differ with respect to characteristic attitudes and behaviors from persons living in another type of social area.[30]

A striking example of variations in health status among people in different areas of a city is provided in a study of two New York City boroughs, Brooklyn and the Bronx.[31] The Department of Health has divided New York into health areas, each consisting of two or three census tracts. Using Census Bureau data, Struening and his colleagues correlated information about the average background characteristics of the people living in the health areas [e.g., their unemployment rates and median family income, proportion of persons divorced or separated, proportion of persons who recently migrated from the South (mostly black) or from abroad (mostly Puerto Rican)] with health and crime rates. Differences among the residential areas were largely attributable to environmental conditions, defined in terms of the average background characteristics of the population used in the study. That is, in both boroughs poorer levels of health were reported in areas characterized by lower income and high unemployment, high proportions of divorced or separated individuals, high proportions of people from the South or abroad, and so on. Thus by describing the areas of a city in terms of their average socioeconomic characteristics, the investigators established important relationships between health status and the neighborhood environment.

The critical issue raised by this study is the need to explain systematic variations in indices of health and criminal activity among groups with different background characteristics. That is, why do census tracts or social areas with high unemployment rates, low median family income, a high proportion of divorced or separated persons, and so on, (i.e., with populations characterized by certain background factors) also show more illness and criminal behavior? In the previous chapter personal characteristics were linked to behavioral outcomes through the social climate created by the group. The ecological studies of crime and delinquency and mental disorder have, to some extent, tried to test this model by confronting the following questions. Are certain groups of people (i.e., people with particular background characteristics) more prone to illness and/or crime than others? Are illness and crime generated by the "social climate" of certain urban areas—lack of social control, anonymity, and disorganization? Do some groups of people create certain types of environments that in turn foster poor health and criminal activity? We consider these questions in reviewing the ecological studies of crime and delinquency and mental disorders.

Ecological Studies of Crime and Delinquency.   The first systematic ecological studies of crime and delinquency were published in France and England during the first half of the nineteenth century.[32] Crime rates calculated for clusters of geographical regions revealed that criminal offenders were not randomly distributed throughout the population. Rather, particular areas referred to as "low neighborhoods" had high concentrations of criminals. Conditions of poverty and overcrowding, coupled with extensive exposure to crime, were alleged to account for the high crime rates in certain areas. The conclusion drawn from these reports was that social disorganization, or the social climate of the environment, was responsible for the development of criminal behavior. This causal observation was echoed in America in the 1820s and 1830s, when social critics pointed to defective community organization as the basis of crime, mental illness, and other forms of deviance.[33] Attention was focused on the social climate in high crime rate areas rather than on an inherent predisposition to deviant behavior among certain types of people.

Ecological studies of crime and delinquency continued to flourish in the first three decades of the present century. Much of this research was influenced by the Chicago school of urban sociology, which extended Darwinian notions of evolution to the process of city growth and expansion. An essential feature of this theory is that cities have evolved into a series of natural areas in the shape of concentric circles or zones. Each zone is presumably inhabited by people with different background characteristics. The innermost circle was the business area, in which the residents were by and large transients, living in hotels. The second zone, designated the "transition area," was the industrial section, populated primarily by unskilled laborers and their families. The third zone was a residential area inhibited primarily by skilled workers. The outermost concentric circles were upper-middle-class residential neighborhoods.

Within this framework, Shaw and his colleagues examined the distribution of home addresses of several thousand male school truants, juvenile delinquents, and adult offenders.[34] Using various maps of Chicago, they showed that all three rates tended to decrease with increasing distance from the center of the city. The highest rates occurred among the poorest populations, and the lowest rates were found in the high socioeconomic residential zones. In addition, recidivism (relapse) rates also declined with greater distance from the center of the city. Shaw and McKay subsequently found the same pattern of results in Philadelphia, Richmond, Cleveland, Birmingham, Denver, and Seattle.[35]

Like their nineteenth-century predecessors, these ecologists attributed the geographical pattern of social problems mainly to the inherent social climate of the area. Specifically, they suggested that unconventional norms and values endemic to those areas were responsible for the rates observed. This climate developed out of the economic growth and structure of the city itself and was influenced by the poor economic status of the inhabitants of the target areas. As one source of evidence they pointed out that the high crime rate sections of Chicago in 1900–1906 were also the high crime rate sections in 1917–1923, even though the ethnic composition of these areas had shifted. Moreover, they showed that as ethnic groups moved in and out of such areas, the delinquency rates for these groups increased and decreased, respectively.

Other investigators have confirmed the existence of high rate of delinquency areas and the association of delinquency with poverty. In 1954 an ecological study of delinquency in Baltimore disclosed higher rates in census tracts characterized by a lower percentage of owner-occupied homes, lower median rentals, less education, and a 50–50 ratio of whites to nonwhites.[36] (Although the author himself attempted to show that only the home ownership and racial factors were significant under more complex analyses, critics have questioned the validity of the additional procedures and the author's interpretations.) Bordua studied juvenile delinquency in Detroit for the period 1948–1952 and found higher rates in areas with greater overcrowding, a lower percentage of owner-occupied homes, lower median education, and a higher proportion of unrelated individuals.[37] Both investigators explained the differential delinquency rates in terms of the social climate of high rate areas, which they claimed were unstable communities with "a deficiency in the traditional social controls which maintain conventional behavior in stable communities."[38]

Two interesting ecological studies applied the classification scheme developed by Shevky and Bell known as "social area analysis." This technique cuts across geographical boundaries by grouping census tracts along three dimensions of background characteristics: economic status, family status, and ethnic status. Economic status is determined by educational and occupational characteristics. Family status is based on fertility ratios (number of children under 5 years per 1000 females aged 15–44), percentage of women in the labor force, and percentage of single dwelling units; higher family status is associated with relatively high fertility ratios, low rates of working women, and many single-family homes. Ethnic status refers to the proportion of nonwhites and foreign-born per census tract; greater proportions indicate lower status according to this scheme. Each census tract is categorized according to its ranking on all three dimensions.

The first study examined crime and delinquency rates in Lexington, Kentucky, constructed from 1960 arrest reports.[39] Crime rates were higher in census tracts having lower socioeconomic status and higher proportions of nonwhites, although they were independent of family status. Juvenile delinquency rates followed the same pattern except that areas low in family status seemed to function as a deterrent to delinquency, because in both low and high economic status social areas, high family status was coupled with lower delinquency rates. Polk analyzed 1960 delinquency rates in Portland using the social area approach and also discovered higher levels of delinquency in areas low in socioeconomic and family status and high in proportions of nonwhites and foreign-born.[40] Thus the social area analyses directly link configurations of individual background characteristics to criminal behavior.

Chein and his colleagues studied 3500 juvenile New York City narcotics users (males from 16 to 21 years of age) who were seen by the courts or municipal hospitals between 1949 and 1955.[41] Fifteen percent of the census tracts (of the Bronx, Brooklyn, and Manhattan), containing less than 30% of the boys 16–20 years old, contributed more than 80% of the cases. The areas of high drug use were characterized by more impoverished and disrupted families and higher proportions of black and Puerto Rican populations. These areas also tended to have high delinquency rates. Questionnaire data assessing the social climate of high and low drug rate areas revealed some interesting differences. All eighth-grade boys in the one high, one medium, and one low drug rate area were given a questionnaire tapping a variety of attitudes and values. The social climate in the high drug rate area was characterized by negativism, pessimism, unhappiness, mistrust, and a sense of futility. Fewer boys in the low rate area said that they knew a heroin user (17% vs. 32% in the medium and 45% in the high drug rate areas). Thus Chein associated both differential background characteristics and social climate with drug use.

A great deal of ecological evidence indicates that crime and delinquency are not randomly distributed throughout the areas of a city. Higher rates tend to occur among populations with average background characteristics such as low income, low education, and low status occupations. Whether the same pattern occurs for unreported criminal behavior is an open question, and several investigators have been concerned with this issue.[42] Except for the social area analyses, which link criminal activity more directly to personal background factors, most of the crime and delinquency studies have hypothesized that the social climate of high rate areas is responsible for the existence of deviant behavior. The next section reviews ecological studies of mental disorders, in which the debate about the role of average background characteristics comes into sharper focus.

Ecological Studies of Mental Disorders. The first ecological study documenting the spatial distribution of treated mental illness was formulated in the tradition of the Chicago school of urban sociology. The work of Faris and Dunham, based on first admissions to mental hospitals in the Chicago area during the 1920s and 1930s, showed that schizophrenia was concentrated most highly in the center of the city and decreased progressively toward the city's periphery.[43] Shortly after Faris and Dunham's results appeared, Schroeder verified the ecological distribution of schizophrenia in five other midwestern cities.[44] Consistent with traditional ecological interpretations, Faris and Dunham contended that the social climate of disorganized subcommunities fostered isolation and seclusiveness, factors thought to influence the development of schizophrenia. This interpretation triggered a lively debate and many subsequent studies (based on census tract groupings) of the spatial distribution of mental disorders.

The counterargument suggested that schizophrenia is a major defect (intellectual, psychosocial, physiological, and/or genetic) of the *individual;* that is, it is a personal background characteristic, and environmental conditions play only a secondary role. The second view led to the hypothesis that the relatively high rates of schizophrenia in socially disorganized (low status) areas resulted from the movement (or drift) of preschizophrenic persons (persons with particular background characteristics) from higher to lower socioeconomic areas. Thus the question the ecological studies addressed was: does the social climate elicit schizophrenic disorders, as Faris and Dunham contended, or do potential schizophrenics with certain background characteristics drift into impoverished areas because of inability to maintain higher levels of status, or both?

One of the first projects to tackle the person versus environment issue within an ecological framework examined the residential mobility pattern of 305 male schizophrenics from the city of Worcester, Massachusetts, who had been admitted to Worcester State Hospital. The authors found that the highest proportion of patients had come from the central area of Worcester, where the living conditions were poorest. When they considered the home setting in which the patients had lived at the time of their hospitalization (with family members vs. outside family settings), Gerard and Houston found that the ecological pattern was based on "the residential pattern of a minority of patients, the single, separated or divorced men living alone" who had "drifted" into the central area of the city.[45] Patients living with their families, who formed the majority of those admitted, were neither residentially mobile nor concentrated in any particular geographical section. Thus Gerard and Houston contended that it was not the environment (i.e., social climate) per se that produced an excess of mental disorder in the central zone, but the selection of people with certain background characteristics (a minority of the sample) who had gravitated to that area. Without information about whether these patients had moved from better or from similar socioeconomic neighborhoods, they suggested that mobility itself was a background characteristic associated with mental hospitalization.

Several other studies of treated mental disorders have also focused on average background characteristics in interpreting the basic ecological pattern. In a comparison of first-admission patients from two subcommunities of Detroit, Dunham reported three times as many schizophrenics living in an inner-city, impoverished neighborhood compared with a fringe, upper-middle-class district. Comparing patients residing in each community for less than 5 years with those living there longer than 5 years, he discovered that the 3–1 ratio of schizophrenics in the inner city was a function of the more mobile group. The rates for those living in each community longer than 5 years were identical. Thus he contended that the high rate in the impoverished area reflected "the mobility of the cases rather than . . . any conditions that characterize the social organization of a given community."[46] Dunham also noted that since the majority of the schizophrenics had moved from the inner city (as opposed to an outlying area), mobility itself, rather than downward drift of schizophrenic patients, was a background factor directly associated with hospitalization.

Two investigators reexamined the spatial distribution of treated mental illness in Chicago, using Chicago residents admitted to Illinois public and private institutions from July 1, 1960, to June 1, 1961.[47] The spatial pattern described by Faris and Dunham in 1939 was essentially reaffirmed 30 years later, with rates of severe disorders declining with increasing distance from the center of the city. First admissions tended to come from the more affluent subcommunities, but readmissions emanated more frequently from poorer areas. Therefore Levy and Rowitz concluded that the overall ecological pattern resulted from the downward *drift* of schizophrenics from higher to lower income areas—that is, background factors were directly responsible for the spatial distribution of schizophrenia.

Another study of the ecological distribution of treated mental disorder revealed, through an analysis of the average sociodemographic characteristics of Minnesota's 87 counties, that the poorer counties had a higher rate of mental illness than the wealthier counties.[48] No attempt was made to link the socioeconomic characteristics to differential social climates of these counties; rather a direct association between this average background factor and hospitalization rates was described. Thus several ecological investigations connected the observed distribution of treated mental illness directly to personal background factors.

Two ecological studies interpreted their findings as indicating that the *social climate* was responsible for the distribution of hospitalization rates. A survey comparing a low-income area of Boston with an upper-middle-class suburb reported a significantly higher rate of mental hospitalization for severe psychiatric disturbance in the poorer socioeconomic area.[49] The investigators hypothesized that the social climate of suburban families encouraged them to keep members out of the hospital, whereas families in the low-income neighborhood did not adhere to this value system. Another study in which higher public hospital admission rates were found in census tracts with low socioeconomic and educational levels and high rates of marital disruption attributed the results to social disequilibrium or social disorganization prevalent in those census tracts (i.e., social climate) rather than to inherent differences in the personal background characteristics of the inhabitants.[50]

The actual evidence in these studies is inadequate for arriving at a conclusion about the role of either average background characteristics or social climate. No control groups with similar background characteristics, exposed to similar climates, have been studied to ascertain the *unique* factors associated with hospitalization. Thus it is surprising that only two investigations offered *both* explanations for the ecological distribution of treated mental illness. Using the Maryland Psychiatric Case Register, a cumulative record of all contacts for mental illness in that state, Klee and his coworkers showed that psychiatric utilization rates of Baltimore residents were higher in areas composed of persons with low income, low educational levels, and semiskilled occupations.[51] In suggesting that both social climate and individual factors were responsible for these results, they pointed to the social forces (i.e., social climate) in low-income areas, which more readily encourage sick individuals to go to psychiatric facilities, and to a greater level of morbidity in these areas.

Another project compared the residential mobility pattern of schizophrenics hospitalized in the Buffalo, New York, area between 1949 and 1951 with that of a normal control group.[52] Census tracts of the city were divided into four quartiles according to the average rent per tract. The schizophrenic sample's residential history was traced back over a 20-year period; and controls were chosen from the original residential locations and traced forward 20 years. By this method, the authors found no difference in the geographic mobility pattern of the two groups. Although the schizophrenics were concentrated in the low-rent areas, their rate of upward (or downward) residential mobility was not substantially different from that of the nonhospitalized control group. Since both the schizophrenics and their controls were exposed to the same environments by and large, the findings could have resulted from individual differences. On the other hand, the overall pattern of higher rates in low-income areas suggested that social climate (i.e., social isolation, fear of unemployment, restricted recreational opportunities) was also a significant factor. The authors thus concluded that both sets of factors must be taken into account.

Until now we have concentrated on studies of treated mental illness. It can of course be argued that the process of becoming a mental patient is not random, and treatment data do not reflect the true incidence or distribution of mental illness in the population. It has also been suggested that diagnosis is not independent of social class; psychiatrists may be more willing to attach the "schizophrenic" label to a lower-class person than to an upper-class patient. Furthermore, since most studies did not include patients seen by private practitioners or hospitals, treatment data reflect sampling biases. Similar issues have been raised regarding crime and delinquency data. However a few studies indicate that the ecological patterns of treated and untreated mental illness are very similar.

Five years after Faris and Dunham's work appeared, another study suggested that the ecological pattern these workers described was true for nonhospitalized populations as well. The results were based on men rejected by the Boston Armed Forces Induction Station for reasons of mental disability.[53] Evaluations of the socioeconomic levels of the subjects' communities of origin indicated that the rate of psychiatric disorder increased progressively from higher to lower socioeconomic communities. The authors believed that both average background and social climate factors contributed to this pattern, and they hypothesized that "unfit" individuals (background characteristic) gravitated into poorer communities, and differences in the cultural acceptability of asocial conduct could be identified at different socioeconomic levels (social climate). (Their second explanation runs counter to a later hypothesis that low-income families are *less* tolerant of deviant behavior, thus are more prone to hospitalize their sick members.)

Another major study, carried out by the Leightons in Stirling County, Canada, compared the mental health of people in two "integrated" Canadian communities with that of residents of three ethnically mixed, "disintegrated" communities.[54] Indicators of disintegration included extensive poverty, widespread ill health, and a high frequency of broken homes. Mental health was assessed by responses to questions about such symptoms as psychosomatic ailments (gastrointestinal disorders, cold sweats, trembling hands, headaches) and emotional problems (fear of having a nervous breakdown, excessive worrying, feeling in poor spirits). Again the same pattern of results occurred, with poorer mental health reported in the disintegrated social areas. The Leightons have become well known for their view that social disintegration (i.e., social climate) is a causal agent in mental illness.

Two other sources of evidence support the ecological findings. Studies of the occupational position of diagnosed schizophrenics have revealed that schizophrenia is progressively more prevalent among individuals holding low-prestige, low-income occupations.[55] In addition, surveys of untreated mental impairment have indicated that rates of mental disability increase progressively with decreasing income and occupational status. The major works in this area were the Midtown Study in New York City, which reported a disproportionately high rate of psychological impairment among the lower social classes,[56] and a study of the mental health of factory workers, which found poorer mental health among less skilled than among more skilled automobile workers.[57] These results are an important complement to the ecological findings.

The debate about the role of personal background factors versus the social climate of the environment in the ecological pattern of mental illness has its counterpart in studies of occupational mobility. These investigations have attempted to determine whether the excess of schizophrenia in lower-status occupations results from a loss of status over time (downward occupational mobility) or from the failure of pre-schizophrenic individuals ever to achieve higher level positions. To date, these studies have produced contradictory results.[58]

Thus the ecological evidence points to a consistent pattern for mental illness and for crime and delinquency. The controversy over individual background factors versus social climate will continue until more direct data become available. On the whole, ecological studies of mental illness seem to favor the individual background hypothesis, whereas studies of crime and delinquency are more often interpreted in light of differential social climates. The issues remain unresolved, and the data at hand are insufficient to disentangle them, if in fact they can be disentangled.

The next section pursues another phase of research that illustrates the importance of average background factors for psychological well-being. The issue is one of congruence between individuals and their environment. In educational settings a lack of congruence in major field choice and background characteristics had demonstrable consequences for college students. There is evidence that a lack of congruence along sociodemographic dimensions in neighborhood settings has important social and mental health effects.

Congruence.   Although rates of mental illness, crime, and delinquency vary systematically among areas with different overall characteristics, some studies have found that certain subgroups have higher rates in areas where they are in the minority than in areas where they form the majority. These investigations of congruence have considered race, ethnic group, social class, age, place of birth, and religion.

In their ecological investigation of Chicago, Faris and Dunham learned that the schizophrenia rates for blacks, whites, and the foreign-born were higher for each group in areas where they were in the minority.[59] More specifically, blacks living in white areas had a rate 32% above that for blacks living in black areas, and whites living in predominantly black areas had a considerably higher rate than whites in white areas. Thirty years later Levy and Rowitz carried out a similar analysis of first admissions to mental hospitals in Chicago and confirmed the original results.[60] Blacks living in neighborhoods that were less than 10% black had higher rates than blacks living in areas where they formed the majority. Similarly whites had higher rates in racially mixed or predominantly black neighborhoods than in areas populated primarily by whites. (These results should not be confused with the overall ecological pattern. A "rate" is defined as the number of cases divided by the population at risk. Where fewer persons are at risk, as is the case for blacks living in white neighborhoods and whites living in black neighborhoods, a small number of cases can produce a relatively high rate. On the other hand, a large population base may contribute many more cases overall but still have a smaller *rate*.)

Several other workers have documented the importance of congruence of racial characteristics. Dee verified part of Faris and Dunham's observations by finding a tendency for schizophrenia to occur more frequently among white people living in predominantly black districts of St. Louis.[61] Two ecological studies of diagnosed mental illness and juvenile delinquency in Baltimore found the highest rates for both whites and blacks in census tracts where they constituted a small minority of the population (10% or less).[62] Finally, a study of Lexington, Kentucky, using the social area analysis described earlier, revealed that nonwhite crime and delinquency rates were higher in areas with greater proportions of whites, whereas white rates increased with increasing proportions of nonwhite residents per area.[63]

Mintz and Schwartz related mental hospital admission rates for Italian-born and second-generation Italians from various communities in the Boston area to the percentage of Italians living in those communities.[64] Communities with a higher "Italian" density tended to have *fewer* Italians admitted for severe psychiatric disorders (schizophrenia and manic-depression) than did communities with a lower density of Italians. This finding was independent of the communities' socioeconomic level as indicated by median monthly rentals. Thus there is some evidence that groups who are not congruent with their communities, either racially or ethnically, may have higher rates of disorder than their counterparts living in areas in which they are congruent with the majority.

In an extremely clever analysis Wechsler and Pugh abstracted four background characteristics from approximately 25,000 first-admission records to all psychiatric inpatient care facilities in Massachusetts (excluding patients from Boston).[65] These characteristics included age (15–34, 35–54, 55 +), marital status (married, single, widowed-divorced-separated), place of birth (Massachusetts, United States outside Massachusetts, foreign-born), and occupation (professional, crafts, etc.). Using data published by the Bureau of the Census, they grouped every city and town in Massachusetts (except Boston) on each of these variables and divided the groups into the 16% with the highest proportion, the 68% with the intermediate proportion, and the 16% with the lowest proportion for each specific category. The authors compared hospitalization rates of people who were incongruent with their communities (lived in towns with characteristics different from their own) with those of people who were more similar to their neighbors (e.g., professional workers in towns where the proportion of such individuals was high). Several variables were significant, including age, marital status, place of birth, and certain occupational classifications. Thus for several sociodemographic characteristics, hospitalization rates were higher among groups who were in the minority than among those who resembled the majority.

Another study of congruence suggested that high school students reared in areas where neighboring families had religious affiliations predominantly different from their own manifested more signs of emotional disturbance than children who grew up near families of the same religious background.[66] Catholic students raised in non-Catholic neighborhoods were more likely to have low self-esteem, to feel depressed, and to report more psychosomatic symptoms indicative of anxiety (trembling hands, trouble sleeping, nail biting, headaches) than Catholics raised in predominantly Catholic or half-Catholic neighborhoods. Similar results were reported for Protestants and Jews.

There is fairly consistent evidence indicating that a lack of congruence with one's neighbors can have negative psychological concomitants for subgroups defined by a variety of dimensions. The most common explanation for these results is that incongruent groups experience greater social isolation from other residents. Bell examined the amount of social interaction with neighbors among a random sample of adult males in blue- and white-collar neighborhoods.[67] By comparing the individuals' occupations with the occupations typical of the neighborhood, he learned that blue-collar workers living in white-collar neighborhoods were more isolated than their peers living in blue-collar areas. White-collar workers residing in blue-collar areas were more isolated than their counterparts in white-collar neighborhoods. Thus there is some direct support for the use of the isolation hypothesis to explain the results of congruence investigations.

Comment. In sum, evidence supports the conclusions that the distribution of severe mental illness and criminal activity varies with the average background characteristics of the population. Despite the methodological shortcomings of the research, the results show a higher rate of severe impairment and criminality in the lower social classes and among individuals who are incongruent with their neighbors on one or more demographic variables. Three explanations have commonly been used to account for the skewed distribution of schizophrenia—isolation, stress, and family supportiveness. All three conditions may reflect both background factors that make people susceptible or vulnerable to illness and a social climate that is conducive to illness.

Clinical research has described the important role of social isolation in predicting the onset of schizophrenia and in distinguishing schizophrenia from other emotional disorders. On the average, schizophrenics tend to be unmarried and to have avoided intimate interpersonal contact. The latter characteristic has been attributed to the presence of a *schizoid* personality; that is, detachment and aloofness around others are traits commonly noted in the personal histories of schizophrenics.

One source of sociological validation for the isolation hypothesis comes from the ecological studies of congruence, where higher rates of disturbance occurred among individuals dissimilar from the majority. Odegaard found an increase in hospitalization rates in occupational groups that decreased in size from 1930 to 1946 and, conversely, a decrease in hospitalization rates in occupations that expanded during those years.[68] More evidence comes from an ecological study of Bristol, England, which indicated that the highest rates of mental hospitalization occurred in the areas of the community having the highest ratios of persons living alone.[69] This finding was confirmed in a study of Chicago residents in which rates of mental hospital admissions demonstrably increased with the percentage of persons living alone.[70] In his social area analysis of San Francisco, Bell reported that there was less social interaction among men in the blue-collar neighborhoods than in the white-collar area.[71] These results suggest that people are more isolated from one another in lower-class neighborhoods, which on the average produce greater numbers of hospitalized cases.

This implication was borne out in a study measuring an array of factors pertaining to interpersonal contact and communication in census tracts producing high and low rates of schizophrenia.[72] In interviewing a random sample of the residents of these areas, Jaco discovered that high rate communities displayed more evidence of social isolation. Respondents from high rate areas indicated that they had fewer personal friends and fewer acquaintances, fewer memberships in lodges or fraternal organizations, fewer visits to other areas of the city or out of town, and fewer friends in remote areas. These studies support the contention that isolation is an important factor mediating the relationship between average background characteristics and the development of schizophrenia.

A second explanation for the observed association is that stressful conditions are more prevalent in impoverished communities. In a study of married schizophrenics in the lowest social class, Rogler and Hollingshead discovered that the stresses endured by the clinical group were harsher than those encountered by a matched control sample.[73] Community surveys have indicated that stressful events are more common among respondents with high levels of symptomatology[74] and preceded the onset of symptoms.[75] Dohrenwend has shown that lower-class residents are exposed to a high rate of change or instability, which produces a high level of individual distress.[76] Finally, when high and low status groups *both* experience a high degree of stress in terms of deprivations and disruptions during their lives, greater psychological impairment occurs among the lower-status persons.[77] Thus there is considerable evidence that stressful experiences are more prevalent in low-income groups and may elicit ineffective coping responses within that population.

Degree of family support may be associated with the higher prevalence of treated schizophrenia at the lowest social class levels. The most direct evidence of the role of family environment as a mediator between background characteristics and mental illness has come from studies of posthospital adjustment. Consider the following descriptions of the contrasting levels of support for two patients, both diagnosed schizophrenic, from different socioeconomic backgrounds:[78]

> Mrs. S, a class III [is a] married woman with five children ranging in age from 1 to 12. . . . Mrs S and her husband . . . know more than a dozen neighbors and visit back and forth regularly. . . . Neither Mrs. S nor her husband feels that they should hide the fact of her hospitalization . . . if the

subject of mental illness arises they usually mention Mrs. S's successful treatment. (p. 188)

Miss M., a class V, . . . would like more friends but feels that people avoid her because she has "been up to the state mental hospital." She claims that the friends of her family have not treated her the same since her return. Her sister, with whom she lives, is embarrassed by the thought of the psychiatric hospitalization. . . . Family members are less willing to invite friends to their home and sometimes avoid their friends because they are embarrassed. (pp. 193–194)

Thus one class-related aspect of the family environment is the attitude toward the hospitalized individual once he returns home—lower class families are more reluctant to accept a person back after he or she has been hospitalized. This process begins long before the person is discharged. Even while the patient is still in the hospital, families in lower classes visit and correspond with their relatives less frequently than families of middle-class patients.[79] The expectations about the returned patient's functioning have been described as generally more pessimistic, the lower the socioeconomic level of the family. Such patients are expected to be inactive, isolated, and unable to maintain a job. In homes in which family members have high expectations, "the former patients themselves are also likely to expect more of themselves. . . . These greater pressures for success and for a return to 'normalcy' and to the fulfillment of the prerequisites of [one's] role are likely therefore to be translated into better posthospital performance."[80]

Kohn was impressed with yet another aspect of the family environment that might contribute to unsuccessful coping behavior, role patterning, and socialization.

Many lower class families transmit to their offspring an orientational system too limited and too rigid for dealing effectively with complex changing or stressful situations. This point of view is . . . consonant with recent psychiatric thinking about the family and schizophrenia. . . . What is new is the assertion that these conceptions of reality, far from being unique to families whose offspring become schizophrenic, are widely held in the lower social classes. . . .[81]

Kohn suggested that lower-class families transmit a rigidly conservative outlook that impairs resourceful adaptation, particularly in the potentially schizophrenic individual. It has also been argued that these class-linked value differences exist between patients and therapists and are a hindrance to successful psychiatric treatment.[82] Hence the potential mediating influence of the family environment may be important in both the development and duration of schizophrenic episodes.

Practical Applications. Our concern with the role of average background characteristics in defining the qualities of an environment has led us to two separate areas of research, educational studies and social epidemiology. Within each of these traditions, average group differences in demographic and personality characteristics were associated with variations in social climate and behavioral outcomes. To untangle the causal nexus involved in these relationships would require more carefully designed studies than are now available. Even within the limitations of our current knowledge, however, this approach contains relevant practical applications.

One basic use of average background characteristics is in supplying information about an environment. For example, most colleges publish annual descriptive statistics of the new freshman class and of the student body as a whole. These data provide the prospective applicant with information about the sex, racial, religious, and ethnic group composition of the school, the percentage of students in each major field, median college board scores, and so on. Thus they present guidelines for deciding where to apply to college by giving applicants a basis for judging how well they will fit in with other students in the various institutions (see Chapter 12).

On a personal level, knowing that other people in an environment share certain experiences and problems may provide a more balanced perspective. College students often feel that their problems are unique and unrelated to the environment, and that they must cope on their own. However some problems are widely shared by a person's peers. For example, a survey of shyness among 800 high school and college students revealed that 42% considered themselves to be shy and two-thirds of that group saw their shyness as a problem.[83] The knowledge that many of one's peers are shy may in itself alleviate some of the distress associated with shyness. Similarly many students in highly competitive academic communities have feelings of low self-esteem, whereas in other settings, in which the average ability level is lower than their own (i.e., former high schools, subsequent occupational settings), the same individuals feel confident and assertive. The magnitude of the problems of shyness and low self-esteem suggests that interventions should be directed at the environment as well as at selected persons.

People moving into a new community can make use of census tract information in selecting neighborhoods in which they feel comfortable. Thus a retired couple might wish to move into an area with a high proportion of retired couples and a low proportion of young children; others might prefer neighborhoods with a particular ethnic group composition. Census tract tables containing relevant statistics are publicly available and can help people make such decisions.

Aggregate data have also been used in planning for community services. Health surveys have repeatedly shown that inner-city areas with average background characteristics such as low income and education and high unemployment, have the highest rates of illness and mortality. This information contributed to the creation of neighborhood health centers in these areas. In addition, once services were offered, comparisons between the background characteristics of patients seen at a clinic with the general population of the target area can be used to identify selective patterns in utilization and to encourage programmatic responses to particular community needs. One such study, which compared children seen by the mental health unit of a neighborhood health center during a 3-year period with children residing in the neighborhood, revealed a disproportionate number of clinic users in the 10–14 year age bracket, male, and white.[84] These (and other) results were used to justify the development of new interventions aimed at male adolescents and to reexplore the referral patterns of the underrepresented Spanish-speaking children.

Thus we see that knowledge of the average background characteristics of setting participants has several practical implications because it provides a basis for inferring other characteristics of an environment and for judging one's own role within the setting.

REFERENCES

1. Johnson, D. *The social psychology of education.* Holt, Rinehart & Winston, New York, 1970, p. 230.
2. Linton, R. *The cultural background of personality.* Appleton-Century-Crofts, New York, 1945.
3. Holland, J. *The psychology of vocational choice: A theory of personality types and model environments.* Blaisdell, Waltham, Mass., 1966.
   Holland, J. *Making vocational choices: A theory of careers.* Prentice-Hall, Englewood Cliffs, N.J., 1973.
4. Cronbach, L. J. *Essentials of psychological testing,* 2nd ed. Harper & Row, New York, 1960, pp. 406–439.
   Strong, E. K. *Strong Vocational Interest Blank manual,* revised by D. P. Campbell. Stanford University Press, Stanford, Calif., 1966.
5. Holland, *op. cit.,* p. 9.
6. Astin, A. and Holland, J. The Environmental Assessment Technique: A way to measure college environments. *Journal of Educational Psychology,* **52:**308–316, 1961.

Astin, A. Further validation of the Environmental Assessment Technique. *Journal of Educational Psychology*, **54:**217–226, 1963.

7. Astin, A. Differential college effects on the motivation of talented students to obtain the Ph.D. *Journal of Educational Psychology*, **54:**63–71, 1963.

8. Pace, C. R. *College and University Environment Scales: Technical manual*, 2nd ed. Educational Testing Service, Princeton, N.J., 1967.

9. Hearn, J. and Moos, R. Social climate and major choice: A test of Holland's theory in student living groups. *Journal of Vocational Behavior*, in press, 1976.

10. Holland, J. Explorations of a theory of vocational choice and achievement: II. A four-year predictive study. *Psychological Reports*, **12:**547–594, 1963.

11. Holland, J. Explorations of a theory of vocational choice and achievement: VI. A longitudinal study using a sample of typical college students. *Journal of Applied Psychology*, **52** (Monograph Supplement): 1–37, 1968.

12. Astin, A. Effect of different college environments on the vocational choices of high aptitude students. *Journal of Counseling Psychology*, **12:**28–34, 1965.

13. Astin, A. and Panos, R. *The educational and vocational development of college students.* American Council on Education, Washington, D.C., 1969.

14. Brown, R. Manipulation of the environmental press in a college residence hall. *Personnel and Guidance Journal*, **46:**555–560, 1968.

15. Strong, *Strong Vocational Interest Blank, op. cit.,* 1966.

16. Freedman, M. The passage through college. In N. Sanford (Ed.), Personality development during the college years. *Journal of Social Issues*, **12:**13–28, 1956.

17. Davie, J. S. Satisfaction and the college experience. In B. M. Wedge (Ed.), *Psychosocial problems of college men.* Yale University Press, New Haven, Conn., 1958, pp. 15–44.

18. Holland, Explorations of a theory of vocational choice and achievement, *op. cit.*

19. Williams, J. E. Conflict between freshmen male roommates. Research Report No. 10–67, University of Maryland, Counseling Center, College Park, 1967. Cited in Holland, *Making vocational choices, op. cit.,* p. 67.

20. Astin and Panos, *op. cit.*

21. Holland, Explorations of a theory of vocational choice and achievement, *op. cit.,* p. 35.

22. Newcomb, T. *The acquaintance process.* Holt, Rinehart & Winston, New York, 1961, p. 13.

23. Astin, A. *The American college.* American Council on Education, Washington, D.C., 1968.

24. Moos, R. and Gerst, M. *University Residence Environment Scale Manual.* Consulting Psychologists Press, Palo Alto, Calif., 1974.

25. DeCoster, D. Housing assignments for high ability students. *Journal of College Student Personnel*, **7:**10–22, 1966.

26. Centra, J. The college environment revisited: Current descriptions and a comparison of three methods of assessment. Educational Testing Service Research Bulletin, Princeton, N.J., 1970.

27. Astin, *op. cit.*

28. Lilienfeld, A., Pedersen, E., and Dowd, J. *Cancer epidemiology: Methods of study.* Johns Hopkins Press, Baltimore, 1967, p. 3.

29. Plunkett, R. J. and Gordon, J. E. *Epidemiology and mental illness.* Basic Books, New York, 1960.

30. Shevky, E. and Bell, W. Social area analysis. In G. Theodorson (Ed.), *Studies in human ecology.* Row, Peterson, Evanston, Ill., 1961, p. 233.

31. Struening, E., Lehmann, S., and Rabkin, J. Context and behavior: A social area analysis of New York City. In E. Brody (Ed.), *Behavior in new environments.* Sage Publications, Beverly Hills, Calif., 1970, pp. 203–215.

32. Voss, H. and Petersen, D. Introduction. In H. Voss and D. Petersen (Eds.), *Ecology, crime, and delinquency.* Appleton-Century-Crofts, New York, 1971, pp. 1–44.

33. Rothman, D. *The discovery of the asylum.* Little, Brown, Boston, 1971.

34. Shaw, C. R. and McKay, H. Juvenile delinquency in urban areas: Research; and juvenile delinquency in urban areas: Theory. In H. Voss and D. Petersen (Eds.), *op. cit.*, pp. 79–99.

35. Shaw, C. R. and McKay, H. *Social factors in juvenile delinquency.* Government Printing Office, Washington, D.C., 1931.

36. Lander, B. Towards an understanding of juvenile delinquency. In H. Voss and D. Petersen (Eds.), *op. cit.*, pp. 161–174.

37. Bordua, D. J. Juvenile delinquency and "anomie": An attempt at replication. In H. Voss and D. Petersen (Eds.), *op. cit.*, pp. 175–187.

38. Lander, *op. cit.*, p. 173.

39. Quinney, R. Crime, delinquency, and social areas. In H. Voss and D. Petersen (Eds.), *op. cit.*, pp. 263–272.

40. Polk, K. Urban social areas and delinquency. In H. Voss and D. Petersen (Eds.), *op. cit.*, pp. 273–281.

41. Chein, I., Gerard, D., Lee, R., and Rosenfeld, E. *The road to H.* Basic Books, New York, 1964.

42. Gold, M. Delinquent behavior in an American city. Wadsworth, Belmont, Calif., 1970.
   Gold, M. Undetected delinquent behavior. *Journal of Research in Crime and Delinquency,* **3:**27–46, 1966.

43. Faris, R. E. and Dunham, H. W. *Mental disorders in urban areas.* University of Chicago Press, Chicago, 1939.

44. Schroeder, C. Mental disorders in cities. *American Journal of Sociology,* **48:**40–47, 1942.

45. Gerard, L. and Houston, L. Family setting and the social ecology of schizophrenia. *Psychiatric Quarterly,* **27:**90–101, 1953.

46. Dunham, H. W. *Community and schizophrenia: An epidemiological analysis.* Wayne State University Press, Detroit, 1965, p. 161.

47. Levy, L. and Rowitz, L. *The ecology of mental disorder.* Behavioral Publications, New York, 1973.

48. Vail, D., Lucero, J., and Boen, J. The relationship between socioeconomic variables and major mental illness in the counties of a midwestern state. *Community Mental Health Journal,* **2:**211–212, 1966.

49. Kaplan, B., Reed, R., and Richardson, W. A comparison of the incidence of hospitalized and non-hospitalized cases of psychosis in two communities. *American Sociological Review,* **21:**472–479, 1956.

50. Bloom, B. A census tract analysis of socially deviant behaviors. *Multivariate Behavioral Research,* **1:**307–320, 1966.

51. Klee, G. D., Spiro, E., Bahn, A., and Gorwitz, K. An ecological analysis of diagnosed mental illness in Baltimore. In R. Monroe, G. Klee, and E. Brody (Eds.), *Psychiatric Epidemiology and Mental Health Planning.* American Psychiatric Association, Washington, D.C., 1967, pp. 107–148.

52. Lapouse, R., Monk, M., and Terris, M. The "drift" hypothesis in socioeconomic differentials in schizophrenia. *American Journal of Public Health,* **46:**978–986, 1956.

53. Hyde, R. and Kingsley, L. The relation of mental disorders to the community socioeconomic level. *New England Journal of Medicine,* **231:**543–548, 1944.

54. Leighton, D., Harding, J., Macklin, D., Macmillan, A., and Leighton, A. *The character of danger.* Basic Books, New York, 1963.

55. Hollingshead, A. and Redlich, F. *Social class and mental illness: A community study.* Wiley, New York, 1958.

    Turner, R. J. and Wagenfeld, M. O. Occupational mobility and schizophrenia: An assessment of the social causation and social selection hypotheses. *American Sociological Review,* **32:**104–113, 1967.

    Rushing, W. Two patterns in the relationship between social class and mental hospitalization. *American Sociological Review,* **34:**533–541, 1969.

56. Srole, L., Langner, T., Michael, S., Opler, M., and Rennie, T. *Mental health in the metropolis: The Midtown Manhattan study.* McGraw-Hill, New York, 1962.

57. Kornhauser, A. The mental health of the factory worker. In H. Wechsler, L. Solomon, and B. Kramer (Eds.), *Social psychology and mental health.* Holt, Rinehart & Winston, New York, 1970, pp. 730–753.

58. For a thoughtful review of these studies, see B. P. Dohrenwend and B. S. Dohrenwend. *Social status and psychological disorder: A causal inquiry.* Wiley-Interscience, New York, 1969.

59. Faris and Dunham, *Mental disorders in urban areas, op. cit.*

60. Levy and Rowitz, *The ecology of mental disorder, op. cit.*

61. Dee, W. An ecological study of mental disorders in metropolitan St. Louis. Cited in Schroeder, Mental disorders in cities, *op. cit.,* p. 45.

62. Klee et al., *op. cit.*
    Lander, Towards an understanding of juvenile delinquency, *op. cit.*

63. Quinney, Crime, delinquency, and social areas, *op. cit.*

64. Mintz, N. and Schwartz, D. Urban ecology and psychosis: Community factors in the incidence of schizophrenia and manic-depression among Italians in greater Boston. *International Journal of Social Psychiatry,* **10:**101–118, 1964.

65. Wechsler, H. and Pugh, T. Fit of individual and community characteristics and rates of psychiatric hospitalization. *American Journal of Sociology,* **73:**331–338, 1967.

66. Rosenberg, M. The dissonant religious context and emotional disturbance. *American Journal of Sociology,* **68:**1–10, 1962.

67. Bell, W. The utility of the Shevky typology for the design of urban sub-area field studies. In G. Theodorson (Ed.), *Studies in human ecology.* Row, Peterson, Evanston, Ill., 1961, pp. 244–252.

68. Odegaard, O. The incidence of psychoses in various occupations. *International Journal of Social Psychiatry,* **2:**85–104, 1956.

69. Hare, E. H. Mental illness and social conditions in Bristol. *Journal of Mental Science,* **102:**349–357, 1956.

70. Galle, O., Gove, W., and McPherson, J. Population density and pathology: What are the relations for man? In R. Moos and P. Insel (Eds.), *Issues in social ecology.* National Press Books, Palo Alto, Calif., 1974, pp. 136–153.

71. Bell, *op. cit.*

72. Jaco, E. G. The social isolation hypothesis and schizophrenia. *American Sociological Review,* **19:**567–577, 1954.

73. Rogler, L. and Hollingshead, A. *Trapped: Families and schizophrenia.* Wiley, New York, 1965.

74. Myers, J. K., Lindenthal, J. J., and Pepper, M. P. Life events and psychiatric impairment. *Journal of Nervous and Mental Disease,* **152:**149–157, 1971.

75. Myers, J. K., Lindenthal, J. J., Pepper, M. P., and Ostrander, D. R. Life events and mental status: A longitudinal study. *Journal of Health and Social Behavior,* **13:**398–406, 1972.

76. Dohrenwend, B. Social status and stressful life events. *Journal of Personality and Social Psychology,* **28:**225–235, 1973, p. 233.

77. Langner, T. and Michael, S. *Life stress and mental health.* Free Press, New York, 1963.

78. Myers, J. K. and Bean, L. L. *A decade later: A follow-up of social class and mental illness.* Wiley, New York, 1968.

79. *Ibid.*

80. Dinitz, S., Lefton, M., Angrist, S., and Pasamanick, B. Psychiatric and social attributes as predictors of case outcome in mental hospitalization. *Social Problems,* **8:**322–328, 1961.

81. Kohn, M. Class, family, and schizophrenia: A reformulation. *Social Forces,* **50:**295–304, 1972, p. 300.

82. Hollingshead and Redlich, *Social class and mental illness, op. cit.*

Levinson, D. and Gallagher, E. The relevance of social class. In H. Wechsler, L. Solomon, and B. Kramer (Eds.), *Social psychology and mental health.* Holt, Rinehart & Winston, New York, 1970, pp. 318–326.

83. Zimbardo, P., Pilkonis, P., and Norwood, R. The social disease called shyness. *Psychology Today,* **8**(12):68–70, 1975.

84. Novack, A., Bromet, E., Neill, K., Abramovitz, R., and Storch, S. Children's mental health services in an inner city neighborhood. I. A three-year epidemiologic study. *American Journal of Public Health,* **65**:133–138, 1975.

CHAPTER TEN

Social Climate: The "Personality" of the Environment

The Social Climate Perspective. The social climate perspective assumes that environments, like people, have unique "personalities." Social environments can be portrayed with a great deal of accuracy and detail. Some people are more supportive than others. Likewise, some social environments are more supportive than others. Some people feel a strong need to control others. Similarly, social environments can be extremely rigid, autocratic, and controlling. Order, clarity, and structure are important to many people. Correspondingly, many social environments strongly emphasize order, clarity, and organization. People make detailed plans regulating and directing their behavior. Likewise, environments have overall programs that regulate and direct the behavior of the people within them.

Almost everyone intuitively believes that the social environment or social climate has a significant impact on the people functioning in it. Many feel that the current social climate in the United States fosters aggressive and criminal behavior. One can cogently argue that every institution in our society attempts to set up social environments to maximize certain directions of personal growth and development. Families, social groups, business organizations, secondary schools, colleges and universities, military companies, psychiatric treatment programs, correctional institutions, and communes all arrange social environmental conditions they hope will maximize "desirable" behaviors (and presumably minimize "undesirable" ones).

The Lester and Mitchell Families. Consider two families who live in physically similar homes on the same block in a middle-income suburban area. Both include four immediate family members: mother, father, teenaged son, and teenaged daughter. At first glance these two families appear to be very much alike, but this impression changes radically when information about the social environment or the "personality" of the families is provided.

The Lester family has a strong sense of belongingness and togetherness. The members get along well together, have a good deal of fun as a family unit, and are involved in and proud of their family. Family members help and support one another and generally feel able to tell other members about personal problems and uncertainties. The Lesters feel relaxed and comfortable at home and show warmth and physical affection toward one another. Laughter, spontaneous discussions, and spur-of-the-moment activities are prevalent. Each of the Lesters is actively involved in hobbies, sports, and other recreational activities. A visitor sees tennis rackets, fishing gear, baseball gloves, and other sports equipment around the house. The Lesters often go to movies, and they participate in outdoor activities such as sports events, camping, and hiking. There always seem to be friends at the house, joining in for dinner or some activity.

The Lesters also emphasize a moral and religious orientation. They attend church regularly. The Bible is often read and discussed in their home, although it is not taken literally. Prayers are said before meals. The family often talks about the religious meaning of Christmas, Easter, and other holidays. Moral and ethical issues are openly discussed and debated, with the express purpose of defining a practical and useful set of ethical standards for each individual. Family members respect and try to emulate others who have high moral and ethical principles.

Our second family, the Mitchells, has a quite different social environment or "personality." The Mitchell family is very well organized. Each family member has certain chores or duties at home and follows a fairly regular schedule every day. Neatness and orderliness are paramount virtues. Family activities are carefully planned, and the household runs on the principle of "a place for everything, and everything in its place." For example, dishes are usually done immediately after eating, being on time is a matter of crucial importance, and financial planning, budgeting, and allowances are handled with extreme care. There is a high degree of clarity and consistency in this family. The family has explicit rules (e.g., the amount of allowances and the number of nights out for each child) which are generally mutually set and agreed on. Each family member has specific defined responsibilities around the home. There is very little confusion, changing of minds, and spur-of-the-moment activity in this family. Thus the Mitchell family is highly predictable. If confusion or uncertainty occurs, open family discussions usually straighten things out. Father is considered the head of the household, but he and his wife usually agree on all important matters anyway.

The Mitchells set very high goals for themselves. Each one feels that it is important to be the best at whatever he does. Getting ahead in life is considered essential, and school grades and promotions are often discussed. Self-improvement is a cardinal virtue, and everyone strives to do things just a bit better the next time. The family believes in competition and tries hard to succeed. Perhaps its motto is: "if a job is worth doing, it's worth doing well." Intellectual and cultural activities are also strongly emphasized. The Mitchells frequently read books and magazines and have intellectual discussions about political and social issues. They go to lectures, plays, and concerts, and actively participate in artistic and other craft activities. Classical music, art, and literature are emphasized (e.g., father plays the violin and mother the piano). The Mitchells often read a book and discuss it over the dinner table or in the evening.

The Lester and Mitchell families clearly have very different "personalities." The adolescent children in these families will develop very differently, likely engaging in different activities, having different values, and organizing their own later families in very different ways. The Lester family is characterized by involvement, cohesion, belongingness, and mutual support, by open, spontaneous, expressive activity, and by active recreational pursuits and an emphasis on moral, ethical, and religious development. This family does not place heavy stress on achievement or intellectual and cultural activities, nor does it value order and regularity or a careful and clear structuring of family activities and rules.

The Mitchell family stands in sharp contrast. They strongly emphasize order, organization, and neatness, clarity of expectations, and consistency and strictness of rules and procedures. The Mitchells are oriented toward academic achievement and success and toward a broad intellectual and cultural education. But success is not to be "bought at any price"; the emphasis is on achievement through inner control, excellence, and competence. The Mitchells are relatively indifferent to active recreational pursuits, and they consider organized religion to be largely irrelevant to their everyday life. Although the family has a certain degree of cohesion, family members tend to do their jobs routinely. The emphasis is somewhat more on competition among family members than on support, and there is relatively little careless joking and spontaneous activity. This simple example of two contrasting families conveys the concept and potential impact of social climate. Two families that superficially appear similar may be quite different in actuality. One family was not "doing better" than the other. Parents and children in both families were active, successful in their chosen pursuits, and generally satisfied with their family lives. We do not wish to make value judgments about families but to illustrate widely divergent family styles and climates.

Measuring Social Climate.   Pace has demonstrated the importance of the social climate of a college or university. [1] Although each college has its own special atmosphere and establishes its own particular image, only certain information about a college is commonly available. It is easy to find out the size of a college, whether it is coeducational, where it is located, when it was founded, what degrees it offers, whether it is public or private, religious or nonsectarian, what it costs, and so on. Pace points out that having learned the answers to all these questions, one really knows very little that is important about a college.

> Suppose one asked the same kinds of questions about a prospective college student: What is his height and weight, sex, residence, age, vocational goal, religious affiliation and his family income. Knowing all these things one is still left in ignorance about what kind of a person the prospective student really is. The important knowledge concerns his aptitudes and interests, his motivations and emotional and social maturity. In short the crucial knowledge concerns his personality. So, too, with a college the crucial knowledge concerns its overall atmosphere or characteristics, the kinds of things that are rewarded, encouraged, emphasized, the style of life which is valued in the community and is most visibly expressed and felt. (p. 45)

Popular and professional writers have tried to capture the "personalities" of different social environments. Almost every biography and autobiography attempts to capture the essential elements of the family environment, which was presumably responsible for the outstanding achievements of its subject. For example, John Stuart Mill describes how his father carefully controlled his education and helped him develop his intellectual interests. [2] He remembers how he studied his Greek lessons in the same room as his father, who was then writing a history of India. The senior Mill patiently explained the meaning of each new Greek word, even though the child's constant interruptions must have slowed down the completion of the writing. Bertrand Russell tells of his grandmother's intense care for his welfare, which "gave me that feeling of safety that children need." [3] In describing his grandmother, Russell states that "her fearlessness, her public spirit, her contempt for convention and her indifference to the opinion of the majority have always seemed good to me and have impressed themselves upon me as worthy of imitation" (p.

18). Russell also wrote of how his brother tutored him in Euclid, which was "one of the greatest events of my life, as dazzling as first love. I had not imagined that there was anything so delicious in the world" (pp. 37–38). Albert Einstein and Winston Churchill had similar recollections of academic and intellectual "press" in their early lives.

Mahatma Gandhi was exposed to certain environmental press that must have been important in his later life. His father and grandfather were known to be men of principle. Gandhi described his father as "incorruptible, truthful and brave" and as having a "reputation for strict impartiality."[4] Gandhi described his mother as deeply religious and saintly. She often made arduous vows and fasted for long periods of time. Once she vowed not to eat unless the sun appeared. Gandhi and his sister and brothers watched for the sun, and when it appeared through the clouds they rushed into the house and announced that their mother could now eat. But her vow required her to see the sun for herself, and she went outdoors; but by then the sun was hidden again. "That does not matter," she cheerfully comforted her children, "God does not want me to eat today" (p. 22). These examples illustrate the potential importance of early family environment on later development.

Vivid and insightful case studies of the impact of positive and negative social environments have been compiled by many writers. In *Death at an Early Age* Jonathan Kozol vividly described how the physical and social environments in the Boston public schools had a shockingly destructive impact on the hearts and minds of black children.[5] In Ken Kesey's *One Flew Over the Cuckoo's Nest* psychiatric patients responded adaptively to a rigidly structured ward setting that required them to submit to the authority of Big Nurse.[6] In sharp contrast, a warm supportive therapist and a constructive humanitarian hospital setting facilitated the recovery of a young schizophrenic girl in *I Never Promised You a Rose Garden.*[7]

Biographers, sociologists, anthropologists, physicians, and popular novelists have described social environments in exhaustive detail. Their reasons for doing so, like their feelings about the impact of different social environments, have varied. However they all agree on one central point: the social climate within which an individual functions has an important impact on his attitudes and moods, his behavior, his health and overall sense of well-being, and possibly even his ultimate personal fate.

But how can the "blooming, buzzing, confusion" of a natural social environment be adequately assessed? Many procedures have been developed. One of the earliest and most interesting experimental studies of the impact of group social climate was carried out by Kurt Lewin and his associates.[8] They were interested in the differential effects of authoritarian, democratic, and laissez-faire social climates on the behavior of 10-year-old boys in various activity groups. Clubs were organized on a voluntary basis. The boys in the autocratic groups were either very aggressive or very apathetic. When aggression occurred it was usually directed toward scapegoats within the groups. None of it was directed toward the autocratic leader. But the repressive influence of the autocratic leader often caused apathy and lack of aggression. For example, two groups changed radically under different leadership climates. Group 1 ("secret agents") showed moderate aggression under a democratic climate, decreased aggression in an autocratic climate, a "rebound" effect on the day of transition, and a decrease in aggressive activity when the democratic climate was reinstituted. Group 4 ("law and order patrol") also exhibited low levels of aggressive behavior in the autocratic climate, a "rebound" effect on the day of transition, a moderate level of aggression under laissez-faire, and a relatively low level of aggression in a democratic climate. The results conclusively demonstrated that the behavior of the same boys changed markedly depending on the social or leadership climate of their group.

Using a somewhat different approach, Withall developed a Social Emotional Climate Index that allows investigators to place teachers' statements into seven different categories, including (1) commend or express approval of a student's behavior, (2) help a student to organize his ideas and plans more clearly, (3) limit or direct student behavior by advice or recommendation, and (4) punish or disapprove of the student's behavior.[9] Withall observed a group of seventh-grade students in regular social science, English, science, and mathematics class sessions. The differences among the classroom climates created by the different teachers were substantial. There was some variation in the day-to-day climate in each classroom, but over time each teacher created an overall consistency in the atmosphere in her classroom. For example, one teacher often punished or disapproved of student behavior (about 25% of her remarks were coded in this category), and she tended to limit students' choices of action and to control the classroom situation. Withall concluded that the students had to cope with quite different psychological climates as they went from class to class.

Much of the more recent empirical work in this area derives directly or indirectly from the contributions of Henry Murray. Murray pointed out that the concept of personality need could describe the general course of individual behavior but that this "leaves out the *nature of the environment,* a serious omission."[10] Murray classified environments in terms of the benefits (satisfactions) and harms (obstructions, dissatisfactions) they provided. He selected the term *press* to designate a directional tendency in an object or situation and he concluded that

One can profitably analyze an environment, a social group or an institution from the point of view of what press it applies or offers to the individuals that live within or belong to it. . . . Furthermore human beings in general or in particular can be studied from the standpoint of what beneficial press are available to them and what harmful press they customarily encounter (p. 120).

Pace and Stern extended the concept of environmental press by applying the logic of "perceived climate" to the study of the "atmosphere" at colleges and universities.[11] They constructed the College Characteristics Index (CCI) to measure the global college environment by asking students to act as reporters about that environment. The students' task was to answer "true" or "false" to items covering a wide range of topics about the college (student-faculty relationships, rules and regulations, classroom methods, facilities, etc.). Similar approaches have been used by several other investigators.[12]

The Social Environments of University Student Living Groups. An example of the construction and interpretation of one of our social climate scales may help to illustrate the logic underlying the measurement of social climate. The University Residence Environment Scale (URES) measures the salient features of student living group environments. We used several methods to gain a naturalistic understanding of living group climates and to obtain an initial pool of questionnaire items. Meetings were arranged with groups of dormitory residents to discuss perceptions of their individual houses and their likes, dislikes, and general observations on dormitory living. Written accounts of university life were searched to identify additional dimensions along which living groups might vary. Observations by university housing personnel were solicited. These sources resulted in a 274-item initial questionnaire.

Data from 74 residence halls representing a wide range of student living units were used to construct a final 100-item form. Coeducational dormitories, men's dormitories, and women's dormitories were included, as were fraternities. Houses were sampled from various types of colleges and universities (e.g., private universities, religious universities, state colleges, a medical school). The residence halls varied in size from fewer than 20 to more than 300 students. We chose a random sample of students from the 74 houses and used various criteria to select items for inclusion in the final form. Each item had to relate highly to its own subscale. The subscales had to show only low to moderate interrelationships. Each item had to discriminate among different living groups.[13]

Table 10.1 presents the resulting 10 subscales, each measuring one important dimension of the social environment of university student

Table 10.1   Social Climate Dimensions Characterizing University Student Living Groups

Relationship Dimensions

1.	Involvement	Degree of commitment to the house and residents; amount of interaction and feeling of friendship in the house
2.	Emotional Support	Extent of manifest concern for others in the house; efforts to aid one another with academic and personal problems; emphasis on open and honest communication.

Personal Development Dimensions

3.	Independence	Diversity of residents' behaviors allowed without social sanctions, versus socially proper and conformist behavior
4.	Traditional Social Orientation	Stress on dating, going to parties, and other "traditional" heterosexual interactions
5.	Competition	Degree to which a wide variety of activities such as dating and grades are cast into a competitive framework
6.	Academic Achievement	Extent to which strictly classroom and academic accomplishments and concerns are prominent in the house
7.	Intellectuality	Emphasis on cultural, artistic, and other scholarly intellectual activities in the house, as distinguished from strictly classroom achievements

System Maintenance and System Change Dimensions

8.	Order and Organization	Amount of formal structure or organization (e.g., rules, schedules, following established procedures) in the house; neatness.
9.	Student Influence	Extent to which student residents (not staff or administration) perceive they control the running of the house, formulate and enforce the rules, control use of the money, selection of staff, food, roommates, policies, etc.
10.	Innovation	Organizational and individual spontaneity of behaviors and ideas; number and variety of activities; new activities.

living groups. The Involvement and Emotional Support subscales measure *Relationship* dimensions. These dimensions measure the degree to which students and staff support and help each other and the degree to which they are involved in the house and its activities. The second group of subscales assess *Personal Development* dimensions, measuring the emphasis on developmental processes fostered by college living. Independence and Traditional Social Orientation measure the emphasis on personal and social maturation. Competition, Academic Achievement, and Intellectuality assess the emphasis on different aspects of academic growth. The last three subscales—Order and Organization, Student Influence, and Innovation—are *System Maintenance* and *System Change* dimensions. Our dimensions are system-oriented in that they obtain information about the structure of the organization within the house and about the processes and potential for change in its overall functioning.

Each item identifies characteristics of an environment that exert a press toward Involvement, or Academic Achievement, or Innovation, and so on. For example, a press toward Involvement is inferred from the following items: "People in the house often do something together on weekends" and "There is a feeling of unity and cohesion here." A press toward Academic Achievement is inferred from these items: "People around here tend to study long hours at a stretch" and "In the evening many people here begin to study right after dinner." A press toward Innovation is inferred from items like these: "In this house people often do unusual things" and "Around here there is a minimum of planning and a maximum of action."

Examples of Contrasting Residence Halls.   Figure 10.1 illustrates the differences among student residence halls by comparing the URES results for an undergraduate coed theme house and a men's medical student house. The theme house was programmatically organized around the area of international relations. Great stress was placed on intellectual discussions of world problems, and an active program of invited speakers and new activities was continually in motion. The faculty advisor, who lived in the house and was a strong influence, informally indicated that he wanted the students to be the intellectual and academic elite of the university. By contrast, the medical students were quite uninterested in any activities not directly related to their academic pursuits. Many of them commented that the house was more like a hotel than a dormitory.

The URES profiles indicate the extreme differences in the social climate of the two houses. There are large differences (more than 4 standard deviations) between the houses on Involvement and Emotional Support, with the coed theme house perceived as much higher. These results are illustrated by answers to URES items like "Very few people here participate in house activities," on which every student in the medical student house answered "true," whereas every student in the theme house

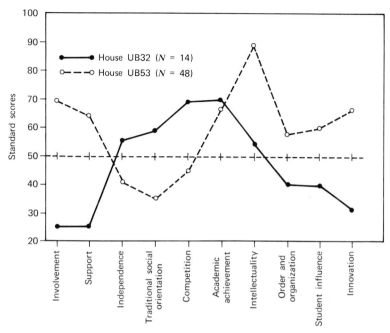

Figure 10.1 University Residence Environment Scale profiles for medical student and coed theme houses.

answered "false." Similar discrepancies appear on all Personal Development dimensions (except Academic Achievement).

The two living units have a similar emphasis on Academic Achievement, but the theme house stresses Intellectuality much more heavily than the medical student house. This discrepancy is reflected in items like "The people in this house generally read a good deal about intellectual material other than class assignments." Ninety-six percent of the theme house respondents answered "true" to this item, whereas only 23% of the medical students gave this response.

There are also large differences on the System Maintenance and System Change dimensions, with the theme house showing much higher scores on all three. For example, 94% of the students in the theme house answered "true" to the item "House officers are regularly elected in the house," but every medical student responded "false" to this item. Similarly, on the Student Influence subscale every student in the theme house agreed with the statement "The students formulate almost all the rules here," but only 21% of the medical students agreed to the same statement. Clearly the differences between the two houses are very large. The theme house has a warm, supportive, innovative, and intellectual social environment. The medical students describe their social environment as unsupportive, competitive, and achievement-oriented. It is reasonable to suppose that these two social environments affect the students living in them quite differently.

Underlying Patterns of Social Environments. Vastly different social environments can be described by common or similar sets of dimensions belonging to three broad categories: Relationship dimensions, Personal Development dimensions, and System Maintenance and System Change dimensions.[14] These categories of dimensions are similar across many environments, although vastly different settings may impose unique variations within the general categories.

Relationship dimensions identify the nature and intensity of personal relationships within the environment. They assess the extent to which people are involved in the environment, the extent to which they support and help one another, and the extent to which there is spontaneity and free and open expression among them. The basic dimensions are very similar in different environments, as indicated in Table 10.2. Each social environment has an Involvement or Cohesiveness dimension. Cohesiveness in families reflects the extent to which family members actively participate and are emotionally concerned with the family (e.g., sense of belongingness and togetherness). Involvement in a work milieu indicates the workers' concern about and commitment to their jobs, and the amount of enthusiasm and constructiveness they display in the work setting. Involvement in a classroom measures the students' attentive interest in class activities and participation in discussions. Involvement in a psychiatric treatment environment measures how active and energetic patients are in the day-to-day functioning of the program (e.g., pride in the program, feelings of group spirit, and general enthusiasm).

The degree of Support present in an environment is especially important. For example, Emotional Support in student living groups reflects the extent of manifest concern for others in the group, efforts to aid one another with academic and personal problems, and emphasis on open and honest communication. Support in a psychiatric treatment program measures the extent to which patients are encouraged to be helpful and supportive toward one another and the supportiveness of staff toward patients. Peer Cohesion and Staff Support in military companies assess the degree of friendship and communication among enlisted men and between officers and enlisted men, and the degree to which officers attempt to help and encourage enlisted men.

A separate Relationship dimension of Expressiveness or Spontaneity is identified in some environments. This dimension is not separately identified in all environments for two reasons. First, certain environments (e.g., military companies) differ so little in Expressiveness that this dimension simply does not discriminate among them. Second, Expressiveness is sometimes very highly related to one of the other Relationship dimensions (e.g., to Emotional Support in university living groups and to Peer Cohesion and Staff Support in work milieus). Thus there are basically three *Relationship* dimensions that characterize all environments: Involvement, Support, and Expressiveness.

Personal Development dimensions assess the basic directions along which personal growth and self-enhancement tend to occur in the particular environment. These dimensions vary somewhat among different environments depending on underlying purposes and goals. For example, in families these dimensions indicate the directions along which families may wish to develop—for example, Independence (the extent to which family members are encouraged to be self-sufficient and to make their own decisions), Intellectual-Cultural Orientation (the importance the family attaches to discussions about political, social, and cultural issues), and Moral-Religious Emphasis (the significance to the family of ethical and religious issues and values).

University student living groups have personal growth goals somewhat different from families, thus a different set of Personal Development dimensions are identified in them (e.g., Independence, Competition), as discussed earlier. Psychiatric and correctional programs emphasize still other yet related areas of personal growth. In these environments the Personal Development dimensions assess a program's overall treatment goals—for example, Autonomy (the extent to which people are encouraged to be self-sufficient and independent), Practical Orientation (how well the program orients an individual toward training for new jobs, looking to the future, setting and working toward concrete goals, etc.), and Personal Problem Orientation (the extent to which individuals are encouraged to be concerned with their feelings and problems and to seek to understand them). Thus Personal Development dimensions differ across environments depending on their basic purposes and goals.

System Maintenance and System Change dimensions, which are relatively similar across all the environments, evaluate orderliness, the clarity of expectations, the degree of control, and the responsiveness to change. The basic dimensions are Order and Organization, Clarity, Control, and Innovation. For example, an assessment of Clarity in a work milieu will tell the extent to which workers know what to expect in their daily routines and how explicitly rules and policies are communicated. Clarity in a

Table 10.2 Common Social Climate Dimensions Across Environments

Type of Environment	Relationship Dimensions	Personal Development Dimensions	System Maintenance and System Change Dimensions
Community settings			
Families	Cohesiveness	Independence	Organization
	Expressiveness	Achievement Orientation	Control
	Conflict	Intellectual-Cultural Orientation	
		Recreational Orientation	
		Moral-Religious Emphasis	
Social, task-oriented, and therapeutic groups	Cohesiveness	Independence	Order and Organization
	Leader Support	Task Orientation	Leader Control
	Expressiveness	Self-Discovery	Innovation
		Anger and Aggression	
Work milieus	Involvement	Task Orientation	Work Pressure
	Peer Cohesion	Competition	Clarity
	Staff Support		Control
			Innovation
			Physical Comfort

Educational Environments			
University student living groups	Involvement Emotional Support	Independence Traditional Social Orientation Competition Academic Achievement Intellectuality	Order and Organization Student Influence Innovation
Junior high and High school classrooms	Involvement Affiliation Teacher Support	Task Orientation Competition	Order and Organization Rule Clarity Teacher Control Innovation
Treatment settings			
Hospital and community programs	Involvement Support Spontaneity	Autonomy Practical Orientation Personal Problem Orientation	Order and Organization Clarity Control
Total institutions			
Correctional	Involvement Support Expressiveness	Autonomy Practical Orientation Personal Problem Orientation	Order and Organization Clarity Control
Military companies	Involvement Peer Cohesion Officer Support	Personal Status	Order and Organization Clarity Officer Control

classroom assesses the emphasis on following a clear set of rules and on students knowing the consequences if rules are not followed.

Some variations occur in these dimensions in different environments. Order and Organization and Clarity may merge into one dimension (e.g., in university living groups and work milieus). A separate dimension of Innovation (System Change) is identified in only some environments, either because there is relatively little Innovation in the environment (e.g., military companies) or because Innovation is linked to Expressiveness and Spontaneity in certain environments (e.g., families). A unique dimension of Work Pressure, which appears in work environments, measures the emphasis on pressure, deadlines, and time urgency in the work milieu. This dimension is not particularly relevant to the other environments.

The ability to identify similar underlying dimensions along which very different social environments can be characterized is quite important. It means that these environments can be compared, particularly in terms of Relationship and System Maintenance and System Change dimensions. This may eventually help us determine why an individual does very well in one environment but quite poorly in another. For example, consider the important life transition that occurs for an adolescent boy or girl who goes away to college. How similar will the dormitory environment be to the student's family environment? How similar will the college classroom be to the student's high school classrooms?.

Our initial family examples serve as illustration. The two children in the Lester family are accustomed to strong emphasis on involvement, support, expressiveness, active recreation, and ethical and religious concerns. Achievement and intellectuality are not stressed in their family, nor are order, clarity, or control. It is unlikely that the Lester children would do well in a college that did not have a strong sense of cohesion, involvement, and support. Even if they were able to function in such an environment, they would probably be dissatisfied, lonely, and alienated. A high-pressure college that emphasizes achievement, competition, and intellectuality also would not be good for them. They should probably find a relatively small college in which all students are urged to participate in activities, and achievement and intellectuality are stressed in a balanced rather than an all-inclusive manner. Recreational and religious pursuits should be available.

The two children in the Mitchell family would look for a very different college. Cohesiveness, support, and expressiveness are not quite as important as to the young Lesters. They might feel trapped and uncertain of how to handle themselves in a small cohesive living group, in which it would be difficult not to socialize. They could easily be labeled as deviant in such a group, since they prefer more solitary and individual pursuits. These students would do quite well in a university that plays to their strengths by emphasizing achievement, competition, and intellectuality, and such an institution should not be difficult to find. However the Mitchells do stand a risk. They might choose an environment that is disorderly, disorganized, confused, and generally lacking in adequate rules and regulations. Whereas the Mitchells might initially like this atmosphere, they would probably experience difficulty soon, since they have never learned to function in such an environment. Real-life situations are, of course, considerably more complicated than this. But our example illustrates some of the important issues in assessing and selecting environments.

In any case, social environments may be conveniently categorized along three common sets of dimensions, and this overall conceptualization holds for a wide variety of environments.[15] We turn now to the evidence on the differential impact of social environments. The three categories of dimensions provide a convenient framework for the integration of the relevant findings.

The Impact of Social Environments.   As we pointed out earlier, social environments are active and directed with respect to their inhabitants. People have plans or personal agendas that impel their behavior in specific directions. Environments have programs that organize and shape the behavior of their inhabitants. Social environments have differential impacts on the people who live and function in them. Some of the current evidence regarding this impact is examined here. Three related categories of outcome criteria are considered. First, we take up criteria such as satisfaction and morale and personal feelings (anxiety, depression, anger). Second, we examine evidence relating to objective outcome criteria, such as achievement levels in high school and college and the outcome of psychiatric treatment. Third, we focus on health-related criteria, analyzing evidence that physical and/or mental symptoms may occur more frequently in certain social environments.

Satisfaction, Moods, and Performance.

Family and Work Settings.   Family environments are often measured by two major parental attitudes: acceptance versus rejection (a Relationship dimension) and high versus low control (a System Maintenance dimension). Acceptance and permissiveness (low control) seem to bring about the best results, although there are some notable exceptions. Sheldon and Eleanor Glueck studied 500 delinquent and 500 nondelinquent boys. Rejecting, hostile, and indifferent parental attitudes were more frequent in the delinquent families. Overly lax, erratic, and overly strict forms of discipline were more frequent in the families with delinquent children. The delinquent boys were much more likely to feel rejected at home, often stating that they were not adequately recognized or appreciated.[16] Many other studies suggest that rejecting parents who use either overly strict or overly lax discipline are more likely than others to have delinquent children.[17]

Summarizing some of the consequences of different kinds of parental discipline, Becker found agreement among many studies and concluded that "Children of dominating parents were better socialized and more courteous, obedient, neat, generous and polite . . . they were also more sensitive, self-conscious, shy and retiring."[18] Children from low control homes were "more disobedient, irresponsible, disorderly in the classroom, lacking in sustained attention, lacking in regular work habits, and more forward and expressive" (p. 191). Thus children from low control homes may be more impulsive and undisciplined, but they may also show greater curiosity and creativity. Kagan and Moss found that children raised under conditions of restrictive control were submissive and timid, particularly in their early years.[19] Parental control may have less impact as children get older, probably because of the greater influence of environments outside the family. In another study, observations on two Israeli nurseries showed that dependent, passive behavior was more common among children who resided in a highly structured nursery than among children who lived in a less highly structured one.[20] Thus we have indications that acceptance has beneficial effects and restrictive control has largely harmful effects, especially in the early years.

A wealth of literature shows that the quality of personal interactions in the work environment, particularly with supervisors, is related to job satisfaction and performance. For example, the job performance of a group of hard-core unemployed individuals has been studied.[21] The group was predominantly male, black, relatively uneducated, with an average duration of unemployment prior to job placement of 15 weeks. Individual background and attitudinal characteristics were not related to job performance. A 2-week orientation program had no demonstrable effect on attitudes toward work or job performance. The only correlate of the work effectiveness and behavior was the supportiveness of the organizational climate in which the individual was placed. People who felt their work climate was supportive were rated more favorably by their supervisors on dimensions such as competence, congeniality, friendliness, and conscientiousness. Unfortunately support from peers and support from supervisors were the only organizational climate dimensions assessed, and the impact of Personal Development and System Maintenance dimensions remains unknown.

Another study revealed that general satisfaction with the work milieu was related to Managerial Support and New Employee Concern (Relationship dimensions), the degree of Agent Independence (Personal Development dimension), and the degree of Managerial Structure (System Maintenance). These findings held for both life insurance agents and their managers.[22]

In some intriguing work, Schneider learned that bank customers decide to switch their bank accounts on the basis of generalized perceptions they have of the bank. A 13-item climate questionnaire was used to obtain data from 674 account holders in two retail and two commercial banks. Items descriptive of employee behavior were found to be highly related to customers' intentions to switch their accounts. Customers who felt that the bank employees were friendly and supportive ("The bank employees bend over backward to provide good service" and "The atmosphere in my bank is warm and friendly") were least likely to wish to switch accounts.[23] These two items also discriminated between the perceptions of people who actually switched their accounts and those who did not. Account holders who had switched their accounts for service-related reasons viewed the bank and its employees much more negatively than did customers who maintained their accounts. Schneider also discovered that the more objective characteristics of customers (size of account, type of account, distance from bank, length of time with bank, sex, number of bank services used) and of the bank itself (waiting time, size of accounts, procedure of queueing customers) were unrelated to climate perceptions.

Most of the results in family and work environments deal with Relationship dimensions, which are usually positively related to valued outcomes. Even though some control is needed in every environment, however, there is little dependable information on the effects of Personal Development and System Maintenance dimensions.

Educational Settings. Colleges with a high sense of Community and Awareness (Relationship dimensions) have a high proportion of students who feel a strong emotional attachment to the college. In addition, it is rare for students to report not having participated in any extracurricular activities in college environments that are high on Cohesion.[24] Peterson and his colleagues related dimensions of institutional functioning to seven factors of student protest in a sample of 50 institutions. Student radicalism as a protest factor was highly related to Human Diversity and

Concern for Improvement of Society (Personal Development dimensions). The other relationships that emerged were generally predictable: the absence of senior faculty and the quality of instruction were protest issues in institutions with a low emphasis on undergraduate learning. Classified research was a protest issue in institutions with a high emphasis on concern for advancing knowledge.[25]

The social environments of high school classrooms have been linked to student satisfaction and mood. Students are more satisfied in classrooms characterized by high student involvement, by a personal student-teacher relationship, by innovative teaching methods, and by clarity of rules regarding classroom behavior.[26] Students feel more secure and interested in classrooms that emphasize the Relationship dimensions of Involvement, Affiliation, and Teacher Support. Students report feeling angrier in classrooms low in Teacher Support and Order and Organization. Teacher Support is a particularly important dimension in high school classrooms, as might be expected.

The classroom in which students felt that much material was learned was both similar to and different from the "satisfying" classroom. Although Involvement, Teacher Support, and Rule Clarity were highly emphasized, the former kind of classroom was also high on Competition and Order and Organization. Thus the picture of the classroom in which students report a great deal of content learning combines an affective concern with students as people (Relationship dimensions) with an emphasis on working hard for academic rewards (Competition) within a coherent organized context (Order and Organization and Rule Clarity).

Other work indicates that the classroom social environment may mediate classroom learning.[27] Both cognitive and noncognitive learning criteria were measured in 144 high school physics classes. The cognitive criteria included a test on understanding science and a test of general physics knowledge. The noncognitive criteria included measures of interest in science, voluntary participation in physics activities, and interest in physics. Students in classes characterized by high satisfaction and low friction did much better on all three noncognitive learning criteria. Students in high Difficulty classes did much better on all three cognitive learning criteria. Thus classes seen as more difficult and competitive (Personal Development dimensions) gained more on physics achievement and science understanding, whereas classes perceived as more satisfying and as having less friction and apathy (Relationship dimensions) gained more on science interest and activities.

Students express greater satisfaction, show more interest in their course material, and engage in more course-relevant activities in classes that are high on Relationship dimensions. Students feel they learn more, and actually do learn more, in competitive and intellectually challenging classrooms. There is some evidence that teachers who establish socially cohesive classrooms give higher average grades, whereas teachers in classrooms high on Teacher Control give lower average grades. If so, it is no wonder that students feel more secure, interested, and satisfied in the former classrooms!

Psychiatric Treatment Settings. Work on individual and group psychotherapy has focused almost exclusively on Relationship dimensions. Certain important therapist qualities are related to improvement in almost all types of psychotherapy; and three characteristics of an effective therapist have emerged from the divergent viewpoints: (1) an effective therapist is authentic or genuine, (2) an effective therapist is able to provide a safe, trusting, and secure atmosphere through his own acceptance of and warmth for the client, and (3) an effective therapist has an accurate emphatic understanding of the patient. Truax and Mitchell state: "These ingredients of the psychotherapeutic relationship are aspects of human encounters that cut across the parochial theories of psychotherapy and appear to be common elements in a wide variety of psychoanalytic, client-centered, eclectic or learning theory approaches to psychotherapy."[28]

When these qualities are present in a relationship, positive personality change is likely to follow. Negative change or personality deterioration is likely to occur when they are absent. The evidence that counselors who are emphatic, warm, and genuine are effective with their clients seems to hold up with a wide variety of clients, from hospitalized schizophrenics to college underachievers and juvenile delinquents. These personal qualities are clearly Relationship dimensions. Empathy, warmth, and genuineness are part of the overall quality of the relationship between the patient and therapist exactly as Involvement, Support, and Expressiveness have to do with the overall quality of the relationships among individuals in a social milieu.

Some studies have related the social or treatment environments of psychiatric programs to treatment outcome. Programs with high dropout rates (i.e., many patients leaving against medical advice) have few social activities, little emphasis on involving patients in the program, and poor planning of patient activities. Patients in these programs do not socialize much together, and they have a lot of free time with little or no guidance. Staff discourage criticism from patients and are unwilling to act on patients' suggestions.

Programs with high release rates (patients are discharged rapidly) typically emphasize preparedness for getting out of the hospital, for training patients for new kinds of jobs, and for making concrete practical plans. There is a fair amount of Staff Control, but staff are personally interested in the patients and tell them when they are making progress. There is little emphasis on Expressiveness, in that patients rarely argue with one another and they keep their disagreements to themselves. Neither patients nor staff see much support in these programs.

Programs that keep patients out in the community the longest emphasize the free and open expression of feelings, particularly angry feelings. Staff think it is a healthy thing to argue, are seen arguing among themselves, and sometimes start arguments in group meetings. Patients are expected to share their personal problems and feelings with one another and with staff. The environment also emphasizes Autonomy and Independence, a Practical Orientation, Order and Organization, and a reasonable degree of Staff Control.

In terms of our three categories of dimensions, programs with high dropout rates have little emphasis in either the Relationship or the System Maintenance areas. Programs with high release rates are relatively strong in the System Maintenance areas and in Practical Orientation. They also have moderate emphasis on Involvement. Programs that keep patients out of the hospital the longest emphasize both the Relationship and System Maintenance dimensions, and the Personal Development dimensions, particularly Autonomy and Practical Orientation. The results of several similar studies of psychiatric treatment outcome are generally corroborative.[29]

The evidence shows that the qualities of the relationships in individual and group therapy are highly related to positive evaluation of treatment and to positive personality change. The results on the Relationship dimensions in studies of treatment programs are strikingly similar. Thus positive relationship qualities may be essential in mediating positive personality change in all types of psychiatric treatment.

Correctional and Military Settings.   We have conducted three studies in juvenile correctional institutions.[30] Our results were quite clear-cut. As the emphasis on the three Relationship and the three Personal Development dimensions increases, residents like one another and the staff more and feel that they have greater opportunities for personal growth in the program. However as Staff Control increases, residents like one another and the staff less and feel that they have less to gain from the program.

We have also studied military basic training companies. Enlisted men generally felt less anxious, depressed, and angry in companies that emphasized Involvement, Cohesion, Support, and Personal Status. Enlisted men were most likely to feel hostile in companies in which Officer Support was low. The men were most likely to feel depressed in companies in which Peer Cohesion was low. The dimension of Officer Control had a pervasive effect on the men's moods; that is, enlisted men felt much more anxious, depressed, and angry in companies in which Officer Control was high. Dimensions of company environments were also related to test performance at the end of basic training. Peer Cohesion, Officer Support, and clarity of expectations were the three most important characteristics of high-performance companies.[31]

The dominant findings on the impacts of social environments concern the Relationship dimensions, which are of great importance in such community settings as families and work groups, in educational settings, in psychiatric treatment settings, and in correctional and military settings. The Relationship dimensions have similar effects in different types of social environments. Much less is known about the differential effects of the Personal Development and the System Maintenance dimensions, which have not been generally used in studies of group and institutional impact. More critically, when they have been used, Relationship dimensions have usually not been measured. Thus some of the presumed negative effects of, for example, high parental control, may be more closely related to lack of emphasis on Relationship dimensions (e.g., warmth) than to control per se.

The "Productivity" of Colleges and Universities.   Do some colleges and universities have unusually beneficial effects on personal development, specifically on student levels of aspiration and achievement? If so, what are their unique characteristics? Initial work in this area dealt with the relationship between certain aspects of undergraduate colleges and the postcollege achievement of their graduates. Investigators calculated how likely it was for graduates of different colleges to win graduate fellowships or to earn their doctoral degrees, to be listed in *American Men of Science,* and to be listed as humanistic scholars by the National Academy of Sciences. Not surprisingly, graduates of some universities were much more likely to attain these achievements than were the graduates of others. The highly productive institutions had higher faculty-student ratios, larger libraries, more funds for scholarships and research, and other resources usually assumed to indicate institutional excellence. The conclusion drawn from these studies was that these institutional characteristics enhanced student aspiration and achievement levels.[32]

These findings were criticized on the grounds that there was no control for "student input" factors. Colleges and universities differ widely in the students they enroll. Some institutions enroll a much higher proportion of academically able students than others. Intellectually capable students are much more likely to win graduate fellowships and to earn their doctorates, even if the institution they attend exerts no special influence on them. These considerations led to attempts to relate college environments to college productivity, while controlling for student input factors.

Thistlethwaite completed the first series of these studies, relating the environmental press at different colleges to student achievement. The measure of achievement was the percentage of the college's alumni who later earned doctorates. Thistlethwaite made adjustments to equate colleges with respect to the initial quality of the students. The measure he used was called the Talent Supply Index—the percentage of the college's freshmen class who were National Merit Scholarship finalists. Thistlethwaite then obtained two college productivity indices, one for the natural sciences (NS) and one for the arts, humanities, and social sciences (AHSS). These indices were the discrepancies between a school's *expected* rate of Ph.D. productivity (NS or AHSS), as predicted by its Talent Supply Index, and its *actual* rate of Ph.D. productivity. The discrepancies for a particular school indicates its relative rate of success in stimulating its undergraduates to obtain doctorates of a given type (NS or AHSS). Thistlethwaite argued that this success rate was independent of the quality of the student body.

Scholarly productivity was greater than expected in student cultures characterized by Humanism (e.g., "There is a lot of interest here in poetry, music, painting, sculpture, architecture, etc."), Breadth of Interest (e.g., students report interest in round tables, panel meetings, and other formal discussions), and Reflectiveness ("There would be a capacity audience for a lecture by an outstanding philosopher or theologian"). Scholarly productivity was lower than expected in student cultures characterized by extracurricular Participation (frequent rallies, parades, dances, carnivals, and/or demonstrations) and Aggression ("Hazing, teasing, and practical joking are fairly common").

Thistlethwaite names the following dominant faculty press perceived by students in colleges with high scholarly productivity.

> The following traits seem to characterize faculties outstandingly successful in encouraging undergraduate students to get the Ph.D. in the Arts, Humanities and Social Sciences: (1) excellent social science faculty and resources, (2) a high degree of energy and controversy in instruction, (3) broad intellectual emphasis, (4) frequent contact with students outside the classroom, (5) a flexible or somewhat unstructured curriculum, (6) emphasis upon independent study and the development of a critical attitude, (7) excellent offerings in the arts and drama, and (8) relatively infrequent appraisal of student performance.[33]

The faculty press at schools that were higher than expected in natural science productivity were described somewhat differently, although there was some overlap. Faculty contacts with students were informal and warm

("In talking with students faculty members often refer to their colleagues by their first name"). The faculty emphasized high and exacting academic standards ("The professors really push the students' capacities to the limit"). The faculty also had high standards for evaluating faculty productivity and for selecting new faculty members. The faculty did not closely supervise the students (e.g., students were not required to sit in assigned seats; attendance was not taken), and the teaching was relatively nondirective. Thistlethwaite concluded that the social environments of colleges and universities had an important impact on encouraging students to obtain their doctorates.

Thistlethwaite also reported the results of follow-ups at the end of the second and third years of college of students who had received National Merit Scholarship recognition. For example, students were asked: "Has the level of training you aspire to achieve changed since you entered college?" Students who reported increased levels of aspiration were compared with those who reported no change in aspiration level. The basic results of the previous studies were replicated. Thistlethwaite concluded that:

> Faculties which students perceived as enthusiastic, warm and informal in their relationships with students (affiliative) and as stressing achievement, humanism and independence were associated with more frequent changes in students' plans to seek advanced training in the arts, humanities and social sciences. Faculties which students perceived as enthusiastic and as not exercising great press for compliance were associated with more frequent changes in students' plans to seek advanced training in the natural and biological sciences.[34]

Astin took issue with these findings and also completed extensive work of his own. For example, he studied a sample of National Merit Scholarship finalists and found that students' decisions to pursue a career in science were much more dependent on their initial "input" characteristics (e.g., major field of study, highest academic degree initially sought, verbal aptitude, high school grades) than on the characteristics of the college attended.[35] In another study more than 6000 high-aptitude students were followed for 4 years. Basically "output" (aspiring to the Ph.D. degree) was quite accurately predicted by "input." However coeducational liberal arts colleges (e.g., Oberlin, Pomona, Reed, Swarthmore) were "overproductive," whereas northeastern men's colleges (e.g., Amherst, Dartmouth, Harvard, Princeton) were "underproductive." Astin concluded: "Ph.D. aspirations appeared to be negatively affected by the size of the student body, percentage of males in the student body and the conventional orientation of the college environment."[36]

In the most ambitious empirical research to date, Astin and Panos studied 36,000 students at 246 institutions. Student input data were obtained on questionnaires at the time of initial matriculation in 1961. Student output data (educational status, aspirations, career plans, etc.) were obtained 4 years later. The student's initial statement of his degree aspirations was the best indicator of his final plans, followed by his academic ability and his initial career choice. The authors concluded that the educational and vocational development of the college student depends much more on his personal characteristics, family background, and interests as a freshman than on the attributes of the college itself. Students at "better" institutions score better on the Graduate Record Examination subtests than do students at "inferior" institutions, but superior performance is mainly attributable to initial superior aptitude rather than to any beneficial effects of the college.[37]

Certain characteristics of the college's social environment had an important impact. For example, institutions high in cohesiveness (students have close friends; social interaction is frequent) had a favorable effect on persistence in college. Institutions low in cohesiveness had unusually high dropout rates. Dropout rates were also high in institutions in which informal dating occurred frequently and career indecision was high. Astin and Panos suggested that selectivity and cohesiveness are important environmental characteristics in relation to students' academic achievement. Students are more likely to complete 4 years of college work and obtain the bachelor's degree if they attend an institution that enrolls academically superior students and has a cohesive peer environment characterized by many close friendships among students.

The college dropout rates were very high; indeed, 44% of the sample decided either to transfer to another institution or to temporarily or permanently drop out of higher education. Most students stated that they withdrew voluntarily, usually because they were "dissatisfied with the environment." Astin and Panos point out that "apparently much of the time and energy that high school students' parents and counselors expend in trying to find the 'right' college is wasted effort" (p. 8). Also, entering freshmen's choices of probable major fields and future careers were highly unstable. Approximately 75% of the students altered their career plans at some point during the 4 years. These findings suggest that the influence of the college social environment may be quite substantial.

The issues raised in this series of studies are not yet resolved. In recent work Rock, Centra, and Linn found that a high proportion of the differences among 95 colleges in student academic achievement (output) was predictable from the academic aptitude of students at entrance (input). However colleges that had higher income per student and larger proportions of doctoral-level faculty tended to do better. In addition, among colleges with relatively high income per student, the smaller colleges did better than the larger ones.[38]

In a second study Centra and Rock[39] measured achievement on the Graduate Record Examination and discovered that: (1) students at colleges high in faculty-student interaction overachieved in humanities and natural sciences, (2) students at colleges with high curriculum flexibility scores overachieved in the natural and social science areas, (3) students at colleges with good cultural facilities overachieved in humanities but underachieved in natural sciences, (4) challenging colleges produced students who overachieved in humanities. These results led Centra and Rock to make the following statement.

> Some of the results reinforce popularly held notions: in particular that students learn more than might be expected if they feel that instructors are readily accessible, interested in teaching and interested in students as individuals. . . . Also related to overachievement were college environments in which students perceived freedom in choosing courses and could try out a variety of courses before selecting a major. (p. 633)

The results are similar to those Thistlethwaite had obtained 12 years earlier.

To summarize, student input factors are importantly related to student aspiration and achievement levels. Academic performance in high school predicts academic performance in college, which in turn predicts academic performance in graduate school. However the evidence indicates that the social environment of the college the student attends is also important. Colleges emphasizing Relationship dimensions (e.g., faculty-student interaction, peer cohesion, energy and controversy in teaching) have a positive impact on students. Colleges emphasizing Personal Development dimensions (e.g., humanism, breadth of interest, reflectiveness, broad intellectual emphasis, independent study and criticism, high standards, challenge) also tend to do better. College qualities such as excellent faculties, first-rate course offerings, and the presence of cultural facilities, foster personal growth press because of modeling and other interpersonal influences. College selectivity relates to personal growth press, particularly academic emphasis, intellectuality, competition, and challenge. Curriculum flexibility is related to personal growth press because it implies an emphasis on student autonomy and independence. Thus the evidence that high emphasis on Relationship and Personal Growth dimensions fosters student aspiration and achievement is relatively persuasive.

Physical Health and Well-Being.   A physician advises a harried executive with high blood pressure to spend a week in the country. A pediatrician recommends that an underdeveloped, neglected child be sent to a foster home. An allergist encourages an asthmatic patient to find a job with more human contact. A heart specialist urges an overworked administrator to delegate some of his responsibilities. Each of these health professionals is responding to the belief that the social environment has an important impact on health. In this section we briefly highlight evidence linking the social environment to indices of individual health. Three dimensions of the social environment are discussed: (1) the Relationship dimension of Support, (2) the Personal Development dimension of Autonomy or Responsibility, and (3) the System Maintenance dimension of Work Pressure.

Support.   Support is clearly a crucial dimension of the psychosocial environment, especially with regard to maturing organisms. Spitz' classic study of children raised in a foundling home and in a nursery related maternal and social deprivation to increased infant mortality, susceptibility to disease, retardation in growth, and failure to achieve developmental milestones. Spitz studied 130 infants in two institutions with comparable quality of food and levels of hygiene. In the foundling home the infants were cared for by nurses, whereas in the nursery they were cared for by their mothers. In contrast to nursery children, foundling home children were extremely susceptible to disease. Almost all the foundlings had histories of intestinal infection, although the home maintained excellent conditions of hygiene, including bottle sterilization. Contrary to what would be expected, older children—those who had been in the home longer—were more likely to die during a measles epidemic than younger children. In addition, growth levels, talking, and walking were severely retarded in the foundling home children.[40]

MacCarthy and Booth describe a syndrome that resembles Spitz' "hospitalism" but occurs in children living at home with their parents. The most prominent abnormalities are dwarfism and subnormal weight/height ratio, with little if any evidence of malnutrition. Behavioral features include inability to play, bodily neglect, apathy, and subnormal intelligence levels. In a study of 10 mothers of these children, seven were judged by a child psychiatrist to have rejecting attitudes toward their children. Two of the remaining mothers were judged "inadequate"—one because of subnormal intelligence and the other because of neurotic depression. In most cases the symptoms, including dwarfism, reversed themselves when the child was removed from home and placed in the hospital, where presumably the staff had at least a minimally supportive attitude.[41]

Some authors criticize the assertion that deprivation of maternal love or support is responsible for the physical, emotional, and intellectual abnormalities in these rejected children. Instead they argue that a deficiency in the amount of stimulation (visual, tactile, vestibular, or social) required for normal development is chiefly to blame.[42] There is evidence from the animal literature that handling can increase developmental and growth rates, and much of the evidence cited earlier could be fitted into the hypothesis of insufficient stimulation. The most reasonable interpretation of the available data is that normal development cannot proceed without certain kinds and certain quantities of stimuli. A supportive psychosocial environment, particularly for infants and young children, consists of some of these stimuli, occurring predictably from the same persons and in sufficient quantity.

Lack of support may also have varied physiological concomitants in maturity. The loss of a mate can represent a sudden severe loss of support. Parkes and his colleagues followed the death rates of 4486 widowers of 55 years of age and older for 9 years following the death of each one's wife. Of these, 213 died during the first 6 months of bereavement, 40% above the expected death rate for married men of the same ages. Death rate from degenerative heart disease was 67% above expected. The mortality rate dropped to that of married men after the first year. Since only 22.5% of the husbands' deaths were from the same cause as the wives' deaths, it is unlikely that a jointly unfavorable environment was the chief cause of the phenomenon. The authors argue that "the emotional effects of bereavement with the concomitant changes in psycho-endocrine functions" accounted for the increased death rate.[43]

A supportive environment may influence the effects of predisposing factors to disease such as stress, lack of exercise, large consumption of animal fat, and cigarette smoking. A series of studies in an Italian-American community in Roseto, Pennsylvania, revealed that the death rate from heart disease was remarkably low despite the prevalence of predisposing factors. A 12-year study of this community of 1700 people indicated that death from heart disease occurred at a rate of less than half that of neighboring communities. Many relatives of Roseto residents who were living in urban and suburban areas around New York and Philadelphia, however, were later found to die from heart disease before the age of 50. In Roseto during the same period there was only one death from heart disease before the age of 47, and most of the deaths occurred in men and women in their seventies and eighties.

Among the living, evidence of heart disease appeared in some persons in their forties and fifties in all neighboring communities but not in Roseto, at least for men under 55 years of age. There was a greater incidence of obesity in Roseto compared with other neighborhoods, and there also appeared to be a higher incidence of high blood pressure among Roseto men. In spite of this there was little difference in documented hypertensive disease. The diet of Roseto inhabitants was relatively high in calories, including animal fat. Cigarette smoking was as prevalent among men in Roseto as in other communities.

The most dramatic differences between Roseto and its surrounding communities were found in its social environment. The study indicated that Roseto was cohesive and mutually supportive, with strong family and community ties. The social environment emphasized the overriding concern of the inhabitants for their neighbors, mutual support, understanding, and unfailing sustenance in time of trouble. The investigators concluded that "emotional support from the environment somehow provides protection."[44] Recent follow-up studies indicate that Roseto has become "Americanized," that the residents are more concerned with making money and succeeding, and that family and community support is disappearing. It may be coincidental, but the town's heart attack rate is now well above the national average.

Autonomy and Responsibility.   Within any given social environment, roles and duties exert differential pressures on people. Some people have greater responsibility than others. Some environments have a greater press toward responsibility for all members than others (e.g., a disarmament conference vs. a cookout). There is evidence that responsibility is associated with important physiological changes. Miller and his colleagues studied hormone secretion and self-reported anxiety in the two-man crews of jet aircraft during practice carrier landings. The pilots who had exclusive control of the aircraft had greater hormone responses than the passive radiomen. This held even though the radiomen reported greater anxiety on the self-report measures than the pilots. Another study found 17 to 20% higher heart rates in active pilots manning aircraft than in the passive copilots at their sides; the difference reversed itself when pilot A became passenger and pilot B took charge of the aircraft.[45]

When key National Aeronautics and Space Administration personnel were suddenly given additional responsibility—for example, put in charge of a project or called on to deliver a report at a high-level meeting—sharp increases in heart rate resulted. The medical director of the project wrote that "something we simply call responsibility often results in extremely high cardiac rates and is probably a much larger factor in rate changes than was formerly thought."[46] Even top executives, with long experience in the handling of responsibility, almost invariably have marked heart rate increases when given additional responsibility.

Responsibility is a complex social environmental dimension. The evidence demonstrates that responsibility for the avoidance of physical threat to oneself or others can produce physiological stress responses. Assuming responsibility for more symbolic outcomes (e.g., delivering a good report) may also cause physiological changes. Thus even responsibility that is seen as ego-enhancing and positive by the individual may elicit increased activation of some physiological mechanisms. Such activation is not invariably aversive for the organism, however. More work is necessary to determine when, for example, heart rate or hormone elevations become detrimental, and what aspects of responsibility are most conducive to aversive levels of activation.

Work Pressure. Rosenman and Friedman have identified a behavior pattern they believe is associated with high risk of coronary artery disease. The coronary-prone behavior pattern, designated Type A, as distinguished from the low-risk Type B, is characterized by extreme aggressiveness, competitiveness, and ambition, along with feelings of restlessness and a profound sense of time urgency. In one prospective study some 3,400 men free from coronary disease were rated Type A or Type B without knowledge of any biological data. Two and one-half years later, type A men aged 39 to 49 years had 6.5 times the incidence of coronary disease as Type B men in the same age group.[47] Although their early work has been criticized on methodological grounds, Rosenman and Friedman's findings have received general support in the critical literature.

Type A persons are engaged in "a relatively chronic struggle to obtain an unlimited number of relatively poorly defined things from the environment in the shortest period of time." Rosenman and Friedman believe that the contemporary Western environment encourages development of this pattern, which represents the interaction of environmental influences and individual susceptibilities. The authors argue, however, that this pattern may not occur if a Type A individual is removed to a Type B setting.[48]

Caffrey has been able to rank environments according to the degree to which their "atmospheres" encourage Type A behavior. He had three physicians rate 14 Benedictine and 11 Trappist monasteries. The individual monks were also rated by their abbots and peers. Caffrey showed that groups of monks having a higher proportion of Type A's living in Type A environments and taking a high fat diet had the highest prevalence rates of coronary disease.[49]

Caffrey's work, in connection with that of Rosenman and Friedman, points to the existence of a dimension of the social environment associated with coronary artery disease, at least in predisposed individuals. We propose the term *work pressure* to include the kinds of environmental influence that encourage the sense of time urgency experienced by the Type A personality.

The association of work pressure and coronary disease gains support elsewhere in the literature. For example, French and Caplan studied male white-collar workers over a 3-day period. They telemetered heart rate, measured serum cholesterol, and had observers rate behavior. "Quantitative work overload," as indexed by the observers' ratings, was positively correlated with serum cholesterol. Subjective measures of work overload were related to both physiological measures.[50]

The dimension of work pressure can be distinguished in practice as well as in principle from the responsibility dimension already discussed. For example, Type A pattern and Responsibility emerged as distinct dimensions in an analysis conducted on Caffrey's monastery data. Responsibility and work pressure may have a cumulative, noxious effect. In fact, the monks with the highest incidence of coronary disease, the Benedictine priests, achieved the highest ratings of Type A pattern and of responsibility. Air traffic controllers, who work under extreme time pressure and with the responsibility for hundreds of lives, have higher risk and earlier onset of hypertension and peptic ulcer than a control group of airmen second class.[51]

The relative contribution of work pressure and responsibility in the etiology of cardiovascular disease and peptic ulcers remains to be determined. But the possibility of identifying distinct social environmental dimensions allows us to frame this kind of question, with its implications for the differential diagnosis and treatment of persons and environments.

What do these studies tell us about the impacts of social environments? People are more satisfied and tend to perform better when the Relationship areas are emphasized. They are also less likely to drop out, be absent, and report that they are sick. People also tend to do better in environments that emphasize the Personal Development dimensions, but there may be some personal costs involved. Students learn more but are absent more often in classrooms emphasizing competition and difficulty. Patients do better in treatment programs that stress Autonomy and Practical Orientation. Students learn more in universities that attach great importance to independent study, high standards, criticism, and breadth of interests. But greater responsibility and greater work pressure have certain negative physiological concomitants—greater arousal and increased probability of cardiac dysfunction. The same kinds of effects must also occur in patients who are pushed out of hospitals and in students who are pushed to the limits of their performance capacities.

Order and clarity generally have weak but positive impacts on satisfaction, moods, and performance. Control generally has a negative impact, but this depends on both the rigidity of the control and on the age and developmental maturity of the people involved. Rigid control is less palatable with advancing maturity.

Future research will need to assess the effects of relationship-oriented "benevolent" control on groups of individuals in different institutions. For example, there is evidence that autistic children react more favorably to highly structured situations.[52] Autistic children who are functioning on a higher developmental level are better able to use relative lack of structure than are those functioning on a lower developmental level. Thus high control may be necessary and beneficial with certain individuals. The clearest conclusion is that in all social environments studied to date, satisfying human relationships facilitate personal growth and development. We know that "love is not enough," however; thus the effects of Personal Development and System Maintenance dimensions merit further study.

Selecting and Transcending Environments.   The growth of new institutional environments has increased the need for accurate descriptions of these environments. Many people feel that institutions know much more about the individuals they wish to recruit or place than those individuals know about the institution. For example, colleges know more about the characteristics of entering students than new students know about the colleges they plan to enter. Social workers and other program staff know more about the characteristics of new patients than these patients know about the programs they are entering.

It is widely agreed that currently available descriptions of social environments are inadequate. The environment is usually described as it is seen by a small and unrepresentative sample of the people in it (e.g., a company manager or administrator). In addition, no "feel" of how the environment actually functions is provided. For example, Jansen discovered that the descriptions of half-way houses for psychiatric patients did not give an accurate picture of the programs she actually visited, and "on visiting such houses I was struck by the discrepancies between writeups and actual practices."[53] Speegle found that the college environment as described by college catalogs was not congruent with students' perceptions of the environments. None of the catalogs he studied furnished descriptions of the informal social atmosphere of the respective colleges.[54]

Social climate scales may be useful in accurately portraying social environments. Program descriptions should systematically tell about the various dimensions included in the Relationship, Personal Development, and System Maintenance and System Change areas. Information about the social climate of an environment should help people to select more accurately the specific social environments most beneficial to them.

Prior information about new social environments can enhance the accuracy of individuals' expectations, thus reduce dissatisfaction, maladaptation, and dropout. For example, work in both individual and group psychotherapy has shown that providing systematic information about the therapy helps to socialize an individual and increases the probability of positive outcome. The presentation of information about social environments to prospective members should reduce discrepant perceptions and expectations and enhance successful adaptation in the environment.

Information about the social climate can also be returned to the participants in an environment, since feedback often motivates people in an environment to seek to change it.[55] Feedback and discussion sessions maximize the involvement of each individual in the definition and facilitation of change. For example, students can decide to increase the emphasis on Emotional Support in a living group, teachers to increase the emphasis on Rule Clarity in classrooms, parents to increase the emphasis on Independence in families. Information about the current environment, and how it differs from an ideal environment, helps people change their social environments in desired directions. At its best it enables some individuals to achieve a new competence, that of being able to change and control their own environments. In our view, the practical applications of the concept of social climate make it one of the most exciting and potentially useful ways of characterizing environments.

REFERENCES

1. Pace, C. R. Implications of differences in campus atmosphere for evaluation and planning of college programs. In R. Sutherland, W. Holtzman, E. Koile, and B. Smith (Eds.), *Personality factors on the college campus*. University of Texas Press, Austin, 1962.

2. Mill, J. S. *Autobiography.* Columbia University Press, New York, 1924 (original edition, 1873).

3. Russell, B. *The autobiography of Bertrand Russell 1872–1914.* Little, Brown, Boston, 1967 (quotation from p. 18).

4. Fischer, L. *The life of Mahatma Gandhi.* Macmillan, New York, 1962 (quotation from pp. 21–22).

5. Kozol, J. *Death at an early age.* Houghton Mifflin, Boston, 1967.

6. Kesey, K. *One flew over the cuckoo's nest.* Viking, New York, 1962.

7. Greenberg, J. *I never promised you a rose garden.* Holt, Rinehart & Winston, New York, 1964.

8. Lewin, K., Lippitt, R., and White, R. Patterns of aggressive behavior in experimentally created "social climates." *Journal of Social Psychology,* **10:**271–299, 1939.

9. Withall, J. The development of a technique for the measurement of social emotional climate in classrooms. *Journal of Experimental Education,* **17:**347–361, 1949.

10. Murray, H. *Explorations in personality.* Oxford University Press, New York, 1938.

11. Pace, C. R. and Stern, G. An approach to the measurement of psychological characteristics of college environments. *Journal of Educational Psychology,* **49:**269–277, 1958.

12. Findikyan, N. and Sells, S. Organizational structure and similarity of campus student organizations. *Organizational Behavior and Human Performance,* **1:**169–190, 1966.

13. Gerst, M. and Moos, R. The social ecology of university student residences. *Journal of Educational Psychology,* **63:**513–522, 1972.

14. Moos, R. *Evaluating treatment environments: A social ecological approach.* Wiley, New York, 1974, Ch. 14.

15. *Ibid.*

16. Glueck, S. and Glueck, E. *Unravelling juvenile delinquency.* The Commonwealth Fund, New York, 1950.

17. Bandura, A. and Walters, R. *Adolescent aggression.* Ronald Press, New York, 1959.

18. Becker, W. Consequences of different kinds of parental discipline. In M. L. Hoffman and L. W. Hoffman (Eds.), *Review of child development research,* Vol. 1. Russell Sage Foundation, New York, 1964 (quotations from p. 191).

19. Kagan, J. and Moss, H. *Birth to maturity.* Wiley, New York, 1962.

20. Faigin, H. Social behavior of young children in the kibbutz. *Journal of Abnormal and Social Psychology,* **56:**117–129, 1958.

21. Friedlander, F. and Greenberg, S. Effect of job attitudes, training and organization climate on performance of the hard-core unemployed. *Journal of Applied Psychology,* **55:**287–295, 1971.

22. Schneider, B. and Bartlett, C. Individual differences and organizational climate, II: Measurement of organizational climate by the multitrait multirater matrix. *Personnel Psychology,* **23:**493–512, 1970.

23. Schneider, B. The perception of organizational climate: The customers' view. *Journal of Applied Psychology,* **57:**248–256, 1973.

24. Pace, R. *College and University Environment Scales: Technical manual,* 2nd ed. Educational Testing Service, Princeton, N.J., 1969.

25. Peterson, R., Centra, J., Hartnett, R., and Linn, R. *Institutional Functioning Inventory: Preliminary technical manual.* Educational Testing Service, Princeton, N.J., 1970.

26. Trickett, E. and Moos, R. Personal correlates of contrasting environments: Student satisfactions in high school classrooms. *American Journal of Community Psychology,* **2:**1–2, 1974.

27. Walberg, H. Social environment as a mediator of classroom learning. *Journal of Educational Psychology,* **60:**443–448, 1969.

28. Truax, C. and Mitchell, K. Research on certain therapist interpersonal skills in relation to process and outcome. In A. Bergin and A. Garfield (Eds.), *Handbook of psychotherapy and behavior change: An empirical analysis.* Wiley, New York, 1971.

29. Ellsworth, R., Maroney, R., Klett, W., Gordon, H., and Gunn, R. Milieu characteristics of successful psychiatric treatment programs. *American Journal of Orthopsychiatry,* **41:**427–441, 1971.

30. Moos, R. *Evaluating correctional and community settings.* Wiley, New York, 1975, Ch. 7.

31. *Ibid.,* Ch. 12.

32. Knapp, R. *The origins of American humanistic scholars.* Prentice-Hall, Englewood Cliffs, N.J., 1964.

    Knapp, R. and Goodrich, H. *Origins of American scientists.* University of Chicago Press, Chicago, 1952.

    Knapp, R. and Greenbaum, J. *The younger American scholar: His collegiate origins.* University of Chicago Press, Chicago, 1953.

33. Thistlethwaite, D. College press and student achievement. *Journal of Educational Psychology,* **50:**183–191, 1959.

    Thistlethwaite, D. College environments and the development of talent. *Science,* **130:**71–76, 1959 (quotation from pp. 74–75).

34. Thistlethwaite, D. College press and changes in study plans of talented students. *Journal of Educational Psychology,* **51:**222–234, 1960 (quotation from p. 233).

35. Astin, A. Undergraduate institutions and the production of scientists. *Science,* **141:**334–338, 1963.

36. Astin, A. Differential college effects on the motivation of talented students to obtain the Ph.D. *Journal of Educational Psychology,* **54:**63–71, 1963 (quotation from p. 63).

37. Astin, A. and Panos, R. *The educational and vocational development of college students.* American Council on Education, Washington, D.C., 1969.

38. Rock, D., Centra, J., and Linn, R. Relationships between college characteristics and student achievement. *American Educational Research Journal,* **7:**109–121, 1970.

39. Centra, J. and Rock, D. College environments and student academic achievement. *American Educational Research Journal,* **8:**623–634, 1971 (quotation from p. 633).

40. Spitz, R. *Hospitalism in psychoanalytic study of the child,* Vol. 1. International Universities Press, New York, 1945.

    Spitz, R. Hospitalism: A follow-up report. In *Psychoanalytic Study of the child,* Vol. 2. International Universities Press, New York, 1947.

41. MacCarthy, D. and Booth, E. Parental rejection and stunting of growth. *Journal of Psychosomatic Research,* **14:**259–265, 1970.

42. Casler, L. Maternal deprivation: A critical review of the literature. *Monograph of the Society for Research in Child Development,* **26:**1–64, 1961.

43. Parkes, C., Benjamin, B., and Fitzgerald, R. Broken heart: A statistical study of increased mortality among widowers. *British Medical Journal,* **1:**740–743, 1969.

44. Bruhn, J., Chandler, B., Miller, M., Wolf, S., and Lynn, T. Social aspects of coronary heart disease in two adjacent ethnically different communities. *American Journal of Public Health,* **56:**1493–1506, 1966.

45. Miller, R., Ruben, R., Clark, B., Crawford, W., and Arthur, R. The stress of aircraft carrier landings, Part 1: Cortical steroid responses in naval aviators. *Psychosomatic Medicine,* **32:**581–588, 1970.

46. *Journal of the American Medical Association* (editorial). Responsibility brings jump in pulse **201:**23, 1967.

47. Rosenman, R., Friedman, M., Straus, R., Wurm, M., Jenkins, O., and Messinger, H. Coronary heart disease in the Western Collaborative Group Study: A follow-up experience of two years. *Journal of the American Medical Association,* **195:**86–92, 1966.

48. Friedman, M. *Pathogenesis of coronary artery disease.* McGraw-Hill, New York, 1969.

49. Caffrey, B. Reliability and validity of personality and behavioral measures in a study of coronary heart disease. *Journal of Chronic Disease,* **21:**191–204, 1968.

50. French, J. and Caplan, R. Organizational stress and individual strain. In A. Marrow (Ed.), *The failure of success.* AMACOM, New York, 1973.

51. Cobb, S. and Rose, R. Hypertension, peptic ulcer and diabetes in air traffic controllers. *Journal of the American Medical Association,* **224:**489–492, 1973.

52. Schopler, E., Brehm, S., Kinsbourne, M., and Reichler, R. Effect of treatment structure on development in autistic children. *Archives of General Psychiatry,* **24:**415–421, 1971.

53. Jansen, E. The role of the halfway house in community mental health programs in the United Kingdom and America. *American Journal of Psychiatry,* **126:**142–148, 1970.

54. Speegle, J. College catalogs: An investigation of the congruence of catalog descriptions of college environments with student perceptions of the same environments as revealed by the College Characteristics Index. Doctoral dissertation, Syracuse University, Syracuse, N.Y., 1969.

55. Moos, R. *Evaluating treatment environments, op. cit.,* Ch. 14.

PART FOUR

Toward an Optimum
Human Milieu

CHAPTER ELEVEN

Utopian Environments[a]

Utopias: Real and Ideal. We have tested different perspectives concerning the physical and social environment. We now suggest an additional approach to comparative analysis: an evaluation of the linkages between theories of the environment and the study of human utopias. After reviewing these diverse systems of thought, we proceed to a detailed discussion of three utopias: two literary, *Utopia* by Thomas More and *Walden II* by B. F. Skinner, and one experimental, the Oneida Community of New York State, 1848–1880. Our method of analysis follows the conceptual scheme used in the preceding chapters. Thus we examine each utopia in terms of its physical geography and architecture, organizational structure, human aggregate, social climate, and so on.

Visions of ideal environments have attracted humanity ever since God dismissed Adam and Eve from Paradise. How have utopian environments been described? Is there any consistency in their characteristics? All utopias are necessarily free of crowding and noise and air pollution, but what are the ideal architectural and physical design characteristics of a human environment? Are certain geographic and weather conditions more conducive to a utopian environment than others?

What is the best kind of organizational structure? How should the government, the economy, and the family be structured? What types of people should live there? Can all types of people be integrated within one ideal environment? What kinds of behavior settings should be included? Finally, what should the social climate of an ideal human community be

[a] This chapter is co-authored by Robert Brownstein and Rudolf Moos.

like? Are cohesiveness and spontaneity sufficient, or is some measure of order and control essential?

Is it possible to establish ideal living environments for human beings, or do the twin problems of inherent environmental limitations and human needs for stimulation, variety, and change preclude the development of a static social system? Architects need not inhabit the buildings they design; the designers of utopias need not live in the environments of their dreams. Given our "ego-centered" perspective, we must ask how an individual might react to the ideal communities so graphically portrayed by scholars and visionaries.

Environmental Thought.   Environmental theory is earth-bound science. With some early exceptions (the use of astrological and mystic elements in ancient hypotheses), the study of man's environment has involved empirical classification, examination of data, formation of hypotheses, testing of data, and generalized conclusions. Although limited in its capacity to conduct experiments, environmental thought has increasingly demonstrated high degrees of scientific rigor in its approach, including recent applications of quantification and computer analysis.

Environmental theories have stressed nature's ability to limit mankind's ambitions and achievements. The first geographic inquiries reached overtly determinist conclusions. Geographic factors directed human responses; man's mode of economic organization, political system, religion, and personality were traced to environmental causes. Determinist arguments subsequently encountered opposition from possibilist and probabilist theory. Human choice did play a role in history. But here again, the environment presented limits. Human choices had to be made among options the environment permitted. When choices are examined to predict the likelihood of their success, the margin of flexibility left to man may be narrow indeed.[1]

With the rise of ecological analysis and new quantitative techniques, the study of the environment delved deeper and with greater exactitude into the world surrounding man. This perspective revealed the complexity and strength of the boundaries to human action, rather than indicating any shortcut to the transcendance of natural limitations. Caught in an ecosystem web of food chains and energy flows, man must act with caution lest he interfere with a balance he cannot reestablish, or initiate trends he cannot later control. Thus new analytical approaches might enable man to maximize his chances in the game of survival against the environment. But he would still be "dealt" an environmental "hand" of land, resources, and weather with which even the best player might find it difficult to win.

Most recently ecological analysts have been unusually strident in their insistence that environmental factors in human planning cannot be over-looked without catastrophic consequences. Limits have been ignored in the past, but the difficulty of responding to future environmental conditions may thus have been compounded. An example of this problem is provided by the Club of Rome's manifesto, published as *The Limits to Growth*. They argue, in a message technical in style but apocalyptic in scope,

> If the present growth trends in world population, industrialization, pollution, food production, and resource depletion continue unchanged, the limits to growth on this planet will be reached sometime within the next one hundred years. The most probable result will be a rather sudden and uncontrollable decline in both population and industrial capacity.[2]

Utopian Thought.   In contrast to the scientific method of environmental thought, the utopian perspective is visionary, restrained only by human desire and imagination. Its sole method of investigation involves reflecting on what is and conceiving of what could be. Nevertheless it is possible to define a utopian work, and to distinguish it from a mere plea for social reform or other expression of political philosophy.

Utopias have the following fundamental characteristics. First, they are holistic. Their intent is to portray the essential elements of an entire social order. Second, they are functional. That is, they do not merely express ideas or values but incorporate such notations into ongoing institutions. Third, they are idealist. Their authors assume that social perfection is conceivable; they seek not a better society but the best society, the end point of human achievement. Finally, they are intentional, describing a society ordered according to a basic guiding plan.[3]

Utopias have a rich history. The specific features of flawless societies range along an enormously long gamut of institutions, structures, and organizations. Such diversity is to be expected, considering the disparity in the life styles of the inventors of utopias, as well as the progressive changes in human cultural evolution which render one century's utopia the next century's reality (especially in matters of technology). Yet interestingly, some elements in even the first utopias occur frequently in subsequent works, including the most modern.[4]

Although several of the lectures of the biblical Hebrew prophets contain utopian features—at least a belief in the final messianic triumph of righteousness—the first full examples of literary utopias are credited to the ancient Greeks. Of these, the work of greatest import is Plato's *Republic*. Writing during a period of decline in Athens, Plato envisioned a perfect city-state, whose structure was both ethical and pragmatic. Society would be divided into three castes, philosophers, warriors, and workers, each one demonstrating a specific value: wisdom, courage, and temperance, respectively. If each caste diligently carried out the duties for which it was best suited, justice, the harmony of the whole social order, would result. In accordance with Plato's idealist philosophy, it is the philosophers, those most capable of comprehending the "good" through contemplation, who rule. To ensure the disinterested application of their wisdom, they enjoy all things in common, including women, children, and property. The working class, on whose labor the economy of the state is based, plays no role in its government. Also, Plato readily acknowledged the need for deception and censorship to ensure that the workers would not harbor beliefs that interfered with social stability.[5]

During the medieval period there occurred a lengthy lapse in utopian thinking. Within Christendom, man's deepest hopes and desires were projected beyond this world to a heavenly future, and utopia became supplanted by theology. Even St. Augustine's *City of God* concentrated more on man's ideal relation to God than on the struture of social institutions.

Utopian thought achieved a spectacular resurrection with the decline of feudalism and the beginning of the Renaissance. Numerous works were completed that differed radically from one another but presented some commonalities distinct from their classical predecessors. An ethical civilization was still the ultimate objective, but the new writers devoted greater attention to the economic requirements for the "good" life, recognizing the significance of a sound agricultural base for a utopian city. Manual labor was deemed a civic duty rather than being relegated to a lower caste. Thomas More's *Utopia,* said to be the first in the new humanist vein, is discussed below. Other notable efforts at redesigning man's conception of a superior social order included Tomasso Campanella's *City of the Sun* and Francis Bacon's *New Atlantis.*[6]

Nineteenth-century utopias strongly reflect the influence of the French Revolution and the Industrial Revolution. Monarchy having been swept aside, capitalist and proletarian waged war over the productive spoils of technology and the open market. For the first time, equality of abundance appeared to be realizable, and utopian writers, now "shamelessly materialistic," fervently pursued that goal. Among the early socialist visions was Etienne Cabet's *Voyage to Icaria.* Written while its author was in exile for his antigovernment activities in France, it depicts a society in which the marriage of science and state power provides material well-being for all in an atmosphere of equality and brotherhood. The price for these economic benefits is every vestige of individual freedom. All aspects of life in Icaria—diet, clothing, architecture, education—are determined by committees of experts. Literature and art are subjected to vigorous censorship.

Edward Bellamy's *Looking Backward,* an enormously popular utopian novel, depicted a socialist order only slightly less regimented than Cabet's. Unlike earlier works that located utopia in some remote geographical region, Bellamy has his narrator fall into hypnotic sleep in 1887 to awaken in the utopian year 2000. Gradual monopolization of capitalist industry is to eventually result in a single gigantic trust, a state enterprise that controls the entire American economy. In consequence, the labor force is nationalized, forming an industrial army into which all are conscripted at 17 and discharged at 45. Bellamy's use of the "army" image is no accident, for the combination of equality in the ranks and efficient organization, common to military institutions, is precisely what he finds attractive. Production is regimented, but consumption becomes a realm of freedom. State warehouses are amply stocked to provide for citizens' material needs, with technical innovation assuring the availability of ample goods to satisfy the soldier-workers' tastes.[7]

Nineteenth-century dreamers became so enamoured with utopian prospects that many attempted to create experimental utopian communities. The enormous supply of open and underpopulated land in North America was seemingly waiting to give birth to a new civilization. Cabet launched several ultimately unsuccessful efforts to develop small-scale Icarias in Texas and Illinois. Other communities with a religious basis were set up by Shakers, Zoar separatists, Hutterites, and Perfectionists. A settlement of the latter group, the Oneida Community, is discussed below.

Modern utopias are an unusual literary event. Theodore Hertska's *Freeland–A Social Anticipation,* written in 1890, was an attempt to preserve a free enterprise economy based on individual self-interest yet avoiding poverty and class domination. An economist by profession, Hertska suggested an amalgam of mechanisms and regulations, usually involving taxation and credit, to assure all citizens access to land and capital and free entrance into the industry of their choosing. He hoped by these means to achieve the historical liberal dream of making each man's pursuit of his personal interests compatible with social welfare.[8]

H. G. Wells, the British social theorist, produced several utopias among his speculative works. In *Modern Utopia* he followed Hertska in attempting to design conditions that would assure popular welfare without threatening personal liberty. This did not prevent him, however, from advocating centralization. In fact, he was unique in insisting that utopia could only take place on a world scale, never in a single nation or isolated community. Perhaps because he was so much a man of the twentieth century, his visions are less extravagant in their promises than those of his predecessors. For example, Wells viewed nature as unmanageable and potentially dangerous. He also felt that a segment of the human populace would prove hopelessly criminal and would have to be exiled to prison islands. Yet in his ideal government Wells progressed no further than Plato. Ruling utopia would be a class of specially educated samurai with a life style unique to their mission; in brief, modernized philosopher-kings.[9]

As the twentieth century progresses utopian writing is becoming increasingly scarce. World War I was the turning point that cured the West of unwarranted optimism. Recent events have continued to discourage expectations of an ecstatic future. Yet, phoenixlike, utopias continue to arise. In the dawn of the Atomic Age, just following the carnage of World War II, B. F. Skinner came forward with a new and controversial utopia, based on his theories of learning and conditioning. His novel *Walden II* is analyzed below.

Thomas More's Utopia.   One of the leading intellectuals of late medieval Christendom, Thomas More (1478–1535) combined in a single career the successful practice of law, diplomacy, politics, and scholarship, at a time of religious dispute and social dissension. An older feudal order faced supersession by the forces of economic and cultural individualism. The rise of capitalism thrust much of the English population into poverty; and political conflict reached to the ranks of the Church and its leadership. In such a context, traditional conceptions of social structure and values stood open to critical evaluation. More chose to criticize indirectly, through comparison. His essay *Utopia,* completed in 1516, depicted a perfect human society whose institutions contrasted markedly with contemporary English practice.[10]

Geography and Architecture.   Utopia is a small crescent-shaped, man-made island. Island status itself, combined with the existence of a single navigable channel in the large bay between the horns, and a naturally "fortified" coastline, ensures the military security of the region. The presence of numerous harbors permits the easy establishment of commercial relationships with friendly foreigners. More limited his interest in geographic factors to issues of foreign trade and military defense. There is no mention in *Utopia* of the impact of geographic variables on any other human characteristics. The island's population is concentrated in 54 cities, which are large and well built and relatively evenly distributed throughout the nation. They are as similar as terrain will permit. "He that knows one of their towns," More writes, "knows them all."

Amaurat, the city in which Utopia's supreme council meets, is centrally located. Much like the island itself, Amaurat is designed to facilitate commerce and defense. Nearby rivers provide access to traders as well as protection from land attack. A thorn-filled ditch encloses the sides of the city not opening onto the river. Amaurat is surrounded by thick high walls that support towers and forts.

Stable urban planning is assured through the regulation of population density at every level of social organization. No family may have fewer than 10 or more than 16 members, and no city may have more than 6000 families. Imbalances are corrected through population transfer or, if necessary, territorial expansion on the nearby mainland. The rationale for these particular densities is never stated. Presumably economic welfare is the primary objective, and it was recognized that overpopulation would strain food resources and underpopulation would restrict labor and intensive production.[11]

Organizational Structure.

Government.   Government consists of several levels. Magistrates, or Syphogrants, the lowest ranked public officials, are elected from a constituency of 30 families. For every 10 Syphogrants there is elected a higher magistrate, the Tranibor. Above the Tranibors reigns a single Prince, chosen by the Syphogrants in secret ballot. Political decisions are generally made by the council of Tranibors, which meets every few days in consultation with the Prince. Two Syphogrants attend these sessions. Particularly important issues may be referred to the entire body of Syphogrants or to the whole populace in assembly.[12]

To Thomas More, Utopian political organization preserved the liberty of the people against enslavement or tyranny. This was accomplished, however, through a hierarchy of sub-elites who would resist one-man rule, rather than through genuine popular control. The fundamental electoral unit is the family, not the individual, and as is demonstrated below the Utopian family is highly autocratic. Also, Utopia prohibits political discourse outside formal assemblies, a measure that precludes the minimal level of interpersonal debate necessary to mobilize organized opposition to established power.

Economy.   Productive economic activity is completely socialized. The means of production are under community control, and everyone (officials, priests, and full-time students excepted) is required to work. Each citizen follows a particular trade, usually inherited from his father; however vocational change in the social interest is permissible. Whatever job a worker has, his work day is organized according to the same schedule. Everyone works a 6-hour day, 3 hours before dinner and 3 afterward. Then follows the evening meal, after which, at 8:00 p.m., the populace retires for 8 hours sleep. The time not accounted for is left to individual discretion within morally acceptable limits.[13]

Distribution of economic resources is also socially determined. The mechanism of distribution is usually direct and simple. Every city is divided into four parts, each having a central marketplace. From the goods stored there, the fathers from neighboring families select what they desire. Payment is never required. It is assumed that no one will appropriate more than he needs, since the public surplus is always available to satisfy future needs.

A distribution system of this type presumes at least a level of affluence such that people regularly find available the goods they need. The reasons for that expectation, despite the 6-hour work day, are twofold. First, the personal desires of Utopian citizens are not exorbitant, since no status is attached to the possession of material wealth. Second, almost the entire population works; there are no idle rich or social parasites.

Family.   In Utopia the family is the basic social unit. It is both the smallest functional political entity and the economic focal point for production and for distribution. Families are multigenerational; parents, male children, and their wives live together, and female offspring move off to reside with their husbands. Authority resides with the patriarch. Unless senile, the eldest male serves as governor. Other family members must respect the general rule of deference that wives serve husbands, children their parents and youth their elders.

Patriarchal dominance does not extend to polygamy. Only monogamous relationships are deemed legitimate, with societal sanctions employed to ensure the stability of marital unions. For example, premarital sexual activity is severely punished, and divorce requires the (rarely granted) approval of the city council.

Both the extensiveness of the family's role and the determination to preserve it as an institution stem from More's perspective on the foundations of social order. Apparently he believed that people must be integrated into the large community not as individuals but through membership in a small, tightly organized subgroup.

Education.   Basic education of children is the province of the priests, who are less concerned with scholastic achievement than with moral development. More writes "They use all possible methods to infuse very early into the tender and flexible minds of children such opinions as are both good in themselves and will be useful to their country." These include "that religious dread of the supreme Being, which is the greatest and almost the only incitement to virtue."

Still, not all instruction is in the hands of clerics. Vocational training apparently takes place within the family. Also, many Utopians continue to improve intellectually through independent reading as adults, although only a small, select number are permitted to pursue full-time scholarship.[14]

Human Aggregate.   Utopia's people are divided into three distinct statuses: slave, citizen, and official. The first category includes persons acquired by purchase abroad, prisoners seized in battle, volunteers from other countries (who prefer servitude in Utopia to the conditions in their homeland), and Utopia's own criminals, who are treated worse than the others. All slaves are deemed inferior creatures whose welfare is secondary to that of citizens.

Despite their economic equality and the political equality of their families, Utopia's citizens are themselves stratified according to age and sex, with status and power the prerogatives of males and elders. The officials possess political power but few of the usual accoutrements, since they receive minimal economic privilege or compulsory honors. In terms of general competence, Utopians are literate and intelligent, tending to emphasize practical and technical knowledge over abstract theory. All are trained in agriculture, and most are masters of a trade as well.[15]

A Behavior Setting: The Dining Hall.   Utopians take their meals together in large halls serving up to 30 families. Almost every aspect of their dining reflects a concern for stratification and order. Work connected with food preparation is performed by social inferiors, "the uneasy and sordid" tasks by slaves, the rest by women. Seating in the hall takes place according to a formal pattern. At the main table is located the magistrate and his wife, any priest residing in the area, and one or two of the oldest other persons present (Utopians always eat four to a table). Men sit next to the wall. The table's open side is reserved for women, to permit them to exit with ease if they become ill, as in pregnancy. Children under 5 eat with their nurses; those from 5 to the age of marriage serve the tables or stand by eating in silence. All others are seated to ensure a thorough mixture of age groups so that the older may restrain the younger from indecent gestures.

Meals are organized according to a definite program. Immediately following a trumpet blast announcing the dinner hour, the Utopians hear a lecture on morality—ideally one so short that it is neither unpleasant nor tedious. Older persons receive priority as the dishes are brought out; after they are served, the others are treated equally. The elders always initiate the conversation at the table. Despite the order and regulation, Utopians seek to incorporate in their dining periods those pleasures compatible with their moral code. For example, music is often played during supper, and at some tables fragrant ointments are sprinkled and perfumes burned.[16]

Social Climate.

Personal Growth.   The highest personal goal for a Utopian is his own ethical development. Several of the society's practices testify to the significance of this objective. Meals begin with a lecture on morality. Reading, for both moral and intellectual edification, is the most common leisure pastime. Religion of some kind is a prerequisite for full social acceptance. One should not assume, however, that this necessarily results in an ascetic or puritanical society. Personal pleasure is morally desirable when it does not interfere with the needs of the community, the welfare of others, or the personal health of the individual.

Thus the pursuit of pleasure is profoundly tempered by rational and religious qualifications, rendering this activity compatible with orderly social relationships. From a rational perspective, it makes no sense to pursue a pleasure that brings a great deal of pain or to allow a lesser pleasure to stand in the way of a greater one. This attitude keeps the unbridled quest for satisfaction within the law, for violations would bring on considerable subsequent pain. The widespread religious belief in the immortality of the soul and in some form of divine judgment also encourages individuals to forego small satisfactions on earth, thereby increasing the prospect for greater rewards on an eternal scale.

The Utopians do not rely on personal conscience for the translation of their morality into practice. Rather, they employ socialization, sanctions, and the pragmatic structuring of situations such that ethical behavior is satisfying and misbehavior detestable. For example, Utopia possesses vast stores of precious metals that might prove enticing enough to corrupt either the leadership or the citizenry. To avoid any lapse in moral standards, gold and silver serve two purposes only: they are used in the manufacture of chamber pots and manacles for slaves. Thus materials which might have been irresistible temptations become objects of universal contempt.[17]

Personal Relationships.   Many aspects of Utopian society reinforce social cohesion. Family relationships pervade so many areas (work, religion, warfare) that there are few situations in which the individual must stand alone. Citizens regularly participate in significant communal activities, particularly dining and religious worship. Although there is more than one faith, all public prayer occurs at the same time, in the same place, and in a manner acceptable to all. Furthermore, individuals have a common experience and basis for solidarity in their 2 years of compulsory agricultural labor.[18]

However, these factors may be outweighed by powerful divisive forces. The subordination of women and youth must be considered a point of political tension. Family loyalty may conflict with public welfare, as when families are broken up or forced to move to achieve suitable population density. In such cases commitment to the family may erode commitment to the nation. Finally, and most important, the existence of a slave class, whose interests and desires must always be alien to those of the citizens, ensures that Utopia can never experience full social harmony.

System Maintenance and System Change. The Utopians perform admirably with regard to the clarity of their regulations. "They have but few laws, and such is their constitution that they need not many . . . . Every one of them is skilled in their law, for as it is a very short study, so the plainest meaning of which words are capable is always the sense of their laws."[19] As a consequence of this clarity, there are no lawyers, and in the few situations in which disputes occur, each citizen is qualified to plead his own case.

Regimentation is a normal element in Utopian life. Housing and clothing are uniform. Everyone in the city has the same work schedule. Large groups eat the same food at the same time (although one is free to dine alone). Travel between cities requires a passport. Violations of these regulations result in severe penalties. Even activities that appear to permit free choice have a measure of restrictiveness. One can choose a new job, but only with public agreement that the new skill will be socially valuable. A citizen is free to enjoy leisure after work, but there is major social pressure insisting that leisure time be used constructively for reading, attending lectures, or voluntary labor.

To maintain its rigidly structured social system, Utopia requires the application of sanctions against those who violate its norms and laws. Public opinion constitutes one punitive force—atheists, for example, are despised as "men of base and sordid minds." Minor offenses may be handled within the family. Parents have the right to discipline their children, and husbands their wives. More serious transgressions result in trial before the local Syphogrants, who determine guilt or innocence. The central council of the city, however, decides on the appropriate penalty, always tempering punishment according to the circumstances surrounding the infraction.[20]

Prospects for innovation and change in Utopia are ambiguous. On the one hand, the society is uniform and regimented. On the other hand, Utopia has experienced technological change—the manufacture of paper and the art of printing are cited as techniques adopted from foreign sources—and Utopian religion sanctions change for the better. The crucial issue is the extent to which Utopia will tolerate its own transformation. More provides no specific answer. However the groups empowered to define the acceptability of potential alteration (i.e., the religious and political leadership) are unlikely to approve changes that might endanger their authority.

The Oneida Community. To understand the background of the Oneida Community, one must know something of the life and thought of John Humphrey Noyes. A convert to evangelical Christianity at the age of 19 (in 1831), Noyes gave up a career in law to enter the ministry. He received a license to preach from the seminary at Yale in 1833. Once his unorthodox religious views became known, however, teachers and fellow students demanded his resignation. There followed a brief period of despair, but Noyes regained his confidence, married, and returned to his family's home in Putney, Vermont, determined to create a community that would translate his theories into practice.

Perfectionism, the new Protestant sect Noyes helped establish, unfolded gradually. One of its central convictions was that the Second Coming of Christ had already taken place, (in A.D. 70, at the time of the destruction of Jerusalem) albeit on the spiritual rather than the material plane. Hence the Kingdom of Heaven on Earth, and individual spiritual perfection, had been a real possibility for 18 centuries. To be sure, the achievement of perfection required great study, prayer, and faith. Moreover, it in no way ensured sinless behavior. Man, Noyes argued, possessed an inner and an outer self, and the purity of the former offered the possibility but not the certainty of the purity of the latter. This point is crucial, because the understanding that perfection in behavior is a challenge, rather than an automatic correlate of spiritual perfection, led Noyes to attempt the design of a community that would be conducive to sinlessness in action.[21]

Noyes' Perfectionist colony at Putney lasted 9 years (1838–1847) and eventually included 28 adults and 7 children. This small but dedicated brotherhood accepted theocratic government, organized a joint economy, and after some time, embraced group marriage. Moral outrage over the latter practice caused the group to hastily disband in fear of mob violence. Nevertheless, Noyes did not give up his convictions. Joining other Perfectionists with the remainder of his Putney followers, he attempted once again to bring God's Kingdom to earth, this time on a small property near Oneida Creek in Madison County, New York.

Geography and Architecture. Lying at the northern end of a secluded valley almost precisely in the center of New York State, the lands of the Oneida settlement offered the potential of a viable community existence. There was fertile soil for farming, ample water power for industry, woodlands for providing construction material, and meadows on which to pasture livestock. Although the winter was rigorous, a variety of crops could be cultivated, including numerous fruits and vegetables. In addition, easy contact with urban and commercial centers could be maintained through the Oneida Railroad Depot, just 3 miles away on the Utica–Syracuse line.[22]

The central edifice at Oneida was the Mansion House, a multistory structure that housed the entire membership and included public rooms, recreational rooms, and functional areas (kitchens, business offices, etc.). Numerous other buildings were gradually erected on Oneida's property; their sites and design reflected pragmatic, economic considerations. When the community's industries prospered, a new stone Mansion House was constructed to replace the wooden original. More luxurious than its predecessor, it included steam heat and an elaborate meeting hall.

Features of both Mansion Houses suggest that the Perfectionists had some consciousness of the effects of architecture on social relationships. The entire membership resided in a single building, assuring frequent interaction, as befitted a close, familylike community. In addition, public space was both extensive and more comfortable than private rooms, an arrangement that encouraged social contact to take place in the open, under general scrutiny.[23]

Organizational Structure.

Government. Although the community exerted considerable power over its membership, regulating innumerable aspects of their lives, decision-making procedures were amorphous and difficult to systematize. The Perfectionists accepted the Bible as a constitution but acknowledged that it required interpretation. They credited accumulated wisdom and the "suggestion of experience" as the sources of their unwritten by-laws.

Noyes employed four mechanisms to direct what amounted to a theocratic despotism. First, he surrounded himself with a clique of older "central" members on whom he could rely and to whom he could delegate authority.Second, Noyes appointed the members of a massive committee network, established to administrate specific economic and social sectors. Participation on the committees was widespread, and many members thus had the opportunity to play a role in community management. Third, meetings of the entire membership took place every evening. On these occasions Noyes delivered "home talks," developing points of Perfectionist theology and elaborating on their relationship to everyday living. Particularly important issues of community policy were placed before the membership for decision. Every member had the right to debate and vote on the question, but Noyes and the central members usually dominated the discourse. Finally, the Perfectionist system of mutual criticism, which provided for group examination of members' character and behavior, could be used as a political weapon. Not only did it provide the leadership with extensive knowledge of each member's actions, it permitted those most competent at criticism (Noyes was unsurpassed) to legislate values, feelings, and actions for members on an individual basis.[24]

Economy.   The Perfectionists initially based their economy on agriculture. Farming did not provide sufficient income to meet their needs, however, and they turned to a multitude of commercial and industrial enterprises. One of these, the manufacture of animal traps, attracted a mass market, bringing relative economic prosperity to the community. Everyone at Oneida worked—men, women, children, and the leadership. All jobs were considered honorable, and Noyes himself labored as a blacksmith and farmer. The community endeavored to make work both productive and satisfying. One technique was frequent job rotation, modified by a concern for efficiency. Another tactic, the organization of work bees, brought mobs of members together to finish a long and dreary task in one quick, energetic, social effort. With the expansion of Oneida's industry it became necessary to hire outside labor to perform the more routine and menial functions. The community's members eventually became a collective of managers, holding almost exclusively supervisory positions.

Oneida distributed its economic resources on an egalitarian basis (to members, not employees). Members lived in similar rooms, dined at a common table, and received the same small allowance for clothing and incidentals. Oneida's standard of living varied with the community's economic success. There were several lean years in the first decade, but once the trap business developed, Oneida consistently increased its wealth and weathered two national financial panics. Indeed, Oneida's economy proved to be its most long-lasting component. After the community collapsed in 1880, its industries were reorganized as a joint stock company that continues to this day.[25]

Family. At Oneida each man became the husband of every woman, and each woman the wife of every man. This system of complex marriage involved a lifetime commitment, including the obligation to provide mutual economic support and the responsibility for child rearing. Selection of sexual partners followed a theological principle termed "ascending and descending fellowship." Ideally, sexual activity took place as ascending fellowship, a contact between a spiritually inferior person and his or her spiritual superior. Of course every ascending relationship was also a descending relationship for the higher party, but it was assumed that the latter, being superior, could withstand the impact. In practice ascending fellowship resulted in greater sexual opportunity for the older and more spiritually advanced of the membership. Finally, complex marriage has to be understood as a mode of group interaction. Each member was married to every other; hence any effort to form an exclusive attachment with one member of the opposite sex constituted neglect of one's commitment to the rest of the community and was strictly prohibited.

Partly for reasons of economy and partly to relieve women from the burden of unwanted pregnancies, Oneida adopted male continence as a method of birth control. This required the male to exercise sufficient restraint to prevent ejaculation during intercourse. In 1869, however, the community qualified its opposition to population growth and began a program of selective breeding. Referred to as stirpiculture (from the Latin *stirps,* meaning stock), this system followed Lamarckian premises and sought to genetically transfer the accumulated spiritual wisdom of Oneida's elders to its next generation. Noyes, who fathered nine stirpicults, exercised control of the committee that determined the suitability of members for parenthood.

Prior to the advent of stirpiculture, Oneida had already acquired significant numbers of children. Youngsters from all sources were raised communally in the Children's House, an area distinct from the adult quarters. Contact between natural mothers and their children was infrequent and strictly regulated. The community endeavored to restrict the degree of affection between parent and child, just as it sought to prevent exclusive love from developing between adults.[26]

Education. Education at Oneida involved several levels geared to the varying needs of students of different ages and abilities. The community's youngest children enjoyed life in a nursery, where they received little or no formal teaching. Children from 7 to 12 acquired a primary education, as well as instruction in Perfectionist beliefs, norms, and practices. Like their elders, they held daily meetings, had work bees, and engaged in mutual criticism. Despite increased work responsibilities, adolescents and young men carried on part-time but systematic schooling. Higher education and technical training could not be provided at Oneida, owing to the lack of competent teachers. Many of the community's most intelligent young men entered Yale to pursue programs in medicine, law, architecture, and mechanical engineering.[27]

Human Aggregate.   Oneida's first members, long-time Perfectionists and/or veterans of Putney, were ideally suited to follow Noyes in a communitarian venture. To ensure that the motivation of prospective newcomers included commitment to Oneida's religious principles rather than a desire for free sexuality or economic support, the community subjected candidates to long periods of examination, criticism, and probationary status. Although inquiries concerning admission were numerous, Oneida accepted so few newcomers that in the period between 1851 and 1878 its membership increased by only 100 persons.[28]

Formal stratification according to class or caste was virtually unknown at Oneida, yet there did exist three factors—level of spiritual achievement, age, and sex—which divided the populace into distinguishable groups. Those in the first category, Noyes and his central members, were considered the community's elite and had special privileges in terms of access to decision making and opportunities for sexual fulfillment. Age proved a divisive force, since young members whose experiences differed widely from those of their elders tended to view Oneida's religious values critically. Finally, although the community's women enjoyed a degree of status that was progressive for the nineteenth century, they were never considered the equals of males and had to accept subordinate positions.[29]

A Behavior Setting: The Dining Hall.   As the community expanded its financial base, built new buildings, and grew in population, the physical structure of its dining facilities underwent modification. Beginning with a single long table extending through the dining room, facilities improved until, in 1870, Oneida became capable of feeding the entire membership at one sitting.

Dining practices involved only a few regulations. For example, each member entering the hall was required to accept the next available seat, regardless of his preferences for meal time companions. Community manners, however, did not require a rigid decorum; in fact, one source observed, "pleasant, conversational buzz is good music while eating." The time and mode of food preparation varied according to members' tastes and values; waiters might be replaced by a buffet or full dinners given up for a religious fast. Menus also varied, depending on Oneida's finances and its changing theories regarding the effect of certain foods on personal characteristics.[30]

Social Climate.

Personal Growth. To Noyes and his Perfectionists, the purpose of creating a community was to further the development of an ideal human type, based on their religious convictions. Faith in God and obedience to His word constituted the fundamental elements in this vision. Perfectionist thought, however, defined sinlessness as an "inner" state, achieved through spiritual experience. "Outer" life had also to be raised to a commensurate level of righteousness. The process of consistently bettering one's outer life, known as improvement, required balanced advancement in all aspects of activity: work, moral behavior, intellectual progress. Improvement was expected to go on without end; no matter what the task, one could always do better, and all efforts in this direction merited community praise. An additional element in the Perfectionist ideal concerned commitment and service to the community. Members were to relate to their fellows in a spirit of love, thinking less of themselves and more of the needs of the group. Possessiveness in persons or property met with strong condemnation. Oneida's membership sought to avoid all selfish conduct; any and all manifestations of greed, egoism, or ambition were criticized.[31]

Personal Relationships. High among the goals of the Oneida Community was the desire to maintain an intense degree of cohesion among members, and many of the Perfectionists' social practices served to reinforce that objective. Daily meetings brought the entire membership together to hear elaborations of their faith; work bees demonstrated the satisfaction of comradeship in labor; mutual criticism generated a bond of unity as each person subjected himself to the judgment of his associates. Moreover, the members shared a common home, a common table, and common mates in complex marriage. Oneida's values also supported cohesiveness. As competition was criticized, sharing was encouraged. The community demanded that each member direct his affections toward the group as a whole rather than toward any segment of it.

Oneida's atmosphere was neither solemn, rigid, nor puritanical. On the contrary, the Perfectionists relished a spontaneous, flexible, and vital existence. Jobs rotated frequently, and large groups felt free to drop what they were doing and help out at a work bee. Meetings varied greatly in form and content. Games, music, and dancing were enormously popular activities which might erupt at any moment.

Despite the above-mentioned factors, conflict did occur at Oneida, eventually causing the community to dissolve. At its root was a generation gap brought on by differences in attitude, status, and privilege between young and old. The correlation between spiritual achievement and advanced age denied the community's young men full stature in decision making. It also prevented them from entering into sexual relations with women their own age. Differences in ideology added to the tension. Those with scientific training at the university level could not fully accept Oneida's theological doctrines. Yet it was just such religious beliefs that were offered as justification for the elders' domination of community life.[32]

System Maintenance and System Change.   Oneida placed great restrictions on individual liberty. Everyone had an obligation to abide by the community's moral code. Morality was not necessarily dull or joyless, but one had no choice but to be moral. The community's system of criticism stood ready to correct any deviation from the norm. In addition, private choice in consumption was virtually nonexistent, except for a small allowance. Sexual activities were also regulated. Community norms determined both with whom one had relationships (ascending fellowship) and the method of birth control (male continence). It must be emphasized that all these restrictions were voluntarily accepted. Oneida's members could leave the settlement whenever they desired. However their religious faith predisposed them to willingly tolerate community control over their lives.

Oneida relied almost exclusively on its system of mutual criticism as a mechanism of social control. Those who criticized might be a select committee of spiritually advanced individuals, or the entire membership. If Noyes was present he usually played a major role in directing the session. Many members requested criticism as an aid to self-improvement. However a member was advised to submit to criticism if the leadership felt his activities warranted correction. Only Noyes stood immune to criticism from others, although he publicly criticized himself at times.

A meeting to perform criticism was generally informal but to the point. Critics would simply tell the person being criticized in a totally candid manner what they considered his failings to be. One's actions, attitudes, values, and emotions all might be the subject of judgment. For example, members could be criticized for idleness, irresponsibility, dogmatism, lack of self-respect, or involvement in an exclusive love affair. Receiving criticism could be an excruciating experience, causing strong men to sweat. Once the ordeal had been concluded, however, the subjects usually reported great exhilaration and happiness, a feeling of being cleansed. Indeed one former member later maintained, "I would gladly give many years of my life if I could have just one more criticism from John H. Noyes."[33]

Always a rebel and innovator, Noyes built Oneida as a genuinely experimental community in which new ideas and techniques were welcomed. Perfectionist theory sanctioned this outlook. The lot of man was to improve—not to stagnate—and improvement implied progressive change. Thus the community's members brought a spirit of creativity and ingenuity to their endeavors. Through trial and error and consistent inventiveness, they devised methods of mechanizing aspects of trap manufacture formerly carried out by hand. New household devices were created, including a dishwasher. Even social practices were put to experimental test. For example, the community's diet was varied in an attempt to promote better physical well-being. Similarly, faith healing was introduced, and later rejected as not yet effective.[34]

There was one area in which Oneida did not tolerate innovation. Although its religious beliefs permitted flexibility, the community could not be flexible on the question of the validity of religion. When young men with scientific training, including Noyes' own son Theodore, professed agnosticism, they introduced an ideological challenge utterly incompatible with community values, and no compromise was possible.

Skinner's Walden II.   *Walden II* is an attempt to design a perfect society according to the tenets of a psychological theory of learning. Written by B.F. Skinner in 1948, it suggests that behaviorism, a recent and controversial approach to the understanding of human conduct, can produce techniques of social management with the capacity to usher in a new "golden age." The behaviorist perspective asserts that people's actions can best be comprehended as their responses to the stimuli they perceive. Each response has some consequence for the organism, depending on the environment in which it acts. The central notion is that responses that are positively reinforced tend to be repeated. The validity of the hypothesis that negative reinforcement decreases the probability of a response is recognized as less certain.

From behaviorism as a method of understanding behavior, one can logically derive a method of controlling behavior. If human responses are governed by the kind and degree of reinforcement they lead to, anyone who can control the pattern of reinforcement can control the probability of response—that is, how people will behave. Following this reasoning, behaviorist techniques are employed in Walden II to regulate an entire community, thereby creating a utopia.

Geography and Architecture. Walden II is located close to a river in a rural valley surrounded on three sides by wooded hills. Beyond this meager description, plus a few adjectives affirming the "pleasant" character of the region, there is little discussion of the area's natural environment.[35] Surprisingly, in light of the author's commitment to a theory that explains behavior in terms of responses to external stimuli, no effort is made to analyze the impact of different geographic factors on human social organization, nor to explain the rationale for the selection of the site for Walden II.

Functional and pragmatic considerations recieve first priority with regard to the physical design of the community. A central main building, various farm buildings, and several workshops are placed to permit effective operation with minimal mutual interference. Within the central building are residence rooms, dining halls, schools, children's quarters, reading rooms, art studios—actually, rooms for every need the members might wish to satisfy in their "home." This elongated structure contains numerous tiers and wings, all interconnected to allow indoor access to services and recreational facilities during inclement weather. Aesthetically pleasing public areas are the focal points of social interaction. Members' rooms (each has his own, including husbands and wives) furnish a domain of peace, quiet, and privacy.

The central living facility seems to impose an architectural limit on total community population. Also, the structure of the main building has been planned to restrict population density in specific locations. For example, Walden II's largest auditorium holds a maximum of 200 persons, one-fifth of the membership. This limit reflects the community's distaste for crowds, which are deemed an ineffective and undesirable mode of securing excitement and social contact.[36]

Organizational Structure.

Government. Government in Walden II is constitutional, although the constitution is never fully described. Political decisions are made by Planners and Managers. The Planners hold general authority and have responsibility for the overall welfare of the community. They initiate basic policy, review the performance of Managers, and carry out some judicial functions. Managers are specialists in control of specific economic and social sectors, such as food, health, play, dining, and labor. The rise to managerial status takes place through gradual advancement in some field of expertise, in a manner akin to civil service. Together, Planners and Managers can define the scope of their own power. A unanimous vote of the former, combined with a two-thirds majority of the latter, is sufficient to amend the constitution.

Political life at Walden II virtually ceases once one moves beyond the realm of the officials. Community members neither elect representatives, debate issues, nor support policy alternatives. A member may make an individual protest against a decision he opposes, but he is prohibited from attempting to mobilize support for his position by arguing about the issue with others. Skinner's rationale for this overtly undemocratic system is that a science of behavior makes possible a science of government. Such a science has the capability of experimentally determining which programs will provide the greatest satisfaction for the individual and success for the community. Of course like all sciences, the science of government is best left to the experts.

Despite the absence of popular participation, it is claimed that residents of Walden II need have no fear of despotism. The community's leaders have no weapons, army, or police apparatus. On the contrary, their only mechanism for securing compliance with their decisions is positive reinforcement. Thus they will only be obeyed if obedience leads to greater happiness than rebellion.[37]

Economy. As a collective, Walden II owns and controls the means of production within the community. Its productive activities include agriculture, community services, and small industry. Jobs are allocated according to a labor credit system. Each member, male and female, owes the community 1200 labor credits a year; the credits are earned by doing work. The average rate of "pay" is one credit per hour, but the credit value of different jobs varies with their desirability. Thus an extremely pleasant job that many members are glad to carry out, such as working in the flower garden, earns only 0.1 credit an hour, whereas labor in the community sewer system receives 20 credits per hour. Under this system, Walden II's members are free to choose whatever job they wish. The laws of supply and demand presumably ensure that the available workers are distributed among the necessary assignments.

Distribution in Walden II is solidly egalitarian. Food, clothing, and medical care for every member are provided by the community. No one, regardless of his job or official position, receives extra privileges. Also, since the only private property permitted consists of objects members bring with them when they join, no one can accumulate wealth. The members reject conspicuous consumption; thus Walden II has little difficulty producing enough to meet its needs.[38]

Family.   Relationships between men and women at Walden II are monogamous. Couples usually marry while in their teens, there being no economic or social reasons for delay. Selection of mates, though essentially a matter of personal preference, is also an object of serious community concern. Once an "engagement" takes place, the couple visits the community's Manager of Marriages who proceeds to examine their interests, school records, and medical backgrounds. If any significant discrepancy in intelligence or psychological temperament is discerned, the Manager advises against marriage, and the recommendation is usually accepted.

Once married, the husband and wife begin a family life markedly different from that normal to American culture. At Walden II the family has no economic function, no division of labor (housekeeping has been communalized), and no childraising responsibilities. As a result, its only basis for existence is mutual affection. Neither mate is dependent on the other, for they both have identical social obligations and privileges, labor credit requirements, and status vis-à-vis the community. Long-term family stability is the norm, but conflict and extramarital affairs do occur. If counseling cannot effect a reconciliation, divorce is reluctantly granted.

Walden II encourages its members to have children, and raising and educating the young is a communal enterprise. Parents visit and play with their offspring, but such contacts are kept to a minimum. Child rearing, like so many other aspects of life at Walden II, is considered a science that requires the talents of skilled practitioners. Needless to say, an untrained mother is hardly adequate for this complex task. Moreover, the community desires a child to develop broad affective ties throughout the membership rather than intense love for its natural parents alone.[39]

Education.   Education begins in the community's Lower Nursery, where newborn infants are kept in large, glass-walled cubicles with controlled temperature and humidity. Life is fairly idyllic during this period, although a few minor discouragements are introduced to extend a child's perseverance. Children from 1 to 3 years are assigned to the Upper Nursery, a relatively similar arrangement, except that cubicles are replaced by small, group sleeping rooms.

Children from 3 to 6 undergo further ethical training, which is actually instruction in emotional development. As an example, one lesson teaches the principle "Get thee behind me, Satan"; in less theological phraseology, it conditions a child to endure delay of gratification with minimal unpleasantness. The lesson involves training a child to reduce his own discomfort when he is handed a lollipop but forbidden to eat it for a specified length of time. Such techniques as thinking of something else, engaging in distracting activity, or hiding the desired object are satisfactory responses to the problem.

While ethical instruction goes on, children move forward in other aspects of the educational process. They gradually acquire independence in daily activity, eventually moving from dormitories to adult quarters at age 17. At the same time, they are completing their academic training in a schoollike facility, which nevertheless lacks an institutional atmosphere. Since conditioning has reinforced the young people's natural curiosity, all that is needed is to provide them with the techniques of learning and let them go their own way. Full-time education generally concludes at the undergraduate level. However professional training (outside Walden II) is permitted for those who desire it, and materials for ongoing adult education are available.[40]

Human Aggregate.   Walden II was founded by a young doctor of psychology aided by a small number of committed associates. Membership is open to all, with a few exceptions (admission is denied to criminals and presumably to those who cannot pass the community's medical exam). New recruits must agree to obey the Walden code and to waive claims to any community property other than that which they bring with them on entrance. Within these limits, Walden II and its sister communities accept applicants as fast as they can be assimilated without endangering the stability of community life.

On becoming a member of Walden II, an individual finds himself in a society almost completely without status distinctions. To be sure, there is some functional differentiation. All members are divided into the occupational categories of Planner, Manager, scientist, or worker, and subclassifications thereof. However none of these divisions has meaning in terms of status in the community. All occupations have equal value. All titles are eliminated.

Community training probably produces a common personality structure among second-generation members. Such a structure is never fully outlined, but several of its elements are nonetheless quite apparent. For example, despite their having been conditioned, Walden II's members are clearly not automatons, performing the behavioral equivalent of salivation on cue. Rather, they are candid and lively. Their emotional repertoire emphasizes energy, affection, and tolerance at the expense of jealousy, ambition, and envy.[41]

A Behavior Setting: The Dining Hall.   Several small dining halls (combined capacity of 200) serve the Walden II membership. Each has its own decor, ranging from early American to Swedish to simulated English inn to modern. The diversity has a purpose. Eating in these dining halls effectively accustoms the community's children to housing interiors they may encounter outside Walden II.

The informal, self-service dining halls are designed to minimize discomfort and maximize efficiency. Although they must service a population five times their maximum capacity, the dining areas are rarely congested because the community encourages its members to adopt staggered living schedules. Meal hours are spread out to cover all the various personal timetables. Selection of one's living and eating schedule is totally unregulated. The community assumes that simply publicizing the hours when facilities are less crowded will automatically result in individual changes of preference in favor of such periods.[42]

Social Climate.

Personal Growth.   As part of its attempt to develop a perfect society, Walden II seeks to create a new man, with new motives and capacities. Fundamentally, Walden II's ideal member is capable of achieving personal happiness without interfering with the happiness of others. To accomplish this goal, he acquires a set of ethical values, or, in behaviorist terminology, he develops certain techniques of self-control. First the individual must learn to accept social equality; he must eliminate any desires that require someone else's defeat as an element in his satisfaction. Second, he must conquer feelings of jealousy and pride; thus the disappointments that cannot be avoided, such as the inability to attract a lover as well as someone else, can be accepted without resentment. Walden II members should demonstrate warmth, openness, and affection. At worst, they may be merely tolerant of their fellows; a preferable stance is that of offering encouragement and support to others.[43]

Personal Relationships.   Human relationships in Walden II are highly cohesive, despite the almost complete absence of activities in which the entire community participates. The major base for community loyalty is the members' belief that life at Walden II is highly satisfying and clearly preferable to living elsewhere. Gratitude for services performed by other members is never personalized but always extended to the community as a whole. There is also a lack of self-conscious subgroups or associations that might interfere with communal harmony. A significant factor in reducing tendencies toward subgroup identity and organization is the extent of equality in income, status, and privilege throughout the membership.

Cursory examination of life at Walden II reveals a markedly unregimented society. People may choose their own jobs, set their own hours, interact with whom they please, pursue whatever hobby interests them, and read any book in the library. There are some restrictions. Everyone must obey the Walden Code, the community's moral guidelines. At work one must follow the orders of the branch manager, but if this individual's decisions are not to one's liking, it is always possible to work at something else the following day. Members have no personal income, and their consumption choices are limited to whatever variety the community provides. Considered as a totality, these conditions hardly seem to be stifling.

However the appearance of spontaneity conceals the reality of prior psychological conditioning. Community members have been trained to act and to feel in prescribed ways. Whether such a background necessarily excludes all subsequent spontaneity is a question involving complex philosophical issues beyond our scope. Let us simply observe that Walden II's Planners acknowledge that their conditioning techniques determine the behavior, motives, and values of the membership. Since this control is exercised through positive reinforcement rather than through coercion, the Planners insist that those they govern do not feel forced to perform acts against their will. On the contrary, Walden II members experience the feeling of free action and free choice, the feeling that they are selecting that behavior which makes them happiest.[44]

System Maintenance and System Change.   The Walden Code is maintained to systematize the Do's and Don't's of community life. Some of its provisions include a prohibition against gossip and a ban on discussing the community with outsiders. In their typically professional manner, Walden II's managers devise special procedures for keeping the membership aware of these rules. Posting a notice in an appropriate place may prove sufficient for simple ordinances. More serious and complex statutes are likely to be discussed in weekly meetings.

The contents of the Walden Code are continually revised in accordance with experimental innovation and reports of member dissatisfaction. Enforcement of the code is based on the community's theory of the nature of man. According to behaviorism, men are neither naturally good nor naturally evil; they are however, malleable. Consequently Walden II employs operant conditioning as its major method of securing compliance with rules. By creating situations in which individuals are positively reinforced for following the statutes, the community induces voluntary observance of its precepts.

Nevertheless Walden II's conditioning processes are not foolproof, and on rare occasions members violate regulations. The infractions are usually minor, and rule violation is considered a symptom of personality disturbance rather than a crime. Those who break regulations are never punished or forced into obedience; they are referred to the community's psychologists for treatment. Since most mental or emotional disorders are discovered at a relatively early stage, therapy is usually successful.

Innovation is extremely common at Walden II, and the community registers delight at each new successful technique or invention. Whether the problem is the design of a tea cup or the elimination of awkwardness in social conversation, scientific experimentation is lauded as the pathway to satisfactory solutions and community betterment. As a result, all habits, customs, practices, and values are deemed fair game for Walden II's researchers. The only major restriction on innovation is that before new proposals are implemented they must prove themselves through rigorous experimentation based on the scientific method.[45]

Critical Analyses of Utopian Perspectives.   We are now in a position to evaluate the utopias just described. Are they cognizant of man's dependence on the environment? In what ways have they sought to cope with its challenges? Can the social orders designed withstand the criticisms of the antiutopians?

In general, all three utopias demonstrate only superficial understanding and treatment of man's relationship to the environment. More's *Utopia* is unique in seriously considering the question of location, particularly in terms of prospects for defense and trade. More recognized the vital importance of providing for an agricultural base to sustain his urban centers, although his treatment of this problem is sketchy. He primarily is concerned with assuring an adequate labor supply for the farmlands; other aspects of agriculture—techniques of cultivation, weather, and so on—do not receive attention.

Probably Utopia's most serious defect is its mechanism for guaranteeing a balance between agricultural productivity and population. More is aware of the possibility of overpopulation, but his remedy is military expansion into neighboring lands. Logically, of course, there is a fixed limit beyond which this policy cannot extend. More important for the short run, continued successful expansion requires the ability to maintain military superiority over foreign states.

Oneida's Perfectionists directed little attention to the environmental attributes of their community site, and they paid a heavy price for their oversight. Even though they were fortunate in acquiring fertile land with an ample water supply, their best efforts were insufficient to maintain a viable economy based on agriculture. Partly as a result of large amounts of capital made available to them, as well as the inventiveness of some of their neighbors, they escaped financial disaster and transformed themselves into a prosperous industrial enterprise. But industry proved to have side effects detrimental to Bible communism, including the necessities of hiring a separate class of employee outside the community and of sending the community's young to universities for technical education.

One might have expected Walden II to reflect increased concern for environmental issues. But to the contrary, Skinner's treatment of the environment is cursory. There is no detailed discussion of local geographic factors that might aid or hamper the growth of a community. The implication is that Walden II type settlements can exist anywhere. There is no indication that Skinner realizes that the transition from a single, small, isolated community to a national federation of communities involves qualitatively distinct environmental challenges, both social and physical. Not the least of these is the requirement that a nationwide utopia be capable of controlling its own growth, disposing of its wastes, and so on.

Although Skinner is thought to be an archenvironmentalist, his relative disregard of larger environmental issues poses difficulties. He forgets that societies are basically organizations to assure survival in a natural environment. There is a complex network of ecological forces that literally constitutes the ground on which Walden II rests. It is very unlikely that it will ever be possible to condition away earthquakes, hurricanes, crop failures, and other natural disasters.

In the development of *Walden II*, the novel, fortune shines on the young idealists. Money somehow appears; skills are somehow mastered. Although the first members have not experienced behavioral conditioning themselves, there are no severe social or organizational difficulties. The list could go on and on. In fact, one could legitimately dismiss this aspect of Skinner's fantasy simply on the basis of reasonable skepticism based on experience in the same culture from which Walden II was to have grown. But much better evidence is available.

Skinner's novel encouraged some individuals to attempt the development of a Walden II of their own, and one group has published an account of its first years. They encountered numerous problems for which their model did not provide solutions. How does a rural commune acquire sufficient revenue to subsist, much less expand? How much maintenance do vehicles used regularly on country roads require? Who is supposed to know how to provide that maintenance? What does a community do when a member falsifies his labor credit reports and attacks the labor manager when the fraud is discovered? Through enormous effort and perseverance, the builders of the experimental Walden II have managed to keep their community in operation. But they have not progressed very far on the road to a golden age, nor do they appear likely to move much farther.[46]

What about critiques of the internal workings of utopia? Do our examples reveal that utopia denies human freedom? Are these societies static and stagnant? Have they eliminated all conflict but also all progress? Each of the utopias offers a distinct aggregate of institutions and values relevant to these questions. In none of them, however, does the potential for human development appear very promising. In fact, the survival of the utopias themselves seems unlikely.

More's Utopia is the most static and stable of the three. It is authoritarian, but with sufficient dispersion of power to avoid the excesses of despotism. As a slaveholding culture, however, it has within it a significant group of people whose interests are best served by the society's downfall. The factor most likely to result in Utopia's historical demise is that it is both preindustrial and expansionist.

More deliberately sought to avoid the conflict endemic in the bourgeois economic order by creating in Utopia an uncomplicated socialism based on agriculture and craft production. However as Utopia's population rises, she must expand to survive, and to expand, she must have military superiority over her neighbors. More expected such superiority to derive from the ingenuity of Utopia's leaders and the dedication of the soldiers. Yet on this point the historical lesson is clear. It was commonplace in the early years of European imperialism for stable and successful empires to find themselves suddenly defenseless before the military technology that capitalism had placed at the disposal of the Western states. One can almost imagine Utopia's legions marching out to confront the artillery and rifles of British regulars. The conclusion of the lesson is worth remembering. A static society in an unstable world is the waiting victim of more aggressive cultures whose dynamic institutions have generated increased technological and economic power.

Oneida encountered problems of a different kind in its attempt to deal with issues of authority, freedom, and innovation. The Perfectionist structure essentially reduced to one-man rule. However dictatorship was made palatable by theology, and Oneida's members willingly served Noyes as they willingly served God. Moreover, this was a despotism ideologically committed to improvement and technical innovation.

But static theology and a dynamic economy and technology made for an unstable social mixture. The community inevitably faced a problem of succession. Noyes' advancing age signified the passing of an entire generation, and the young community members, with secular educations, lacked the orthodox faith of their parents. Thus they were both unsuitable as leaders and unwilling to accept continual second-class status in relation to the "spiritual" superiors. The bond of common belief disintegrated just when it was needed most.

In addition, Oneida's economic structure no longer reinforced a commitment to group living. In its effort to adjust to the demands of an industrialized market economy, the community had transformed itself from a society of comrades working together to a colony of managers who supervised their employees during the day and returned to their "communist" home at night. The mutual dependence of work in a common endeavor had been replaced by the more passive and autonomous relationship of common ownership. When religious leadership collapsed, there no longer existed a rationale for superimposing a communitarian social structure over a capitalist economic base. A joint stock company could operate as profitably as a utopia, and Oneida became just another business in a competitive economic system.

For Walden II, freedom is no problem; it is a myth. It is said that man has always been conditioned by his environment. Behaviorism simply brings such conditioning under human control. There is no difficulty with political power, since politics has ceased to exist. Government is a science, and questions relevant to it are solved experimentally. Finally, when innovation is carried out with proper scientific rigor, it supplies solutions to all other problems rather than being a source of difficulty.

How are we to evaluate such claims? It may be possible using behaviorist parlance to define away freedom, but it is less simple to eliminate power in this way. Walden II's Planners have virtually unlimited capacity to control the behavior, the motivations, and the thoughts of the membership. Lord Acton's warning that power corrupts can be translated into behaviorist terminology—the environment produced by the exercise of power may elicit increasingly ruthless and immoral responses from those who experience it. Skinner's dismissal of this issue is particularly disturbing, because the first Planners will have received their conditioning in twentieth-century America rather than in the Walden II children's quarters.

In his use of innovation in Walden II, Skinner gives science a task for which it is utterly unsuited—the development of a community's ethics. To be sure, the experimental method can be used to assist in reaching a goal already set. But science alone cannot select objectives for humanity; it cannot design a utopia. Over the long run, Walden II furiously provides answers without any means of ascertaining the value and meaning of questions. Walden II will apparently innovate continuously without ever reaching or defining a goal. Stasis will have been conquered, only to be replaced by perpetual and purposeless motion.

The Antiutopians.   In light of the utopian theorists' commitment to human perfection, it may seem surprising that their projections have engendered a formidable array of opponents. The critics do not represent a mere aggregate of those who disagree with one or another facet of one or another utopia. Rather, they object to the utopian effort. Thus the Russian philosopher Nicolas Berdiaev argues, "Utopias appear to be much more capable of realization than they did in the past. And we find ourselves faced by a much more distressing problem. How can we prevent their final realization?"[47] What reasons lead men of good will to vehemently reject the prospect of utopia?

We can note only briefly some of the more frequent and intense objections. First there is the conservative reaction. All utopias imply criticism; none fully legitimate the society in which they are created. Those who are defenders of the status quo, who believe that the society is as good as is humanly possible, interpret the drive to utopia as a futile and dangerous quest that risks decline and degeneracy without prospect of success.

Second, there is the romantic critique. Utopias are rational; they are orderly efforts to form societies according to specific principles and hypotheses. They come into conflict with those who demand the triumph of the aesthetic, a world open to uninhibited spontaneity, creativity, and self-expression. The imagination is without rational or moral limits, and that minimal coherence necessary to every planned society may be perceived as a restriction on the vitality of art.[48]

A third basis of opposition to utopia concerns the prospects for human freedom in a perfect society. To the extent that they prescribe a new social order, all utopias deny people the opportunity of determining their own destiny. Beyond this general coerciveness, specific political and social structures common to many utopias can be considered threats to human freedom. Utopias often include a monolithic and centralized state apparatus, powerful enough to defend the perfect society and to provide for the popular welfare, but also powerful enough to crush any possible dissent. This central control may be lodged in the hands of an intellectual elite, or it may be buttressed by technology, the basis of Orwell's nightmare of *1984*.[49]

In addition, science and technology represent to antiutopians potential dangers, regardless of their connection to some totalitarian administration. The very machines that yield abundance may require the society that depends on them to orient its social life to their operational requirements. Indeed, Engels, in a characteristically determinist but unusually pessimistic declaration, suggested that the following sign be hung above the entrance to any industrial factory: "Abandon all autonomy ye who enter here."[50] The needs of men must be subordinated to the needs of the engines of production.

Still another criticism of utopia is directed toward the notion of pure social perfection. Once a perfect order has been established, there is no longer any basis for improvement or innovation: utopia must remain a static society, ever faithful to its ideal routine. Such a state denies to its members that creative impulse which motivated the utopian writers themselves, the desire to change the world for the better. Without such progressive movement, a society could only permit the perfection of uniformity and stagnation.

A fifth reason for viewing utopia with dismay involves the quality of "perfected" human life. The many elements of this argument include the contention that neurosis is the fundamental source of great art, as well as the elitist view that abundance would be an unspeakable bore. But a deeper thesis suggests that human happiness and pleasure cannot be wholly divorced from pain and unhappiness. There is a dialectical relationship between the poles of experience; one state cannot be known without the possibility of encountering its opposite. An effort to eliminate the depths of despair may restrict the heights of ecstasy. We believe that this view explains the astounding speech of the Savage in Aldous Huxley's antiutopian novel *Brave New World:*

> But I don't want comfort. I want God, I want poetry, I want real danger, I want freedom, I want goodness. I want sin. . . . I'm claiming the right to be unhappy. . . . Not to mention the right to grow old and ugly and impotent; the right to have syphilis and cancer; the right to have too little to eat; the right to be lousy; the right to live in constant apprehension of what may happen to-morrow; the right to catch typhoid; the right to be tortured by unspeakable pains of every kind. . . . I claim them all.[51]

Up to this point we have discussed sociological, philosophical, and political objections to utopia. Are some antiutopian positions related to environmental theory? Of course certain of the arguments just presented can be supported by an analysis of environmental factors. For example, the contention that utopian writers ignore historical men and forces can be broadened to include a charge of similar treatment of natural law. Rarely is a utopia premised on a concrete analysis of the ongoing interaction of living people and an actual environment, and the social implications thereof.

The argument that utopias attempt the unmanageable task of controlling all human experience can be reinforced by reference to the complexity of the interaction between man and nature. Dynamic ecosystems, of which human societies are a part, cannot necessarily be manipulated to serve the needs of every conceivable social institution or the whims of political leaders. Ecosystems can be modified, but changes in one area may bring adverse ecological consequences in another. As botanist Paul Sears observes, "Too often utopian writers have failed to appreciate that spontaneous interplay—to them lost motion—is essential to a flexible and enduring biological and social system. They are like engineers who insist upon too tight a range of tolerance and thus condemn a mechanism to become frozen in the course of operation."[52]

Environmental theory discourages any predilection toward a static social order. Ecosystems may be in equilibrium, but they are in an open and moving equilibrium that responds to ongoing macro changes in geology, weather, and other environmental factors. In the face of such environmental pressures, human planners must eventually make adjustments, or find their schemes adjusted involuntarily.

The most powerful environmental criticism of utopia concerns the ability of the planet to provide sufficient resources to support its human population. From this perspective, Thomas Malthus is the arch antiutopian. His thesis stipulated that prosperity inevitably encourages increased human reproduction. Any rise in the standard of living would inevitably be brought down again by the pressure of additional mouths to feed. Mankind was doomed to chronic poverty because of unrestricted population growth. Needless to say, with world population expected to reach 7 billion in the year 2000, the ghost of Malthus is still with us, as are other predictors of doom by overpopulation.[53]

The social devices usually relied on by utopians to eliminate poverty and guarantee abundance lead precisely to those institutional arrangements most suspect to antiutopians. Thus technological innovation to improve production, centralized economic and political organization under technocratic control, and state power sufficient to regulate human reproduction, may all contribute to meeting man's desires for material well-being. But these are also the possible agencies of uniformity, stagnation, and tyranny. Thus critics of utopia depict mankind as facing a Hobson's choice: life in poverty, or subordination to the technical and social organization that can assure abundance.

At this point one might conclude that the critique of utopia is devastating. Each of man's efforts to create a perfect social order is flawed and/or undesirable. But such an evaluation is premature. The reader is urged to take one more look at our utopias. This time, instead of seeking perfection, consider whether there are suggested specific institutions, values, or processes superior to those in our present society. For if utopias have failed in the quest for an ideal civilization, they nevertheless reveal innumerable ways in which the status quo might be improved.

For example, Oneida and Walden II suggest that children can be raised communally without psychological damage and with enormously increased efficiency. Many Americans who were stunned in 1956 when the

Soviet Union orbited the first space satellite had assumed that a communist society would be incapable of technical or scientific creativity. The Bible communists of Oneida had demonstrated a century before that a communal economy could give rise to technological innovation, even to innovations threatening to the community's values. Thomas More's endorsement of a socialist economy and religious toleration were likewise ahead of the times. This list could be extended. Indeed, Auguste Comte, the founder of positivism, insisted, "There is no Utopia so wild as not to offer some incontestable advantages."[54]

The environment, technology, existing political and social relationships, and so on, set parameters that limit the future of mankind. Utopians err in assuming that limits do not exist, and they are doomed to failure when they reach for the sky. Yet they provide a valuable service. For the point at which man can move no farther is not known in advance. On the contrary, it appears historically as the interaction between human desire and imagination and the structure of the material world. It is through the quest for utopia that we reach these outer boundaries and learn of the range of possibilities for experimentation and change. Oscar Wilde said it well. "A map of the world that does not include Utopia is not worth even glancing at, for it leaves out the one country at which Humanity is always landing. And when Humanity lands there, it looks out, and seeing a better country, sets sail. Progress is the realization of Utopias."[55]

REFERENCES

1. See Chapter 2 for a more detailed discussion of these issues.
2. Meadows, D. H., Meadows, D. L., Randers, J., and Behrens, W. W., III. *The limits to growth*. Signet, New York, 1972, p. 29.
3. For discussions of the nature of the utopian genre, see Lewis Mumford, *The story of utopias* (Viking, New York, 1922), pp. 11–26; Glenn Negley and J. Max Patrick, *The quest for utopia* (H. Schuman, New York, 1952), pp. 2–8; J. O. Hertzler, *The history of utopian thought* (Macmillan, New York, 1923), pp. 257–269.
4. In all cases, the best way to comprehend a specific utopia is to read it in its entirety. Those with only a cursory interest in the subject are referred to the following texts, most of which combine excerpts and commentary: Marie Louise Berneri, *Journey through utopia* (Beacon Press, Boston, 1950); Mumford, *op. cit.;* Negley and Patrick, *op. cit.;* Hertzler, *op. cit.*
5. Mumford, *op. cit.*, pp. 29–56; Negley and Patrick, *op. cit.*, pp. 259–261; Hertzler, *op. cit.*, pp. 7–120; Berneri, *op. cit.*, pp. 1–45.
6. Mumford, *op. cit.*, pp. 59–60, 103–109; Negley and Patrick, *op. cit.*, pp. 313–347, 360–378; Hertzler, *op. cit.*, pp. 69–74, 121–127, 146–165; Berneri, *op. cit.*, pp. 52–58, 88–102, 126–137.

7. For general discussions of nineteenth-century utopias, see Mumford, *op. cit.*, pp. 151–168, 178–183; Negley and Patrick, *op. cit.*, pp. 551–579, Hertzler, *op. cit.*, pp. 181–186, 204–208; Berneri, *op. cit.*, pp. 207–234, 243–281.

8. Hertzler, *op. cit.*, pp. 236–244; Negley and Patrick, *op. cit.*, pp. 106–135.

9. Hertzler, *op. cit.*, pp. 244–254; Mumford, *op. cit.*, pp. 183–189; Negley and Patrick, *op. cit.*, pp. 226–250; Berneri, *op. cit.*, pp. 293–308.

10. Negley and Patrick, *op. cit.*, pp. 262–267; Berneri, *op. cit.*, pp. 58–61.

11. Gallagher, Ligeia (Ed.), *More's Utopia and its critics*. Scott, Foresman, Chicago, 1964, pp. 22–25.

12. *Ibid.*, pp. 23, 26–27.

13. *Ibid*, pp. 27–28, 23–24.

14. *Ibid.*, pp. 37, 62–64.

15. *Ibid.*, pp. 27, 46, 49.

16. *Ibid*, pp. 32–33.

17. *Ibid.*, pp. 38–44.

18. *Ibid.*, pp. 63, 65.

19. *Ibid.*, p. 49.

20. *Ibid.*, pp. 28, 48, 59.

21. Parker, Robert A.. *A yankee saint*. Putnam, New York, 1935, pp. 15–117; Carden, Maren L. *Oneida: Utopian community to modern corporation*. Johns Hopkins Press, Baltimore, 1969, pp. 1–17.

22. Robertson, Constance Noyes. *Oneida Community: An autobiography, 1851–1876* Syracuse University Press, Syracuse, N.Y., 1970, p. 30; Nordhoff, C., *The communistic societies of the United States*. Hillary House, New York, 1960, p. 262.

23. Muncy, Raymond Lee. *Sex and marriage in utopian communities*. Indiana University Press, Bloomington, 1973, pp. 177–178; Robertson, *op. cit.*, pp. 30–45.

24. Robertson, *op. cit.*, pp. 14–15, 134, 214–215; Nordhoff, *op. cit.*, p. 279; Carden, *op. cit.*, pp. 46–49, 85–86.

25. Robertson, *op. cit.*, pp. 212–264; Nordhoff, *op. cit.*, pp. 261–264, 279–285; Parker, *op. cit.*, pp. 205–210; Carden, *op. cit.*, pp. 39, 41–43, 66.

26. Muncy, *op. cit.*, pp. 173–192; Carden, *op. cit.*, pp. 49–65; Robertson, *op. cit.*, pp. 281–283, 311–358.

27. Kanter, Rosabeth Moss. *Commitment and community*. Harvard University Press, Cambridge, Mass., 1972, p. 14. Carden, *op. cit.*, pp. 93–94, 67–69; Nordhoff, *op. cit.*, pp. 284–285; Robertson, *op. cit.*, pp. 173–187.

28. Robertson, *op. cit.*, pp. 90–91, 348–349, 336, 23; Estlake, Allan. *The Oneida Community*. George Redway, London, 1900, pp. 33–34.

29. Estlake, *ibid.*, p. 10; Carden, *op. cit.*, pp. 67, 94–96; Parker, *op. cit.*, pp. 263–264.

30. Parker, *op. cit.*, p. 97; Robertson, *op. cit.*, pp. 31, 41–45, 84, 87, 140, 156–167.

31. Kanter, *op. cit.*, p. 15; Robertson, *op. cit.*, pp. 51, 58, 117; Parker, *op. cit.*, pp. 110–112; Carden, *op. cit.*, pp. 23–25.

32. Carden, *op. cit.,* pp. 93–98; Nordhoff, *op. cit.,* p. 286; Robertson, *op. cit.,* 46–47, 66, 78, 83.

33. Robertson, *op. cit.,* pp. 128–149; Parker, *op. cit.,* pp. 215–224; Carden, *op. cit.,* pp. 71–86; Estlake, *op. cit.,* p. 68.

34. Carden, *op. cit.,* pp. 65–71; Nordhoff, *op. cit.,* pp. 285–286; Robertson, *op. cit.,* pp. 228–229.

35. Skinner, B. F. *Walden II.* Macmillan, New York, 1948, pp. 15–17, 21.

36. *Ibid.,* pp. 23–27, 40–45, 79, 154, 247.

37. *Ibid.,* pp. 54–55, 68–69, 195–196, 232–236, 263–292.

38. *Ibid.,* pp. 51–53, 63–64, 75–80, 172.

39. *Ibid.,* pp. 131–137, 140–148.

40. *Ibid.,* pp. 96–101, 107–108, 113–124.

41. *Ibid.,* pp. 25–28, 55–56, 78–79, 88–94, 101, 127, 133, 139–141, 160, 162, 223–226, 233–237, 249–250.

42. *Ibid.,* pp. 46–50.

43. *Ibid.,* pp. 57, 102–103, 127, 141, 174–177, 237.

44. *Ibid.,* pp. 54, 57, 90, 147, 169–170, 199–200, 257–264.

45. *Ibid.,* pp. 29–30, 172–175, 196–199.

46. Kinkade, K. *A Walden Two Experiment.* Morrow, New York, 1972.

47. Berdiaev's statement is used as an introduction by Aldous Huxley in his antiutopian novel *Brave New World* (Harper & Row, New York, 1946).

48. For a fuller analysis of the conservative and romantic critiques of Utopia, see Judith Shklar, *After Utopia* (Princeton University Press, Princeton, N.J., 1957).

49. Two of the most famous antiutopian novels, Huxley's *Brave New World (op. cit.)* and George Orwell's *1984* (Secker & Warburg, London, 1951) depict totalitarian states of the future.

50. *Marx & Engels: Selected works.* Foreign Languages Publishing House, Moscow, 1962, p. 637. Also see Eugen Weber, The anti-Utopia of the twentieth century. In George Kateb (Ed.), *Utopia.* Atherton Press, New York, 1971, pp. 82–83.

51. Huxley, *op. cit.,* p. 288. See Kateb, *op. cit.,* pp. 17–19, and George Kateb, *Utopia and its enemies* (Free Press of Glencoe, London, 1963), pp. 17–19.

52. Sears, Paul. Utopia and the living landscape. In Frank Manuel (Ed.), *Utopias and utopian thought.* Houghton Mifflin, Boston, 1966, pp. 146–147.

53. See Malthus, T. R., *An essay on population* (J. M. Dent, London, 1914); D. V. Glass (Ed.), *Introduction to Malthus* (Frank Cass, London, 1959), and Ann Ehrlich and Paul Ehrlich, *Population, resources, and environment* (Freeman, San Francisco, 1970).

54. Berneri, *Journey through utopia, op. cit.,* introductory quotations preceding p. 1.

55. *Ibid.*

CHAPTER TWELVE

Coping with Environmental Impact

In Chapter 1 we pointed out that a social ecological approach views the environment from the perspective of the individual. We now attempt to derive conclusions and to develop practical guidelines regarding human environments. Each of us is involved in selecting and coping with a diversity of everyday environments. Each of us must make choices regarding environments every day. Should I go to this university, or that one? Should I move to this city, or that one? Should I take this job, or that one? Should I join this group, or that one? Should I send my child to this day care facility, or that one?

Two related developments, by increasing the available range of environmental options, have dramatically increased the necessity of individual choice. First, there is increasing openness and flexibility in our society. More women are working and entering professional life. Residential change is increasingly common (e.g., about half of all American families move at least once during a 5-year period). Alternate life styles—urban communes, single-parent families, and open marriages—also broaden individual choice. In an open society such as ours, where our task is "not . . . adapting to what *is*, but . . . working out what *is to be*,"[1] each individual faces more choices than ever before.

Second, technological advances and economic well-being have resulted in an overabundance of attractive stimuli and life choices. Lipowski has suggested that our society offers too many attractive options and thereby promotes the development of conflict between incompatible approach tendencies. Conflict is generated when there is a diversity of equally attractive alternatives with no relevant information allowing one to arrive at realistic choices.[2]

People usually base their environmental choices on inadequate or incomplete information. This often leads to selecting an "incompatible" environment. The high turnover and dropout rates characteristic of most environments indicate that the environments people select often become seriously unsatisfactory. For example, Astin and Panos found that 44% of the college students they studied either transferred to another institution or temporarily or permanently dropped out of higher education.[3] Employee alienation, low morale, and high dropout and turnover rates are prevalent in many work environments.[4] Psychiatric treatment programs often have dropout rates ranging between 25 and 60%.[5]

We have shown that environments have differential impacts on people. This suggests that it would be helpful to have more accurate and complete information about the entire range of common human environments. Four other converging lines of evidence support this conclusion. First, investigators who have observed the same people in different real-life settings have almost invariably concluded that both characteristics of settings and the interactions between persons and settings consistently account for substantial proportions of the variance in a wide range of individual behaviors.[6]

Second, the failure to systematically include environmental and setting variables in understanding behavior has severely limited the accuracy of prediction. For example, Arthur reviewed personnel prediction studies in military organizations and discovered that the predictive validity of psychological tests and other background characteristics varied over different adjustment and performance criteria and in different subject populations. He wrote that there is currently a "sound barrier" effect, since "no matter how much information about the individual one adds to the predictive equation, one cannot bring the correlation coefficient between individual characteristics and prediction criteria much above about .40."[7] The nature of the environment in which behavior is to take place must be carefully considered if more accurate predictions of human performance are to be made. Similar conclusions have been derived in other areas—for example, the prediction of violent behavior[8] and the prediction of absconding or runaway behavior from correctional institutions.[9]

Third, psychiatric and correctional treatment outcome studies indicate that there is little or no relationship between a person's behavior in and out of an institution. Ellsworth and his colleagues obtained data on the outcome of psychiatric hospitalization as perceived by staff and by schizophrenic patients and their relatives. Surprisingly, no congruence appeared between patients' initial hospital adjustment and their community behavior before admission. In addition, there was very little relationship between staff-rated adjustment at the time of hospital release and family-rated adjustment only 3 weeks later.[10]

Sinclair studied the characteristics of British probation hostels. He defined the failure rate of a hostel as the proportion of boys who left as the result of an absconding or an offense. The failure rates of 46 regimes varied from a low of 13.5% to a high of 78.1%. The differences in failure rates among the regimes could not be explained by either the personal background characteristics or the previous criminal histories of the boys. In fact, Sinclair noted

> that 17 years previous experience counted as little in comparison with the immediate impact of the hostel environment while the boys were in it. But the gratifying evidence of a hostel's ability to influence its present residents for good carries with it a less welcome corollary. If the effects of 17 years of family training can be modified almost overnight, how long can we expect the impact of one year's hostel training to last? It is not surprising that when boys have left the hostel it is not usually the differences in their past hostel environments that count, but the differences in the environments to which they go.[11]

These results indicate that individual background characteristics and behavior or improvement within an institution do not adequately predict postinstitutional behavior. Since the community environment to which a patient must adapt is quite different from the institutional or program environment, it may be unreasonable to expect a significant relationship between institutional treatment and community outcome. The inevitable conclusion is that the community settings in which released residents must function critically affect their postinstitutional behavior and outcome. Thus these studies lend further support to the notion that the sociophysical milieu is an important determinant of behavior.

Fourth, the selection of environments, particularly long-term and enduring environments, may make an enormous difference in personality development. Skeels' work indicates that the placement of institutionalized children into supportive adoptive homes can make a remarkable difference in their later occupational achievement and income, in their marital and family status, and so forth (see Chapter 1). It is highly unlikely that these children would have achieved the level of development they did if they had remained institutionalized.[12]

Bronfenbrenner and his colleagues have made comparative studies of socialization in more than a dozen countries. In summary, Bronfenbrenner states:

> In the course of this work I encountered for the first time a phenomenon I had not previously experienced as a researcher: nonoverlapping distributions between groups of subjects. In other words, in certain respects children brought up in different cultures were markedly different in their behavior. So much so that one could identify their country of origin on the basis of their behavior with virtually no error. Moreover, such cross-cultural variability had implications of social as well as scientific significance: the young human organism, it appeared, was exceedingly malleable; there was hope for the future.[13]

These results support the conclusions that environments may have very important impacts and that people can develop and grow in response to favorable environmental conditions. One cannot overemphasize the extent to which human environments may shape their inhabitants, thus the importance of adequately selecting the environments in which people function. Systematic information about social and physical environments is of utility precisely because people vary their behavior substantially in accordance with the characteristics of their social and physical settings.

Choosing and Creating Environments. Some of the evidence presented, particularly in relation to the differential effects of enduring environments, comes close to supporting a hypothesis of environmental determinism (see Chapter 2). Of course it is also true that people can cope with and master their environment. In addition, environmental possibilities are not static. New developments continually open up new possibilities. People can select their own environments, and even when there is a strong environmental influence, the individual may have a choice about "succumbing" to it. In fact, environments may have differential impacts mainly because people select the environments that are likely to have certain impacts. In this view, the evidence presented for environmental impact is really evidence that people differentially choose environments that have the impact they desire. For example, Wachtel points out that

> the understanding of any one person's behavior in an interpersonal situation solely in terms of the stimuli *presented* to him gives only a partial and misleading picture for, to a very large extent, these stimuli are *created* by

him. They are responses to his own behaviors, events he has played a role in bringing about, rather than occurrences independent of who he is and over which he has no control.[14]

Wachtel is saying that a great deal of a person's environment is engendered by his own behavior. Thus people create certain social environments, which then "reciprocate" by fostering certain behaviors and attitudes. Human behavior is both chosen and caused. People actively select and create their own environments. Environments also actively select and "create" their own people. In addition, people seldom have adequate power to change the environmental conditions other people have created. This is particularly true for young children and for the aged, but it is also generally the case in any environment featuring an imbalance of power. Residents in most correctional facilities have limited power to change their sociophysical environment. This is also true of patients in most psychiatric programs, of students in most junior high and high school classrooms, of employees in most work situations, and even of the individuals in many families. Although people are not passively molded by their environment, neither is their environment passively molded by them.

These considerations support the notion that increased information about human environments can enhance human coping and personal growth. Each individual must choose the most beneficial course of action for him (i.e., the most beneficial environment or set of environments). This problem of selecting the most advantageous environmental option links the geographic theory of possibilism (see Chapter 2) to the other social sciences. We must be able to identify the quantity and quality of information an individual has about his environment. A person who is unaware of an environmental option or of a characteristic of the environment cannot consider this characteristic in making a decision. How we perceive an environment (i.e., the information we have about it) determines what that environment will be like for us.

For example, Betty Meggers derived a new dimension on which environments could be characterized—their agricultural potential[15] (see Chapter 2). When she used the new dimension she was able to relate the environment (the agricultural potential) to the development of culture. Thus new environmental dimensions may allow us to develop new perspectives and to identify previously obscure relationships. Finally, satisfaction and functioning in an environment depend as much on the expectations of the individual as they do on the characteristics of the milieu. Satisfaction is a "negotiated settlement" between what an individual wants and expects and what an environment has to offer. Morale and performance can change because the individual's expectations or perceptions change (i.e., his information changes), or they can change because the environment itself changes.

We have attempted to demonstrate the need for an increase in the availability of information about environments. We have pointed out that defining environments in new ways may lead to new verifiable generalizations. We have argued for a pluralistic position; that is, the environment must be defined in broad terms, and potential dimensions must be drawn from radically different environmental concepts. Both social and physical environmental dimensions are necessary. We attempt now to increase people's feelings of freedom and control by providing them with information that is useful in coping with their everyday environments. In the next section we briefly review some tentative conclusions about environmental impact. These are not established facts; they are reasonable hypotheses or working guidelines that should help individuals gather relevant information about the environments in which they must function.

Tentative Conclusions Regarding Human Environments.

The Weather and Human Behavior.

1. The work on heat and human behavior indicates that heat tends to reduce performance levels. It may also increase the variability of performance. These effects depend on intervening variables such as the level and quality of supervision, the degree of acclimatization to heat, whether performance is measured in the morning or afternoon (heat makes more difference in the afternoon, probably because people are more tired), and the intelligence of the individual (heat seems to affect less able students more).

2. Excessive heat is related to increased urban mortality rates. Again, there are many mediating factors, including the age and physical condition of the individual, and whether air-conditioning is available.

3. Excessive heat may facilitate hostility and violence; for example, heat is one factor that contributes to urban riots. There is also a tendency for people to be rated as less attractive under hot (and subjectively uncomfortable) conditions.

4. Certain aspects of the weather may have a stimulating or arousing effect. High and/or rising pressure has been related to better health and better performance. Low and/or falling pressure has been related to a decrease in perceptual-motor performance and an increase in accidents, physical symptoms, and dispensary visits. Cool, calm days with low humidity appear to be best for performance.

5.   Various winds, including the Chamsin in Israel and the Foehn in the Alps, seem to have negative effects on health and performance. One study found that accident rates went up in the 4-hour periods preceding the onset of the Foehn, suggesting an anticipatory effect.

6.   There are seasonal variations in social indices such as police calls and admissions to mental hospitals. For example, fair weather is generally associated with increased police activity. Social indices such as hospital admissions and suicides appear to be higher in the summer than in the fall and winter. Possible mediating variables include increased heat, more daylight hours, and social variables such as children being on vacation and more interpersonal contact and interaction in the summer. There is also some evidence that more suicides may occur in conditions of falling pressure or pressure variability.

7.   There is substantial individual variability in thermal comfort standards (i.e., in what is a comfortable temperature). As usual, there are a host of mediating variables (sex and age of individual, type of clothing, type of work being performed) to be considered.

8.   There are strong, long-standing human beliefs regarding the full moon. It is thus plausible to assume that the full moon has some effects on human activity which are mediated in part by the amount of light it casts.

Climate and weather variables have generally been treated as stressful. This conceptualization is related to findings like performance decrements, increased hospital admissions, and suicide and mortality rates. Somewhat smaller and more naturally occurring mood and performance changes related to day-to-day variations in weather variables are probably quite prevalent and are in need of further study. Performance enhancement and other adaptive effects may also occur. This is consistent with Huntington's belief in the stimulating effects of certain climatic conditions and with Lynn's suggestion that climatic conditions may have a facilitating effect on economic growth. The same climatic conditions may have both adaptive and maladaptive effects; thus further work on the weather and human behavior should assess both enhancements and decrements in mood and performance variables.

An important issue relates to the role of compensatory or adaptive behavior in coping with, and thus possibly masking, weather effects. Within broad limits, people can get used to almost any climate and temperature. It is possible that man may adapt too well to his own successful efforts in controlling his microclimate (e.g., air-conditioning) and ecoclimate (e.g., control over the weather). Greater control means less variability in environmental conditions, thus reduced adaptive capacity.

These tentative conclusions, and the overall conceptualizations of weather effects, may be helpful to individuals in choosing and planning environments. The knowledge that excessive heat may lower attractiveness ratings and increase irritability or aggression should caution people against making hasty judgments under hot conditions. This may be relevant to employer hiring and firing decisions. Some people may find that their mood and judgment fluctuate with certain changes in climatic conditions. These people may even discover that anticipatory effects occur and that it is useful for them to monitor their behavior in relation to climatic changes.

For example, Kritzinger was concerned about the possible danger of solar activity and established the SOWELA broadcasts to warn certain medical patients about potentially threatening solar events. The warnings, on a numerical scale from 1 (insignificant) to 9 (powerfully threatening), were disseminated on the radio like smog warnings for the benefit of pregnant women, persons suffering from pulmonary hemorrhages, and so on.[16] One problem with an early warning system of this type is that some people become so anxious and tense that the solar activity (or whatever they are being warned against) meets their expectations and becomes "powerfully threatening." In this connection, present-day smog warnings probably have both beneficial and harmful effects.

Information about seasonal variations in police activity, mental hospital admissions, and the use of recreational facilities can help managers make decisions about vacation schedules and monthly or quarterly allocation of hospital budgets. The general conceptualization of weather effects can help the individual, the planner, and the social science researcher in formulating and understanding various mood and performance changes that may be related to weather variables.

Architectural Variables: Physical Space and Building Design.

9.   Distance is related to friendship formation and the use of recreational, social, and other public facilities. It is important to distinguish between physical and functional distance, but it is clear that distance is a prime variable in determining whether people will meet and whether they will develop and continue a friendship. Mediating variables must be taken into account. For example, the life cycle phase of the individual is important, and friendship formation in special interest groups (e.g., a gourmet society) may transcend distance variables.

10.   The organization of space into closed versus open cubicles is related to mood and behavior. People in closed cubicles interact more and usually have higher morale and a greater feeling of personal security. However individuals who are incompatible with the group are more likely to become "social isolates"; that is, a closed cubicle situation may be more

detrimental for people who do not fit in. Open cubicles may result in wider friendship choices and less personal animosity, since people are not arbitrarily thrown together. Similar conclusions hold for open versus enclosed office settings.

11.   The design and arrangement of buildings and urban environments may facilitate or inhibit social interaction and the development of a cohesive climate. For example, a building may encourage interaction through a compact layout and the provision of central areas in which people can gather. Osmond's distinction between sociopetal and sociofugal environments allows us to conceptualize the results in this area. For mental hospital wards, Osmond favors radial designs which he feels encourage interaction by eliminating hallways and furnishing central recreation and meeting areas.

12.   The arrangement of chairs and other furniture may also facilitate or inhibit social interaction. This conclusion is drawn from work on furniture rearrangements on psychiatric wards, experimental studies that manipulated the distance between chairs and their relative orientations, and other types of research. These effects are mediated by variables such as the personality traits of the individuals (e.g., affiliation, sensitivity to rejection) and the degree of cohesion within the group.

13.   It may be possible to control deviant student behavior by seating arrangements in a classroom; for example, a teacher might seat a troublesome student between two very well-behaved students. An office manager could facilitate the adaptation of an introverted office worker by placing that individual close to two extroverted workers. On the other hand, it is possible to inhibit social interaction by separating the most extroverted and talkative individuals. Seating and other spatial arrangements may have important behavioral correlates.

14.   The provision of amenities such as carpets may decrease "inappropriate" (incongruent) behaviors (e.g., incontinence, excitability, irritability) in institutional settings. This probably occurs because patients associate carpets and other similar amenities with familiar home and community environments.

15.   Interpersonal judgments may be affected by the characteristics of the room in which the judgments take place (e.g., judgments of people are more negative in ugly physical environments). This finding has implications in such situations as jury deliberations and job interviews.

16.   There may be positive effects of relocation from slum housing to better public housing facilities. The extent to which these effects relate to the change in architectural and physical conditions is unclear. In addition, relocation often changes people's life styles and disturbs extended family networks and friendship patterns. The evidence indicates that suburban

land use patterns are more compatible (congruent) with some life styles than with others.

17.   Crime rates seem to increase in close approximation to building size and height. This effect may be independent of both interpersonal density and the number of units per housing project. Low-rise architectural designs may create "defensible space" by fostering feelings of protective ownership and increasing awareness of territorial boundaries.

18.   People develop cognitive maps of the environments in which they live. These cognitive maps are related to the social class, ethnic, and intellectual characteristics of people, as well as to their residential locations. People use environments in ways that are congruent with their mental images of those environments.

19.   If a building or housing area does not provide the facilities necessary for important functions, people will try and adapt other facilities, to ensure that they can do what they want to do.

Individuals can use information and cues from the physical design and architectural characteristics of environments. For example, a person may be able to control his social role by choosing a seat at a table, or a position in a room, which will probably put him in a leadership role. The intersystems congruence model raises the important possibility of selecting environments that will be congruent with the behavior an individual wishes to perform.

There are large individual differences in perceptions and cognitions about the architectural environment. Cities vary in their architectural characteristics, but people vary even more in describing the architectural characteristics of one city. Rooms differ in the characteristics of their physical design, but people disagree even more markedly in describing the physical design of one room. Since different individuals often perceive the "same" architectural environment quite differently, it is unlikely that there exists any simple architectural impact.

Population Density, Crowding, and the Use of Space.

20.   Areas of high population density have disproportionately higher indices of social pathology, such as crime and mortality rates, than areas of low population density. Clearly this does not mean that population density "causes" crime and social pathology. Cities may attract more aggressive people and/or may have environments that provide more opportunity for aggression. Higher crime rates in denser city areas may be mediated through social climate effects (e.g., anonymity, greater tolerance for deviant behavior, greater feelings of isolation and frustration).

21.   Population density can be separated into various components.

Interpersonal press (inside-dwelling-unit density) seems to be related to such indices of social pathology as juvenile delinquency, even after the effects of socioeconomic status have been controlled. Social climate may mediate the impact of density; for example, adolescents may have a high degree of autonomy from parental controls, thus may be more susceptible to peer influence, in an overcrowded living unit.

22.   There seems to be a U-shaped relationship between inside density (specifically, persons per room) and mental illness. There is probably a minimum amount of living space necessary for optimum health and social adaptation; however living alone may engender feelings of isolation and alienation.

23.   Complaints about lack of space and privacy are related to the social composition of the living unit. One study revealed that complaints were related to the number of families in the living unit rather than to the number of people. There are also more complaints on higher floor levels of buildings, presumably because the occupants of upper-story dwellings cannot escape one another as easily as can ground-floor occupants.

24.   Surprisingly, high living unit densities may restrict rather than facilitate socializing. Families living in more crowded conditions are less likely to invite others into their living unit. Similarly, there may be less social interaction in double than in single rooms in college dormitories. These findings also relate to the feelings of loneliness and alienation often found in more crowded settings.

25.   Experimental work suggests that short-term experiences of crowding have little or no effect on task performance variables. However evaluations of other people may become more negative, and aggressive behavior may increase, as social and/or spatial density increases. These effects may be a function of the size of the group; that is, aggressive behavior may increase as the number of people who are required to interact with each other increases.

26.   There are consistent sex differences in reaction to crowding. Males in small crowded rooms are more competitive and harsh, feel less pleasant and friendly, and like other participants less than males in large uncrowded rooms. Female subjects produced opposite results, being more cooperative and perceiving their experience as more pleasant and other subjects as more likable and friendlier, in small than in large rooms. These results have potential practical implications. They suggest the possibility that dormitory rooms or office spaces for females might be made smaller than those for males. Perhaps one should consider the sex composition of a jury and/or of other decision-making groups in relation to the crowding conditions.

27.   People have "body-buffer" zones that signal the need for a certain

amount of personal space. When this space is "invaded" people usually move away, although they may verbally defend their space and/or react in a more aggressive and violent manner.

28.   Important individual and cultural differences are associated with the need for space. Males seem to need more personal space than females. Violent prison inmates may be more sensitive to the physical closeness of other people. Children dying of leukemia may have and want increased physical space between themselves and their caretakers. Different cultural and subcultural groups have quite different personal space expectations.

The model we presented of human crowding phenomena may be useful because it conceptualizes both overcrowding and undercrowding as discrepancies from expectations that can lead to psychological and physiological stress. This serves to link the crowding area with work on the stressful effects of excessive stimulation and input overload, and work on understimulation and sensory deprivation. The model points out that physical or spatial variables alone are not adequate to explain crowding phenomena, and the interaction of the physical environment, the social environment, and personal background factors must be considered both in understanding which individuals will perceive a setting as crowded or uncrowded and in recognizing the types of stress-reducing or adaptive responses (e.g., perceptual, cognitive, or behavioral modes) that will be utilized. Finally, the model makes it clear that within reasonable limits, high population density or crowding may positively enhance human diversity and creative stimulation.

Noise and Air Pollution.

29.   There are various negative reactions to community noise (annoyance, anxiety, sleep disturbances, etc.). There generally is habituation over time, and there are large individual differences.

30.   Airport noise can disturb sleep patterns, quiet reading, communication patterns, and the watching of television. It may also cause headaches, insomnia, irritability, and other mild psychosomatic complaints. It may increase marital disagreements, and perhaps arguments and tension between parents and children. These effects occur mainly in areas very close to airports (e.g., housing tracts located near airport runways).

31.   The experimental work on noise has disclosed effects similar to those reported in community and airport noise studies. There may be less participation, less attentiveness, more hearing problems, greater disagreement and tension, sleep loss, poor judgment, lack of alertness, and so

on, under noise conditions. The findings show that there are behavioral and not just attitudinal or mood effects. Performance decrements seem to occur more readily under conditions of high than of low task difficulty, and during unpredictable rather than predictable noise.

32.   There may be behavioral aftereffects of noise; that is, task performance decrements sometimes occur after the cessation of noise. This suggests, for example, that people may be more irritable and more prone to insomnia, headaches, and other psychophysiological symptoms after they have been exposed to noise. In fact, there may be adaptational costs to noise exposure (e.g., moderate irritability) of which we are unaware precisely because we do habituate and adapt to noise.

33.   There are reasonably consistent negative effects of carbon monoxide exposure. Several experimental studies have found measurable performance decrements even at low carbon monoxide levels.

34.   Variables such as reaction time and signal detection may be impaired under the levels of carbon monoxide commonly found in urban freeway driving. However it is not clear whether there is a direct relationship between carbon monoxide levels and automobile accidents. In addition, behavior decrements may occur before mood or symptom changes develop—that is, without the individual being aware of the change.

35.   Epidemiological studies indicate that certain morbidity and mortality rates (respiratory symptoms, cardiovascular disease, and cancer) are related to air pollution. There is an air pollution syndrome consisting of symptoms such as headache, fatigue, irritability, insomnia, impaired judgment, and difficulty in concentration. There is also a small group of normal healthy individuals who react with particular sensitivity to air pollution, which exacerbates colds, coughs, headaches, eye and throat irritation, and other minor ailments.

36.   Normally occurring levels of carbon monoxide may affect people with angina pectoris and other heart disease problems. Specifically, patients were not able to exercise as long without pain after they had breathed freeway air. In addition, the duration of pain was longer after exposure to carbon monoxide.

37.   Cigarette smoking causes significant indoor air pollution, and heavy cigarette smokers are often exposed to levels of carbon monoxide much higher than are commonly found outdoors, even under very smoggy conditions. People who do not smoke but who breathe smoke-filled air (passive smokers) are also exposed to significant amounts of carbon monoxide and other pollutants. Importantly, cigarette smokers may be particularly strongly affected by high atmospheric carbon monoxide.

These results have some practical implications. For example, did the people who bought houses under airport runways fully realize the extent, duration, and disruptiveness of airplane noise? Perhaps one could present information on tape recordings that would give people a more accurate idea of what the noise is actually like. Since low levels of carbon monoxide may affect perceptual-motor performance, it is possible that policemen, pilots, taxicab drivers, and air traffic controllers (particularly if they are smokers) may be adversely affected by the ambient carbon monoxide levels in their work settings. These individuals might be given regular reaction time and other perceptual-motor tests.

The findings on noise and air pollution indicate the existence of adaptational costs of which individuals are unaware, and regular changes in environments may provide useful information. For example, some people may experience frequent headaches or other minor physical symptoms, a low level of chronic irritability, or performance decrements; because of adaptation over time however they may not fully recognize these conditions as "effects." If the individuals were able to live in a quiet, smog-free environment for a short time, they might realize the detrimental effects noise and air pollution actually have on them. Of course this would probably make it more difficult for them to readapt to their regular life settings.

The fact that we can adapt to noise and air pollution does not mean that we should adapt. Dissemination of information regarding the effects of noise and air pollution may help individuals judge why they are feeling irritable, depressed, and so forth. It may also help arouse public concern and increase the probability of positive action. The startling fact that a high proportion of the population has carboxyhemoglobin levels above those set by the Air Quality Control Standards indicates that such action is long overdue.

Behavior Setting Theory and Research.

38.   The behavior setting is the only unit we have discussed that has both physical and social environmental properties. "Intermediate" in size, it is a unit that can "mediate" between a person and an organization. It is a naturally occurring unit through which an individual can better understand his environment.

39.   The idea that continual interaction between the people in a setting and other aspects of the setting produces a stable patterned (i.e., congruent) state of affairs is important. The four types of "circuits" (goal circuits, program circuits, deviation-countering circuits, and vetoing cir-

cuits) represent "feedback loops" that help us to understand how settings are maintained and why the behavior of individuals within settings exhibits such remarkable stability.

40.   Certain behavioral and attitudinal consequences occur when environments are "undermanned." People perform more activities in undermanned settings, and they are required to accept more positions of responsibility. These settings have a greater "claim" on people, because they require more effort and because relatively more difficult and important tasks are assigned to the occupants. It is less likely that a person will achieve great proficiency at any one task, since each person must fulfill several tasks. Each person has greater functional importance in the setting, more responsibility, and a greater feeling of functional self-identity. However there may be greater feelings of insecurity, since each person is in greater jeopardy of failing to carry out the tasks assigned him—and the tasks are more important for the maintenance of the setting.

41.   Marginal individuals may be particularly affected by the forces just enumerated. For example, marginal students in large schools (i.e., schools with relatively overmanned settings) may have a much lower sense of obligation to the school than do nonmarginal students. Perhaps undermanned settings should include more people who are only marginally qualified to function in them. These settings make a greater "claim" on people and may thus enhance their self-esteem and integration into a group. This finding has important implications for people who are introverted and/or marginal, who have difficulty initiating social relationships, who are recurrent dropouts or misfits, and so on.

42.   Recent extensions of the theory of undermanning provide new concepts by which to analyze behavior settings (i.e., maintenance minimum, capacity, applicants). This raises important new ideas about how under- and overmanned settings can be defined and changed. For example, one might change an overmanned to an undermanned setting simply by adding new performance roles. Again, this stratagem may be of particular importance for marginal individuals who are most at risk as dropouts and most in need of environmental supports.

43.   One study revealed that students from small high schools participated in more areas than students from large high schools, but these differences did not carry over to the students' college experiences. Instead the size of the college itself was related to participation in college. This indicates that the effects of the immediate environment are most critical. The theory itself suggests that generalization is most likely to occur for students who have leadership roles in overmanned settings. These students are more likely to feel enhanced competence and self-

esteem, and they should be more likely to become leaders in other settings.

44. Personality variables such as neuroticism and extroversion relate to how individuals select behavior settings. For example, inhibited individuals may spend more time in their rooms and less time in socialization areas than do more highly extroverted and action-oriented individuals. There are also sex differences in the use of different behavior settings. Behavior setting surveys may provide useful information about the specific differences between the daily lives of males and females, of introverts and extroverts, of low- and high-ego-strength individuals, of black and white high school students, and so on.

45. Behavior setting taxonomies suggest variables that can be useful in characterizing behavior settings. The variables include the authority system to which the setting belongs, the predominant action patterns, the age and sex characteristics of the setting inhabitants, and the duration and frequency of occurrence of the setting. These variables are important in providing information about the range of settings available in particular locations and organizations. They can also be used to compare environments such as small cities, factories, and hospitals. For example, one study disclosed that there were very few settings in which people could interact across age and sex roles. This raises the possibility of developing new settings in which men and women of varying ages could be accommodated.

The behavior setting is an important eco-behavioral unit. People can be easily "sensitized" to behavior settings and to the characteristics that differentiate among them. The behavior setting is a "logical" unit that everyone can immediately understand. Behavior setting observations or interviews might be useful as information-obtaining devices about the everyday lives of people, and as teaching devices to help sensitize people to the attributes of settings that most significantly affect their daily lives.

The work on undermanned environments has especially important practical implications. This information can be useful to an individual in choosing a setting, or to a parent or social worker in placing a child. It can help in planning meetings, in organizing the committee structure of an academic department, in establishing a new teaching program, and in similar endeavors. In addition, it can be useful in deciding what kinds of change might promote certain behavioral experiences. For example if one knew the number of organizational positions at different levels of "penetration" (responsibility), these positions could be carefully allocated to different participants. It would be possible to ensure that no one participant filled too many positions and that each participant became involved in at least a minimal leadership role.

Organizational Structure and Change.

46.   Organizations can be thought of as environments that influence the behaviors and attitudes of the people who participate in them. The four models of organizational functioning we presented (scientific management, human relations, structuralism, and open systems) highlight variables that should be considered by managers and employees in understanding organizational environments. These four perspectives suggest potentially useful dimensions for analyzing environments and for planning, facilitating, and evaluating change.

47.   The results on organizational size are highly consistent. As plant and work group size increase, morale and attitudes become less positive, and absenteeism is more frequent. Other variables such as productivity and turnover rate are less consistently related to size.

48.   The results on organizational shape (i.e., span of control) are less clear. Theoretical considerations suggest that employees will like flat organizations (high span of control) better than tall organizations (low span of control). The theory suggests that when a supervisor is responsible for more employees he will supervise each employee less closely, leading to greater employee autonomy and satisfaction. However a greater span of control may lead to more distant relationships, and to controls based on general rules and regulations rather than on employees' needs. Low span of control may result in better communication, more cohesive supervisor-employee relationships—thus, in effect, in greater employee autonomy.

49.   Automation initially produces lower morale, greater isolation among workers, and feelings among workers of diminished importance and less confidence in coping with the job (i.e., the machine). Workers also feel a greater lack of control over the pace and style of their work and increased mental and emotional fatigue. There is some evidence that morale increases with time after the introduction of automation.

50.   Small size and high staffing in mental hospitals and correctional institutions relate to early release of patients and rapid turnover. Social climate may function as a mediating variable between these structural factors (size and staffing) and organizational impact (turnover rate). There is a need to develop more specific measures (e.g., the staff-patient attention ratio) that can capture the behavioral concomitants of these and other organizational factors.

51.   The effects of size and staffing may be mediated by the personal-

ity characteristics of the individuals in a setting. For example, since introverted individuals may have particular difficulty in coping with many people, small settings may be especially beneficial for them.

The overall model proposed is useful in the analysis of environmental impact. Intermediate factors "condition" or mediate organizational impacts and the results of change attempts. Thus, for example, in understanding the potential impact of an organizational factor such as work group size, we must take into account the role concomitants of the people involved (blue-collar vs. white-collar workers), average background and personality characteristics (educational level, degree of self-esteem), and the social climate of the work group. As a related condition, we must realize that it may be easier to change one of the intermediate factors (e.g., social climate) to effect a particular organizational impact (satisfaction, absenteeism) than to change an organizational factor (size). The model suggests that organizational factors may have effects that vary at different levels of the organization (e.g., students may be alienated by large universities, whereas faculty consider college size a mark of high status). In addition, an organizational factor may engender both positive and negative consequences; for example, students in large universities may feel alienated and isolated but also more satisfied with the available range of academic and extracurricular opportunities.

Significantly, the negative effects of certain organizational variables can be counteracted by paying attention to the mediating variables. For example, large work groups can be reorganized into several somewhat smaller groups, thereby making additional leadership roles available to employees. This strategem would probably increase employees' identification and satisfaction with the work group and the organization.

Richard Tanner Johnson's recent work indicates that the foregoing considerations may have practical implications for predicting the impact of the different organizational structures used by recent presidents in organizing the White House staff.[17] Johnson suggests that presidents Nixon and Eisenhower needed structure and order, a strong Chief of Staff, and advisers in specialist roles. This created bureaucratic machinery that screened out conflict. Unfortunately such a system gets the facts but fails to consider the attached emotions (e.g., public reactions), and a president who relies on it may respond inappropriately to the public mood. Franklin Delano Roosevelt apparently liked conflict and had no structure at all. Johnson believes that this system is conducive to generating new ideas. The teamwork approach, used by John Kennedy, lies between these extremes. The problem is that a closed system of mutual support may occur, and advisers may feel so good about being on a team that they fail to ask hard questions of one another. Thus decisions that appear to be drastically incorrect in retrospect can be unanimously approved (e.g., the Bay of Pigs invasion of Cuba). Johnson points out that every president who has used the formal bureaucratic approach has had problems with scandals, and the system Richard Nixon used "set him up" for the Watergate disaster. Regardless of whether Johnson's analysis is accurate, it provides a fascinating example of how people might use information about organizational structure and impact in formulating practical policies.

The Human Aggregate.

52.   The major utility of Holland's formulation of six types of work environment is that it links vocations (professions, major choices) with personality and attitude traits. This is relevant to high school and college counselors, to employers engaged in job recruitment and placement, and to people selecting majors and/or places to work.

53.   The other concepts that Holland uses (e.g., consistency, homogeneity, and congruence) also provide important information about environments. In general, students who are congruent with the majority are more satisfied and stable in terms of their vocational plans than are incongruent students. However the potential impact of these dimensions may vary in relation to the personality and background characteristics of the individual. For example, one study revealed that women but not men were more satisfied with a college if their interests were congruent with the college environment, suggesting that congruence effects may be stronger for women than for men. Sex differences in reactions to environments indicate the potential utility of different environmental selection guidelines for men and women.

54.   The studies we reviewed supported the notion that congruence, homogeneity, and consistency have important effects. These are variables people should take into account in selecting environments. Homogeneous college environments produce high stability of major choice but may have lower morale than more heterogeneous environments. Heterogeneous colleges have a diverse student population, giving a student a greater opportunity to find congenial friends than he would have had at a college populated largely by a single personality type. In a similar vein, high-ability students, living in close proximity in homogeneously assigned residence halls, may perform better academically than scattered high-ability students. Low-ability students, assigned to a residence in which there is a concentration of high-ability students, may do somewhat worse than scattered low-ability students. Thus environmental dimen-

sions such as homogeneity may have quite dissimilar effects on different groups of people.

55. People have a tendency to become more like their environments (i.e., more like the majority of the other people in their milieus). This notion of progressive conformity raises the important possibility that people could select environments in relation to the kinds of changes they wanted to make in themselves. A person who wants to learn to cook quite naturally enrolls in a cooking class. A person who wants to become more assertive might consider participating in an environment that strongly rewards assertiveness. Perhaps people could select environments not only as a way of maximizing congruence but also as a way of maximizing the probability of personal development in particular directions. Individual potential might be maximized by having people choose new environments that are "optimally incongruent."

56. Epidemiological research indicates that various indices of social pathology are more prevalent in lower socioeconomic living areas. The related work on social drift versus social selection represents one possible model for dealing with the problems of man-environment interaction. Do the social environments of disorganized communities create conditions conducive to social pathology? Are certain types of people more prone to crime or illness than others? Or do some types of people create social conditions that naturally foster social pathology? Each of these processes occurs, and current evidence is not sufficient to disentangle them.

57. Epidemiological studies provide additional evidence that an individual's degree of congruence with a group has important implications. People living in areas in which they do not share the dominant racial, religious, or socioeconomic characteristics of the population have high rates of mental illness and associated symptoms. For example, one study discovered less social interaction among blue-collar families living in white-collar neighborhoods, and among white-collar families living in blue-collar neighborhoods.

58. There are many mediating factors to be taken into account in explaining human aggregate effects. For example, the differences among male, female, and coed universities, and male, female, and coed student living groups support the conclusion that average background characteristics (sex composition) and homogeneity affect the social climate. The three major explanations of the higher prevalence of schizophrenia in lower socioeconomic areas also yield suggestions about potential mediating variables. Environmental conditions that reinforce isolation and/or make interpersonal contact more difficult may facilitate the development of unhealthy mental symptoms. Lower-class environments may predispose individuals to develop certain psychological symptoms because of

their highly stress-producing characteristics. Finally, the social environment of an individual's family or work setting (cohesion, support, the intellectual and cultural orientational system provided) may mediate the impact of different "human aggregates."

Social Climate.   The social climate perspective identifies three types of dimensions that can sensitize organizers and consumers of environments about what to look for in analyzing social settings. The three types of dimensions (Relationship, Personal Development, and System Maintenance and System Change) provide a useful format for characterizing and understanding the confusing complexity of social environments. These dimensions may help an individual select a wide range of environments in which to participate in his everyday life.

59.   Rejecting, hostile, and indifferent parental attitudes, and overly lax, erratic, or strict discipline may have harmful effects. However children of high control parents are better socialized and more courteous, obedient, neat, generous, and polite. They are also more sensitive, self-conscious, shy, and retiring. Children from low control homes are more disobedient, irresponsible, disorderly, and lacking in sustained attention and regular work habits. They are also more expressive and outgoing, tending to show greater curiosity and creativity.

60.   Students feel more secure, interested, and satisfied in classrooms that emphasize involvement, affiliation, and support. Classrooms in which students report a great deal of content learning combine an affective concern with students as people and an emphasis on working hard for academic rewards, within a coherent organized context.

61.   Colleges that emphasize Relationship dimensions (faculty-student interaction, peer cohesion) have a positive impact on students. Colleges stressing Personal Development dimensions (e.g., humanism, breadth of interest, reflectiveness, broad intellectual emphasis, independent study, and criticism) also tend to have more productive students.

62.   Emphasis on Relationship dimensions is helpful in all types of psychotherapy and is related to low dropout rates on psychiatric wards. Programs that keep patients out of the hospital the longest emphasize the Relationship and System Maintenance dimensions in addition to Autonomy and Practical Orientation. This suggests that satisfaction may be most highly related to Relationship dimensions, but "objective" progress may need a somewhat more complex and carefully constructed type of social milieu.

63.   The work on correctional and military settings also indicates that the emphasis on cohesion and support has a beneficial impact on satisfac-

tion, morale, and mood. High control is associated with poor morale and greater anxiety, depression, and anger. However high performance in both settings appears to depend on a combination of support (warmth) and strictness (control).

64.   There are some relationships between social environmental stimuli and physical health and well-being. Lack of support is related to developmental retardation in children and possibly to a higher incidence of heart disease in men and a higher-than-expected death rate in widows and widowers. Autonomy, responsibility, work pressure, and time urgency are related to physiological arousal and dysfunction. The research in this area raises the issue of how the effects of stressful environments can be ameliorated. How can we modulate and control the degree of stress in the environment and/or the stress effects that occur?

In general, the dominant findings on the effects of social climates concern what we have termed the Relationship dimensions, which appear to exert a consistent positive influence on morale and satisfaction in all environments. However more objective behavioral and performance effects (academic learning in classrooms, test scores in military companies, etc.) may depend on a combination of warm and supportive relationships, an emphasis on specific directions of personal growth, and a reasonably clear, orderly, and well-structured milieu. It appears that too much emphasis on personal growth may have destructive effects (e.g., "the failure of success"), and overly rigid control may inhibit curiosity and spontaneity.

In practical terms, each individual should probably participate in a variety of social environmental conditions, particularly in relation to the Personal Development dimensions. It may be easier for a person to cope with an environment that is low on the Relationship dimensions (e.g., lack of support) if he or she also participates in an environment high on these dimensions (i.e., one in which there is high support). Similar considerations may hold for the System Maintenance and System Change dimensions. An unruly child might be placed in a high control environment until his behavior becomes somewhat better controlled whereupon he might be placed in a more expressive milieu. Children could be assigned to different environments on the basis of the personal traits these environments foster.

The work on social climates suggests that detailed case studies of environments might be useful. In fact, it is surprising that so few "biographies" of environments exist. Important knowledge about the "natural history" of social settings could be derived from longitudinal case studies of particular hospitals or wards, student living groups, and so on. This work might clarify the extent to which architectural and physical design variables, and the background characteristics of people (i.e., the human aggregate), set limits on social climates and treatment environments.

The data on physical and mental health effects of social environments support the notion that certain environmental characteristics have both positive and negative concomitants. An individual wants to increase autonomy and independence because this engenders personal growth. But autonomy and independence may relate to work pressure and time urgency, thus having negative physiological concomitants. When people are pushed to the limits of their performance capacities, they may experience both personal growth and success and physiological arousal and dysfunction. It is therefore especially important for people to obtain information about the probable health effects of potentially stressful milieus.

The Utility of Information–Seeking.   The major ways of conceptualizing environments discussed in this book, as well as the tentative conclusions just presented, can be useful in supplying information to help people select and change environments. This is especially relevant because people have a basic coping tendency to seek and utilize information in major life crises and transitions.[18] For example, Silber and his colleagues studied a group of competent high school graduates as they prepared for their freshman year in college.[19] The students made many attempts to obtain information about the new situation (correspondence with the college, reading college catalogs, talking with college friends, visiting campuses, talking with counselors and teachers, etc.); they wanted information about the new roles they would be asked to perform and future difficulties they might encounter. Information seeking is also an important coping mechanism in other major life transitions—marriage and divorce, migration and relocation, retirement and aging.[20]

Prior information about environments can enhance the accuracy of people's expectations, thus reducing the incidence of dissatisfaction and turnover. For example, work in individual and group psychotherapy has demonstrated that providing systematic information about the therapy helps to socialize an individual and increases the probability of positive outcome.[21]

Relocation is considered a major stress for elderly people, and there is some evidence that the death rate may increase after forced moves. Prior information about living environments to which elderly people will be relocated may help them to adapt to and cope with the new setting.[22] Jasnau noted an increased postrelocation death rate among elderly patients who received little or no psychological preparation for a mass move within a hospital, whereas those who received personal attention had a lower-than-expected death rate after the move.[23] Novick showed that the relocation of chronically disabled geriatric residents could result in a postrelocation death rate that was lower than the prerelocation rate if the relocation program included attention to the residents' fears, maintenance of familiar relationships and belongings, and so on.[24] Similarly, Leiberman has discovered that psychological preparation is useful in easing the misery commonly associated with relocation of the elderly.[25]

Matching Student and College Preferences. The results of many investigations of the beneficial effects of "anticipatory guidelines" strongly support the utility of increasing the amount and accuracy of environmental information. The environmental descriptions that are available to fill these needs are usually compiled by people who wish to present "their" environment in a positive light. Thus currently available descriptions of environments do not give an adequate picture of the environments.[26] For example, students are known to have unclear expectations about social life on campus, about the wealth of curricular and extracurricular activities, about how hard they will have to study, and about the degree of competition they will face.[27]

Holland has pointed out that students choose colleges the way consumers buy cars. They must deal with their own ignorance and misconceptions as well as with misleading advertising.[28] Given these conditions, it has been suggested that accurate, easily understood descriptions of colleges might be extremely useful. For example, Pace has summarized College and University Environment Scales (CUES) results for different types of colleges (denominational, teachers', etc.).[29] A student can complete a special form of CUES by indicating how strongly he hopes each item will be true or false. He can then compare his preferences with the typical responses in various types of colleges.

Baird[30] cites experiences with the Questionnaire on Student and College Characteristics (QSCC), which assesses students' perceptions of their respective college and students' reports of their own activities, interests, and backgrounds.[31] This instrument also provides information on the restrictiveness of rules, the extent of faculty-student interaction, the degree of student activism, the emphasis on the nonacademic aspects of college, the flexibility of the curriculum, and the intellectual rigor of the college. The institutions involved were furnished free tests and scoring services and were encouraged to use the results as an aid in describing themselves to prospective students. Baird reports that only about a quarter of 200 colleges involved made extensive use of their QSCC results.

More than half did not use the results at all, and another 9% made only very limited use of them. Thus even a free, voluntary program could not induce colleges to reveal what their students thought of them. Baird points out that many colleges, anxious about declining enrollment and rising costs, may be forgiven if they fear the loss of students due to negative impressions of their respective institutions.

Matching People with Living and Working Places.   Many attempts are being made to provide more adequate information to individuals attempting to select new environments. For example, one approach is being developed to match home buyers and sellers by a "computer mating" procedure. The parties fill out separate questionnaires with more than 300 features detailing what the buyer wants in a home and what the seller has to offer. The buyer's needs are then matched up with the details of each home for sale. The computer procedure finds the homes that come closest to what the buyer wants and prints out a complete description. A substantial side benefit is that the computer service takes only a 2% commission, compared to the 6 or 7% real estate broker's fee. The idea was developed by George Militzer, who believes that the computer matching formula may spread nationwide, since it will give prospective buyers and sellers better information.[32]

Apartment guides, which represent a somewhat similar venture, have been published in many large American and European cities. One guide covers several counties in the San Francisco Bay Area and includes information about the acceptability of children and pets and the availability of environmental amenities such as wading pools, tire swings, day care centers, and dog runs. These guides are useful for people moving into a new area, particularly since they yield information about the types of people already living in an apartment complex or condominium (e.g., students, swinging singles, young marrieds, empty nesters, or the elderly).[33]

Sandler has suggested a "cafeteria approach" to the problems of repetitive and monotonous jobs and employee alienation. Many companies have assumed that the needs of executives should be a factor in determining the nature of the compensation package and that the investment made by the organization would be recouped through effective performance. These assumptions are just as reasonable for blue-collar as for white-collar workers. In the cafeteria approach, employees select the compensation package they feel is most beneficial to them.[34]

This approach can be extended to other aspects of work organizations, and it may hold the promise of increased satisfaction for both the organization and its employees. The introduction of the modified work week and flexible working hours, for example, would permit employees to select the hours they work, as long as they abide by certain rules regarding starting and quitting times and total hours worked. The use of flexible working hours may enhance employee satisfaction and reduce tardiness and absenteeism. The cafeteria approach might also be used in grouping people according to their needs and aspirations and in helping employees to choose more satisfying jobs and work styles.

Other enterprising individuals have suggested the possibility of selecting a likely mate from a television screen in the privacy of one's home. A West German television station is reported to have started a marriage market program on a monthly basis. People are interviewed by a television reporter who elicits information about their private lives, jobs, and hobbies, and the kind of person they would like to marry. Viewers are shown pictures of the candidates' homes and surroundings to help them form an impression. Other possibilities being considered include the use of television to help find foster parents for orphaned or homeless children.[35]

Maximizing Available Environmental Information.

Various innovative procedures might be used to help people adjust to new environments. People could be specifically trained to perceive environments in as many ways as possible. An environment that is stagnant given one perspective may be growth-enhancing given another. Planned exposure to individuals with radically different conceptions of environments may be useful in this regard. For example, students in law, medicine, engineering, economics, and geography revealed basic differences in the manner in which they conceptually organized environmental information, as well as in their knowledge about air pollution and in their perceived professional roles.[36] Radically different town plans were created by students who assumed different positions in the community (e.g., homeowner, school superintendent, police chief, shopping center manager), suggesting that role-playing techniques may usefully broaden people's environmental perspectives.[37]

Environmental games, which clarify the potential range of available environmental choices and their probable effects, could be developed. Gould has illustrated the potential utility of game-playing situations pitting "man against environment." His logic was that man and nature were opposing players in a competitive zero-sum game (see Chapter 2), but other types of simulation games might also be useful.[38]

Other possibilities include the development of courses concerned with learning to understand and cope with difficult environments. Since selecting the "right" environment is an important "life skill," high schools and colleges should consider offering regular courses to dispense systematic information about various environments and their impacts. Roger Barker has pointed out that we have very little "real world" knowledge about playing, about laughing, about talking, about being valued and devalued, about conflict, about failure, and so on.[39] A compendium of information along these lines—and particularly about the environments in which these and other activities occur—would be very valuable.

Information about environments could also be presented through the use of tape recordings, videotapes, or movies. Techniques of this kind are being used in the rapidly expanding field of health care education.[40] People who have lived in different environments could supply prospective inhabitants with realistic and practical information about these milieus.

The data on "cognitive maps" indicate that a person will seldom enter areas that are cognitively undifferentiated. This raises the possibility of systematically increasing people's information about unfamiliar city areas. For example, guided tours may enhance the probability that people who do not use certain areas of the city will begin to use them. Information-giving techniques could be systematically employed to make unfamiliar urban areas and other types of environments more inviting.

People could actively plan to place themselves in diverse environments. Adaptability and coping competence may be related to the variability of environmental conditions in which an individual has learned to function. These considerations underscore the need for a general taxonomy or typology of environments, to help ensure that an individual has experienced environments that differ substantially on important dimensions. In this sense, people should consider making regular periodic changes in environment.

One procedure that is gaining popularity in this connection is job swapping. For example, two airline executives were reported to have successfully concluded a month-long job swap. One man was a district sales manager for American Airlines and the other managed airport services at the San Francisco International Airport. Both men felt that they were able to make improvements in the other's operations, but they concluded that executives swapping jobs must be completely compatible and convinced of the utility of the switch. Vacations or short leaves of absence could be used to explore new environments in this manner.[41]

Trial experiences in environments may prevent hasty changes to new settings on the basis of inadequate or faulty information. For example, the Saab automobile company's shift from conventional production line to group assembly procedures, in which employees have more control over work routines, has been hailed as a promising way of counteracting the monotony and boredom of regular assembly line work. However five of six American automobile workers who worked in the Saab plant in Sweden preferred the conventional production line system, in part because it was more relaxed and did not require continuous concentration.[42]

A number of investigators have suggested that changes in perceiving environments may open up new perspectives and new possibilities. For example, many preventive mental health programs have established the importance of anticipatory guidance for individuals who are undergoing life transitions. Prior information about the problems and reactions individuals will experience is believed to enhance their coping and adaptation processes and to beneficially affect the ultimate outcome.[43] The Widow-to-Widow program is a preventive project primarily designed to reach young widows before they have serious problems and to help them in making the difficult adjustments necessary to their new status. The widow "caregiver" can offer newly widowed women information, advice, and understanding in a way nonwidows seldom can.[44] Such programs are often helpful perhaps mainly because they provide important information.

Krumboltz and Thoresen indicate that it is possible to specify the process in which an individual should engage if he is to maximize the probability of arriving at a wise decision. The process includes considering several courses of action, exploring relevant information about the potential outcome related to each alternative, and weighing the information obtained in an attempt to make a rational decision. These authors devised counseling and modeling procedures that successfully increased the information-seeking behavior of students with regard to their own educational and vocational decisions.[45]

Modeling might also be used to change or ameliorate certain impacts of environments. For example, one study (cited in Chapter 3) indicated that an aggressive model could facilitate aggression under hot or high-temperature conditions. An environmental effect may be more likely when someone is modeling the behavior that is supposed to occur. Conversely, it may be less likely to occur if an opposite or incompatible behavioral effect is being modeled. Prestigious and socially powerful models may have substantial impact in this regard. Models who are physically present may not be significantly more effective than models presented on audio- or videotapes.[46] Thus a prestigious social model who engages in a positively reinforced activity may be highly effective in controlling desired environmental impacts.

Environmental Quality and the Quality of Individual Lives. At a more general level, many people have suggested that information on overall environmental quality be compiled on an index basis analogous to currently available economic indices such as the Gross National Product. A Canadian Environmental Quality Index (EQI) consists of four separate indices representing air quality, water quality, land quality, and the quality of miscellaneous aspects of the environment. Each has several subindices; for example, the land quality index includes six subindices —overcrowding in cities, characteristics of forests, access to park land, erosion, strip mining, and sedimentation. The EQI is not simply a "pollution index." It attempts to take into account environmental benefits as well as problems and aesthetic considerations as well as those related to health.[47]

A subindex of relative accessibility to regional and national parks incorporates people's perceptions of distances from environmental benefits or problems. The inclusion of indices of human perception may give a much more accurate portrayal of the actual effect of environmental conditions on people's lives. Although the overall index value is purely relative, once a value has been established, a higher or lower value at a subsequent measurement would indicate that on the average environmental conditions were getting better or worse. Thus an EQI might measure the "environmental health" of a country.

A related approach has recently been used to rank America's 50 largest cities in terms of their "quality of life." Twenty-four indices were selected to represent seven basic areas: crime (murder, rape, and robbery rates), health (e.g., death rates from influenza and pneumonia), affluence (e.g., median income, percentage of housing units owned by occupants), housing (e.g., percentage of housing units lacking some or all plumbing facilities), educational and professional achievement (e.g., percentage of individuals 25 and older who are high school and/or college graduates), atmosphere (e.g., micrograms of particulate matter per cubic meter of air), and amenities (e.g., places of amusement and recreation per 100,000 residents). Not everyone will agree with the conclusion, derived from the averaged indices, that the best and worst American cities are Seattle and Newark, New Jersey, respectively. However such information should be useful in evaluating cities and in following their future development or decay.[48]

In this connection, Campbell and Converse have said that economic measures should not be accepted as the sole criteria of desirable development, remarking on the need for other indicators which reflect living conditions in a wider sense.[49] They suggest that social indicators should function as guides by which social development can be directed toward established goals. Social indicators should help in assessing the effectiveness of social institutions and social programs and should furnish information for predicting the outcome of important social decisions. Social indicators can only serve to measure the quality of life if our current measures for external conditions are supplemented with measures of how the environment is experienced by the individual.

Substantial progress is being made in developing psychologically oriented measures of the quality of life, which basically assess the environment as perceived by the individual.[50] Zifferblatt and Hendricks have recently written that broad social problems, such as the population explosion, can be solved only if they are conceptualized, and relevant programs are implemented and evaluated, at the level of the individual.[51] Massive energy consumption may indeed not be necessary to maintain current living standards,[52] but it will take societal programs aimed at changing individual perceptions and behaviors to implement the needed changes. When attempting to solve global problems, the individual and his environment always represent the most important planning unit.

Although we have been duly warned about ecological disaster, most people are less concerned about what may happen in the distant future than they are with more immediate developments. This is partly because people do not fully appreciate their own ability to influence and control the future. Involvement in the future could be enhanced by disseminating information about the extent to which we can control our own future development. People must be made aware that they can make a difference in the future course of human events. In this sense, it is important to develop methods for presenting information about alternative lines of environmental development in a way that will arouse people's interest and lead them to sustained effective action.[53]

Sommer has discussed the need for environmental educators or managers, that is, people who help individuals or organizations maximize the utilization of existing environments.[54] Environmental educators can teach people about their environment, how to conceptualize its component parts and their interrelationships, and, most importantly, how to understand and control its potential impact on their everyday lives.

Useful materials to stimulate people's creativity and problem-solving abilities in these areas are being developed.[55] Levinson and Yanofsky have described how environmental education programs may instill a new measure of hope even in inner-city youth living in decay-ridden urban environments.[56]

Environmental education should begin at the level of the individual and his immediate surroundings. Each individual must feel competent to change and control at least some portion of his immediate environment. In fact, people usually can change their own home or apartment, their classroom or office, and even their street or neighborhood, at least to some degree. In this connection, Steele has provided a diagnostic scheme for the analysis of the man-made physical environment and has suggested some methods for enhancing environmental competence by "increasing people's ability to both *use* the potential of settings and *choose* settings appropriate to their needs."[57] Furthermore, feedback about the social climate of an environment can both motivate people and furnish guidelines to help them successfully change their environments in directions they themselves desire.[58]

Sommer feels that there is no sharp distinction between solving broad ecological problems and improving one's immediate sociophysical milieu.

> One step toward solution . . . is to involve people in a problem-solving stance toward problems in their homes, schools, offices, and neighborhoods. This will inevitably mesh into larger environmental issues, but they are originally perceived at a scale where there is some likelihood of success. I would like to suggest that for most people the logical starting place is the person's immediate environment, where the scale of problems is manageable and the effects of his efforts are apparent."[59]

These applications of environmental information (i.e., its use to select and change social environments) are directly linked to concepts of problem solving, coping, and adaptive behavior. Every person has needs for involvement, efficacy, and for the competence to predict and control his own environment.[60] The ideas presented here are consonant with these important needs. Their use may help some individuals achieve a new competence—that of being able to change and control their own environments. If all else fails, we can at least build our own playgrounds![61]

Toward an Environmentally Based Utopia. In this book we have discussed both environmental and utopian thought. Environmental theory is earthbound and oriented to reality. Its objective is the discovery of laws and relationships that typify the dynamics of nature and the interaction between man and his environment. Modern work in this area emphasizes scientific procedures: empirical classification, examination of data, formation of hypotheses, testing of data, and generalized conclusions. The aim of environmental theory is not to create an ideal environment but to comprehend the actual environment. It does not attempt to evaluate the processes of nature but to accurately identify them—to specify how things are, not how they ought to be. Essentially, environmental thought has demonstrated the ability of nature to limit the ambitions and achievements of mankind.

Unlike environmental theory, utopian thought ignores the reality of the existing natural and human order in favor of a condition that does not now exist but could perhaps come to be. It is a visionary perspective restrained only by the extent of human hopes and dreams. Its method of investigation is reflection on the limits of the possible, combined with imagining what is ultimately most desirable. Utopias are not specifically concerned with what is, except as a take-off point. They seek to picture future worlds superior to the contemporary one.

Utopian thought and environmental thought have developed quite separately. Yet each is deeply concerned with the way men conceive of the future, particularly how they conceive of future relationships between man and his environment. On further analysis, environmental and utopian thought appear to have certain common underlying principles and assumptions. It is our final thesis that these two seemingly divergent modes of thought complement and mutually enhance each other. Both are necessary if we are to solve our current ecological crisis creatively.

Human ecologists have applied the notion of homeostasis and balance on a global scale to man and the ecosystem that sustains him. Their findings indicate that for generations man has been disturbing the ecological balance of his habitat. Most relevant here is the realization that his behavior cannot continue indefinitely. At some point—the precise timetable being a matter of dispute—natural balance will be restored. The processes of homeostasis may be catastrophic from the human point of view: excess population leading to famine, resource shortages causing war and the collapse of industry, pollutants poisoning entire populations. In the logic of ecology, the creature that makes its habitat unlivable destroys itself. To survive, men must reconstruct their political, economic, and social activities, and their values, to restore their equilibrium with the environment.

At first reading this ecological perspective appears highly deterministic. Nature (via ecosystems) requires that man obey its rules or pay an incalculable price. Closer examination reveals that the ecologists still leave substantial room for man to shape his own destiny. Unlike pure determinism, ecological theory does not insist that an environmental impetus accounts for a human response. On the contrary, its major assertion is that human action inevitably leads to environmental consequences. The environment limits man's activities because these consequences cannot be continually postponed or avoided. However the possibility of attempting new modes of action with different consequences remains. Indeed, it is the existence of such options that accounts for the ecologists' determined efforts to effect change in modern social institutions.

What new practices will permit a restoration of ecological balance? No single blueprint has been suggested; however several major changes in human social organization are commonly discussed as necessary elements for an environmentally stable planet. First and foremost is control of human population. Second, environmental balance requires a steady-state economy. As opposed to contemporary growth-oriented systems, this refers to a mode of organization typified by a relatively constant population and stock of physical wealth with a minimal rate of through-put (i.e., depletion of resources through use). A steady-state society would probably exhibit a low birthrate, a low death rate, a low level of production, a low level of consumption, and a high life expectancy. In addition, the totally egalitarian distribution of goods and resources would almost certainly be politically and practically essential.

Third, man's ecosystem is planet size, as indicated by the "Spaceship Earth" analogy. To carry that analogy one step further, spaceships cannot afford to have their passengers fighting over the controls. Ecological balance requires the organization of human and material resources on a world scale, which is hardly likely to result from consultations between sovereign and potentially hostile nation-states. Hence world order is considered a prerequisite for environmental stability.

Finally, a society desiring to maintain ecological balance will require a new set of values. To a large extent Western man's ethos defines progress in quantitative terms. National goals are ever higher levels of industrialization and consumerism; nature remains the helpless object of man's insatiable passion for increased productivity. Clearly such an outlook is incompatible with a steady state. Ecologically responsible people will have to conceive of themselves as partners rather than masters of nature, and new goals will have to replace those which are irrevocably linked to growth. The substance of such new ethics, however, is probably the aspect of an environmentally stable social order that ecologists are least competent and least likely to predict.

Utopian thinkers agree in principle with this analysis of the fundamental changes necessary to improve the quality of human life. In fact utopian thinkers usually espouse a qualitative, holistic, and carefully planned change emphasizing a steady-state economy and the egalitarian distribution of goods, population control, world order, decreased emphasis on work, and an entirely new value system. We earlier described utopias as holistic, functional, idealistic, and critical (see Chapter 11). Each of these qualities also characterizes environmental thought. Environmental thought is critical. By suggesting the need for a new society qualitatively distinct from the current one, it calls attention to the shortcomings of current practices. Environmental thought is holistic. The intent is to portray the essential elements of an entire social order. Environmental thought is functional—that is, the goal is not merely to express ideas or values but to incorporate these notions into ongoing institutions. Environmental thought is idealistic in that it assumes that a better world order is conceivable. Environmental thinkers want to construct the best society, which is, of course, a society in which man lives in homeostatic balance with the nature. Thus current environmental thought shares certain basic perspectives with utopian thought. Our analysis of Utopia, Oneida, and Walden II indicated that the creators of these communities had only a superficial understanding of man's relation to the environment. The realism and practicality of ecosystems concepts could enhance the productivity of utopian thought.

Kanter has identified several basic beliefs that prompted the development of utopian communities.[62] The first belief is that human perfectibility is possible, that the tensions and conflicts existing in social situations are inflicted on man by the conditions of society rather than from man's inner being. A second idea is a belief in the value of order and planning. Carefully structured utopian communities can coordinate human affairs to the ultimate benefit of each individual. Third, people can live together harmoniously, even as man's social world must potentially be harmonious with natural laws. Utopian thinkers also value experimentation and innovation. Finally, utopian communities take pride in their uniqueness and cohesion as a group. These basic values are shared by some environmental activists.

This analysis suggests that utopian and environmental systems of thought can be compatible and complementary. Ecosystems concepts indicate practical limits within which man must operate. But as pointed out earlier, ecosystems concepts do not "determine" the relationship between man and the environment. There is room for choice and change. Utopian thinking provides the ideals, the models, and the overall guiding perspectives. Utopian thinking clarifies the basic alternative value systems by which future societies can be constructed.[63] Utopias supply a positive future image that can give us direction. Our best hope for the future may be in a fusion of the visionary goals of utopian thinkers with the practical policies espoused by environmental advocates. Their visions of our future world are surprisingly congruent.

REFERENCES

1. Raush, H., Goodrich, W., and Campbell, J. Adaptation to the first years of marriage. *Psychiatry*, **26:**368–380, 1963 (quotation on p. 372).

2. Lipowski, Z. J. Surfeit of attractive information inputs: A hallmark of our environment. *Behavioral Science*, **16:**467–471, 1971.

3. Astin, A. and Panos, R. *The educational and vocational development of college students.* American Council on Education, Washington, D.C., 1969.

4. *Work in America.* Report of a Special Task Force to the Secretary of Health, Education, and Welfare. MIT Press, Cambridge, Mass., 1972.

5. Moos, R. *Evaluating treatment environments: A social ecological approach.* Wiley, New York, 1974, Ch. 8.

6. Ekehammar, B. Interactionism in personality from a historical perspective. *Psychological Bulletin,* **81**:1026–1048, 1974.

7. Arthur, R. Success is predictable. *Military Medicine,* **136**:539–545, 1971 (quotation on p. 544).

8. Megargee, E. The prediction of violence with psychological tests. In C. Spielberger (Ed.), *Current topics in clinical and community psychology.* Academic Press, New York, 1970, pp. 98–156.

   Monahan, J. The prediction and prevention of violence. In Proceedings of the Pacific Northwest Conference on Violence and Criminal Justice. Issaquah, Wash., December 6–8, 1973.

9. Chase, M. The impact of correctional programs. Absconding. In R. Moos, *Evaluating correctional and community settings.* Wiley, New York, 1975.

10. Ellsworth, R., Foster, L., Childers, B., Arthur, G., and Kroeker, D. Hospital and community adjustment as perceived by psychiatric patients, their families and staff. *Journal of Consulting and Clinical Psychology Monograph,* **32,** No. 5, Part II, 1968.

11. Sinclair, I. Hostels for probationers. Her Majesty's Stationery Office, London, 1971, p. 78.

12. Skeels, H. Adult status of children with contrasting early life experiences: A follow-up study. *Monograph of the Society for Research in Child Development,* **31,** 1966.

13. Bronfenbrenner, U. The ecology of development. *American Psychologist,* in press, 1976 (quotation on pp. 1 and 2 of the manuscript version).

14. Wachtel, P. Psychodynamics, behavior therapy and implacable experimenter: An inquiry into the consistency of personality. *Journal of Abnormal Psychology,* **82**:324–334, 1973.

15. Meggers, B. Environmental limitations on the development of culture. *American Anthropologist,* **56**:801–824, 1954.

16. Kritzinger, H. Der Sinn Meiner SOWELA-Meldungen. *Krankenhausarzt,* **26**:12–13, 1953.

17. Johnson, R. T. *Managing the White House: An intimate study of the presidency.* Harper & Row, New York, 1974.

18. Hamburg, D. and Adams, A. A perspective on coping behavior: Seeking and utilizing information in major transitions. *Archives of General Psychiatry,* **17**:277–284, 1967.

19. Silber, E., Hamburg, D., Coelho, G., Murphey, E., Rosenberg, M., and

Pearlin, L. Adaptive behavior in competent adolescents: Coping with the anticipation of college. *Archives of General Psychiatry,* **5:**354–365, 1961.

20. Moos, R. (Ed.). *Human adaptation: Coping with life crises.* Heath, Lexington, Mass., 1976.

21. Yalom, I. *The theory and practice of group psychotherapy.* Basic Books, New York, 1970.

22. Kasl, S. V. Physical and mental health effects of involuntary relocation and institutionalization on the elderly—A review. *American Journal of Public Health,* **62:**377–384, 1972.

23. Jasnau, K. F. Individualized versus mass transfer of nonpsychotic, geriatric patients from mental hospitals to nursing homes with special reference to the death rate. *Journal of the American Geriatric Society,* **15:**280–284, 1967.

24. Novick, L. Easing the stress of moving day. *Hospitals,* **41:**64, 1957.

25. Leiberman, M. A. Relocation research and social policy. Based on a paper given at the Symposium on Long-Term Care, Gerontological Society, November 7, 1973, Miami Beach, Fla.

26. Moos, R. *Evaluating treatment environments: A social ecological approach.* Wiley, New York, 1974, Ch. 11.

27. Feldman, K. and Newcomb, T. *The impact of college on students, Vol. 1.* Jossey-Bass, San Francisco, 1969.

28. Holland, J. Determinants of college choice. *College and University,* **35:**11–28, 1959.

29. Pace, C. R. The use of CUES in the college admissions process. College Entrance Examination Board Report No. 11, University of California, Los Angeles, 1966.

30. Baird, L. The practical utility of measures of college environments. *Review of Educational Research,* **44:**307–329, 1974.

31. Centra, J. Development of the questionnaire on student and college characteristics. Research Memorandum, 68–11, Educational Testing Service, Princeton, N.J., 1968.
Centra, J. The college environment revisited: Current descriptions and a comparison of three methods of assessment. Research Bulletin, 70–44, Educational Testing Service, Princeton, N.J., 1970.

32. *San Francisco Examiner,* October 20, 1974, page A.

33. *Palo Alto Times,* November 26, 1974, page 16.

34. Sandler, B. Eclecticism at work: Approaches to job design. *American Psychologist,* **29:**767–773, 1974.

35. *San Francisco Chronicle,* October 16, 1974, page 10.

36. Barker, M. Information and complexity: The conceptualization of air pollution by specialist groups. *Environment and Behavior,* **6:**346–377, 1974.

37. Baird, J., Degerman, R., Harris, R., and Noma, E. Student planning of town configuration. *Environment and Behavior,* **4:**159–188, 1972.

38. See, for example, Gamson, W. *SIMSOC, Simulated society participant's manual.* Free Press, New York, 1969.

39. Barker, R. *Ecological psychology: Concepts and methods for studying the environment of human behavior.* Stanford University Press, Stanford, Calif., 1968.

40. Feiner, A. Health care and education: On the threshold of space. *Science,* **186:**1178–1186, 1974.

41. *Palo Alto Times,* October 14, 1974, page 8.

42. *San Francisco Chronicle,* December 25, 1974, page 5.

43. Caplan, G. *Principles of preventive psychiatry.* Basic Books, New York, 1964.

44. Silverman, P. The widow as a caregiver in a program of preventive intervention with other widows. *Mental Hygiene,* **54:**540–547, 1970.

45. Krumboltz, J. and Thoresen, C. The effect of behavioral counseling in group and individual settings on information-seeking behavior. *Journal of Counseling Psychology,* **11:**324–333, 1964.

46. Bandura, A. *Principles of behavior modification.* Holt, Rinehart & Winston, New York, 1969, Ch. 3.

47. Inhaber, H. Environmental quality: Outline for a national index for Canada. *Science,* **186:**798–805, 1974.

48. Louis, A. The worst American city. *Harpers,* **250:**67–71, January 1975.

49. Campbell, A. and Converse, P. Social change and human change. In A. Campbell and P. Converse (Eds.), *The human meaning of social change.* Russell Sage Foundation, New York, 1972.

50. The "Quality of Life" concept: A potential new tool for decision-makers. Environmental Protection Agency, Office of Research and Monitoring, Environmental Studies Division. *An anthology of selected readings for a symposium at Airlie House.* Warrenton, Va., August 1972.

51. Zifferblatt, S. M. and Hendricks, C. G. Applied behavioral analysis of societal problems: Population change, a case in point. *American Psychologist,* **29:**750–761, 1974.

52. Mazur, A. and Rosa, E. Energy and life style. *Science,* **186:**607–610, 1974.

53. See, for example, Klausner, S. *On man in his environment.* Jossey-Bass, San Francisco, 1971, Ch. 8.

54. Sommer, R. *Design awareness.* Rinehart, San Francisco, 1972.

55. See, for example, Wurman, R. and Gallery, J. *Man-made Philadelphia: A guide to its physical and cultural environment.* MIT Press, Cambridge, Mass., 1972; and Our Man-made Environment Series, Group for Environmental Education, Philadelphia, and the MIT Press, Cambridge, Mass., 1973.

56. Levinson, E. and Yanofsky, S. After the water is clean (or not), then what? How? and why? *Social Education,* **35:**67–73, 1971.

57. Steele, F. *Physical settings and organization development.* Addison-Wesley, Reading, Mass., 1973 (quotation on p. 123).

58. Moos, R. *Evaluating treatment environments, op. cit.,* Chs. 4 and 11.

59. Sommer, *op. cit.*, pp. 31–32.

60. White, R. Motivation reconsidered: The concept of competence. *Psychological Review,* **66:**297–333, 1959.

   White, R. *The enterprise of living: Growth and organization in personality.* Holt, Rinehart & Winston, New York, 1972.

61. Hewes, J. J. *Build your own playground! A source book of play sculptures, designs and concepts from the work of Jay Beckwith.* Houghton Mifflin, Boston, 1974.

62. Kanter, R. *Commitment and community: Communes and utopias in sociological perspective.* Harvard University Press, Cambridge, Mass., 1972.

63. Sarason, S. *The creation of settings and the future societies.* Jossey-Bass, San Francisco, 1972.

Author Index

Abe, K., 81
Acton, Lord, 387
Alexander, B. K., 154
Alihan, M., 11
Altman, I., 168, 231–232
Appleyard, D., 178
Aristotle, 39–40, 257
Aronow, W. S., 202
Arthur, R., 395
Astin, A. W., 291, 293, 295, 297, 343–344, 395
Augustine, Saint, 362
Auliciems, A., 78–79
Azrin, N. H., 186

Back, K., 112
Bacon, F., 362
Bailey, K. G., 164
Baird, L. L., 227–228, 417
Barash, D. P., 163–164
Barker, R. G., 21, 213–244
Baron, R. A., 91–92, 175–176
Barrett, R., 261
Bates, M., 100–101
Baumgartel, H., 261
Baxter, J. C., 132, 162, 168
Bay, A. P., 118
Beard, R. R., 193
Becker, F. D., 157
Becker, W., 336
Bedford, T., 86

Bell, W., 298–299, 301, 309, 310–311
Bellamy, E., 363
Beloff, J. S., 277
Berdiaev, N., 388
Berke, J. (quoted), 76–77
Blashfield, R. K., 219–221
Blauner, R., 266
Bock, H., 83
Booth, E., 346
Bordua, D. J., 301
Bowman, I., 48, 49–50
Bragdon, C. R., 181
Brezowsky, H., 90
Bronfenbrenner, U., 396–397
Brunhes, J., 48, 63, 66
Brunswick, E., 20
Buckle, H. T., 42–43
Buechley, R. W., 89
Burrows, A. A., 181

Cabet, E., 362, 363
Caffrey, B., 349–350
Calhoun, J. B., 153–154
Campanella, T., 362
Campbell, A., 422–423
Campbell, D. T., 243
Caplan, R., 350
Carson, R., 26
Cassell, E. J., 200
Centra, J., 344–345
Chein, I., 302

Chovin, P., 194
Christian, J. J., 154
Clarkson, J. D., 46
Clayton, G., 194
Clevenger, S. V., 94
Club of Rome, 361
Cohen, J., 272
Cohen, S. I., 201–202
Converse, P., 422–423
Cowen, E., 217
Cowen, M., 190
Craik, K. H., 217
Cummings, L. L., 263

Darwin, C., 9, 20, 30
David, T. G., 135–136
Davis, D. C., 154
Deanovich, B. F., 162
DeCoster, D., 296
Dee, W., 308
Demolins, E., 41–42, 64, 66
Derogatis, L. R., 166
Desor, J. A., 169
Dexter, E. G., 78
Diamond, S., 132
Digon, E., 83
Dohrenwend, B., 311
Downs, R. M., 132–133
Dubos, R., 153, 154
Duff, D. F., 165
Duncan, O. D., 58–59, 63
Dunham, H. W., 303, 304, 308
Durkheim, E., 82–83, 257

East, W. G., 52
Eddy, G. L., 237–238
Ehrlich, A., 27–28
Ehrlich, P. R., 27–28, 155
Einstein, A., 19
Ellsworth, R., 395–396
El Salmi, A. M., 263
Empey, J., 165
Engels, F., 388
Epicurus, 40
Espy, J., 96
Eyre, S. R., 57–58, 63

Faris, R. E., 303, 304, 308
Farrell, B., 234–235
Febvre, L., 47

Felipe, N. J., 163
Festinger, L., 112
Firey, W., 12
Flyger, V., 154
Freedman, J. L., 148–149, 155, 157
French, J., 350
Freud, S., 18–19
Fried, M., 131
Friedman, M., 349–350

Gagge, A. P., 85–86
Galle, O. R., 147, 149, 150, 151, 152
Gandhi, M., 324
Gans, H. J., 114, 130, 131
Gerard, L., 303–304
Gerst, M. S., 296
Getzels, J., 122
Gibson, F. W., Jr., 164
Gierasch, P., 98
Glass, D. C., 187–189
Gleicher, P., 131
Glueck, E., 336
Glueck, S., 336
Good, L. R., 118
Gould, P. R., 61–62, 419
Gove, W. R., 147, 149, 150, 151, 152
Gover, M., 89
Graeven, D., 182
Grandstaff, N., 193
Graves, T., 167
Griffin, A., 81–82
Griffitt, W., 91, 156, 157
Gropius, W., 24
Grotjahn, A., 14
Gump, P. V., 216–217, 226–227, 242–243

Haase, R. F., 168
Hackney, J. D., 193–194
Haeckel, E., 9, 55
Hall, E. T., 161–162, 167
Hammond, K., 20
Hare, E. H., 151
Harrell, T., 259
Hart, R. H., 197
Hartnett, J. J., 164
Hauck, P. A., 82
Hawley, A. H., 9, 11
Hazard, J. N. (quoted), 109–110
Hearn, J. C., 291–292
Heller, N. B., 80

Hendricks, C. G., 423
Hersey, J., 141–142, 170
Hertska, T., 363
Herzog, A., 150
Hickish, D. E., 84–85
Hildreth, A. M., 166
Hill, A. D., 60, 63
Hinkle, L. E., 15
Hippocrates, 13–14, 39–40, 73, 93
Hobbs, P. V., 97
Holahan, C. J., 120–121
Holland, J. L., 286–296, 412, 417
Hollander, J. L., 77–78
Hollingshead, A., 311
Holt, J., 136
Horowitz, M. J., 165
Houston, L., 303–304
Hunt, E. A., 178–179
Hunt, R. S., 99
Huntington, E., 45, 46, 73–75, 99, 101, 102, 400
Hutt, C., 159, 160
Huxley, A., 389

Ibn Khaldun, 40
Indik, B. P., 261

Jaco, E. G., 311
Jacobs, J., 147–148, 170
James, R., 81–82
Jansen, E., 351–352
Jasnau, K. F., 416–417
Jesness, C. F., 273
Johnson, R. T., 411–412

Kagan, J., 336
Kahn, R., 151
Kanter, R., 427
Karmel, L. J., 127
Karon, M., 165
Kasmar, J. V., 124
Katzell, R., 261
Kellog, W., 99
Kesey, K., 324
Kinzel, A. F., 166
Klee, G. D., 305
Klevansky, S., 155
Kirkbride, T., 24–25
Knight, D., 275
Kohn, M., 312

Kounin, J. S., 242–243
Kozol, J., 324
Kritzinger, H., 401
Krueger, A., 80
Krumboltz, J., 421
Kuper, L., 112–113

Lansing, J. B., 115
LaVerne, A. A., 197
Lawler, E. E., 263
Lawton, S., 92
LeCompte, W. F., 235–237
Le Corbusier, 24, 169–170
Leiberman, M. A., 417
Leighton, A., 306–307
Leighton, D., 306–307
Le Play, F., 41
Levinson, E., 423
Levy, L., 150, 304, 308
Lewin, K., 19–20, 21, 324–325
Lieber, A. L., 94
Likert, R., 252
Linn, L., 270
Linn, R., 344–345
Lintell, M., 178
Lipstreu, O., 265
Lombard, G., 258
Lombroso, C., 90
Loo, C., 159, 160
Lyman, S. M., 161
Lynch, K., 134
Lynn, R., 76, 400

MacCarthy, D., 346
McCusker, K., 166
McKay, H., 300–301
McKennell, A. C., 178–179
McNall, P. E., 85
McPherson, J. M., 147, 149, 150, 151, 152
Malin, J., 59–60, 64–65
Malthus, T. R., 390
Marans, R. W., 115
Markey, M. J., 168
Markham, S. F., 75
Markland, R. E., 80
Marris, P., 130–131
Marx, B. S., 122
Marx, K., 17, 40, 252–253, 257
Maslow, A. H., 123
Mason, O., 12

Mayo, E., 258
Meggers, B., 54, 63, 64, 65, 398–399
Mehrabian, A., 132
Michelson, W., 11, 92, 132
Milgram, S., 146, 153
Militzer, G., 418
Mill, J. S., 323
Miller, R., 348
Mills, C. A., 74–75, 77 (quoted), 83, 99, 101
Mintz, N. L., 123, 308–309
Mitchell, R. E., 150, 151
Moos, R. H., 271–272, 275, 291–292, 296
Moos, W. S., 79–80
More, T., 359, 362, 364–370, 384, 386, 391
Moss, H., 336
Muecher, H., 79
Mumford, L., 4
Murray, H., 19, 325–326
Myrick, R., 122

Nevins, R. G., 85
Newcomb, T., 295
Newman, O., 123
Novick, L., 417

Oechsli, F. W., 89
Orwell, G., 388
Osborn, R., 94–95
Osmond, H., 119–120, 122, 402
Ozerengin, M., 190

Pace, C. R., 291, 323, 326, 417
Panos, R., 293, 295, 343–344, 395
Pantleo, P. M., 82
Park, R., 10
Parker, T., 261
Parkes, C., 347
Parsons, T., 219
Pavlov, I., 21
Pellegrini, R. J., 165
Pepler, R. D., 87–88
Perlin, S., 151
Petersen, W. F., 73
Peterson, R., 337
Plato, 361–362
Pokorny, A. D., 83–84, 94–95
Polk, K., 302
Porter, L. W., 260, 263
Price, R. H., 219–221
Provins, K. A., 88

Pugh, T., 309

Radke, L. F., 97
Ramsey, J. M., 194–195
Rappaport, R. A., 56–57, 63
Ratzel, F., 44
Raush, H. L., 243, 394 (quoted)
Reed, K., 265
Revans, R. W., 257–258, 260–261
Rigler, D., 165
Ritter, C., 40–41
Rock, D., 344–345
Rogler, L., 311
Rohles, F. H., Jr., 85, 100
Rosenman, R., 349–350
Ross, M., 156
Roth, E. M., 154
Rowitz, L., 304, 308
Rush, B., 93–94
Russell, B., 323–324

Saegert, S., 121
Sagan, C., 98
Sandler, B., 418
Sargent, F., 15
Schachter, S., 112
Schaefer, V., 96–97
Schmitt, R. C., 147–149
Schneider, B., 337
Schneider, S., 99
Schoggen, M., 234
Schroeder, C., 303
Schuman, S. H., 89–90
Schwartz, D., 308–309
Scott, M. B., 161
Sears, P., 390
Seashore, S., 261
Sells, S. B., 80, 84
Semple, E. C., 44
Shakespeare, W., 93
Shaw, C. R., 300–301
Sherin, C. R., 94
Sherrod, D. R., 155
Shevky, E., 298–299, 301
Siegel, J., 263
Siegel, S. M., 118
Silber, E., 416
Sinclair, I., 396
Singer, J. E., 187–189
Sinnett, R., 237–238

Skeels, H. M., 23, 396
Skinner, B. F., 21–22, 359, 364, 377–384, 385, 387
Smith, A., 264
Sobol, R., 261
Sommer, R., 110, 136, 157, 162, 163, 423, 424
Sorokin, P. A., 37, 46–47, 64
Spate, O. H. K., 51
Speegle, J., 352
Spinetta, J. J., 165
Spitz, R., 22–23, 346
Spivack, M., 121–122
Sprout, H., 47, 48–49
Sprout, M., 47, 48–49
Stanley, J. C., 243
Stea, D., 132–133
Sterling, T. D., 197–198
Stern, G., 326
Steward, J., 13
Stewart, B. C., Jr., 81
Stoddart, D. R., 55–56
Stokols, D., 142–145, 158
Stratton, L. O., 165
Struening, E., 272
Suedfeld, P., 183–184

Talacchi, S., 258–259
Tatham, G., 53–54
Taylor, F. W., 250–251, 267
Taylor, G., 53–54
Theodorson, G. A., 12
Thistlethwaite, D., 342–345
Thomas, F., 39
Thoresen, C., 421
Toon, O., 98
Toynbee, A., 4–9, 28, 30
Trabert, W., 77
Tromp, S. W., 100
Tuke, W., 16
Turner, E. (quoted), 108–109
Turner, F. J., 59, 64

Ullmann, L. P., 270, 272, 275
Ungeheuer, H., 79
Ury, H. K., 195

Vaizey, M. J., 159, 160
Veitch, R., 156, 157
Villerne, L. R., 14
Virchow, R., 14
Vitruvius, 40

Wachtel, P., 397
Wallace, A. F. C., 131
Wallis, W. E., 50
Ward, L. M., 183–184
Watson, O. M., 167
Weber, M., 17, 252–253
Wechsler, H., 309
Wells, H. G., 363–364
Wertheim, G. A., 193
White, L. E., 126–127
Whyte, W. H., 113–114, 130
Wicker, A. W., 169, 222, 225–226, 228–233, 234–235
Wilde, O., 391
Wildman, R. W., 81
Will, D. P., Jr., 80, 84
Willems, E. P., 228, 235–237, 240–243
Willmott, P., 128
Wilner, D. M., 129
Wilson, V. (quoted), 76–77
Wissler, C., 49
Withall, J., 325
Wolff, H. G., 15
Woodhead, M. M., 185–186
Woodward, S., 16
Wooldridge, S. W., 52
Worthington, M. E., 165
Worthy, J. C., 262–264
Wyndham, C., 86–87
Wyon, D. P., 88, 102

Yanofsky, S., 423
Yeostros, S. J., 78
Yoshida, K., 198
Young, M., 128

Zamarin, D. M., 181
Zehner, R. B., 115
Zeidberg, L. D., 199
Zlutnick, S., 168, 231–232
Zifferblatt, S. M., 423

Subject Index

Absenteeism, 260–261, 268, 269, 350
Academic achievement, 296–297, 326–330, 333, 338–339, 341–345
Accidents, 79–81, 100, 194–196, 298
Adaptation, 29, 127, 274–278, 411, 419–421
  to climatic conditions, 86–87, 102, 400–401, 407
  to crowding, 145–146, 153, 170
  to noise, 181–182, 184, 189–190, 407
  to overmanning, 232–233, 408
  to physical design, 126–127, 403
Adaptation, group, 11–12, 61, 251, 253–254
Age differences, 131, 195–196
  in utopias, 367–368, 374, 376
Aged, relocation of, 416–417
Aggressivity, 157–159, 166, 324–325
  and physical conditions, 78, 80–81, 89, 90–92, 94, 157–159
Agricultural potential, 54, 56–57, 63, 398
Agriculture, 49–52, 60–62
Air conditioning, see Climate, interior
Air pollution, 58–59, 191–295, 406–407
Aircraft noise, 180–182, 405, 407
Anxiety, "national," 76. See also Stress
Alcoholism, 76
Architecture, 23–26, 108–137, 215–216, 401–404
  and crowding, 150, 152, 169

  in utopias, 364–365, 371, 378, 380, 381–382
Automation, 264–266

Barometric pressure, 77–81, 83–84, 99
Behavior settings, 169, 213–247, 407–410
  in utopias, 367–368, 374–375, 381–382
Bereavement, 347, 421

Cancer, 191, 199, 204
Carbon monoxide, 191–205, 406–407
Cardiovascular diseases, 201–204
"Challenge and response" (Toynbee), 7–8, 30
Children, 126–127, 235, 314, 398, 415, 419
  aggressivity of, 159, 160, 324–325
  development of, 14, 22–23, 396–397
  and housing, 129, 131, 150, 151, 159, 160
  misbehavior of, 78, 109, 127, 415
  and social climate, 336, 346–347, 351, 396–397
  in utopias, 366–367, 370, 373–374 passim, 390
Cities, 128–129, 134–135, 144–145, 146–153, 169–170, 224–225, 422
Class differences, 110, 235, 294, 300–302
  and health, 297–299, 303–312
  and space, 131–132, 148–149, 152
  in utopias, 361–362, 367, 369–370, 371–372, 382

Classrooms, 122–123, 127, 183, 398
  as behavior setting, 220, 223–224
  social climate of, 325, 333, 338–339
Climate, 5–9, 36–69, 73–107. *See also*
    Weather
Climate, interior, 75, 78–79, 84–89, 156–
    157
Climate modification, 98–99, 102–103
Cognitive maps, 132–134, 420
Cohesiveness, *see* Relationship dimensions
College Characteristics Inventory (CCI),
    290–291, 326
College and University Environment Scale
    (CUES), 291, 417
Colleges and universities, 228, 256, 286–297
  selection of, 313, 351–352, 412, 416–418
  social climate of, 286–297, 323, 326,
    337–338, 341–345
Competition, *see* Personal development,
    dimensions of
Congruence, 31, 111, 126–127, 131–137,
    222–224, 395
  in colleges, 292–294, 412
  in neighborhoods, 307–312, 413
Control, *see* System maintenance and change
    dimensions
Control, feeling of, 145, 156, 189. *See also*
    "Environmental competence"
Coping, *see* Adaptation
Cornell Family Illness Study, 199–200, 203
Correctional facilities, 273–274, 333, 340,
    396
Crime, 46, 146–153, 166, 299–302, 307
  and physical design, 109, 123, 129
  in utopias, 364, 369–370, 383–384, 385
Crowding, 141–174, 403–405
Culture, 12–13, 42, 397
  as mediator, 12, 46, 54, 60–61, 152,
    167–168

Darwinism, 9, 20, 55
Decision-making, 51–52, 61–62, 252, 286–
    296, 419, 421
  and comfort, 91, 400, 404
Density, 144, 146–151, 153–161, 168–170,
    403–404
Determinism, 397–398
  geographical, 39–47, 50–54, 65–66, 360–
    361
Distance, 112–115, 132, 164–167

Division of labor, 12, 42
  in modern organizations, 17–18, 249–251,
    253, 274
Dormitories, 115–117, 169, 183–184, 237–
    238
  social climate of, 291–292, 326–330, 333
Driving and pollution, 194–196, 202–203

Ecological studies, 298–312
Ecology, 9–10, 55–57, 360–361, 389–391
  cultural, 13
  human, 10–12, 31, 55–60
  social, 29–32, 394–397
Economic organization, 41–42, 57, 248–269
  in utopias, 363, 365–366, 372–373, 379,
    384–387
Education (in utopias), 366–367, 373–374,
    380–381
Emotional state, 118–124, 179, 183–184,
    224–227, 336–337
  and climate, 77, 81–82, 91, 99, 401
"Environment," definitions of, 37–38, 55,
    63–64, 119–122, 214–216, 229–231
Environmental Assessment Technique, (EAT),
    290–293, 295
"Environmental competence," 409–410,
    423–424
Environmental Description Scale (EDS), 124–
    125
Environmental Force Unit (EFU), 234–235
Environmental planning and change, 135–
    136, 223–224, 252, 268–269, 352, 409–
    411, 423–427
  resistance to, 135–136, 223–224
"Environmental press," 19, 324, 325–326,
    328, 342. *See also* Social climate
Environmental taxonomies, 217–222, 288–
    289, 332–333, 409, 420
Environments, ideal of optimum, 4, 7–8,
    40–44, 74–76
  information about, 351–352, 398–399,
    416–424
  and utopias, 359–364
Epidemiology, 15, 297–314. *See also* Health

Factories, 184–185, 249–252, 257–269,
    420–421
Family climate, 311–312, 320–324, 332–
    333, 334–336, 346–347, 398
Family life, 42, 128–130, 149–150,

221, 234–235
in utopias, 366, 369, 373, 380
Foehn, 77–80
Free will, 38, 65, 66
Freedom, personal, 368–369, 371–372, 379, 382–383, 386–387, 388
Friendship formation, 111–118, 128–129
Furniture arrangement, 109–111, 119–123, 125–127

Game theory, 61–62, 419
Geography, 5–10, 29–30, 36–69, 74–76
of utopias, 364–365, 371, 378, 384–385, 389–390
Gestalt psychology, 19–20
Governments (in utopias), 365, 371–372, 378–379, 386, 390

Health, 13–16, 148, 182, 190–205, 297–299, 306–309, 346–351
and weather, 39, 73, 76–84, 89–90, 200–201
Health care, 15, 276–278, 314
in utopias, 374, 377, 378
Heart diseases, 201–203, 347–351
Heat, see Temperature
Homicide, 89, 94
Homogeneity, 295–296, 308–310
Hospitals, 118–122, 125–126, 235–237, 271–272, 324, 333. See also Mental hospitals
Housing, 112–117, 127–131
Human aggregate, 284–319, 367, 374, 381, 412–414
Human relations school, 18, 250–252, 253, 267, 275
Humidity, 77–81

"Incongruence," 126–127, 308–311
Independence, see Personal development dimensions
Individual differences, 88, 233, 286–297
in air pollution tolerance, 194, 200–201
in crowding response, 145, 170
in disease susceptibility, 10, 89, 349–350
in environmental perceptions, 110, 131–135, 419–421
in noise response, 179–180, 182, 189
in personal distance, 132, 164–167
and setting effects, 395–396, 403

and setting selection, 237–238, 395
Infant mortality, 199, 298
Information, environmental, 351–352, 398–399, 416–424. See also Selection
Innovation, see System maintenance and change dimensions
Interior design, 115–127
Involvement, see Relationship dimensions

Juvenile delinquency, 273–274, 299–302, 308, 335–336, 340, 396

Kuder Preference Record, 286

Ladino culture, 60–61
Leadership, 324–325
Levittown (Pa.), 114, 130
Los Angeles, 13, 89, 181
smog in, 58–59, 198, 201–202

Management, scientific, 249–251, 253, 266–267, 274–275
"Manning," under- and over-, 169, 224–233, 408–410
Marxism, 17, 43–44
Mediating factors, 38, 64–65, 88, 144–145, 169–170, 254–257, 266–269, 411
acclimatization, 102, 170
social environments, 82–83, 271–272, 311–312, 338, 411, 413–414
Medical sociology, 15, 297–314
Mental hospital admissions, 81–82, 94–95, 100, 148–149, 303–305, 308–312
Mental hospitals, 16, 24–25, 118–122, 125–126, 269–272, 275, 395–396. See also Psychiatric programs
Mental illness, 16, 76, 93–95, 119, 144–153, 303–312. See also Schizophrenia
Midtown Study (New York City), 307
Midwest Psychological Field Station, 213 passim, 242
Military barracks, 115–116
Military companies, 333, 340–341
Modeling, 92, 234–235, 421
Moon, 93–95
Mortality rates, 89–90, 148–149, 346–347, 416–417
and air pollution, 196, 198, 199, 201–202, 298
Multi-factor explanation, 45, 57–59,

65–66, 100, 110
need for, 145, 405. *See also* Mediating
factors

Nashville Air Pollution Study, 199, 203
National character, 39–40, 43, 59–60, 73,
76, 167–168
Naturalistic methods, 213 passim, 235–235,
238–243
Neighborhoods, 129–130, 298–302, 307,
310. *See also* Cities; Suburbs
Neodeterminism, 52–54, 65. *See also*
Determinism
New York City, 89, 199–200, 203, 307
Noise, 175–190, 405–407

Obligation, sense of, 153, 228–229
Offices, 117–118, 177–178, 184–185, 350,
404
Oneida Community, 363, 370–377, 384
passim
"Open systems" approach, 253–254, 268,
276–278
Order and organization, *see* System
maintenance and change dimensions
Organization, 9–10, 16–18, 58–59, 248–
283, 410–412. *See also* Economic
organization

Pain, 77–78
Park Forest (Ill.), 113–114
Participation, 92, 130, 224–233, 259
by users, 136, 252, 268–269, 418–419,
423–424
in utopias, 365, 369, 371–372, 379
Perceptions of environments, 110, 135,
419–421
Performance, 155–156, 160, 184–188,
336–337
and air pollution, 192–196, 203
and Weather, 77–79, 86–88, 100, 399–
401
Personal development or growth, 413
dimensions of, 291–292, 326–335 passim,
341–345, 414–416
in utopias, 368, 375, 382
Planning, *see* Environmental planning and
change
Play areas, 126–127, 131
Pollution, 27, 385, 422. *See also* Air
pollution

Population, 58
distribution of, 52, 56–58, 365, 384
growth of, 27, 141–142, 168–170, 231–
233
in utopias, 361, 364–365, 373, 384–385,
390–391
Possibilism, 47–51, 53–54, 64, 65, 66, 398
Pragmatism, 50–52, 65
Privacy, 108–109, 129, 145
in utopias, 371, 373, 376–377, 378
Private property, 42, 366, 372–373, 375,
379
Probabilism, 50–52, 65
Productivity, 18, 249–252, 257, 269, 372
"Progressive conformity," 292–294, 413
Proxemics, 161–168
Pruitt-Igoe (St. Louis), 128
Psychiatric programs, 118–122, 125–126,
237–238, 324, 339–340, 351–352, 395.
See also Mental hospitals

"Quality of life," 421–423

Race differences, 87, 132, 152, 168, 235
Racial incongruence, 308–309
Radiation, solar, 76, 401
Rain, 80, 96–97
Recreational facilities, 115
Reinforcement, 22
in utopias, 368–370, 377 passim
Relationship dimensions, 291, 326–335
passim, 414–416
in utopias, 368–369, 375–376, 382–383
Religion, 45, 221, 229, 366–377, 386
Religious incongruence, 309
Relocation, 127–131, 416–417
Residences, group, 108–109, 111, 237–238,
273–274, 396. *See also* Dormitories
Resources, natural, 26, 27, 47, 48, 49, 59–
60
Respiratory disease, 197–201, 203
Responsibility and health, 348–349

Satisfaction, 157, 264–266, 293–294, 382–
383, 386–387
and organizations, 256, 258–264, 268–
269, 278
and social climate, 336–339, 344, 395
Schizophrenia, 165–166, 190, 303–312,
413
Schools, 220, 226–229, 285–286, 324

design of, 122–123, 127, 136
Selection, of members by settings, 30, 225, 237–238, 284–285, 341–344, 374, 381, 412
of settings by members, 31, 182, 237–238, 313, 351–352, 370–371, 374, 381, 394–395 passim, 419–421 passim
Sex differences, 85, 156–160, 164–167, 238, 404, 412
in social climates, 296, 326–330
in utopias, 367, 374
Size, 226–229, 257–258, 270–278, 345
of utopias, 364–365, 378, 384–385
Smog, see Air pollution
Smoke, cigarette, 197, 200, 204, 406
"Social area" analysis, 12, 298–299, 301–302, 308
Social climate, 285–286, 296, 303–312, 320–356, 414–416
and academic achievement, 296–297, 326–330, 333, 338–339, 341–345
and crime, 300–302, 307, 308
of settings, 256, 268, 271–275, 291–292
in utopias, 368–370, 375–377, 382–384
Social Climate Scales, see University Residence Environment Scale; Ward Atmosphere Scale
Social disorganization, 146–153
Social Emotional Climate Index, 325
Social isolation, 310–311
Solar radiation, 76, 401
Space, see Architecture; Crowding; and Density
personal, 161–168, 170
"Space fetishes," 12
Staffing, 270–278
Status, 163–164, 367–368, 374, 376
Stimulation, environmental, 7–8, 30, 416
by density, 169–170, 405
by noise, 185, 190
by undermanning, 224–233
by weather, 74–76, 98–99, 101–102, 400
Stimulus deprivation, 22–23, 405
Stimulus enrichment, 23, 30
Storminess, 74–80, 83, 95–99. See also Barometric pressure
Streets, 113–115, 128, 221, 178
Stress, 29, 101–102, 347–351, 400–401
and crowding, 141–146, 149–153, 162–167, 170

and noise, 175–190
Strong Vocational Interest Blank (SVIB), 286, 293–294
Structuralism, 252–253, 267–268, 275–276
Student and College Characteristics, Questionnaire on (QSCC), 417–418
Suburbs, 128, 130, 131, 147, 305
Suicide, 76, 82–84, 94
Supervisor-employee ratios, 250, 254, 262–264
Support, see Relationship dimensions
System maintenance and change dimensions, 292, 326–335 passim, 414–416
in utopias, 369–370, 376–377, 383–387, 390–391

Technology, 47–49, 57–61, 63–65
unforeseen consequences of, 49, 66, 102–103
in utopias, 372, 377, 384, 386, 387, 388, 390–391
Temperature, 75 passim, 84–93, 100, 156
interior, 75, 78–79, 87–89
and pollution, 191, 196–197, 200, 204
Territoriality, 161–162
Traffic, 178, 179, 183–184
and pollution, 191–192, 194–196, 202
Turnover, 395
by workers, 261–262, 268, 269
by patients, 269–272, 276

"Undermanned" environments, 169, 224–233
Universities, see Colleges and universities
University Residence Environment Scale (URES), 291–292, 326–330
Urban renewal, 25, 128–131
User participation, 136, 252, 268–269, 418–419, 423–424
Utopia (T. More), 362, 364–370, 384 passim
Utopian thought, 359–393, 424–425

Veterans Administration hospitals, 270, 272, 275–276
Violence, 89, 94. See also Aggressivity
Vocational Preference Inventory (VPI), 287
Vocations, 286–297

Walden II (Skinner), 364, 377–384 passim
Ward Atmosphere Scale (WAS), 271–272

Wealth: accumulation of, 42–43, 47
  distribution of, 42–43, 365–366, 372–
    373, 379
Weather, 39, 73–107, 399–401
  control of, 95–99, 102–103
  and pollution, 191, 196–197, 204
Wind, 77–80
Women, 128, 130, 131, 133–134, 220
  and social climate, 296, 326–330

Workers, 411, 420–421
  motivation of, 249–253, 372
  participation of, 252, 268–269, 418–419
  satisfaction of, 336–337, 411, 418. *See also*
    Automation; Productivity
Work milieus, 398, 420–421
  social climate dimensions, 332–333, 336–
    337, 350.   *See also* Factories; Offices
Work pressure, 349–350

DATE DUE